REVISITING RENTAL HOUSING

JAMES A. JOHNSON METRO SERIES

JAMES A. JOHNSON METRO SERIES

The Metropolitan Policy Program at the Brookings Institution is integrating research and practical experience into a policy agenda for cities and metropolitan areas. By bringing fresh analyses and policy ideas to the public debate, the program hopes to inform key decisionmakers and civic leaders in ways that will spur meaningful change in our nation's communities.

As part of this effort, the James A. Johnson Metro Series aims to introduce new perspectives and policy thinking on current issues and attempts to lay the foundation for longer-term policy reforms. The series examines traditional urban issues, such as neighborhood assets and central city competitiveness, as well as larger metropolitan concerns, such as regional growth, development, and employment patterns. The James A. Johnson Metro Series consists of concise studies and collections of essays designed to appeal to a broad audience. While these studies are formally reviewed, some will not be verified like other research publications. As with all publications, the judgments, conclusions, and recommendations presented in the studies are solely those of the authors and should not be attributed to the trustees, officers, or other staff members of the Institution.

REVISITING RENTAL HOUSING

Policies, Programs, and Priorities

NICOLAS P. RETSINAS
ERIC S. BELSKY
Editors

JOINT CENTER FOR HOUSING STUDIES
Harvard University
Cambridge, Massachusetts

BROOKINGS INSTITUTION PRESS
Washington, D.C.

Copyright © 2008
THE BROOKINGS INSTITUTION
1775 Massachusetts Avenue, N.W., Washington, DC 20036
www.brookings.edu

Library of Congress Cataloging-in-Publication data
Revisiting rental housing : policies, programs, and priorities / Nicolas P. Retsinas and Eric S. Belsky, editors.
    p. cm.—(James A. Johnson metro series)
  Summary: "Reviews the contributing factors and primary problems generated by the operation of rental markets. Dissects how policies and programs have—or have not—dealt with the primary challenges, what improvements—if any—have been gained, and the lessons learned in the process. Looks to potential new directions in housing policy"—Provided by publisher.
  Includes bibliographical references and index.
  ISBN-13: 978-0-8157-7411-2 (pbk. : alk. paper)

  1. Rental housing—United States. 2. Housing policy—United States. I. Retsinas, Nicolas Paul, 1946– II. Belsky, Eric S. III. Title.

  HD7288.85.U6R48 2008
  333.33'8—dc22   2007048079

Digital Printing

The paper used in this publication meets minimum requirements of the American National Standard for Information Sciences—Permanence of Paper for Printed Library Materials: ANSI Z39.48-1992.

Typeset in Adobe Garamond

Composition by Circle Graphics
Columbia, Maryland

Contents

Part II: What Happened? Current Rental Housing Policy

Part III: Moving Forward: New Directions in Rental Housing Policy

Acknowledgments

This book is the product of a conference exploring the role rental housing plays in the nation's housing market on economic, policy, community, and personal levels. The goal of raising the profile of rental housing on the national agenda was successfully accomplished, but only with the assistance of several dedicated parties. Principal funding for the symposium was provided by the MacArthur Foundation, to which we are indebted for seeing the value of sponsoring an event dedicated to researching, uncovering, and understanding the issues related to rental housing, especially the supply and preservation of decent, affordable rental housing. We were fortunate to have worked with an extraordinary group of colleagues from the MacArthur Foundation, all of whom contributed to making this project such a success. We would especially like to thank Erika Poethig, Michael Stegman, and Debra Schwartz for the formative role they played in shaping the research questions addressed in this book.

At the Joint Center for Housing Studies, we would like to thank Rachel Drew and Daniel McCue for their stewardship of the conference and the broader rental initiative that led up to the conference. Both were closely involved in every aspect of the work that led up to this book and instrumental to the success of the endeavor. We also want to thank Pamela Baldwin, Laurel Trayes, William Apgar, Elizabeth England, Angela Flynn, Nancy Jennings, and Jackie Hernandez for their hard work and dedication to this project. In addition, we owe a debt of gratitude to each of the following leaders in the field, who gave freely of their time and shared with us ideas that we incorporated into the design of the conference: Rachel Bratt of Tufts University, Shekar Narasimhan of Beekman Advisors, Sandra Newman of Johns Hopkins University, and Stuart Rosenthal of Syracuse University.

Of course, this book would not have been possible without the exceptionally strong papers that were prepared by the contributors. We went to the best and the brightest in the field, and the result is a set of papers that is meticulously researched and cogently argued. Furthermore, the moderators and discussants of the papers at the conference added enormous value and insight. In addition to the book's contributors, a group of representatives from the rental industry, academic, and advocacy communities advised us early in the process and deserve special recognition: Bruce Katz of Brookings; Doug Bibby and Mark Obrinsky of the National Multi Housing Council; Thomas Bozzuto of the Bozzuto Group; Glen Canner and Sheila Maith of the Federal Reserve Board; Sheila Crowley of the National Low Income Housing Coalition; Larry Dale of Newman Financial Services; Wendy Dolber of Standard & Poor's; Anthony Downs of Brookings; Conrad Egan of the National Housing Council; Denise Kiley, formerly of CharterMac; Judd Levy of Community Development Trust; George McCarthy of the Ford Foundation; Jenny Netzer of MMA Financial; Michael Petrie of P/R Mortgage Capital Company; David Reznick of Reznick, Fedder, and Silverman; and Ron Terwilliger of Trammell Crow Residential.

Finally, we wish to thank Joan Retsinas and Cynthia Wilson once again for always being there for us and encouraging us to do our best work.

REVISITING RENTAL HOUSING

Introduction: Why Rental Housing Is the Neglected Child of American Shelter

ANTHONY DOWNS

Although almost one-third of all American households rent their shelter, rental housing is the neglected child of American life. In fact, the number of renter-occupied housing units actually increased by 1.1 million from 2000 to 2005, though the nation's total number of housing units (including vacant units) rose by 8.6 million in the same period (Census Bureau 2000, 2005a). Owning one's home is fundamental to the American dream. Although millions of well-off households voluntarily choose to rent, rental housing is basically considered second class. Even more significant, America's poor are concentrated in rental housing, further degrading its status. Among the 15.12 million poor households in America in 2005, 57.4 percent were renters, and they made up 25.6 percent of all renter households. In contrast, only 8.6 percent of owner-occupant households were poor (Census Bureau 2005b, tables 1A-1, 2-12). Of all poor households, 42.6 percent were owner-occupants, but they had substantially more accumulated wealth on average than poor renters.

In November 2006 Harvard's Joint Center for Housing Studies and the MacArthur Foundation sponsored a symposium focused on the nature and condition of rental housing in the United States. Over a two-day period, fifty academic and industry housing experts met in Cambridge, Massachusetts, to present papers analyzing every aspect of rental housing. This introduction presents an overview of the symposium's general findings.

Income Differences between Renters and Owners

The concentration of poor households in rental housing is illustrated by the difference in incomes between renters and homeowners. In 2005 the median income among renter households was $27,051, just under half the $55,571 median among owner-occupant households (Census Bureau 2005b, table 2-12). Only 31.7 percent of renter households had incomes of $40,000 or more, compared with 64.4 percent of owner households (Census Bureau 2005b, table 2-12). Renters have lower incomes than owners because, on the average, it costs less to rent than to own one's own home, and ownership requires amassing an initial down payment that many renters cannot afford. Also, renting households typically move much more often than do home-owning households. Renters can be transient, whereas homeowners must buy and sell their properties in order to move. "Moving up" usually requires having increased equity, but renters often lack that option. According to the 2000 census, 38.8 percent of all renter households moved from March 1999 to March 2000, compared with only 10.3 percent of all owner-occupant households (Census Bureau 2000). Households still on the move are more likely to rent than to own and more likely to have lower incomes and shorter employment records than those who have settled down. Among all those who moved between 1995 and 2000, about 58 percent remained in the same county (Census Bureau 2000).

Housing is the single largest expense in the budgets of both renters and owners. According to the Consumer Expenditure Survey for 2005, conducted by the Bureau of Labor Statistics, homeowners spent an average of $54,126 on housing each year, while renters spent $30,462. Spending on all aspects of housing was 31.9 percent of all consumer spending for homeowners and 35.6 percent for renters. For shelter alone, homeowners spent 17.6 percent, and renters 23.95 percent (BLS 2005). Viewing housing spending as a share of total income is unreliable as a measure of housing cost burden, however, because the lowest-income households reported having spent far more than they received as income each year—which implies that their income reporting was erroneous, probably because they omitted credit card debt or gray-market receipts. According to the U.S. Census Bureau's American Community Survey for 2005, 31.9 percent of all renter households had incomes of less than $20,000 a year, and among them, 86.2 percent spent more than 30 percent of their incomes on housing. In contrast, among homeowner households, 12.5 percent had incomes under $20,000 a year, and 68.0 percent of those spent more than 30 percent of their incomes on housing (Census Bureau 2005a).

Locational Differences

Renter households tend to be concentrated in central cities, while owner-occupant households are more prevalent in the suburbs. According to a 2005 American

Housing Survey, 52.2 percent of owner-occupants were suburbanites and 23.3 percent lived in central cities (Census Bureau 2005b). Among renter households, 42.2 percent lived in central cities and 40.3 percent in suburbs. However, because owner households outnumber renter households by more than two to one, owners made up 54.4 percent of all central-city households, 74.1 percent of all suburban households, and 76.5 percent of all households living outside of metropolitan areas (Census Bureau 2005b). These proportions give owner-occupant households substantial political advantages over renters when it comes to influencing local government regulations concerning housing, especially in the suburbs and outside metropolitan areas.

The Impacts of a Huge Inflow of Financial Capital into Housing Markets

This political power has become especially significant because of the immense inflow of financial capital into housing markets in the United States and around the world in the past decade. As a result of the worldwide stock market collapse in 2000, plus several other major economic developments, financial capital fled from stocks into real estate almost everywhere. At the same time, central banks in developed nations increased liquidity in their economies and cut interest rates to forestall a general recession from the stock market crash. Such easing of economic policies encouraged renter households the world over to seek homeownership because of low interest rates, easy credit terms, and rising home prices that promised substantial capital gains. Home builders stepped up production of new housing units to meet this increased demand, but home prices rose rapidly anyway in nearly all developed nations except Germany.

In the United States, median prices of existing homes sold, as measured by the National Association of Realtors, rose 51.1 percent from 1990 to 2000 but then soared 59.6 percent in the six years from 2000 to 2006. In California the median price rose 134 percent during those same six years. Home prices in other nations rose even more. From 1997 to 2006, median home prices rose 82 percent in the United States but 244 percent in Ireland, 184 percent in the United Kingdom, 173 percent in Spain, and 126 percent in Australia.[1] Soaring home prices were not primarily the result of a worldwide shortage of housing but were mainly caused by a massive shift of capital out of stocks and other investments into real properties, including both homes and commercial properties.

This dramatic spurt in home prices had several critical effects upon housing markets. First, it encouraged more and more renters to buy homes both to avoid

---

1. Author's calculations from data in several issues of the *Economist*: March 2003; March 11, 2004; June 3, 2004; September 2, 9, and 30, 2004; and December 11 and 30, 2004.

even higher future prices and to enjoy future increases in home equity. Their desires were furthered by low interest rates and reductions in credit standards for home buyers. In several California housing markets, 35 percent or more of all home mortgages originating in 2006 were negative amortization or interest-only loans. Those markets were San Diego (42 percent), the San Francisco Bay Area (40 percent), Los Angeles (39 percent), Sacramento, and Modesto-Stockton (35 percent) (Rosen 2006). As a result, nationwide, the fraction of households owning their own homes rose from 63.9 percent in 1990 to 67.4 percent in 2000 and to 68.9 percent in 2005.[2]

This shift from renting to homeownership involved a second impact on housing markets: a fall in the demand for rental units. From 2000 to 2005 the number of occupied rental housing units in the United States increased only slightly, by just 1.1 million units, as many renters and newly formed households rushed to buy homes (Census Bureau 2000, 2005a). The number of new home-owning households rose by 4.5 million, four times the total number of new renter households formed. No wonder rental vacancy rates rose notably in this period. Among all rental units, vacancy rates were between 7.1 and 7.9 percent from 1989 to 1998; they then rose quickly to 10.2 percent in 2004 before beginning to decline slightly in late 2005 and 2006 as the home sales market cooled.[3] Among apartments managed professionally in structures with five or more units, vacancies rose from 4 percent in the third quarter of 2000 to 7 percent in the first quarter of 2003 (Rosen 2006).

The third major impact of rising home prices was the enrichment of home-owning households as the market values of their homes shot upward. According to the Federal Reserve Board's Flow of Funds tables, the total market value of real estate held by U.S. households escalated from $6.58 trillion in 1990 to $11.41 trillion in 2000 and to $20.62 trillion in 2006—an increase of 213 percent in sixteen years. Even after subtracting home mortgages and other debts against their homes, the net equity of homeowners in their homes rose from $4.1 trillion in 1990 to $10.5 trillion in 2005—a gain of 160 percent. True, there were about 15 million more home-owning households in 2005 than in 1990 (Census Bureau 1990, 2005a). But correcting for that fact, and also converting home prices from current dollars to constant 2005 dollars, the average net real equity of each home-owning household rose by 36 percent from 1990 to 2005 (Federal Reserve Board 2007; Census Bureau 1990, 2005b).

In reality, home buyers, home builders, realtors, lenders, mortgage bankers, and almost all other practitioners in real estate transactions never think in constant dollars—only in current dollars; only economists correct for inflation. I

2. Census Bureau (2007a).
3. Census Bureau (2007a).

know, because I have been in the real estate business for more than fifty years. So most households who have owned their own homes during the past decade or more believe—correctly—that they have experienced large increases in the net market values of their homes. This is especially true in those regions where prices have risen much faster than the national average—such as California, Florida, Honolulu, and northeastern seaboard metro areas.

This enrichment has been a major incentive for additional renters to shift into homeownership during the past decade. It has also stimulated a large increase in consumer spending on goods and services unrelated to housing, using money borrowed against their home equities by refinancing mortgages at lower rates or taking out home equity loans.

The fourth major impact of rising home prices has been a devastating decline in the affordability of housing for millions of households. One group consists of those households living in regions with high housing costs who managed to scrape together enough money to buy homes during the past decade. In places like California, Boston, and Miami, those first-time buyers had to wait longer to amass their down payments, and they then got smaller, less luxurious homes, most likely located much farther from where they work, than did people buying homes in less costly regions like much of the Midwest and South.

An even larger group suffering from affordability problems consists of millions of renters who would like to become homeowners but cannot afford to do so. In spite of easy credit terms and low interest rates, soaring home prices have put ownership out of their reach because their incomes have not risen anywhere nearly as fast as housing prices. In 1990 the median household income in the United States in current dollars was $29,943; in 2004, it was $44,334 (Census Bureau 2006). That is a gain of 48.1 percent in the same period that the median price of existing homes sold, also in current dollars, rose by 101.3 percent.[4] In real terms in 2005 dollars, median incomes rose only from $43,366 in 1990 to $45,817 in 2004, or 5.7 percent, while median home prices were rising from $137,507 in 1990 to $191,478 in 2004, or 39.3 percent.[5] Whichever way you look at it, incomes lagged far behind home prices during those fourteen years.

However, the ability of low-income households with slow-growing incomes to buy homes with fast-rising prices was greatly expanded by changes in credit requirements. Interest rates on thirty-year, fixed-rate conventional home mortgages fell from 10.13 percent in 1990 to 5.87 percent in 2005, slashing monthly payments.[6] Credit terms were eased, with interest-only loans, lower or no down payments,

4. Author's calculations of 1990 and 2004 data from the National Association of Realtors.

5. Author's calculations of 1990 and 2004 data from the National Association of Realtors.

6. Freddie Mac, "Primary Mortgage Market Survey" (www.freddiemac.com/pmms/pmms30. htm).

undocumented income declarations by borrowers, option or negative amortization loans (in which payments were less than interest but the unpaid interest was added to the amount to be amortized later), and increases in the total proportion of income that lenders permitted borrowers to use for debt repayment. All these changes made it possible for many relatively low-income renters to purchase homes in spite of the fact that home prices were rising much faster than household incomes. That is a key reason why homeownership rose so fast, especially from 2000 to 2005, even though housing prices were soaring. However, the situation of renters was, and is, much worse in regions with the highest housing costs, where incomes did not rise much faster than the national average but housing price increases were double or triple the national average.

Moreover, rents also rose significantly in the same period. The median asking rents for vacant units in the United States was $371 a month in 1990 but increased to $483 in 2000 and $633 in 2006, all in current dollars.[7] That is an overall increase of 70.6 percent in sixteen years. In constant 2006 dollars, that rent increase was from $572 to $633, or 10.6 percent.[8] Many renters had difficulty just keeping up with their rents, let alone putting together money to buy a home. Furthermore, unless home prices decline much more than they have since the peak in 2005, this major shift in the relationship between household incomes and housing prices is likely to remain in place for a long time. Hence the decline in homeownership affordability will probably be a permanent fixture of American housing markets.

Another consequence of the rise in homeownership has been the attempts of NIMBYs (proponents of "not in my back yard") to subvert the creation of rental housing and multifamily apartments in thousands of suburban communities. Most local governments are politically dominated by homeowners with no-growth or slow-growth agendas. For suburban homeowners, the market values of their homes are their single largest assets. They want to protect those assets. They also believe that permitting cheaper owner-occupied homes or rental apartments in or near their neighborhoods might lower the market values of their own homes or affect the quality of local public schools. So they pressure their local government officials to prevent construction of such housing nearby. Since those local officials owe their election and reelection to voters, they adopt regulatory barriers and delaying tactics to block creation of low-cost housing—and nearly all rental apartments—in their communities.

In his paper delivered at the conference, Edward Glaeser of Harvard University pointed out that 68 percent of the local communities in Massachusetts had no land whatever zoned for multifamily housing. He and Joseph Gyourko of the University of Pennsylvania did a nationwide analysis of housing prices that concluded that local regulatory barriers were the major cause of high housing prices

---

7. Census Bureau (2007a, table 11A).
8. Census Bureau (2007a).

across the nation (Glaeser and Gyourko 2002). Those barriers also limit the production of rental apartments in the nation's suburbs. As a result, 84 percent of
all the new housing units built from 1990 to 2006 (including mobile or manufactured homes) consisted of single-family units, although an average of 34 percent of all households were renters during that entire period (Census Bureau
2006).[9] Even allowing for the fact that 31 percent of renters live in single-family
dwellings, new home builders undersupplied rental accommodations during the
past sixteen years (Census Bureau 2005b). That is one reason why renters are
more concentrated in central cities than are owners: too many suburbs block new
apartments within their boundaries.

How Federal Housing Policies Support Homeownership

The federal government's housing-related policies strongly favor homeowners over
renters, as indicated by its allocation of financial benefits between those groups.
Independence and homeownership are valued American traditions, so federal policies seek to expand homeownership. That leaves poor renters with only a relatively
small piece of the federal aid pie in the form of Section 8 vouchers, public housing
units, older rental construction subsidies, and other direct federal payments. In
2005 total federal outlays on all renter subsidies amounted to $32.297 billion (in
2006 dollars), as John Quigley notes in chapter 9 of this volume (table 9-1), using
data from the Office of Management and Budget. The Urban Institute's estimate
of such subsidies for 2005 was somewhat larger, as noted below.

In 2005 about 74 percent of all renter households had incomes below the
national median of $44,503, and 43 percent, or 14.6 million renter households,
had incomes below one-half the national median, which would qualify them as
eligible for federal housing aid (Census Bureau 2005b). Yet the federal government provides such aid to only 6.2 million renter households (HUD 2005).
Quigley notes that 70 percent of poor households eligible for federal housing aid
were not served by it, and 40 percent of those who were served did not meet the
official definition of poverty (because income limits for federal housing aid eligibility are higher than poverty income limits).

In contrast, financial benefits to homeowners consist of tax reductions in the
form of deductibility of mortgage interest payments from taxable income, tax
exemptions on profits from the sale of homes that have been occupied as a principal residence for two or more years, and, in many jurisdictions, lower property
tax rates on owner-occupied homes than on rental apartment units. These benefits are not direct federal outlays and therefore do not appear in government
appropriations, revenue statements, or budgets. However, the Urban Institute
has estimated that all the tax benefits to homeowners in 2005 amounted to

9. Census Bureau (2007b).

$146.9 billion, compared with $41.0 billion in aid to renters in the same year.[10] Since homeowners outnumber renters more than two to one, it is not surprising that federal benefits to the former are 3.6 times as large as those to the latter, even though the latter have much lower incomes.

The frustrating aspect of this situation is that most of the benefits to home-owners accrue to those in the highest tax brackets—households who need them least. Those benefits consist of deductions from taxable income, so households who pay the highest tax rates gain the most. As a result, households in the top-most income quintile (20 percent) received 82 percent of the total income tax benefits to all homeowners in 2005, and those in the second-highest quintile got 15 percent of those benefits. Only 3 percent went to the 60 percent of households in the bottom three quintiles, according to estimates made by economists Adam Carasso, Eugene Steuerle, and Elizabeth Bell.[11] Distributing federal tax benefits to homeowners more evenly—perhaps by using a tax credit instead of deductions from taxable income—would be much fairer. In addition, doing so would allow some of current costs to the federal government of housing-related benefits to be shifted to increasing direct aid to low-income renters. They clearly need housing assistance much more than the high-income households who now receive most federal housing-related financial benefits.

The current disparity between federal benefits to owner and renter households sustains the incentive for households to choose owning over renting. Other federal policies, such as maintaining low interest rates, financing mortgages through Fannie Mae and Freddie Mac, and providing Federal Housing Administration mortgage insurance, all favor homeowners over renters. The massive flows of finan-cial capital into housing and other real estate markets exacerbate the economic dilemma of poor renters, even though such inflows will surely not last indefinitely.

Policy Recommendations

What should be done to improve the functioning of U.S. rental housing? Mem-bers of the conference identified four major problems that prevent rental housing markets from working well now:

—The incomes of millions of American households in our free enterprise econ-omy are too low for them to own their own homes and also too low for them to pay for adequate rental shelter. They have to devote so much of their incomes to housing that they cannot afford other necessities, such as health care, transporta-tion, education, and food.

10. Adam Carasso and others, "Improving Homeownership among Poor and Moderate-Income Households," Urban Institute (2005) (www.urban.org/uploadedPDF/311184_improving_homeownership.pdf).

11. Adam Carasso, Eugene Steuerle, and Elizabeth Bell, "How to Better Encourage Home-ownership," Urban Institute and Brookings Tax Policy Center (2005) (www.urban.org/UploadedPDF/311193_IssuesOptions_12.pdf).

—Federal housing-related policies are based upon the widely held economic goal and the political popularity of homeownership, not upon the intensity of housing needs among households. Federal income-tax benefits for homeowners are entitlements, and, since 69 percent of all American households were home-owners in 2006, those benefits are several times larger—both in the aggregate and per household aided—than all federal subsidy benefits for renters. Yet it is renter households that need housing assistance most acutely.

—In the opinion of most symposium participants, high-poverty neighbor-hoods adversely effect the life chances of persons living there, most of whom are renters. High rates of poverty, crime, drug abuse, broken homes, unemployment, and gang activity combine with low-quality public schools and lack of health care to make living in such areas much more harmful than living in most middle-income neighborhoods.

—Most American suburbs are politically dominated by home-owning majori-ties, who pressure local governments to maintain regulatory barriers against local construction of low-cost single-family homes or any rental apartments at all. Local homeowners fear affordable housing might cause a decline in the market values of their own homes, which are their largest financial assets. This makes it difficult for many low-income households to move out of concentrated poverty areas into suburbs, where they can more easily obtain good jobs and good schools for their children.

The first problem—low household income—is both the most important obsta-cle to providing adequate shelter to poor renters and the most difficult to remedy. Prospects for significantly increasing the wage levels of the lowest two quintiles in the American income distribution are not bright, mainly because of globalization. The continuing inflow of well-trained and low-wage Chinese and Indian workers into the world's industrial and commercial labor markets holds down many Amer-ican wages, too. Foreign workers have expanded those labor forces by roughly 20 percent in the past two decades. I do not think that Congress can push the wages of our low-income sectors up enough, through minimum wage hikes and even an expanded earned income tax credit, to enable low-income American households to afford decent housing. Even significant protectionist tariffs against cheap imports are not likely to cause incomes to rise sufficiently for the lower 40 percent of the income distribution.

Moreover, the flood of financial capital into domestic and international hous-ing markets, especially since 2000, has greatly raised American housing prices. Those prices are now so high that the cost of either subsidizing the wages of the poor or building enough affordable housing would be astronomical. In view of the budgetary pressures now facing the federal government, there is little chance that Congress will agree to provide such subsidies for poor renters. Although the cost of housing in the United States is likely to decrease somewhat in the next few years, I do not foresee a general collapse of housing prices. Most homeowners unable to sell at prices they like will simply withdraw their homes from the market and remain living in them. That will put a floor under housing prices. Yet the relation between household incomes and housing prices has undergone a major structural change in the past decade that is likely to endure for a long time. Both renters and prospective home buyers are adversely affected by that shift.

In theory, the second obstacle—the federal government's bias toward home-ownership in its provision of housing assistance to American households—could readily be solved technically. Congress could change the present mortgage payment deduction from homeowners' taxable incomes to a uniform tax credit for each dollar of mortgage interest paid. That would stop high-income homeowners from getting larger tax benefits for each dollar of mortgage interest paid than low-income homeowners do, as now occurs. If the tax credit were set to produce slightly larger tax benefits for low- and middle-income homeowners than they now receive from tax deductions, the tax benefits flowing to high-income home-owners would be significantly reduced. That saving to the federal government could then be transferred to either an entitlement tax credit for low-income renters (as suggested by John Quigley at the conference) or larger and more broadly distributed housing vouchers and other subsidies already going to renter households. This change would produce a much fairer distribution of federal housing aid and tax benefits at no added cost.

Remedying the problem, however, is a political nonstarter. For decades, the politics of such legislation have prevented its passage, even though consecutive presidential housing commissions have recommended it as fairer and more effective than present policies. Home builders, realtors, landowners, lenders, and others gain higher profits from federal government subsidies of the most expensive housing units, which encourage construction of such units. These groups have always joined together with homeowners in the top income brackets to block even serious consideration of such a federal tax policy change. As mentioned, home-owners constituted 69 percent of all U.S. households in 2006 and represent a majority of constituents in almost all suburban communities, many big cities, and all states. Moreover, many middle-income homeowners who would immediately gain from the tax change suggested above aspire someday to own more expensive homes, so they do not want to increase the future after-tax costs of doing so. Congress will not antagonize the politically powerful interests who benefit from the present blatantly unfair system, so it refuses to consider a much fairer distribution of federal housing tax benefits and subsidies.

The third problem faced by low-income renters is their concentration in high-poverty neighborhoods, mainly in big cities. As Margery Turner and Bruce Katz note in chapter 10 of this volume,

Living in a distressed, high-poverty neighborhood undermines the long-term life chances of families and children. . . . Children who grow up in distressed neighborhoods . . . are less likely to perform at grade level, complete high school, or go on to college. . . . Young people who are surrounded by drug dealing and crime are more likely to become caught up in dangerous or criminal activities. Concentrated poverty also exacerbates the housing-jobs imbalance through which residents of poor neighborhoods are isolated from opportunities for employment and advancement because of distance or poor access to transportation.

How can low-income renters be encouraged—and empowered—to move out of such areas into neighborhoods, probably in the suburbs, where they can gain better access to new jobs, safer environments, and public schools of higher quality? Creating such movements at a large scale is known as the dispersion strategy. Pursuing this strategy inevitably raises the fourth problem, that of regulatory barriers blocking such movements. So I consider both these problems at once.

Turner and Katz propose an extensive array of policy changes aimed at attacking these problems through a combination of federal, state, and local policy initiatives. They suggest that the federal government create substantial financial incentives for state governments to pressure local governments to reduce regulatory barriers to more affordable housing, especially in suburbs. They further recommend that the federal government also expand the existing Low Income Housing Tax Credit and the Home Investment Partnership programs, both to offset losses of affordable units from the standing inventory and to create new affordable units in communities near suburban jobs. To increase the production of affordable housing, both renter and owner occupied, they recommend that existing metropolitan planning organizations expand their planning purview to include regional housing plans as well as regional transportation plans. They stress regional housing plans because they want to shift the creation of new affordable housing away from central cities and poverty areas therein into suburban communities that have up to now resisted entry of such housing.

I believe Turner and Katz are correct in outlining the directions in which public policies ought to move if the nation wants to help low-income households cope with the housing-related problems facing them. But merely pointing out to suburban governments that their local regulatory barriers are unfair and injurious to entire regions is useless; many federal housing commissions have done this in the past, with no visible results. Shifting some genuine power over where housing is built from local governments to state or regional government agencies is the only way to reduce suburban intransigence to acceptance of low-income households. State governments could do this on their own, since they are responsible for the welfare of all the citizens in their states, including the poor. But almost none have shown any inclination toward such a policy. Only Oregon and New Jersey have made some moves in that direction, and New Jersey did so mainly under pressure from state courts.

The basic issue is that most American households are homeowners—which is a good thing—and most do not want to accept low-income households, especially renters, as neighbors. Governments in the United States have been deliberately structured so that local autonomy, through its small-scale democracy, almost always defeats regional planning, with its more comprehensive perspective. The only exception involves planning primarily physical infrastructures clearly regional in nature, such as highways, water and sewer systems, and environmental pollution. No major metropolitan areas engage in true regional planning of housing or even future population growth except Portland, Oregon, possibly the Twin Cities in Minnesota, and those few regions where city and county governments have been merged. Everywhere else, the desire of local citizens to retain complete control over what types of housing are built in their own communities and who lives there remains dominant. Hence no effective planning for overall regional growth is carried out.

Louis Winnick, in his brilliant 1995 paper on why vouchers triumphed over housing production programs and preservation of concentrated-poverty neighborhoods blocked deliberate dispersal of their residents to more outlying areas, notes another factor: "Reproaches 20 years ago by . . . dispersionists over the futility of 'gilding the ghetto' . . . were overwhelmed by an unrelocatable underclass and by the explosive growth in numbers and political standing of salvational organizations, CDCs [community development corporations], Neighborhood Housing Services . . . and its financial backers, the Local Initiatives Support Corporation . . . , the Enterprise Foundation, the Neighborhood Reinvestment Corporation, and major philanthropic foundations. . . . The preservationists have won hands down [over the dispersionists]" (Winnick 1995, p. 100). Of course, the advocates of preserving and improving low-income city neighborhoods rather than helping their occupants disperse were strongly supported by suburban residents opposed to the entry of low-income households into their own territories. That attitude still prevails among most suburbanites today, even though millions of once low-income households of all races and ethnic groups have moved out of cities into suburban neighborhoods as their incomes rose.

This means that making progress against the third and fourth problems noted above will be slow going, involving one small step at a time against strong opposition. The first steps should probably be getting the federal government to create some financial incentives for state governments to pressure local governments into reducing regulatory barriers to lower-cost housing units; conducting well-documented research to determine whether building lower-cost housing and apartments in suburbs actually reduces the values of most housing there, as homeowners fear; developing inclusionary zoning systems that provide significant offsetting benefits for home builders who build affordable new units as a certain percentage of all the units they construct; and trying to create some form of regional housing and growth planning at the metropolitan area level. The last is being done in a nonbinding way in many fast-growth regions. There, leaders are trying to figure out how to cope with looming large-scale growth by increasing densities, in-fill development, and adopting a regionwide perspective.

Where is the political leadership to overcome the opposition to such changes— opposition that already exists and will become even more vehement? Although many more municipalities are now discussing their needs for more affordable housing, few elected officials, home builders, lenders, developers, or voters are willing to support the changes necessary to achieve that goal. The major obstacle to rental housing will remain rooted in the dilemma presented by the low incomes of millions of American households, on the one hand, and high housing prices, defended by most American homeowners, on the other.

Meanwhile, we must keep trying to improve rental housing. It may be a second-class form of shelter in the minds of most Americans, but it is also the starting point for millions of workers seeking better lives for themselves and their children, and a necessity for many others at the bottom of the income scale. In our free country, such low-income renters—and their housing—deserve to be treated with greater respect, acceptance, and support.

References

Bureau of Labor Statistics (BLS), U.S. Department of Labor. 2006. *Consumer Expenditure Survey* (www.bls.gov/cex/).

Glaeser, Edward L., and Joseph Gyourko. 2002. "The Impact of Zoning on Housing Affordability." Discussion Paper 1948. Harvard Institute for Economic Research.

Rosen, Kenneth. 2006. "The Real Estate and Economic Outlook." Paper prepared for the twenty-ninth annual Real Estate and Economics Symposium. University of California, Berkeley, Fisher Center for Real Estate and Urban Economics. San Francisco, November 20.

U.S. Census Bureau. 1990. *60 Years of Decennial Censuses, Homeownership 1900–2000, Historical Tables from the Housing Censuses.*

———. 2000. *Census 2000* (www.census.gov/main/www/cen2000.html).

———. 2005a. *American Community Survey 2005* (www.census.gov/acs/www/).

———. 2005b. *American Housing Survey 2005* (www.census.gov/hhes/www/housing/ahs/ahs.html).

———. 2006. *Current Population Survey* (www.census.gov/cps/).

———. 2007a. *Housing Vacancies and Homeownership* (www.census.gov/hhes/www/housing/hvs/hvs.html).

———. 2007b. *Survey of Construction* (www.census.gov/const/www/).

U.S. Department of Housing and Urban Development (HUD). 2005. *Affordable Housing Needs: A Report to Congress on the Significant Need for Housing.* December.

U.S. Federal Reserve Board. 2007. *Federal Reserve Flow of Funds Accounts of the United States* (www.federalreserve.gov).

Winnick, Louis. 1995. "The Triumph of Housing Allowance Programs: How a Fundamental Policy Conflict Was Resolved." *Cityscape: A Journal of Public Policy and Research* 1, no. 3: 95–121.

1

Overview: Rental Housing Challenges and Policy Responses

ERIC S. BELSKY AND RACHEL BOGARDUS DREW

The nation faces many long-standing rental housing challenges. Chief among these concerns are widespread affordability problems, neighborhood decline, the spatial concentration of poor renters, and exposure to health hazards in the home. Government policies and programs designed to grapple with these challenges have led to some impressive achievements. Although housing quality problems have not been eliminated, the number and share of substandard housing units has been sharply reduced over the past fifty years (Quigley and Raphael 2004; Orr and Peach 1999). Meanwhile, many cities that were losing residents in the 1950s, 1960s, and 1970s have started to recover population (Simmons and Lang 2001). These rebounds were at least in part aided by investments in building and reha-bilitating subsidized rental housing in distressed areas (Ellen and Voicu 2006). On the affordability front, federal programs now subsidize about 1 million public housing rentals, 2 million rentals in privately owned but federally assisted prop-erties, 1 million rentals in properties assisted by tax credits, and 2.1 million rental voucher holders. Annually, outlays for rental assistance and housing block grants top $35 billion, and tax incentives for rental housing total about $6 billion. Most of those living in these subsidized rentals or receiving vouchers spend no more than 30 percent of their income on housing.

Although the federal commitment to rental housing is far from trivial, by most reckonings federal rental subsidies still serve only a small fraction of the population in need (Joint Center for Housing Studies 2006a; Millennial Housing Commission 2002). No more than one-quarter of renter households with federally defined worst-case needs (very low income households spending more than half of their income on rent or living in severely inadequate or crowded conditions) receives a subsidy, whereas almost none of the growing share of low- and moderate-income households shouldering heavy rent burdens gets aid. Federal assistance is also widely seen as falling far short of what is needed to reverse neighborhood decline, eliminate housing quality and crowding problems altogether, and provide greater access to affordable rental housing in moderate- and upper-income neighborhoods and in newer, outlying suburbs. Making matters worse, federal rental assistance has reached a plateau, with increases at best limited to the rate of inflation.

Beyond the failure of rental policy to fully address the problems generated by the operation of rental markets, the long history of federal rental assistance has been checkered by some high-profile failures (Hays 1995). Lost on most is that only a small share of subsidized rental housing fits the stereotype (Finkel and others 2000). Still, the government has also been charged with persistently underinvesting in much of the subsidized, especially public, housing stock it helps fund (Compass Group 2002) as well as with contributing to the concentration of poor households in select neighborhoods by site decisions for large subsidized housing projects (Schill and Wachter 1995; Newman and Schnare 1997; Freeman 2004).

Although state and local governments have been playing an increasingly important and effective role in allocating federal rental assistance, they have not contributed much of their own funds, apart from coming up with required federal matches (Joint Center for Housing Studies 2005). Furthermore, state and local governments often impose regulatory restrictions on land development and residential building, which add to production costs and limit the number, types, and price-points of housing that can be built (Quigley and Rosenthal 2005). Many fault state and local regulations for being an important contributor to several of the rental housing challenges facing the nation today, especially rental affordability problems and the thin supply of rental housing in suburban areas, where job growth is most vigorous (Katz and others 2003).

These developments and trends are dispiriting enough but appear even more so now that the importance of safe, decent, affordable, and geographically balanced rental housing options is coming into sharper focus. It is also increasingly apparent that coping with the problems that rental markets produce could have far-reaching economic and social benefits. More and more research shows that unaffordable rental housing imposes needless additional costs through the negative externalities it creates (Wilson 1996; Newman and Schnare 1997; Glaeser and Sacerdote 2000; Bratt 2002; Galster 2002). By forcing households to make difficult trade-offs like skimping on basic needs, taking long and costly commutes, and accepting substandard housing, unaffordable rental housing is producing negative health and labor outcomes, reducing savings, and placing children at risk.

Mounting, though still limited, evidence suggests that, properly conceived and executed, promising new rental programs can help recipients of rental subsidies achieve better social and economic outcomes by deliberately helping them move and become established in communities richer in opportunity; achieve more-successful welfare-to-work transitions and support workforce development efforts more generally by combining housing with job assistance; and save and build assets by encouraging savings and rewarding extra work effort (Bloom, Riccio, and Verma 2005; Sard 2001; Verma and Riccio 2003; Newman and Harkness 2002; Ludwig and Kling 2005; Leventhal and Brooks-Gunn 2001). Rental housing is finally being seen more fully for what it really is: a vital housing option that can help meet multiple policy objectives and that should not be artificially constrained by government regulations or discouraged by government programs.

This chapter explores the primary problems generated by the operation of rental markets, why addressing these problems is important, what factors contribute to the generation of these problems, and how policies and programs have (or have not) tried to deal with them.[1] Four problems are emphasized: rental affordability; concentration of affordable rental housing in and near city centers; concentration of poor renters and neighborhood decline; and rental housing quality and crowding problems.

A fifth problem is treated separately and first here. This is the basis upon which households make their tenure choices—that is, their decision about whether to own or to rent. Although it may not constitute a problem of the kind the others represent, there is reason to believe that tenure choices may be influenced by cultural factors and perceptions that make people more favorably disposed to homeownership. This can result in tenure choices that leave households either more vulnerable to risks they would not face as renters or with a lower chance of financial benefit. In addition, tenure choice speaks to the critical importance of rental housing as an option. In this sense, a look at the tenure choice and the basis for making it is an important first step in properly construing the importance of rental housing and geographically balanced rental choices.

The Rental Option

The much-covered homeownership boom notwithstanding, more than 34 million American households currently opt to rent. This constitutes more than three in ten households. Every time a household forms or moves, the members of that household must decide whether to own or rent, where to live, the type of home to select, and how much to spend on housing. These decisions are made simultaneously, but

1. By markets, we mean not only the coming together of buyers, sellers, and intermediaries but also the government rules, infrastructure, and programs that play a part in constituting the markets.

the choice of whether to own or rent is distinctive. In 2004 more than 5 million households made this choice as they moved into homes they had not previously occupied.

Distinctions between Owning and Renting

At its most elemental level, renting differs from homeownership in terms of the tenure in which the property is held or used. Renters pay for the right to consume the flow of services that housing provides, including shelter, a location from which to commute and shop, and a neighborhood in which to form social connections and receive public services.[2] For homeowners, housing is both an investment and a consumable good. As an investment, it exposes owners to considerable risk that the property will decline in value or that the cost of repairs and replacements will outpace their ability to pay for them. It also provides the opportunity to earn a return if the home appreciates more in value than it costs to buy and sell it.

Beyond this fundamental and vital distinction is one other: moving from one rental to another does not involve the transfer of property among owners. As a result, transaction costs are far lower for renters, reducing the costs and friction of moving. Renters, like owners, have search costs and moving costs and may have to provide an initial up-front deposit. But they do not have to cover the far steeper costs of paying real estate transfer taxes, the legal costs of closing on a home, the higher due-diligence costs of making sure the property purchased is fit and free of significant hazards, the costs of using a broker (in the vast majority of cases in which one is used), and the costs of applying for a mortgage if the property is financed. It is not uncommon for the combined costs of buying and selling to amount to 10 percent of the home's total value.

The only other important distinction between owning and renting is that owners must come up with the full market value of the property they intend to own up front, whereas renters must cover only the rent for a particular time period, often only between one and three months' worth. This means that most owners must finance the purchase of their homes at least at some point in their lives, which requires them to apply for a mortgage, meet the underwriting standards of the lender, and make a slew of other choices about the type of mortgages to use to finance the purchase of their home. Related to this is the fact that mortgage interest and real estate taxes are tax deductible. Thus for those with payments large enough to benefit from itemizing deductions, owning taps into powerful and costly (to government) tax breaks that are more generous than those available to owners of rental properties.

---

2. Although renting is a form of consumption, where one chooses to rent has implications for human capital formation because it typically determines the quality of the public schools that children attend and the economic value of local social relationships.

In other respects, renting and owning are quite similar. Although laws governing each are different, owners and renters are united in that both can lose their homes for failure to meet financial obligations. And though owners typically have more control over the use of their space than renters, the degree of individual control varies with the type of situation they buy into. Both condominium and homeowner associations often impose multiple restrictions on private rights of use, and local governments invariably impose many others. Additionally, though it is true that rental housing usually provides greater convenience and less responsibility, owners can contract for the same sorts of services. Both condo and owner associations can achieve the same sorts of economies of scale in service provision that residents of larger rental properties enjoy. The real difference is that owners must take responsibility for maintenance of the home and the risks associated with uncertain future maintenance costs, while renters do not and can walk away if displeased with the decisions made by their landlords.

The Importance of Rental Housing

It flows from these fundamental differences that rental housing is a critical housing option—and one that government should have an interest in ensuring is available and that artificial barriers are not put up that slant the playing field toward ownership—for the following important reasons:

—Rental housing reduces transaction costs and hence constitutes less of a barrier to mobility, a fact economists take note of because it allows a speedy adjustment of the labor market when the geographic pattern of labor demand changes.[3]

—Rental housing lowers transactions costs that constitute market inefficiencies and produce deadweight losses.[4]

—Unlike homeowners, renters do not have to assume the risks associated with an undiversified investment in a single primary residence.[5]

—Rental housing provides an opportunity for real estate risk to be pooled and diversified by larger-scale owners better able to manage and professionally assess real estate risk.

—Rents are set in a competitive market, whereas the costs of homeownership depend on the individual mortgage choices made by homeowners.[6]

—By virtue of not requiring a mortgage, rental housing is accessible to more households.[7]

3. See Green and Hendershott (2001).
4. See Haurin and Gill (2002).
5. William N. Goetzmann and Matthew Spiegel (2002) provide a good discussion of the risks associated with the purchase of a home.
6. The move into risk-based pricing of mortgages means that housing costs of homeowners increasingly reflect their individual mortgage choices and credit histories (Belsky and Calder 2004).
7. Underwriting constraints on tenure choices, while loosened over the past ten years, remain. Loan rejections on conventional home-purchase first-lien loans in 2004 were 11 percent for whites, 25 percent for blacks, and 19 percent for Hispanics (Avery, Canner, and Cook 2005, p. 374).

—By virtue of not requiring an individual mortgage, renting can be a better deal for households with impaired or no credit histories because its costs are not usually tied to the past credit history of the renter.[8]

In addition, rental choices also provide opportunities for investors to earn a return on their rental investments. The total value of rental properties was estimated at $2.7 trillion in 2003 (Joint Center for Housing Studies 2006a, p. 1). Rent revenues bring $250 billion annually to landlords, who also spend approximately $50 billion a year to maintain and improve their properties. Fully 4.3 million households in 2004 reported having received at least some income from residential properties they owned, and countless others invest in real estate investment trusts (REITs), limited partnerships, and syndications that own rental properties. The rent revenues reported averaged 11 percent of the total income of these investors (Joint Center for Housing Studies 2006b, p. 23).

Finally, renting can be a better financial choice than owning, especially for those who plan to move again in the near future, because it saves on transactions costs. It is also a better choice during a period of flat or declining house prices and for those who lack the savings to deal with unexpected housing-related repairs, have poor credit histories, or are at special risk for disruptions in income that may force them to move. For owners who resell their homes in a relatively short period of time, the value of their homes may not rise enough to cover the transaction costs, and they may end up spending more on owning than they would have on renting over the same period (Belsky, Retsinas, and Duda 2005; Goodman 1997). Even owners who hold their properties for a longer time may still not see sufficient appreciation if they are forced to sell in a down market (Belsky and Duda 2002). Finally, owners who default on their mortgages may end up in foreclosure and lose their investment altogether.

Given the appeal of renting to those who are most mobile and those excluded from homeownership owing to institutional and economic barriers, it is unsurprising that large shares of young people, people who are in transitional states in their family living arrangements, minorities, the foreign born, and those with low incomes live in rental housing. Indeed, 47 percent of unmarried persons living alone rented their homes in 2005, compared with only 17 percent of married couples. Similarly, 61 percent of householders under the age of thirty-five rented, while 73 percent of thirty-five- to sixty-four-year-olds and 79 percent of seniors owned. Fully three-quarters of white households owned, but only half of minorities did. Finally, 46 percent of divorced or separated householders, and more

---

8. The greater access to rental housing is being jeopardized by the expanded use of credit scores, criminal background checks, and other electronic information to screen tenants in a way that mortgage lenders long have but landlords have not. Although this certainly makes sense from the landlord's point of view, it surely restricts access to rental housing and magnifies the ill effects of failing in homeownership.

than 70 percent of recent movers relocating for financial or employment reasons, rented in 2005.[9]

Still, the attraction of homeownership is deeply ingrained in our social consciousness, with its associations with the American dream and its symbolic demonstration of independence and success. Many regulatory, policy, and financial incentives to homeownership further encourage households to buy. In addition, financial institutions, under increasing pressure in the 1990s to comply with federal regulations, rallied behind a call to expand homeownership by reaching out to low-income and minority communities and individuals.[10] In the early 1990s, under the banners of strengthening communities, supporting children, and helping the poor get a stake in the ownership society, the drumbeat of homeownership turned into a federally coordinated national campaign to boost the homeownership rate, an effort that has been sustained through two presidents.

More recently, the idea of using homeownership as a way for the poor to build assets has taken root. Increasingly, advocates are calling for funding for programs that help low-income households achieve homeownership (Sherraden 1991; Retsinas and Belsky 2005). Even academics are getting into the act. Over the past ten years, there has been a flurry of studies suggesting that homeownership produces stronger communities, more civic-minded citizens, and better outcomes for children, even after controlling for income, wealth, race, and neighborhood effects.[11]

With business, government, scholars, the advocacy community, and the American public all in favor of promoting homeownership, renting runs the risk of getting even less attention in the future than it now receives. Compounding these problems are the often negative perceptions of affordable rental housing (NeighborWorks 2004). This is not to say that individuals should not prefer homeownership or not seek it out. Rather, it means simply that we live in a society that typically predisposes people to think that ownership is the right choice for them and that failure to achieve it is negative. Unfortunately, though we know prob-

9. Numbers in this paragraph are Joint Center for Housing Studies tabulations of the 2005 American Housing Survey (www.huduser.org/datasets/ahs.html).

10. These regulations include the affordable, underserved, and special affordable housing goals of Fannie Mae and Freddie Mac, the Community Reinvestment Act, the Home Mortgage Disclosure Act, the Equal Credit Opportunity Act, and the Fair Housing Act.

11. Holding such critical variables as race, income, and wealth equal, these studies suggest that homeownership generally leads to greater wealth accumulation than renting (Di, Yang, and Liu 2003), reduces behavioral problems and increases the educational achievement of children (Haurin, Parcel, and Haurin 2002), and leads to greater participation in civic affairs (DiPasquale and Glaeser 1999). Furthermore, several studies also indicate that higher neighborhood homeownership rates have a positive influence on child outcomes (Haurin and others 2003; Harkness and Newman 2002) as well as on the probability that a neighborhood will move up or down the income distribution within a metropolitan area (Rosenthal 2004). Though these findings are still subject to criticism and may be less conclusive than some might recognize, they have become highly influential in policy circles (Apgar 2004).

lematic outcomes from homeownership are possible, the literature is largely silent on how many tenure choices, seen from a normative perspective, appear suboptimal for individuals and the nation. What we do know is that consumers make decisions about whether to own or rent based on financial considerations and preferences as well as expectations about how long they plan to stay in a place before moving again (Herbert and others 2004). Financial considerations include the current relative costs of owning and renting and expectations about future house prices and rents. Preferences include having a greater or lesser degree of control over home spending decisions and the time spent on home maintenance and improvement. They also include location preferences that may effectively preclude one or another tenure choice.

Knowing that financial considerations are major factors, however, is a far cry from understanding how households form expectations about the future course of house prices, the returns on alternative investments, the risks of income disruptions, and the risks of unforeseen expenses. If these are systematically biased toward homeownership, as they might well be, by government policies, industry outreach, and cultural factors, then it is likely that many choose to own when their chances of coming out ahead financially would have been better had they rented.[12]

The Nation's Rental Challenges

Rental markets (construed as the actions of buyers, sellers, and intermediaries, the factors that influence these actions, and government interventions in these actions) produce at least four major outcomes that are the cause of policy concern: affordability; availability in and near central cities; concentration of the poor and neighborhood decline; and housing quality and crowding. Table 1-1 summarizes these concerns and the reasons rental markets produce these outcomes.

Rental Affordability Problems

Affordability is by far the most common housing problem facing renters, though its implications for individual and community outcomes have been surprisingly understudied. It is ultimately an elusive concept that demands subjective judgments about what share of income should be spent on housing. By convention, housing expenses that consume more than 30 percent but less than 50 percent of income are considered moderate cost burdens, and expenses that consume more than half of income are severe cost burdens. Very low-income households (those with incomes

---

12. There are several studies that simulate the returns to homeownership under a variety of assumptions about house price appreciation, rent change, holding periods, transactions costs, the performance of alternative investments to owning, and mortgage finance terms (Goodman 1997; Rohe, McCarthy, and Van Zandt 2001). Even the most complete set of simulations (Belsky and Duda 2002) were limited to a handful of metropolitan areas and did not examine holding periods beyond seven years.

Table 1-1. *Summary of Principal Rental Housing Concerns*

Policy concern	Contributing factors	Why it is important
Rental affordability problems —Widespread and increasing —Long-term trend of problems worsening among the bottom income quintile —Primarily low-income and very low-income households afflicted and most harmed —Growing shares of moderate-income households facing rent burdens —Forces trade-offs, including sacrificing basic needs, saving less, having longer travel times and higher travel costs, living in poorer quality housing, and living in poorer quality neighborhoods	Demand-side income problems[a] —Slow rate of real growth in returns to low-wage work —Strong demand for low-wage and part-time workers —Growth at tails of the distribution of occupations as ranked by wages, with flattening in the middle —Size and scope of safety net for elderly and disabled Supply-side problems —Rate of growth in operating costs relative to income —Development and land-use regulations that increasingly add to replacement cost —Development regulations that limit production of higher-density, more modest rentals —Market dynamics that lead to net losses of low-cost rental housing —Rate of growth in rental subsidies and tax incentives relative to need	Equity —making work pay —fulfilling the social contract Human costs of trade-offs —Sacrifice of other basic needs —Lower expenditures on nutrition and health care —Increased financial insecurity for families —Heightened exposure to health risks —Longer commutes and less time with family —Poorer educational outcomes for children Social, public, and economic efficiency costs of trade-offs —Reduced private savings —Increased public health and safety costs —Reduced economic productivity —Increased auto emissions and habitat destruction —Lost investment in the rental capital stock —Higher costs of serving homeless Potential to contribute productively to antipoverty strategies (asset building, workforce development, and the like)
Concentration of rental housing in and near city centers —Exacerbated by continuing dispersion of jobs and housing in metro areas —Places greater distance between supply of low-wage workers and demand for them	Demand-side problems —Renter location choices given public transit constraints —Race- and class-based preferences expressed by "home voters" Supply-side problems	Human costs —Higher unemployment and restricted opportunity for urban low-wage workers —Higher commuting costs and times Social, public, and economic efficiency costs —Higher suburban wage rates for low-wage occupations

Concentration of poverty and neighborhood decline
—Easing nationally but remains significant
—Present in all cities
—Intensifying in many metro areas
—Most severe for minorities, especially African Americans
—Reductions in high-poverty (2 in 5 poor) areas has not been accompanied by a reductions in poverty (1 in 5 poor) areas

Housing quality and crowding
—Severe structural inadequacy reduced
—Incidence sharply higher for low-income households
—Large portion of housing stock still has significant home health hazards (lead paint, asbestos, aluminum wiring, narrow stair treads, and the like)

—Difficulty producing moderate-cost housing in suburbs owing to building, development, and land use regulations
—Political balkanization of metro areas

Demand-side factors
—Race- and class-based preferences
—Competition for preferred locations and housing based on income
—Functional obsolescence of older housing stock
—Social capital formation in poverty areas

Supply-side factors
—Discrimination
—Political balkanization of metro areas
—Physical depreciation of housing
—Comparative costs of greenfield versus infill and brownfield development
—Microeconomics of supplying housing at rents below operating expenses
—Underinvestment in and concentration of subsidized affordable housing in poor communities

Rental affordability problems
Cost to remediate significant hazards
Code promulgation (lack of rehab codes)
Code enforcement
Low average incomes of households that occupy older housing stock

—Greater reliance on school-age workers
—Greater traffic congestion and increased auto emissions

Human costs
—Heightened exposure to health and safety hazards and greater mental stress
—Isolation from economic opportunities
—Poorer educational outcomes, including higher high-school dropout rates
—Increased social problems (such as teen pregnancy)

Social, public, and economic efficiency costs
—Higher social welfare, public health, and safety costs
—Loss of past investments in the rental housing stock
—Negative externalities of underinvestment in housing on neighbors and residents
—Lower workforce productivity
—Costly restoration, revitalization, and redevelopment efforts

Human costs
—Higher exposure to health risks
—Higher potential for loss of household income
—Negative influence on cognitive development

Social, public, and economic efficiency costs
—Higher public health costs
—Reduced worker productivity

a. Many so-called household demand factors reflect the structure of the economy and the nature of labor demand.

of half or less of median income) with severe cost burdens or living in substandard housing or crowded conditions are defined by the federal government as having "worst-case housing needs."

Developed initially as a way of counting housing needs among households with incomes low enough to be eligible to receive rental assistance, the concept of moderate and severe cost burdens has been extended by the broader policy community to households above very low-income cutoffs. Although this approach has underscored the fact that rental affordability problems are creeping into the middle class, it has taken the spotlight off those who stand to lose the most by allocating large fractions of their incomes to housing because their incomes are so meager to begin with.[13]

A principal drawback of these simple measures is that they do not consider trade-offs households often make to lower their housing costs. A household may opt to live in a place with poorer quality schools, for example, or at a great distance from work (Belsky and Lambert 2001). Households make these choices because they find rental housing unaffordable in neighborhoods and locations that meet their preferences. But as a consequence they do not show up among the counts of those with rental affordability problems (Thalmann 2003).

Despite these drawbacks, the traditional measures of rental affordability do an adequate job of measuring the magnitude of the problem and tracking changes in them over time and among subgroups. Rental affordability problems are hardly a new phenomenon. John Quigley and Stephen Raphael (2004) show a steady upward trend in the share of renters with cost burdens and a decrease in the share of units affordable to the lowest-income renters starting as early as the 1960s. The struggle to find decent and affordable housing has only been getting worse in recent years. From 2001 to 2004 alone, the number of renter households with severe cost burdens increased by more than 1 million—including more than 800,000 in the bottom income quartile—for a total of 8.4 million renters. Another 7.6 million renters had moderate but not severe cost burdens. In share terms, the number of severely cost-burdened renters increased by 14 percent over this period, and as of 2004 represented 23 percent of all renters, while those with moderate cost burdens increased 5.5 percent and accounted for 21 percent of all renters. Among renters in just the bottom income quintile, 57 percent had severe and 22 percent had moderate cost burdens (Joint Center for Housing Studies 2006b, p. 36, table A-6).

Rental affordability problems and the material hardships they may trigger are, for obvious reasons, most heavily concentrated among the poor and those with near-poverty incomes. However, many of these households have earnings that are

---

13. As a result, some have argued for switching to a residual approach to defining affordability—that is, in terms of how much is left over after paying for housing to meet other basic needs (Stone 1993; Nelson and Redburn 1994). This approach focuses on cases in which housing costs are so high that they cause material deprivations.

Figure 1-1. *Housing Cost Burdens among the Lowest-Income Households,*
by Household Income Quartile and Equivalent Full-Time Work Ratio, 2005

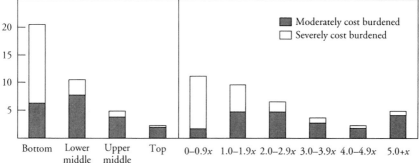

Source: Joint Center for Housing Studies tabulations of the 2005 American Housing Survey.

equal to or above the minimum wage equivalent of full-time work (figure 1-1).
Indeed, nearly 70 percent of all cost-burdened renter households are in the bottom
fourth of the income distribution, and 63 percent have incomes at least equivalent
to that of a single full-time minimum wage job.

WHY RENTAL AFFORDABILITY PROBLEMS MATTER. Heavy public investments to ease rental affordability problems have been justified primarily on equity
grounds. Because the economy does not produce enough jobs with wages high
enough for many to comfortably afford rental housing, government has redistributed income to make up for at least part of the shortfall. But rental affordability
can and is increasingly being justified also by the material deprivations households
suffer when burdened with high housing costs. For example, among households in
the bottom expenditure quartile, those that devote at least 50 percent of their expenditures to housing have less than $400 a month to spend on all other items and end
up spending two-thirds as much on food, half as much on clothes, and one-third
as much on health care as households in the same expenditure group but with less
than 30 percent of expenditures going toward housing. The more burdened
households also spend one-third as much on transportation (see figure 1-2).

Clearly, those who spend less on housing typically trade off commute time and
auto dependence for lower housing costs. These longer commutes create congestion
and degrade the environment through auto emissions. Auto dependence among
those with low incomes is problematic because it exposes them not only to higher
costs but also to greater uncertainty concerning the reliability of the transportation
they may need to get to work. The resulting spatial pattern can undermine the
productivity of workers and the economic competitiveness of regions.

Figure 1-2. *Spending Trade-off between Housing and Transportation, 2005*

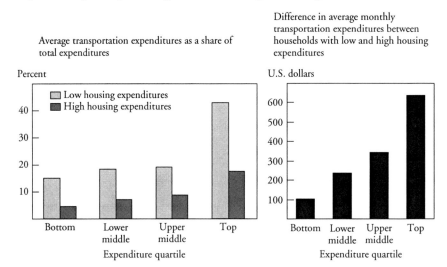

Average transportation expenditures as a share of
total expenditures

Difference in average monthly
transportation expenditures between
households with low and high housing
expenditures

Source: Joint Center for Housing Studies (2005).

It is also evident that spending more on housing leaves less to spend not only on daily essentials but also on savings for the future. As housing cost burdens creep up, private savings and retirement balances suffer. The broader implications of this are significant from the standpoint of future demands on the social welfare system. Yet the important link between savings and rental housing costs is seldom raised as a reason for public leaders to tackle housing affordability problems.

The impact of higher housing costs on health care spending and health insurance enrollment is also cause for concern (Lipman 2005). Spending less on these items leaves households at greater health risk and greater risk of making demands on emergency rooms, which shifts costs to the insured, and on government Medicare and Medicaid programs. To the degree that they result in health problems that might otherwise have been avoided, high housing costs reduce worker productivity and create unnecessary medical costs. Renters with high housing costs also move more frequently (Coulson and Fisher 2002), which, besides being costly, has been linked with poorer educational performance of children (GAO 1994). Affordable rental housing is therefore important for the social and physical well-being of children and the transactions costs that households must bear.

While all these impacts of unaffordable housing have adverse consequences for the households that suffer from them, they also clearly generate negative externalities that have public costs. In an effort to cover rent each month, households can skimp on nutrition, health insurance, and health care expenditures. These, together with trade-offs that entail living in poor-quality housing and neighborhoods, can add to public health costs, influence worker productivity and job retention, add to educational costs, and reduce the educational attainment of children. The impact on savings creates negative externalities since, in the end, social insurance and supports make up at least in part for what households do not save privately. At the extreme, people who cannot afford a rental under any circumstances fall into homelessness.[14]

In addition, rental affordability matters because there is suggestive evidence that affordable rental housing can help achieve better social and economic outcomes for low-income recipients. The most carefully controlled study of welfare-to-work programs, for example, suggests that the availability of stable affordable housing can improve the outcomes of antipoverty efforts (Bloom, Riccio, and Velma 2005). Experience with the Family Self-Sufficiency program, which provides incentives for rental aid recipients to both work and save, strongly suggests that subsidy programs can provide incentives to save and can aid in asset building among the poor (Sard 2001).[15] Affordable rental housing may also reduce the likelihood of getting overextended on credit and having low credit scores, which now govern the cost and availability of mortgage credit and even access to rental housing (Belsky and Calder 2004).

Finally, rental housing is the logical starting point for families and individuals making a variety of different transitions, including out of homelessness, out of foster care, out of prison, and from independent to assisted living. Combined with social services, the extension of the helping hand of an affordable rental in these situations can also lead to improved outcomes for these households with special needs.

CONTRIBUTING FACTORS TO RENTAL AFFORDABILITY PROBLEMS. Although it is possible that the growth of housing cost burdens among low- and moderate-income households reflects a shift in the perceived utility of the flow of services linked to housing (including education, social connections, and access to jobs and amenities), it is more likely a function of shifts in the structure of the economy and the operation of housing markets. Starting with supply constraints, a host of natural features and government-imposed regulations reduce the overall supply of available land and govern the types of housing that can be built. The weight of these supply constraints fall most heavily on lower-income households because they create especially tight restrictions on development of higher-density, more modestly constructed rentals. When the market demands these rentals but is constrained by government from delivering them, low-income households are forced to bid up rents on an artificially constricted supply.

---

14. Indeed, the intuition that unmanageable housing costs for the poor contribute importantly to homelessness is supported by a study by Amy Crews Cutts and Edgar O. Olsen (2002), who find that targeting housing subsidies to the poorest households significantly reduces homelessness.

15. The program allows residents of subsidized housing to save the difference between 30 percent of their initial incomes and any growth in their income, rather than allocating that amount to rent.

Building affordable units is a challenge. The cost to build rental housing has gone up over time, in large measure because of development regulations and restrictions that introduce added expense and delays into the process and prevent developers from building at higher densities (see Schill 2004). Land costs, though inherently local, have been rising overall over the past several decades. Quigley and Rosenthal (2005) find that while direct causal relationships are hard to prove, the presence of restrictions is often correlated with higher land costs, which alter the composition of housing produced by withdrawing land from development, imposing fees and costs, adding to risks, and restricting development densities.

Recently, more sophisticated analyses and better survey data have provided more compelling evidence of an effect.[16] Linking these newer survey data to prices, building permits, demographic change, mobility, and migration patterns, several studies have found that an increase in regulation had a positive effect on prices but a negative effect on affordability (Malpezzi 1996; Malpezzi, Chun, and Green 1998; Somerville and Mayer 2003; Glaeser and Gyourko 2002; Saks 2004). In addition, in Richard Green's (1999) analysis of land-use and zoning regulations in a suburban Wisconsin county, the impact was greater on lower-price houses and thus disproportionately borne by lower-income households. As Michael Schill (2004) points out, however, few studies have been able to conclusively show whether the higher prices associated with development restrictions are the result of these supply constraints or are, rather, a response to the demand for such housing. On balance, however, the evidence strongly suggests that supply constraints from regulations contribute materially to rental affordability problems.

It is really the intersection of supply and demand, however, that produces the affordability problem. On the demand side, those who rely on government income supports often have incomes below the poverty level, and even incomes above the poverty level are frequently insufficient to escape moderate or severe rent burdens. The economy demands low-wage and part-time workers who earn too little in many cases to afford the operating costs of even modest rentals in less than desirable neighborhoods. Even working families that use the earned income tax credit (EITC) spend more than half their income on rent.

Rental affordability problems are growing because the incomes of those most in need of affordable rental housing have not kept pace with increases in the costs of rental housing. From 1993 to 2003, for example, the median income of renters in the bottom quintile of all renters increased nominally by only 20 percent, while the median incomes of all other quintiles grew by at least 30 percent. At the same time, the median rents paid by the lowest-income renters increased by 62 percent,

---

16. A survey by the Wharton School of Business polled more than 1,000 municipalities on their land policies and restrictions, resulting in a comprehensive database for comparative study (Linneman and others 1990).

compared with increases of 32 to 37 percent for all other quintiles.[17] Indeed, for renter households in the top two income quintiles, the growth in median income was actually greater than the increase in their median rents, whereas incomes at the low end of the distribution have stagnated. Only the incomes of those at the top have been keeping pace with the rise in housing costs over the past few decades (Millennial Housing Commission 2002).

The growth in low-wage and part-time jobs with little opportunity for advancement has contributed to the stagnation in income growth at the low end of the income distribution. A recent study (Autor, Katz, and Kearney 2006) demonstrates this U-shaped pattern in the national wage distribution: most jobs are clustered at the low end and a smaller set at the high end, with few remaining in the middle. As the nation has shifted from manufacturing and labor-intensive industries to a more services-oriented economy, the types of middle-income jobs that many households relied on in the past are disappearing. Unfortunately, prospects for reversing this trend are bleak. Of the fifteen occupations expected to generate the most growth in jobs over the next ten years, ten offered median wages of less than $28,570 (Hecker 2005).

Recent losses of affordable rental housing are only exacerbating an already dire situation. On net, 1.2 million units with rents under $400 were lost from 1993 to 2003. As a result, fully 13 percent of the stock affordable to renters with incomes of less than $16,000 was lost in just a ten-year period (Joint Center for Housing Studies 2006a). Affordable rental housing is being lost on net because less low-cost rental housing is filtering down to lower rent ranges than is filtering out of it through rent inflation, on the one hand, and abandonment and loss, on the other (Somerville and Holmes 2001).

Finally, the number of households served with rental assistance has stalled even as the number of renter households with worst-case needs has surged. The number of severely cost-burdened low-income renters has grown from just over 5 million in 1990 to almost 8 million in 2004. At the same time, the number of assisted renter households has barely budged, from just under to just over 5 million. Indeed, from 2000 to 2004 alone, the number of severely cost-burdened low-income renters grew by more than a million, while the number assisted by the Department of Housing and Urban Development did not change at all (Joint Center for Housing Studies 2006a).

Concentration of Affordable Rental Housing in and near Central Cities

The concentration of affordable rental housing in and near central cities has also spawned public policy concerns. It is one of two rental housing challenges— the other being the concentration of poor renters in distressed neighborhoods—

17. Numbers in this paragraph are Joint Center for Housing Studies tabulations of data from the 1993 and 2003 American Housing Surveys (www.huduser.org/datasets/ahs.html).

that is the result of the spatial outcome of the operation of rental markets. Households sort themselves into neighborhoods within jurisdictions and across jurisdictions within a metropolitan area. At the metropolitan level, the operation of the market clearly segregates residential areas by race and income and creates a pattern of greater concentration of renter households and housing near the cores of urban areas.

The concentration of rental housing near city centers is significant. Whereas only 12 percent of owner households in the ninety-one largest metropolitan regions lived within 5 miles of a central business district in 2000, fully 25 percent of renter households did so. In these same ninety-one metro regions in 2000, the median distance from central business districts was 9.4 miles for renters but 13.8 miles for owners. Focusing only on more affordable rentals, in the same year 38 percent of units with rents of $400 or less were within 5 miles of these city centers, while only 17 percent of all occupied homes were in these locations. The concentration of minority renters near city centers is even more extreme (Joint Center for Housing Studies 2006a, pp. 13–15).

WHY CONCENTRATION OF AFFORDABLE RENTALS NEAR CITIES MATTERS. The disproportionate share of rental units, affordable rentals, and minority renters in and near cities matters in large measure because it means that rental options are increasingly restricted to urban locations while employment is increasingly dispersing to suburban locations and low-density areas at the metropolitan fringe. From 1990 to 2000, the share of jobs in the suburbs increased from 39 to 43 percent, while the share in central cities declined from 42 to 39 percent.

The evidence strongly suggests that the dearth of moderate-cost rental housing in the suburbs and the overall pattern of sprawl within which it is embedded is driving up suburban wages for low-wage work and cutting off those most in need of these jobs from access to them. The separation of low-wage renter households from suburban low-wage work has a number of specific outcomes:

—It restricts employment opportunities for these households and may further tilt their tenure choices toward owning, even if renting may suit them better.

—It forces some to make costly reverse commutes.

—It contributes to higher unemployment among city renters.

—It bids up wages for these jobs in suburbs.

It is important to point out, however, that the sprawling pattern of development also means that low-wage renters who do move in search of jobs and find homes to rent in suburbs face steeper transportation costs than they would face if living in cities on or near public transit because they usually must rely on private transportation. This places them at greater risk of missing work and sacrificing other items to cover their combined housing and travel cost burdens. Hence sprawl presents problems for all low-wage workers and generates environmental concerns that are largely independent of the particular form of tenure of dispersed homes.

CONTRIBUTING FACTORS TO THE CONCENTRATION OF RENTAL HOUS-
ING NEAR CITIES. Two principal factors contribute to these uneven spatial
patterns. First, the uneven distribution of rental units, especially of those that are
affordable to low-wage workers, is strongly influenced by restrictive regulations
within suburban jurisdictions, as discussed above. Further testament to what the
market demands but regulations often deny, however, is the pressure of the developers' lobby nearly everywhere to allow them to build at higher density than is
allowed by zoning and subdivision regulations. Although these restrictions directly
add to housing costs, they have a disproportionate impact on renters, who have
lower incomes on average.

Second, it is also likely that the pattern of rental properties reflects the strong
demand for owner-occupied housing by those opting to live in the suburbs. Even
in this regard, however, it is unclear precisely what leads these households to seek
suburban locations. It appears to be motivated, in part, by factors that "push" rather
than "pull." The higher-income households that are more able to afford homeownership may leave cities as a result of perceived urban ills, including crime,
pollution, and low-quality schools. Almost certainly, racial preferences and institutional discrimination also play a role. Conversely, some have argued that the poor
and those with low incomes gravitate to places where they have greater access to
public transportation, usually in neighborhoods that have become distressed and
therefore offer relatively low-cost housing (Glaeser and Gyourko 2005; Glaeser,
Khan, and Rappaport 2000).

In sum, both supply- and demand-side influences give rise to the concentration of rental housing, and especially of more affordable rental housing. The
two sides are, in fact, intricately intertwined, and the choices made by both
consumers and suppliers are heavily influenced by government regulation and
the uneven distribution of public service quality both within and between metropolitan areas.

Concentration of the Poor and Neighborhood Decline

At the extreme, substantial portions of the very poorest renters end up concentrated in the highest-poverty neighborhoods. This concentration of the poor
and the process of neighborhood decline it often generates also give rise to a
series of public policy concerns. The numbers are striking. In 2000, 38 percent
of renters earning less than $20,000 lived in tracts in which at least one in five
households lived in poverty, whereas only 25 percent of all renter households
and 16 percent of all households lived in such areas. Furthermore, while only
2 percent of all households lived in the highest-poverty tracts (those in which
at least two in five households were living in poverty), fully 8 percent of all renter
households with incomes of less than $20,000 lived in them. Living in concen-
trated poverty tracts is also no guarantee of being able to afford housing. Indeed,
even among renters living in the highest-poverty tracts, more than a quarter

had severe housing cost burdens, and fully 43 percent had at least a moderate cost burden in 2000.[18]

The good news is that the incidence of concentrated poverty seems to be declining. From 1990 to 2000, the number of people living in high-poverty census tracts declined by 2.3 million. This decline was far from equal across the country, however, with the South and Midwest experiencing all the decrease while the Northeast remained flat and in the West concentrated poverty actually increased. Similarly, while the inner rings of large metropolitan areas experienced a decrease in population in high-poverty tracts, the metropolitan fringes saw an increase. Unfortunately, concentrated poverty remains persistent and disproportionately distributed across households. High-poverty tracts in 2000 were still home to 10 percent of all poor but a higher 19 percent of black poor and 14 percent of Hispanic poor (Joint Center for Housing Studies 2006b).

WHY CONCENTRATION OF THE POOR AND NEIGHBORHOOD DECLINE MATTER. The relative concentration of the poor is a reflection of broader processes that lead both to pockets of poverty and neighborhood decline and distress. These processes and their outcomes pose two critical challenges to policymakers. First, they isolate the poor away from economic and social opportunities and compound the problems of poverty (Galster and Killen 1995; Kain 1992; Ihlanfeldt and Sjoquist 1998). Second, the disinvestment in housing stock that results from poverty concentrations is wasteful, creates significant negative externalities for neighborhood property owners and residents, and leads to losses of higher-density, more modestly built housing that is not being replaced with similarly affordable housing. Thus the processes of residential segregation by income and race that underpin these outcomes exacerbate shortages of affordable housing, squander past investment in housing, and expose residents to hazards and property owners to falling values.

Areas of concentrated poverty are the front lines both in the battle to preserve low-cost housing and in the battle to tackle some of the nation's most costly social problems. Rental properties in poor areas are at higher risk of deterioration for several reasons. First, the housing in these neighborhoods tends to be older and therefore has a higher concentration of hazards that have since been regulated away in newer homes, such as lead-based paint and asbestos. The cost of remediation of these hazards discourages investment in this stock. Although not directly a problem of poverty concentration, hazards in older homes are more likely to get remediated in higher-income areas, where property values justify the investment. Second, some fraction of landlords will find it difficult to charge rents high enough to cover basic operating and maintenance costs. As some of them elect to reduce maintenance or not recapitalize older properties, they create a

18. Numbers in this paragraph are Joint Center for Housing Studies tabulations of 2000 Decennial Census tract-level data.

disincentive for other owners to invest because the presence of these deteriorated properties reduces the values of surrounding properties. Meanwhile, teen pregnancy rates, the incidence of childhood asthma, high school dropout rates, and crime rates are higher in poverty areas than elsewhere (Wilson 1987, 1996; Altshuler and others 1999; Galster 2002).

In spite of years of study, the premise that the effects of living in extremely poor areas has negative implications for its residents over and above those of having extremely low incomes remains controversial. The most thoughtful and thorough review of the evidence through the early 1990s concludes that it is best to exercise caution in interpreting it, owing to methodological challenges that failed to establish the causal mechanisms through which neighborhood factors influence individual outcomes (Ellen and Turner 1997). Robert J. Sampson, Jeffrey D. Morenoff, and Thomas Gannon-Rowley (2002) reach similar but somewhat more optimistic conclusions.

A number of additional studies conducted since these reviews also suggest that neighborhood effects matter. Xavier de Souza Briggs (1997) finds that depressed levels of social capital in poverty areas lead to negative impacts. Rowland Atkinson and Keith Kintrea (2001) find that concentrated poverty under certain circumstances leads to poorer employment outcomes. Thomas Vartanian and Philip Gleason (1999) have found that neighborhood affects high school dropout rates, especially among those with lower incomes. Bas van der Klaauw and Jan van Ours (2003) find that the effectiveness of welfare-to-work transitions of Dutch youth is reduced in poor areas. Joseph Harkness and Sandra Newman (2002) have found a reduction of the positive effects of homeownership on educational outcomes of children in distressed neighborhoods. Jeffrey Kling and others (2004) find that the Moving to Opportunity program appears to have reduced the criminal activity of women and shifted that of men from violent to property crimes. However, Lisa Sanbonmatsu and others (2004) find that the program did not appreciably increase education test scores of children. Three earlier studies of Moving to Opportunity critically reviewed by Sampson, Morenoff, and Gannon-Rowley (2002) also suggest that moving away from an area of concentrated poverty may improve at least some outcomes (Ludwig, Hirschfield, and Duncan 2001; Katz, Kling, and Liebman 2001; Rosenbaum and Harris 2001).

The most important recent research in this area makes a stronger and more compelling case that concentrated poverty has negative impacts. This research comes from the Project on Human Development and Chicago Neighborhoods. The project was designed to determine why some neighborhoods exhibit signs of social stress and pathology while others do not and to examine the mechanisms by which neighborhood milieus influence a range of human developmental outcomes. The principal finding of the effort so far is that concentrated disadvantage—a high level of poverty and racial segregation—is often associated with poor outcomes, though certain neighborhoods that score highly on collective efficacy, despite these disadvantages, have better outcomes.[19] *Collective efficacy* is a measure of social cohesion and shared norms that predicts how likely residents are to intervene to advance the common good. It is generally, but not always, lower in areas of concentrated disadvantage. In areas where collective efficacy is low, violent crime is more likely, school performance tends to be worse, and birth weights of babies are generally lower (PHDCN 2004).

CONTRIBUTING FACTORS TO THE CONCENTRATION OF POVERTY AND NEIGHBORHOOD DECLINE. Much has been written about how and why housing markets concentrate the poor, and especially poor minorities, into pockets of poverty. The list of reasons is long, and the forces that give rise to these tendencies are reinforcing. Figuring at the center of these explanations are preferences and institutional discrimination. While in part the concentration of the poor is driven by racial segregation because minorities are overrepresented among the poor, society is divided along lines of both race and class (Jargowsky 1997). Just as whites generally tend to avoid areas that have larger proportions of minorities, those with higher incomes tend to avoid areas that have large proportions of lower-income households. Housing markets are competitive, so higher-income households can always outbid lower-income households for housing (DiPasquale and Wheaton 1996). As higher-income households act by choice to live with others more like themselves and with similar preferences and abilities to pay for public services, they segregate residential areas by income (Tiebout 1956; Schelling 1971; Wheaton 1977; Hardman and Ioannides 2004). Kerry Vandell (1995) considers how both demand- and supply-side factors create spatial heterogeneity among urban neighborhoods, drawing on a microeconomic framework to explain why residential segregation occurs. Michael Schill and Susan Wachter (1995) examine how local control of taxes, public services, and land use reinforces and enables spatial stratification by income and race. Both studies find multiple and reinforcing factors that contribute to residential segregation by income, race, and ethnicity.

Beyond the impacts of discrimination and racial and class preferences exercised in a competitive market for desirable housing and locations (Turner and others 2002), the geographic filtering of neighborhoods also isolates low-income households in certain older neighborhoods. As many large metropolitan areas experienced rapid suburbanization in the 1960s and 1970s, high-income households fled inner cities, and the housing they previously occupied filtered down to increasingly lower-income households. With the costs of development of open spaces lower than the cost of developing in cities, new development has tended to take place at the periphery of urban areas. Infill development of land in high-density built-out cities is more limited. Stuart Rosenthal (2004) has done some of the most recent and thorough work on the subject of neighborhood filtering. In

19. Robert J. Sampson, Stephen W. Raudenbush, and Felton Earls, "Neighborhoods and Violent Crime: A Multilevel Study of Collective Efficacy," *Science*, August 15, 1997, pp. 918–24.

his study, neighborhood economic status is a function of the aging of the housing stock and neighborhood externalities. Because development expands out from the centers of cities with time, most of the older housing is located closer to the center of cities. That housing becomes functionally obsolete, and maintenance and upgrading of it will take place only if demand of higher-income groups for the particular area remains strong enough to justify the costs.

As opposed to aging stock, neighborhood externalities can result in much more rapid rates of change if they create "tipping" points. In the context of neighborhood decline, the tipping points most commonly implicated are property abandonment (Sternlieb 1966; Simmons-Mosley 2003), redlining (Massey and Denton 1993), increases in poverty rates and rentership rates (Galster, Quercia, and Cortes 2000; Rosenthal 2004; DiPasquale and Glaeser 1999), white flight (Schelling 1971; Megbolugbe, Hoek-Smit, and Linneman 1996), and homeowner foreclosures (Baxter and Lauria 2000). Threshold effects, however, have not been studied much (Galster, Quercia, and Cortes 2000).

Whether renting plays a causal role in the process or is simply a part of it remains unclear. Indeed, it is easy to overstate the role rental housing plays in the process of neighborhood filtering (Galster, Quercia, and Cortes 2000; Rosenthal 2004). Although homeownership rates are sharply lower in these areas, this reflects the filtering of housing down to those with lowest incomes who are more likely to rent. Other studies have shown that high concentration of low-income homeowners can also be detrimental to a neighborhood if those owners are at risk of widespread foreclosures (Baxter and Lauria 2000).[20] In 2000, even in areas with poverty rates of 40 percent or more, the homeownership rate was 25 percent on average, and in one-quarter of these tracts homeownership rates top 50 percent. Still, the mistaken identification of rental housing with the poor and neighborhood distress has clouded judgments about the suitability of affordable rental housing in middle-class and upper-income neighborhoods and the contribution of dispersed affordable rental housing to healthy housing markets and communities.

Housing Quality and Crowding

Problems of crowded and poor-quality housing often overlap with these other challenges. In an effort to reduce costs, some households live in substandard housing conditions or double up with others in residences too small to effectively meet their needs. Even then, many still continue to pay large shares of their income for housing.

Although the incidence of crowding problems in 2005 was only 4.6 percent among all renters and 3.6 percent among renters in the bottom fifth of the household income quintile, crowding remains a concern. More troubling, despite

20. For more studies on tenure effects in neighborhood decline, see von Hoffman, Belsky, and Lee (2006).

significant reductions over the past fifty years in the incidence of moderate or serious structural inadequacy problems, 11 percent of all renters, and 12 percent of renters in the bottom income quintile, still live in these conditions. A summary of previous reports on federal worst-case needs conducted in 2003 shows progress in reducing crowding and dropping the incidence at least of severe inadequacy to low levels. The share of renters in severely inadequate units declined from 6.2 percent in 1978 to 3.5 percent in 1999, while crowding among renters also fell, from 5.8 to 4.9 percent. Since the number of renters has grown over that same period, however, the number of households suffering from these problems has actually increased (HUD 2003). The types of renters most likely to live in crowded or inadequate housing include families with children, younger households, minorities, immigrants, and those with very low incomes. But even making housing quality trade-offs does not always help enough with affordability. More than 42 percent of crowded households and 46 percent of those in severely inadequate units are cost burdened, compared with 33 percent of households without either problem.[21]

WHY HOUSING QUALITY MATTERS. The consequences of inadequate and crowded housing are far reaching and often disturbing. They include an increase in acute and chronic health problems, more hospital visits and higher medical expenses, lower productivity, lower social participation, and worse outcomes for children in these households.

The literature on housing problems and health outcomes is varied. Many studies focus on a specific kind of health problem or reaction.[22] Others take a broader view. For example, Gary Evans, Nancy Wells, and Annie Moch (2003) look at the relationship between housing and mental health, while Patrick Breysse and others (2004) summarize various studies on the health impact of exposure to poor-quality housing. Stella Lowry (1990) examines the most extreme form of inadequate housing, homelessness, and the health outcomes associated with living on the street.

Many studies of the health outcomes of poor housing link the housing quality in some way to the incomes or poverty level of the household, the cost or subsidy status of the housing, or the quality of the surrounding neighborhood. Examples of recent versions of these studies include Sandra Newman and Joe Harkness (2005), Dolores Acevedo-Garcia and others (2004), Ernie Hood (2005), and James Dunn (2000). Others focus on the hazards in the homes themselves and do not address whether exposure to them is greater or more likely among the poor.[23] These include

21. Numbers in this paragraph are from Joint Center for Housing Studies tabulations of the 2005 American Housing Survey (www.huduser.org/datasets/ahs.html).

22. For an annotated list of scientific research on housing and specific health outcomes, see the Alliance for Healthy Homes (www.afhh.org/hah/HH%20research%20articles%20fact%20sheet%20web.doc).

23. For a summary of literature on the types of household defects that directly contribute to poor health, see Matte and Jacobs (2000).

unintentional injuries from structural defects like broken stairs, ungrounded electrical wiring, exposed radiators, and the absence of smoke detectors. It also includes health problems directly related to poor insulation and heating systems, exposure to disease-carrying pests and rodents, and reactions to mold, asbestos, or lead in the home.

Less studied and understood, but no less important, is the potential ripple effect of these health problems for individuals. Poor health from exposure to housing problems may affect employment opportunities and outcomes for residents, making it difficult to earn the money necessary to improve their homes or move to better ones (Smith 1999). In children, health problems interfere with their education, thereby reducing their later earning potential (Ding and others 2006).

We know less about the direct consequences of crowded housing on social and health outcomes. Beyond increased opportunity for disease transmission, the effects of overcrowded housing conditions in this country have not been recently evaluated. Among the few studies is an early one by Walter Gove, Michael Hughes, and Omer Galle (1979) that controls for socioeconomic factors in evaluating the effect of crowded conditions on mental health, social interactions, and child care, finding a strong negative relationship. A few European studies have addressed this issue more recently, with an emphasis on the impact on children (Office of the Deputy Prime Minister 2004; Goux and Maurin 2003).

CONTRIBUTING FACTORS TO HOUSING QUALITY AND CROWDING PROBLEMS. Many of the problems with rental housing discussed above contribute to the neglect of the rental stock that leads to structurally inadequate conditions. The concentration of affordable housing in particular neighborhoods, as well as the associated clustering of poor and disadvantaged households, discourages investment in these areas. By attracting only low-income and poor renters, the rents that building owners can charge for these units are insufficient to cover even basic operating costs, further discouraging any improvement. And so long as affordability problems persist, households will need to trade off housing quality and size for cost, so some demand exists even for the most substandard properties.

Much of the blame for home health hazards is simply that at the time certain materials were used, such as lead paint or asbestos, they were not known hazards. Ironically, the same codes that have been promulgated to reduce the incidences of known hazards often play a part in keeping owners from making improvements to housing built to earlier standards. If rehabilitation is significant enough, it triggers full compliance with new codes. The costs of this compliance may be larger than landlords can recoup in increased rents. In these cases, landlords do not make the improvements (Listokin and Listokin 2001). Furthermore, standards for mitigation of certain hazards, like lead paint, can be set so high that landlords withdraw units or try to fly below the radar screen rather than comply. At the other extreme, code enforcement of habitability requirements and restrictions on crowding may be laxly enforced.

Rental Housing Policy and Programs

The federal, state, and local responses to these myriad housing challenges have been valiant and critical to improving the lives of millions of Americans and reducing public costs associated with the impacts of these challenges. However, they have plainly not been sufficient to resolve these problems. While some problems, like housing quality, have been dramatically reduced, others, like the concentration of poverty, have only been modestly remedied. Still other problems, like rental affordability and relative concentration of renters near cities, are growing dramatically worse. At the same time, many problems are cropping up in places that used to be more immune to them and among moderate-income households that did not previously suffer from them.

Progress is hard won because dealing with these challenges is extremely expensive and runs counter to powerful social, economic, and political forces. It means addressing people's preferences and biases, entrenched political geographies, the relative costs of developing more open space in the suburbs compared with filling in or reusing space in cities, multiple policy objectives—the pursuit of which lead to land-use and development regulations that can add to housing costs—and, of course, the steep cost of housing itself.

The evolution of rental policy and programs reflects changing economic, social, demographic, and political conditions, on the one hand, and policy experimentation and learning, on the other. Although some are quick to dismiss the valuable lessons that have been learned, it is well to review them and reflect on the ones for which there is now broad consensus and those for which there is not. It is also worth taking stock not only of these policy responses but how they might be used to serve broader purposes than merely helping people afford homes, by focusing instead on opportunities to save on other public costs, reduce human suffering, improve antipoverty program outcomes, and alter the residential patterns that give rise to multiple other policy challenges.

While there are, of course, many ways of grouping the policy responses, we elect here to group them into the following six categories:
—Rental affordability
—Preservation of affordable rental housing
—Redevelopment
—Rental assistance as a stepping-stone to better opportunity
—Regulatory relief
—Housing quality
Conspicuously missing from this list is the issue of informing tenure choices. These difficult intertemporal decisions, which are subject to great uncertainties,

have profound consequences. Yet there are essentially no government policies or programs to inform these choices. Although there are increasing efforts to help educate homeowners about the process of buying a home that may lead some to conclude that homeownership is not right for them, these efforts are part of broader homeownership campaigns that presume ownership is and ought to be the goal.

Rental Affordability

The lion's share of federal outlays on housing are aimed squarely at reducing the number of very low-income households, which suffer the most under the burden of rent expenses that absorb more than 30 percent of income. The voucher, Section 8, public housing, privately owned but assisted, and low-income tax-credit programs are all designed principally to relieve rental cost burdens (though by enforcing suitability standards they also address housing quality). The older project-based programs, including public housing, were also aimed at speeding the replacement of poor-quality housing, but like the others they are now mostly intended to lower rent burdens. The low-income tax-credit program is now used to pursue multiple goals, but affordable housing is first among them. Block grants from the HOME Investment Partnerships and Community Development Block Grant programs also are intended, at least in part, to create more-affordable rental housing.

The primary drawback of these programs in addressing affordability problems is their scale. Getting rental housing assistance is like winning the lottery—the losers languish on long waiting lists and the winners hit the jackpot. Moreover, these programs are nearly all aimed at households earning up to 60 percent of area median incomes, and most are targeted to even lower income levels. Hence the growing difficulty that households earning more than 60 percent of area median income have in trying to pay the higher cost of housing is left unaddressed. In addition, the primary remaining program for rental production—the low-income tax credit—requires other subsidies to make rental housing affordable for any household not exactly at the 60 percent of area median cutoff—an income cutoff of about $26,100 nationally.

Other problems identified with the government effort to relieve affordability problems through tenant-based and project-based subsidies include the following:

—The failure to adequately fund the operating and modernization costs of public housing and of some of the older privately assisted housing programs

—Contributing to rather than ameliorating the concentration of poverty as a result of location decisions that concentrate public housing and other project-based assistance in poor neighborhoods

—Fragmented administration of programs at the state and local levels that lead to diseconomies of scale, multiple program rules, and deadlines that add costs to the development process

—Difficulty recruiting landlords to participate in the tenant-based assistance program

—Insufficient support for apartment seekers who receive vouchers

—Rent formulas that create disincentives to work

—New federal funding rules that force trade-offs that could lead either to fewer households' being served or to shallower income targeting

Despite all these issues, the past fifty years have come close to reaching consensus on a few critical issues about the best way to address rental affordability programs. There is a growing consensus that vouchers are a more efficient way to subsidize renters and that they lead to better spatial outcomes by reducing the concentration of poverty (Khadduri, Burnett, and Rodda 2003). There is also now a tendency to move beyond the debate between tenant-based and project-based assistance and frame it instead in terms of when project-based assistance is valuable and for what aims beyond just relieving rental affordability problems. But there are still unresolved questions, especially related to project-based assistance. Chief among them are how to structure subsidies and programs so that market forces police outcomes to the maximal extent possible and how to design programs that reduce project failures from owners' inability to keep up with maintenance and replacement demands. The tax credit is viewed as less than ideally efficient in terms of dollar-for-dollar delivery of subsidy but far better than any previous programs in leading to successful outcomes, garnering political support, and sparking highly effective state-level and market oversight. From a life-cycle perspective, tax credits may well prove the most successful project-based program yet.

Issues concerning the best way to administer direct federal subsidies and how to select the best entities to own assisted rental properties are still very much in play. Bruce Katz and Margery Turner (2001) have argued, for example, that the current system for administering direct subsidies (vouchers) is splintered and inconsistent. They argue that direct subsidies ought to be administered by regional authorities rather than by local agencies. This not only would make program administration potentially more efficient but would also create much-needed regional authorities to take a regional view of housing needs across metropolitan areas. In addition, there is still a debate over whether federal programs have been devolved to state and local governments to a sufficient extent, as well as whether it makes sense to concentrate more allocation authority at the state or regional level than at the local level (McEvoy 2002; Downs 1994; Orfield 2002; Katz and Turner 2001; Katz and others 2003).

The surprisingly high rate of return of vouchers unused, despite the fact that households may have waited years to receive them, has spotlighted the difficulty that some households have finding suitable rentals (Jones 2001). This has led to calls for increased funding to assist renters in locating suitable voucher-eligible housing and to recruit landlords to participate in the program (Millennial Housing Commission 2002).

Finally, that the renter contribution is set at 30 percent of income means that any additional income a household earns is in a sense taxed at a rate of 30 percent. There is a heavily contested debate over whether this is sufficient to dissuade aid recipients from increasing their incomes (Shroder 2002). An even stronger disincentive to work occurs if recipients cross the threshold of eligibility. Given long waiting lists to regain assistance and the potential for job loss to take a household's income back below the eligibility cutoff, it is feasible that some may avoid taking that chance.

Preservation of Affordable Rental Housing

Programs aimed at preserving assisted rental housing are closely linked to policy and programmatic efforts to address the shortage of affordable housing. These preservation programs are aimed at preserving assisted rental housing at risk of loss through financial failure and neglect, on the one hand, and conversion to higher market-rate rentals in gentrifying neighborhoods, on the other. As just noted, one of the problems associated with some project-based housing has been that it was not funded sufficiently to prevent modernization needs from mounting and to deal with the now accumulated backlog of these needs. But another fundamental problem with virtually all project-based programs is inattention in program designs to preservation of rental housing as affordable in places where investors can reap higher returns by exiting the programs upon expiration of their contracts. As awareness of this problem dawned, efforts were made at first to abrogate contracts and force property owners to stay in the programs. Inevitably, these gave way to programs aimed at providing incentives for owners not to exit rather than placing bans on the exercise of contractual rights.

At the same time, problems of deterioration in a portion of the assisted stock surfaced, along with the problem of getting owners to transfer their properties to new, more suitable owners. Many of these existing owners were in some senses trapped by tax rules that would force large recapture of previously taken tax benefits upon sale of the property. The problem of such "exit taxes" has yet to be addressed and still stands in the way of transfers from one set of owners to others to whom the federal government would be willing to provide subsidies to improve properties in return for long-term restrictions on rent.

Efforts to preserve assisted housing have since been stepped up and improved. Eventually, a mark-to-market program that brings rents to market levels for Section 8 subsidies was established that has been viewed as far more successful in preserving housing and optimizing limited federal resources. Perhaps even more important, and operating on a large scale, are efforts by state housing finance agencies to use tax credits and other resources to prevent subsidized rental housing from exiting the supply of affordable rental housing. The National Housing Trust estimates that state agencies have increased the annual number of federally assisted rental units they have helped preserve from 20,000 units in 2000 to 56,870 units in 2005 (National Housing Trust 2006).

At least as important as the loss of subsidized rental housing on net is the loss of unsubsidized rental housing. As opposed to multiple strategies that are being used to stave off the losses of subsidized rental housing, there is no comparable organized strategy to do the same for unsubsidized affordable rental units. Yet at least three-quarters of very low-income renters live in units that receive no project-based subsidy, tenant-based voucher, or tax-credit assistance whatsoever (Donovan 2002). Although tenant-based vouchers play a positive role in preserving rentals that do not receive project-based subsidies by letting landlords charge rents that support proper maintenance, there is no systematic approach to helping preserve the rest. Properties that receive no federal funds are diverse in ownership, location, style, and property type. The piecemeal and generally limited efforts to address this stock are problematic. Some cities use block grants more actively to provide incentives in the form of direct grants and below-market loans to help owners of properties with no rent restrictions properly maintain their properties. Leading examples are Chicago, which supports organizations like Community Investment Corporation, and New York, which supports organizations like Community Preservation Corporation. Still largely unexplored is the impact of small-grant and below-market loan programs aimed at shoring up small properties on neighborhood conditions and change. While many places do not fund such activities, it is a common use of Community Development Block Grants.

Redevelopment

Rental housing programs aimed at redevelopment of areas of neighborhood distress notoriously took the original form of the "federal bulldozer." Initially, the federal government provided grants to help local government assemble land and raze the properties on it. The land and residential uses that typically succeeded the blighted housing it replaced resulted in drastic net reductions in affordable rental housing in the transformed areas. Worse, little regard was paid to the residents who were displaced from these areas.

Over time, the approach changed to trying to revitalize areas by rehabilitating properties, using new construction selectively to replace nuisance properties, and working with neighborhood groups to come up with redevelopment plans. Some programs, such as the Model Cities and Urban Development Action Grant programs, came and went. But what have endured are special incentives in federal production programs to induce developers to build in distressed areas. Furthermore, states may provide additional incentives to steer tax-credit development to target areas, such as giving extra points in state allocation plans. In addition, Community Development Block Grants and HOME grants have planning requirements that demand public involvement in development plans. These block grants also provide vital funding that state and local governments can use with some discretion to revitalize areas.

Most recently, federal policy has returned to the idea of larger-scale redevelopment. To address the worst problems in public housing, the Housing Opportunities for People Everywhere (HOPE VI) program allows for wholesale redevelopment of large public housing communities, sometimes reaching to planning for areas surrounding these communities. Unlike the federal bulldozer, however, these programs engage local community groups in the planning process; a much more concerted effort is made to deal with displaced residents and to achieve a mix of incomes that includes the very lowest up through moderate-income households. Like the federal bulldozer programs, replacement of affordable rentals is not always one-for-one. However, the ratios are far better than under the older programs, and many of the units not replaced were vacant or on the road to becoming so because they were in such poor condition.

The efforts to redevelop areas in these new incarnations are more positively viewed than federal bulldozer schemes. Studies of HOPE VI suggest that these efforts can have powerful and positive outcomes, though whether they do so depends not only on broader economic conditions in the areas in which they are located but also on how redevelopment plans are formulated and implemented (Salama 1999; Zielenbach 2003). Studies of New York City's ten-year housing plan provide especially compelling evidence that, under the right circumstances, concentrated public investment to reverse neighborhood decline can succeed and create ripples that extend outward from the physical location of the redevelopment projects (Schill and others 2002).

Still, there is much to be learned about this topic. There appears to be an inherent conflict, formulated in the 1960s by the economists John Kain and Joseph Persky (1969) as to whether to "gild" the ghetto or help move people out of these areas so that poverty is less concentrated. But thinking on the subject has matured. The two goals are now viewed not as oppositional but as two parts of the same process of encouraging mixed-income communities. Attention to helping those displaced by urban revitalization helps move these individuals out of poor areas, and attention to income mixing in revitalization projects helps moderate-income households move into high-poverty areas.

Beyond federal intervention and funding to achieve local community economic development and revitalization, some state and local governments have recognized the powerful influence they can have on the redevelopment process by more aggressively attaching nuisance properties and forestalling the financial collapse of distressed properties. Stalling the process of negative externalities from disinvestment in an initially small number of failing properties from spreading to others can stop or slow neighborhood decline. In addition, rapidly recycling properties that have been abandoned or demolished can create opportunities to spark a process of reinvestment. The most sophisticated states provide legal frameworks and support for taking control of nuisance properties; and the most enlightened local governments use a spectrum of tools and coordinated planning to reclaim community assets and put them in the hands of more civic-minded developers. These states and local governments can serve as examples to those who want to get more serious about having effective and coordinated plans to deal with financially distressed and nuisance properties.

Rental Assistance as a Stepping-Stone to Better Opportunity

New uses of rental assistance are deliberately being conceived and tested to move policy beyond the use of programs to merely cap the rent contribution of aid recipients to 30 percent of income, prevent further losses of affordable rental housing on net, and spark redevelopment of distressed areas. In particular, rental assistance is being reinvented as a tool to accomplish the following:

—Move people to areas of greater opportunity and disperse the poor

—Support efforts to make welfare-to-work transitions successful

—Develop the low-wage workforce

—Provide incentives to save and invest in education and build assets

—Provide incentives for recipients of housing assistance to increase their work effort

Indeed, the recent explosion in creativity in the use of rental assistance and in attempts to carefully evaluate their efficacy is noteworthy. These run the gamut from the Family Self-Sufficiency program, which provides incentives to save and work (with savings available for a range of eligible uses); the Moving to Opportunity program, intended to provide special assistance to help aid recipients find rentals in moderate- and higher-income areas; and the Jobs-Plus Community Revitalization Initiative for Public Housing Families program, which bundles housing assistance with workforce development services; to the active experimentation by states in using housing assistance in conjunction with Temporary Assistance for Needy Families to achieve better workforce outcomes for former welfare recipients.

Although not entirely conclusive, the available evidence supports the view that rental housing assistance can more than handle these additional weighty and important goals under the proper circumstances. Although results of the Moving to Opportunity program are mixed, those from one exceptionally well crafted study of the Jobs-Plus housing program suggests that bundling workforce development and housing assistance can be a powerful antipoverty strategy. The numerous studies of Moving to Opportunity lack a true experimental design, and the results are sensitive to how the program has been implemented by local agencies (Goering and Feins 2003; Kling and others 2004). Although there is some cause for optimism on child outcomes and other social measures, labor impacts of Moving to Opportunity have been at best lackluster. Jobs-Plus housing however, has clearly scored some major workforce gains (Bloom, Riccio, and Verma 2005). In addition, most evaluations of linking welfare reform to rental housing assistance have found positive impacts on both employment and earnings (Verma and Riccio 2003).

A range of policies and programs have also been designed to promote integration, but relatively little effort has been made to study the individual and collective impacts of these policies. Policies have been designed both to eliminate discriminatory behavior and to encourage the dispersal of the poor. Although antidiscrimination and fair-housing laws have been on the books for nearly four decades, there is considerable evidence that housing market discrimination, as measured by audit studies, persists. There is also considerable evidence that the Home Mortgage Disclosure Act and Community Reinvestment Act have expanded access to mortgage credit in low-income communities, but high levels of subprime lending in these communities are raising new concerns over fair treatment. Court-ordered desegregation of public housing has occurred in some places and has been effective in reducing the concentration of the poor and moving them to areas with greater opportunities. And although housing vouchers were not initially designed with the intention of dispersing the poor, the shift in federal housing policies toward housing vouchers appears to have diminished the concentration of low-income households.

Regulatory Relief

Federal and state success has been limited in providing relief from the development regulations that channel production into more expensive housing, create costly uncertainty and delays, and restrict overall residential land supply. The federal government has not gotten beyond commissions, clearinghouses of best regulatory relief practices, and studies of the ill effects of many development regulations on the cost and type of housing that gets built or rehabilitated (Schill 2004). While not unimportant, these efforts provide neither carrots nor sticks. The federal government has been reluctant to get involved with issues that are viewed as being in the purview of state constitutions and laws. States, meanwhile, tend to let local governments create most rules governing land use without imposing many requirements. There are exceptions, but these exceptions prove the rule: the rest of the states have done little.[24] Still, the states that have been active have experimented with a variety of different incentives and requirements that have a good chance of overcoming some local regulatory and fiscal barriers.

At the local level, many jurisdictions have acted to deal with the problem of lack of affordable housing (though not specifically rental housing) by passing some form of inclusionary zoning ordinance (Burchell and Galley 2000). Even so, the use of these tools remains limited and tends to be less common in suburban jurisdictions. Furthermore, their impacts on rental housing availability, specifically, have not been studied.

Hence the issue of regulatory relief, although central to rental affordability challenges and the concentration of rental housing near city centers, is only weakly addressed at the present time. Interest in the topic has increased, however, and it seems an issue upon which affordable housing advocates and those opposed to

---

24. Calavita, Grimes, and Mallach (1997); Calavita and Grimes (1998); David Rusk, *Evaluating Inclusionary Zoning Policies* (2002) (www.gamaliel.org/DavidRusk/IZ%20issues.pdf); Krefetz (2001); Listokin and Listokin (2001).

heavy-handed government meddling in housing markets can agree. Nevertheless, efforts to deal with the situation come up against entrenched interests opposed to residential development in general and high-density development in particular. William Fischel (2001), among others, has demonstrated that differences in the provision of public services are capitalized into the value of homes and that owners have an interest in defending those values in a variety of ways, including preventing dilution of the public services that they have in effect paid for in the price of their homes. Fischel notes that the financial interest of homeowners in the small jurisdictions where they exert political control would lead logically to a resistance to development. Indeed, "not in my backyard" sentiment is strong and buttressed by many economic rationales.

Housing Quality

Finally, there are many government interventions aimed at issues of housing quality. In addition to preservation and redevelopment-focused initiatives, the following are targeted at improving housing quality:
    —Funds for remediation of home health hazards, such as lead-based paint
    —Federal, state, and local regulations governing remediation of hazards
    —Building codes and code enforcement programs
    —Special rehabilitation codes
Perhaps the most promising of these approaches is the promulgation of special rehabilitation codes. The Department of Housing and Urban Development has also been behind the creation of model codes specifically for the rehabilitation of existing structures and in 1997 issued the "Nationally Applicable Recommended Rehabilitation Provisions" to guide states and municipalities in creating their own renovation codes. By 2001 a handful of states had enacted codes based on these guidelines.

The great difficulty with interventions aimed at improving quality is that they come at a cost. Vigorous code enforcement can cause landlords to give up on compliance altogether because it is too costly for them, given the rents their tenants are willing to pay. Obligations to remediate certain hazards in rental situations can cause owners to pull their properties from the rental market. Disclosure requirements about hazards reduce the market value of properties, potentially increasing the chances they will be abandoned. This is not to say that these hazards should not be disclosed or that remediation of them in every case is not essential to public health; it only points out the unintended consequences of these rules.

Furthermore, many hazards that government could help reduce are generally not the subjects of programs or policies. Perhaps the most notable and common of these is the presence of high concentrations of allergens that vastly increase the risk of childhood and adult asthma. Asthma is a primary reason for expensive emergency room visits. Lack of a policy in this area—even though dealing with the problem could well be less expensive and surely far more humane—is a major failing.

Conclusions

The rental challenges facing the nation are, at best, persistent, costly, and difficult to address. At worst, many chronic rental problems are expanding, and the prospects for a reversal of this trend are poor, given current economic, social, demographic, and political trends. The economy continues to produce jobs mostly at the tails of the wage distribution, and employers continue to demand millions of part-time low-wage workers. The federal government is facing growing demands on its entitlement programs, with Social Security projected to run a deficit in the not-too-distant future and Medicare and Medicaid costs spiraling out of control. Prospects for substantial increases in income supports or funding for rental subsidies are not great. Social and political trends also do not give much cause for optimism about the nation's capacity to seriously deal with regulatory restraints that distort housing markets and make the production of affordable rental housing difficult.

Meanwhile, household growth over the next decade is expected to be greatest among minorities, the foreign born, and seniors. Indeed, the Joint Center for Housing Studies projects that the minority share of households will increase from 28 percent in 2005 to nearly 35 percent by 2015 (Joint Center for Housing Studies 2006b, p. 3). As a result, several of the groups with the highest propensity to rent, with the lowest incomes, and with the greatest institutional barriers to homeownership will see the fastest growth. The growth in the number of renters overall is expected to be approximately 1.8 million over ten years, depending on whether ownership rate gains stall or advance by age and family type at about the rate of the previous ten years. Meanwhile, the passage of the baby boomers into their sixties and seventies over the next twenty years will lift the demand for special-needs rental housing for the elderly.

The material reviewed in this chapter leads to many findings and conclusions about the challenges ahead, what government could be doing to address them, and why it is important for them to do so. Before ending on a more sober note about the many topics that still demand further research to better inform policy research, we list the most important of these findings and conclusions.

Perhaps most important, it is becoming increasingly clear that tenant-based rental housing assistance can effectively serve a host of public policy purposes. Rental housing assistance can help low-income households better afford their housing and save for homeownership. Providing assistance to help rental-aid recipients search for housing over a wider range of neighborhoods can help them move away from areas of concentrated poverty and increase their access to better social, economic, and educational opportunities. Combining job assistance with rental housing can improve welfare-to-work transitions and help enhance the benefits of other workforce development programs. And providing savings account and credit management skills to recipients of rental housing assistance can achieve better homeownership outcomes for the low-income population.

More-targeted supply-side interventions, meanwhile, can also serve critical policy goals effectively. By encouraging owners of rental properties in transitional neighborhoods to properly maintain and upgrade their properties, targeted investments in the existing unsubsidized housing stock can help arrest the costly process of neighborhood decline. By averting rent increases driven by constrained supplies rather than the costs of production, supply-side programs that ensure an adequate supply of affordable rental housing can also lower the costs of voucher programs. By building on a growing number of best practices at both the state and local levels, local governments can be far more effective in rapidly recycling financially stressed and nuisance rental properties, restoring them to productive community use. By enacting state laws that provide incentives for or impose requirements on local governments to take more seriously the production of affordable rental housing, states can play a pivotal role in overcoming local regulatory barriers (though politics in many states make this unlikely at present, enough states have shown how this can be done to serve as a source of ideas for these other states). By considering possible government-supported equity-side interventions in the small multifamily segment of the affordable rental market, policymakers may be able to find ways to aggregate the ownership of this stock in a federally supported entity that would satisfy public purposes in exchange for public finance.[25]

It is also becoming apparent that it is time to get beyond the "voucher versus production" and "revitalize poor neighborhoods versus disperse the poor" debates in rental policy. In reality, overcoming these divisive dichotomies will allow policymakers to better tune rental housing policies and programs to meet local challenges, avoid ignoring residents displaced by revitalization, and encourage mixed-income communities in poor as well as moderate- and higher-income communities.

At an even more fundamental level, past experience suggests that analysts are quite likely understating the full magnitude of rental affordability problems, and governments are failing both to help inform tenure choices and to acknowledge and address the true long-term costs of supplying rental housing assistance. By attending more seriously to key but seemingly banal questions like how to define rental housing affordability, count worst cases, and judge how little leftover is too little for moderate-income households (as separate from low-income households), the debate over the costs to society as a whole of the lack of affordable rental housing would be enriched. By promoting more-informed choices and leveling the playing field between owning and renting, government could create improved

25. Shekar Narasimhan, "Why Do Small Multifamily Properties Bedevil Us?" Brookings *Capital Xchange* (2001) (www.brook.edu/es/urban/capitalxchange/article8.htm).

outcomes. By acknowledging the lottery-like nature of rental housing assistance as currently structured and the real costs of helping reach the full need, greater focus on what it would take to actually end certain problems rather than simply reduce them could be brought to bear.

Finally, there is still much to be learned that could help improve rental housing policies and programs. While the list of topics worthy of further study is long, we list just a few of the most important here. Most urgently in need of further study are the public and private costs of the lack of affordable rental housing, concentration of poverty, concentration of renters near city centers, and unattended-to issues of housing quality and health. Attempting to quantify the public costs of rental housing challenges would take the discussion a step closer to addressing rental housing policies and programs in cost-benefit terms. Also high on the list of research needs are more experiments to test the impact of attempts to use rental assistance to improve labor outcomes and child outcomes by combining it with job services or helping aid recipients move to opportunity.

Beyond these research needs, there are others that relate to our understanding of the operation of rental markets, especially with respect to the process of disinvestment and its policy implications. First, additional research is required on the determinants of net losses of affordable rental housing stock as well as the comparative costs and challenges of preserving and rehabilitating existing rental housing versus building new rental housing in areas where rentals are being lost. Second, more research is needed to compare the costs of trying to build new housing and rejuvenate neighborhoods with the costs of preventing them from falling into disrepair in the first place. Third, additional research on neighborhood filtering is needed to better predict which communities are at risk of losing housing to abandonment and decline and which are likely to have relative stability in rents and tenure. This would also allow identification of areas ripe for gentrification so that policymakers can find ways to preserve affordable housing in these areas before it becomes more costly to do so. Finally, even though one- to four-unit rental properties make up more than half of the unassisted affordable rental housing stock, there is a virtual absence of studies on the ownership, management, and financing of these properties (Mallach 2006). The study of five- to forty-nine-unit rental properties is similarly limited.

Regulatory impacts on rental markets also warrant further study. Although much has been written on the negative impacts of many regulations on the supply of affordable rental housing, especially in the suburbs, not enough attention has been paid to efforts to use regulations such as inclusionary zoning to instead stimulate the production of affordable rental housing. And despite a growing body of literature on the impacts of regulation on housing costs and the availability of affordable housing, only a handful of recent studies have specifically examined the impact of regulations on rental housing (Malpezzi 1996; Levine 1999; Green 1999; Somerville and Mayer 2003).

Although there is still much to be learned, much is already known about what to do to address the nation's rental housing challenges and the associated problems they create. Building on the lessons of the past, and with a clearer focus on why grappling with these admittedly difficult and daunting issues is so worthwhile, significant progress is possible. But progress will be made only if the political will to do so can be mustered and the commitment to solutions that span all levels of government.

References

Acevedo-Garcia, Dolores, and others. 2004. "Does Housing Mobility Policy Improve Health?" *Housing Policy Debate* 15, no. 1: 49–98.

Altshuler, Alan, and others. 1999. *Governance and Opportunity in Metropolitan America.* Washington: National Academy Press.

Apgar, William C. 2004. "Rethinking Rental Housing: Expanding the Ability of Rental Housing to Serve as a Pathway to Economic and Social Opportunity." Working Paper W04-11. Cambridge, Mass.: Harvard University, Joint Center for Housing Studies.

Atkinson, Rowland, and Keith Kintrea. 2001. "Disentangling Area Effects: Evidence from Deprived and Non-Deprived Neighborhoods." *Urban Studies* 38, no. 12: 2277–98.

Autor, David H., Lawrence F. Katz, and Melissa S. Kearney. 2006. "The Polarization of the U.S. Labor Market." Working Paper 11986. Cambridge, Mass.: National Bureau of Economic Research.

Avery, Robert B., Glen B. Canner, and Robert E. Cook. 2005. "New Information Reported under HMDA and Its Application in Fair Lending Enforcement." *Federal Reserve Bulletin 2005* (Summer): 344–94.

Baxter, Vern, and Mickey Lauria. 2000. "Residential Mortgage Foreclosure and Neighborhood Change." *Housing Policy Debate* 11, no. 3, 675–99.

Belsky, Eric, and Allegra Calder. 2004. "Credit Matters: Building Assets in a Dual Financial Service System." In *Building Assets, Building Credit: Creating Wealth in Low-Income Communities,* edited by N. P. Retsinas and E. S. Belsky, pp. 10–41. Brookings.

Belsky, Eric, and Mark Duda. 2002. "Asset Appreciation, Timing of Purchases and Sales, and Returns to Low-Income Homeownership." In *Low-Income Homeownership: Examining the Unexamined Goal,* edited by N. P. Retsinas and E. S. Belsky, pp. 208–38. Brookings.

Belsky, Eric S., and Matthew Lambert. 2001. "Where Will They Live? Metropolitan Dimensions of Affordable Housing Problems." Working Paper W01-9. Cambridge, Mass.: Harvard University, Joint Center for Housing Studies.

Belsky, Eric S., Nicolas P. Retsinas, and Mark Duda. 2005. "The Financial Returns to Low-Income Homeownership." Working Paper W05-9. Cambridge, Mass.: Harvard University, Joint Center for Housing Studies.

Bloom, Howard S., James A. Riccio, and Nandita Verma. 2005. *Promoting Work in Public Housing: The Effectiveness of Jobs-Plus.* Final Report. New York: MDRC.

Bratt, Rachel G. 2002. "Housing and Family Well-Being." *Housing Studies* 17, no. 1: 13–26.

Breysse, Patrick, and others. 2004. "The Relationship between Housing and Health: Children at Risk." *Environmental Health Perspectives* 112, no. 15: 1583–88.

Burchell, Robert, and Catherine Galley. 2000. "Inclusionary Zoning: Pros and Cons." *New Century Housing* 1, no. 2: 3–12.

Calavita, Nico, and Kenneth Grimes. 1998. "Inclusionary Housing in California: The Experience of Two Decades." *Journal of the American Planning Association* 64 (Spring): 150–69.

Calavita, Nico, Kenneth Grimes, and Alan Mallach. 1997. "Inclusionary Housing in California and New Jersey: A Comparative Analysis." *Housing Policy Debate* 8, no. 1: 109–42.

Compass Group. 2002. *Funding for Production and Preservation of Subsidized Rental Housing.* Report prepared for the Millennial Housing Commission. Washington.

Coulson, N. Edward, and Lynn M. Fisher. 2002. "Tenure Choice and Labour Market Outcomes." *Housing Studies* 17, no. 1: 35–49.

Cutts, Amy C., and Edgar. O. Olsen. 2002. "Are Section 8 Housing Subsidies Too High?" *Journal of Housing Economics* 11, no. 3: 214–43.

de Souza Briggs, Xavier. 1997. "Moving Up versus Moving Out: Neighborhood Effects in Housing Mobility Programs." *Housing Policy Debate* 8, no. 1: 195–234.

Di, Zhu Xiao, Yi Yang, and Xiaodong Liu. 2003. "The Importance of Housing to the Accumulation of Household Net Wealth." Working Paper W03-5. Cambridge, Mass.: Harvard University, Joint Center for Housing Studies.

Ding, Weili, and others. 2006. "The Impact of Poor Health on Education: New Evidence Using Genetic Markers." Working Paper 12304. Cambridge, Mass.: National Bureau of Economic Research.

DiPasquale, Denise, and Edward L. Glaeser. 1999. "Incentives and Social Capital: Are Homeowners Better Citizens?" *Journal of Urban Economics* 45, no. 2: 354–84.

DiPasquale, Denise, and William C. Wheaton. 1996. *Urban Economics and Real Estate Markets.* Englewood Cliffs, N.J.: Prentice-Hall.

Donovan, Shaun. 2002. "Background Paper on Market Rate Multifamily Rental Housing." Report prepared for the Millennial Housing Commission. Washington.

Downs, Anthony. 1994. *New Visions for Metropolitan America.* Brookings.

Dunn, James R. 2000. "Housing and Health Inequalities: Review and Prospects for Research." *Housing Studies* 15, no. 3: 341–66.

Ellen, Ingrid G., and Ioan Voicu. 2006. "Nonprofit Housing and Neighborhood Spillovers." *Journal of Policy Analysis and Management* 2, no. 1: 31–52.

Ellen, Ingrid G., and Margery A. Turner. 1997. "Does Neighborhood Matter? Assessing Recent Evidence." *Housing Policy Debate* 8, no. 4: 833–66.

Evans, Gary W., Nancy M. Wells, and Annie Moch. 2003. "Housing and Mental Health: A Review of the Evidence and a Methodological and Conceptual Critique." *Journal of Social Issues* 59, no. 3: 475–500.

Finkel, Meryl, and others. 2000. *Capital Needs of the Public Housing Stock in 1998: Formula Capital Study.* Report prepared for U.S. Department of Housing and Urban Development. Washington: Abt Associates.

Fischel, William A. 2001. *The Homevoter Hypothesis.* Harvard University Press.

Freeman, Lance. 2004. *Siting Affordable Housing: Location and Neighborhood Trends of Low Income Housing Tax Credit Developments in the 1990s.* Brookings.

Galster, George C. 2002. "An Economic Efficiency Analysis of Deconcentrating Poverty Populations." *Journal of Housing Economics* 11, no. 4: 303–29.

———. 2005. "Urban Decline and Durable Housing." *Journal of Political Economy* 113, no. 2: 345–75.

Galster, George C., and S. P. Killen. 1995. "The Geography of Metropolitan Opportunity: A Reconnaissance and Conceptual Framework." *Housing Policy Debate* 6, no. 1: 7–43.

Galster, George, Roberto Quercia, and Alvaro Cortes. 2000. "Identifying Neighborhood Thresholds: An Empirical Exploration." *Housing Policy Debate* 11, no. 3: 701–32.

Glaeser, Edward, and Joseph Gyourko. 2002. "The Impact of Zoning on Housing Affordability." Discussion Paper 1948. Cambridge, Mass.: Harvard University, Harvard Institute of Economic Research.

Glaeser, Edward L., and Bruce Sacerdote. 2000. "The Determinants of Punishment: Deterrence, Incapacitation, and Vengeance." Discussion Paper 1894. Cambridge, Mass.: Harvard University, Harvard Institute of Economic Research.

Glaeser, Edward, Matthew Kahn, and Jordan Rappaport. 2000. "Why Do the Poor Live in Cities?" Discussion Paper 1891. Cambridge, Mass.: Harvard University, Harvard Institute of Economic Research.

Goering, John M., and Judith D. Feins. 2003. *Choosing a Better Life? Evaluating the Moving to Opportunity Social Experiment.* Washington: Urban Institute Press.

Goetzmann, William N., and Matthew Spiegel. 2002. "Policy Implications of Portfolio Choice in Underserved Mortgage Markets." In *Low-Income Homeownership: Examining the Unexamined Goal,* edited by N. P. Retsinas and E. S. Belsky, pp. 257–74. Brookings.

Goodman, Jack. 1997. "The Costs of Owning and Renting Housing: 1985–1995." Working Paper. Washington: National Multi Housing Council.

Goux, Dominique, and Eric Maurin. 2003. "The Effects of Overcrowded Housing on Children's Performance at School." Discussion Paper 3818. Paris, France: National Institute of Statistics and Economic Studies (INSEE), Center for Economic Policy Research.

Gove, Walter R., Michael Hughes, and Omer R. Galle. 1979. "Overcrowding in the Home: An Empirical Investigation of Its Possible Pathological Consequences." *American Sociological Review* 44, no. 1: 59–80.

Green, Richard. 1999. "Land Use Regulation and the Price of Housing in a Suburban Wisconsin County." *Journal of Housing Economics* 8, no. 2: 144–59.

Green, Richard K., and Patrick H. Hendershott. 2001. "Home-Ownership and Unemployment in the U.S." *Urban Studies* 38, no. 9: 1509–20.

Hardman, Anna, and Yannis M. Ioannides. 2004. "Neighbors' Income Distribution: Economic Segregation and Mixing in U.S. Urban Neighborhoods." *Journal of Housing Economics* 13, no. 4: 368–82.

Harkness, Joseph, and Sandra Newman. 2002. "Homeownership for the Poor in Distressed Neighborhoods: Does This Make Sense?" *Housing Policy Debate* 13, no. 3: 597–630.

Haurin, Donald R., Robert D. Dietz, and Bruce A. Weinberg. 2003. "The Impact of Neighborhood Homeownership Rates: A Review of the Theoretical and Empirical Literature." *Journal of Housing Research* 13, no. 2: 119–51.

Haurin, Donald R., and H. Leroy Gill. 2002. "The Impact of Transaction Costs and the Expected Length of Stay on Homeownership." *Journal of Urban Economics* 51, no. 3: 563–84.

Haurin, Donald R., Toby L. Parcel, and Ruth Jean Haurin. 2002. "Impact of Homeownership on Child Outcomes." In *Low-Income Homeownership: Examining the Unexamined Goal,* edited by N. P. Retsinas and E. S. Belsky, pp. 427–46. Brookings.

Hays, R. Allen. 1995. *The Federal Government and Urban Housing.* 2d ed. State University of New York Press.

Hecker, Daniel E. 2005. "Occupational Employment Projections to 2014." *Monthly Labor Review* 128, no. 11: 70–101.

Herbert, Christopher E., and others. 2004. "Homeownership Gaps among Low-Income and Minority Borrowers and Neighborhoods." U.S. Department of Housing and Urban Development.

Hood, Ernie. 2005. "Dwelling Disparities: How Poor Housing Leads to Poor Health." *Environmental Health Perspectives* 113, no. 5: 310–17.

Ihlanfeldt, Keith R., and David L. Sjoquist. 1998. "Inner-City Concentrated Poverty and Neighborhood Distress: 1970 to 1990." *Housing Policy Debate* 9, no. 4: 849–92.

Jargowsky, Paul A. 1997. *Poverty and Place: Ghettos, Barrios, and the American City.* New York: Russell Sage Foundation.

Joint Center for Housing Studies. 2005. "The State of the Nation's Housing, 2005." Harvard University.

——. 2006a. "America's Rental Housing: Homes for a Diverse Nation." Harvard University.

——. 2006b. "The State of the Nation's Housing, 2006." Harvard University.

Jones, Amy. 2001. *Tools and Strategies for Improving Community Relations in the Housing Choice Voucher Program*. U.S. Department of Housing and Urban Development.

Kain, John F. 1992. "The Spatial Mismatch Hypothesis: Three Decades Later." *Housing Policy Debate* 3, no. 2: 371–460.

Kain, John F., and Joseph J. Persky. 1969. "Alternatives to the Gilded Ghetto." *Public Interest* 14 (Winter): 74–83.

Katz, Bruce, and Margery Turner. 2001. "Who Should Run the Housing Voucher Program? A Reform Proposal." *Housing Policy Debate* 12, no. 2: 239–62.

Katz, Bruce, and others. 2003. "Rethinking Local Affordable Housing Strategies: Lessons from 70 Years of Policy and Practice." Discussion Paper. Brookings Center on Urban and Metropolitan Policy.

Katz, Lawrence F., Jeffrey R. Kling, and Jeffrey B. Liebman. 2001. "Moving to Opportunity in Boston: Early Results of a Randomized Mobility Experiment." *Quarterly Journal of Economics* 116, no. 2: 607–54.

Khadduri, Jill, Kimberly Burnett, and David Rodda. 2003. "Targeting Housing Production Subsidies." U.S. Department of Housing and Urban Development.

Kling, Jeffrey R., and others. 2004. "Moving to Opportunity and Tranquility: Neighborhood Effects on Adult Economic Self-Sufficiency and Health from a Randomized Housing Voucher Experiment." Working Paper 35. Princeton, N.J.: Princeton University, Woodrow Wilson School of Public and International Affairs, Center for Health and Wellbeing.

Krefetz, Sharon. 2001. "The Impact and Evolution of the Massachusetts Comprehensive Permit and Zoning Appeals Act: Thirty Years of Experience with a State Legislative Effort to Overcome Exclusionary Zoning." *Western New England Law Review* 22, no. 2: 381–430.

Leventhal, Tama, and Jeanne Brooks-Gunn. 2001. "Changing Neighborhoods and Child Well-Being: Understanding How Children May Be Affected in the Coming Century." In *Children at the Millennium: Where Have We Come From? Where Are We Going?* edited by Timothy J. Owens and Sandra L. Hofferth, pp. 263–302. New York: Elsevier Science.

Levine, Ned. 1999. "The Effects of Local Growth Controls on Regional Housing Production and Population Redistribution in California." *Urban Studies* 36, no. 12: 2047–68.

Linneman, Peter, and others. 1990. "The State of Local Growth Management." Real Estate Working Paper 81. Philadelphia: University of Pennsylvania, Wharton School of Business.

Lipman, Barbara J. 2005. "Something's Gotta Give: Working Families and the Cost of Housing." Center for Housing Policy. Washington.

Listokin, David, and Barbara Listokin. 2001. *Barriers to the Rehabilitation of Affordable Housing*. Vol. 1, *Findings and Analysis*. U.S. Department of Housing and Urban Development, Office of Policy Development and Research.

Lowry, Stella. 1990. "Housing and Health: Health and Homelessness." *British Medical Journal* 300, no. 6716: 32–34.

Ludwig, Jens, Paul Hirschfield, and Greg J. Duncan. 2001. "Urban Poverty and Juvenile Crime: Evidence from a Randomized Housing-Mobility Experiment." *Quarterly Journal of Economics* 116, no. 2: 665–79.

Ludwig, Jens, and Jeffrey R. Kling. 2005. "Is Crime Contagious?" Working Paper 117. Princeton, N.J.: Princeton University, Center for Economic Policy Studies.

Mallach, Alan. 2006. *Bringing Buildings Back: From Abandoned Properties to Community Assets*. Montclair, N.J.: National Housing Institute.

Malpezzi, Stephen. 1996. "Housing Prices, Externalities, and Regulation in U.S. Metropolitan Areas." *Journal of Housing Research* 7, no. 2: 209–41.

Malpezzi, Stephen, Gregory Chun, and Richard Green. 1998. "New Place-to-Place Housing Price Indexes for U.S. Metropolitan Areas, and Their Determinants: An Application of Housing Indicators." *Real Estate Economics* 26, no. 2: 235–75.

Massey, Douglas S., and Nancy A. Denton. 1993. *American Apartheid: Segregation and the Making of the Underclass.* Harvard University Press.

Matte, Thomas D., and David E. Jacobs. 2000. "Housing and Health: Current Issues and Implications for Research and Programs." *Journal of Urban Health: Bulletin of the New York Academy of Medicine* 77, no. 1: 7–25.

McEvoy, John. 2002. *The Federal Housing Delivery System.* Report prepared for the Millennial Housing Commission. Washington.

Megbolugbe, Isaac F., Marja C. Hoek-Smit, and Peter D. Linneman. 1996. "Understanding Neighborhood Dynamics: A Review of the Contributions of William G. Grigsby." *Urban Studies* 33, no. 10: 1779–95.

Millennial Housing Commission. 2002. *Meeting Our Nation's Housing Challenges.* Report of the Millennial Housing Commission Appointed by the Congress of the United States. Washington.

National Housing Trust. 2006. "More than 152,000 Affordable Apartments Preserved with LIHTCs since 2003." *National Housing Trust Preservation News* (June 27) (www.nhtinc.org/newsletter_archive.asp?month=0507).

NeighborWorks. 2004. "Changing Minds, Building Communities: Advancing Affordable Housing through Communications Campaigns." *NeighborWorks Journal.* Special issue prepared for the NeighborWorks Symposium on Multifamily Excellence. NeighborWorks Training Institute, Minneapolis, Minn., May 5.

Nelson, Kathy P., and F. Stevens Redburn. 1994. "Rethinking Priority Needs for Rental Assistance: Limitations of 'Worst Case Needs.' " Paper prepared for the midyear meeting of the American Real Estate and Urban Economics Association. Washington, June 1.

Newman, Sandra J., and Joseph M. Harkness. 2002. "The Long-Term Effects of Public Housing on Self-Sufficiency." *Journal of Policy Analysis and Management* 21, no. 1: 21–43.

———. 2005. "Housing Affordability and Children's Well-Being: Evidence from the National Survey of America's Families." *Housing Policy Debate* 16, no. 2: 223–56.

Newman, Sandra J., and Ann B. Schnare. 1997. " '. . . And a Suitable Living Environment': The Failure of Housing Programs to Deliver on Neighborhood Quality." *Housing Policy Debate* 8, no. 4: 703–41.

Office of the Deputy Prime Minister. 2004. *The Impact of Overcrowding on Health and Education: A Review of the Evidence and Literature.* Report from the Office of the Deputy Prime Minister. London (May).

Orfield, Myron. 2002. *American Metro Politics: The New Suburban Reality.* Brookings.

Orr, James A., and Richard W. Peach. 1999. "Housing Outcomes: An Assessment of Long-Term Trends." *Economic Policy Review* 5, no 3: 51–61.

Project on Human Development in Chicago Neighborhoods (PHDCN). 2004. "Neighborhood Matters: Selected Findings from the Project on Human Development in Chicago Neighborhoods." Paper prepared for New Directions in Housing Research: An Exploratory Discussion, sponsored by the John D. and Catherine T. MacArthur Foundation. Cambridge, Mass., July 13–14.

Quigley, John M., and Stephen Raphael. 2004. "Is Housing Unaffordable? Why Isn't It More Affordable?" *Journal of Economic Perspectives* 18, no. 1: 191–214.

Quigley, John, and Larry A. Rosenthal. 2005. "The Effects of Land-Use Regulation on the Price of Housing: What Do We Know? What Can We Learn?" University of California, Berkeley, Program on Housing and Urban Policy.

Retsinas, Nicolas P., and Eric Belsky. 2005. *Building Assets, Building Credit: Creating Wealth in Low-Income Communities.* Brookings.

Rohe, William M., George McCarthy, and Shannon Van Zandt. 2001. "The Social Benefits and Costs of Homeownership: A Critical Assessment of the Research." Low-Income Home-ownership Working Paper 00-01. Cambridge, Mass.: Harvard University, Joint Center for Housing Studies.

Rosenbaum, Emily, and Laura E. Harris. 2001. "Low-Income Families in Their New Neigh-borhoods." *Journal of Family Issues* 22, no. 2: 183–210.

Rosenthal, Stuart S. 2004. "Old Homes and Poor Neighborhoods: A Dynamic Model of Urban Decline and Renewal." Syracuse University, Department of Economics.

Saks, Raven E. 2004. "Housing Supply Restrictions across the United States." *Wharton Real Estate Review* 8, no. 2: 43–51.

Salama, Jerry J. 1999. "The Redevelopment of Distressed Public Housing: Early Results from HOPE VI Projects in Atlanta, Chicago, and San Antonio." *Housing Policy Debate* 10, no. 1: 95–142.

Sampson, Robert J., Jeffrey D. Morenoff, and Thomas Gannon-Rowley. 2002. "Assessing Neighborhood Effects: Social Processes and New Directions in Research." *Annual Review of Sociology* 28: 443–78.

Sanbonmatsu, Lisa, and others. 2004. "Neighborhoods and Academic Achievement: Results from the Moving to Opportunity Experiment." Working Paper 492. Princeton, N.J.: Princeton University, Industrial Relations Section.

Sard, Barbara. 2001. *The Family Self-Sufficiency Program: HUD's Best Kept Secret for Promoting Employment and Asset Growth.* Washington: Center on Budget and Policy Priorities.

Schelling, Thomas C. 1971. "Dynamic Models of Segregation." *Journal of Mathematical Sociology* 1:143–86.

Schill, Michael H. 2004. "Regulations and Housing Development: What We Know and What We Need to Know." Paper prepared for the U.S. Department of Housing and Urban Devel-opment's Conference on Regulatory Barriers to Affordable Housing. Washington, April 22.

Schill, Michael H., and Susan M. Wachter. 1995. "The Spatial Bias of Federal Housing Law and Policy: Concentrated Poverty in Urban America." *University of Pennsylvania Law Review* 143, no. 5: 1285–342.

Schill, Michael H., and others. 2002. "Revitalizing Inner-City Neighborhoods: New York City's Ten-Year Plan." *Housing Policy Debate* 13, no. 3: 529–66.

Sherraden, Michael. 1991. *Assets for the Poor: A New American Welfare Policy.* Armonk, N.Y.: M. E. Sharpe.

Shroder, Mark. 2002. "Does Housing Assistance Perversely Affect Self-Sufficiency? A Review Essay." *Journal of Housing Economics* 11, no. 4: 381–417.

Simmons, Patrick A., and Robert E. Lang. 2001. "The Urban Turnaround: A Decade-by-Decade Report Card on Postwar Population Change in Older Industrial Cities." Census Note 01. Washington: Fannie Mae Foundation.

Simmons-Mosley, Tammie X. 2003. "Interdependence Effects of Housing Abandonment and Renovation." *Journal of Real Estate Research* 25, no. 4: 421–30.

Smith, James P. 1999. "Healthy Bodies and Thick Wallets: The Dual Relation between Health and Economic Status." *Journal of Economic Perspectives* 13, no. 2: 145–66.

Somerville, C. Tsuriel, and Cynthia Holmes. 2001. "Dynamics of the Affordable Housing Stock: Microdata Analysis of Filtering." *Journal of Housing Research* 12, no. 1: 115–40.

Somerville, C. Tsuriel, and Christopher J. Mayer. 2003. "Government Regulation and Changes in the Affordable Housing Stock." *FRBNY Economic Policy Review* 9, no. 2: 45–61.

Sternlieb, George. 1966. *The Tenement Landlord*. New Brunswick, N.J.: Rutgers University, Urban Studies Center.

Stone, Michael E. 1993. *Shelter Poverty: New Ideas on Housing Affordability*. Temple University Press.

Thalmann, Philippe. 2003. " 'House Poor' or Simply 'Poor'?" *Journal of Housing Economics* 12, no. 4: 291–317.

Tiebout, Charles M. 1956. "A Pure Theory of Local Expenditures." *Journal of Political Economy* 64, no. 5: 416–24.

Turner, Margery A., and others. 2002. *All Other Things Being Equal: A Paired Testing Study of Mortgage Lending Institutions*. Report prepared for the U.S. Department of Housing and Urban Development, Office of Policy. Washington.

U.S. Department of Housing and Urban Development (HUD). 2003. *Trends in Worst Case Needs for Housing, 1978–1999: A Report to Congress on Worst Case Housing Needs*. Washington (December).

U.S. General Accounting Office (GAO). 1994. *Elementary School Children: Many Change Schools Frequently, Harming Their Education*. Report to the Honorable Marcy Kaptur, House of Representatives.

Vandell, Kerry D. 1995. "Market Factors Affecting Spatial Heterogeneity among Urban Neighborhoods." *Housing Policy Debate* 6, no. 1: 103–39.

van der Klaauw, Bas, and Jan C. van Ours. 2003. "From Welfare to Work: Does the Neighborhood Matter?" *Journal of Public Economics* 87, nos. 5–6: 957–85.

Vartanian, Thomas P., and Philip M. Gleason. 1999. "Do Neighborhood Conditions Affect High School Dropout and College Graduation Rates?" *Journal of Socio-Economics* 28, no. 1: 21–41.

Verma, Nandita, and James Riccio. 2003. *Housing Assistance and the Effects of Welfare Reform: Evidence from Connecticut and Minnesota*. Report prepared for the U.S. Department of Housing and Urban Development, Office of Policy Development and Research. Washington: MDRC.

von Hoffman, Alexander, Eric Belsky, and Kwan Lee. 2006. "The Impact of Housing on Community: A Review of Scholarly Theories and Empirical Research." Working Paper W06-1. Cambridge, Mass.: Harvard University, Joint Center for Housing Studies.

Walker, Christopher, and others. 2002. "The Impact of CDBG Spending on Urban Neighborhoods." Contract C-OPC-18572 UI 06729-006-00. U.S. Department of Housing and Urban Development.

Wallace, James, and others. 1981. "Participation and Benefits in the Urban Section 8 Program: New Construction and Existing Housing." Cambridge, Mass.: Abt Associates.

Wheaton, William C. 1977. "Income and Urban Residence." *American Economic Review* 67, no. 4: 620–31.

Wilson, William J. 1987. *The Truly Disadvantaged: The Inner-City, the Underclass, and Public Policy*. University of Chicago Press.

———. 1996. "When Work Disappears." *Political Science Quarterly* 111, no. 4: 567–95.

Zielenbach, Sean. 2003. "Assessing Economic Change in HOPE VI Neighborhoods." *Housing Policy Debate* 14, no. 4: 621–55.

PART I

What We Know: Rental Market Operations and Outcomes

2

Where Poor Renters Live in Our Cities: Dynamics and Determinants

STUART S. ROSENTHAL

Policies designed to improve rental housing opportunities for the poor differ from other low-income support programs in many ways, but one in particular stands out: housing programs have a direct impact on where poor families can live. This is perhaps self-evident. Nevertheless, where poor families live affects their access to jobs, school quality, and other factors that influence a family's ability to rise up out of poverty. For these reasons, development of low-income housing policy should take into account market forces that govern where the poor live and why. Failure to consider such forces could undermine the effectiveness of low-income housing policies or, at a minimum, increase the cost of attaining goals that prompted housing support policies in the first place. With this in mind, the primary focus of this chapter is to assess and measure those factors that drive the location of poor communities, and especially poor communities in which rental housing is the dominant mode of accommodation. Some further background is in order.

Short History of Rental Housing

For several decades, federal low-income housing programs have been dominated by two quite different strategies: "place-based" construction programs and "tenant-based" voucher (certificate) programs.[1] From 1937 to the early 1980s, the dominant federal low-income housing program was public housing. Under this program, the federal government built roughly 1.3 million housing units in multifamily projects and then delegated management of these projects to local (but federally funded) housing authorities. Roughly 1 million of these units were still in service in 2005. The more recent Low Income Housing Tax Credit (LIHTC) program, begun in 1986, provides construction subsidies to private for-profit developers provided that at least 40 percent of a project's units are leased to low-income families (other rules also apply). As of 2005, more than 1.4 million units had been built through the LIHTC program. In contrast, Section 8 housing vouchers allow beneficiaries to seek housing in the private market with the assurance that the federal government will pay a portion of their rent (up to an amount stipulated by the terms of the voucher). In 2005, more than 1.8 million families received Section 8 vouchers.

A fundamental difference between new-construction and voucher-type programs is their effect on where the poor can live. Because of the durability of housing, public and LIHTC housing programs dictate for years to come where an important fraction of the low-income housing stock will be found within a city. In addition, especially in the case of public housing, there is a tendency to concentrate the poor in low-income areas, reducing access to middle-income amenities. Although the LIHTC program is based on a partnership between government and for-profit entrepreneurs, that program also retains a tendency to concentrate the poor, although arguably less so than does public housing.[2] Voucher-type programs do the opposite by enabling low-income families to search across an expanded set of neighborhoods that lie within their voucher-enhanced economic reach. In principle, this could improve the ability of low-income families to live in neighborhoods with better schools, lower crime rates, and stronger job networks. This could be especially important if job locations or other location-specific opportunities shift over time. Voucher recipients can react quickly to such changes by relocating to different neighborhoods, whereas place-based subsidized housing lives on at its original site.

This chapter provides background evidence that will be useful in thinking about the spatial fixity associated with place-based housing strategies as compared with the spatial flexibility of tenant-based programs. If the poor are restricted to a limited

1. Concerns that place-based programs may crowd out private investment (Murray 1983, 1999; Sinai and Waldfogel 2005; Eriksen and Rosenthal 2007) are well known. The possibility that voucher programs may cause market rents to rise is also apparent (Susin 2002). These are important issues, but they are not the focus of this chapter.

2. In part, that is because 15 percent of occupants of LIHTC housing in the United States are not of low-income status. In addition, LIHTC housing is really more moderate-income as opposed to low-income housing, and nearly one-fourth of the LIHTC projects are located in census tracts in the upper third of the income distribution, with another fourth of the projects in the second third (Eriksen and Rosenthal 2007).

set of neighborhoods for reasons unrelated to the provision of subsidized rental housing, that would reduce any benefits arising from the spatial flexibility of tenant- versus placed-based programs. On the other hand, if the poor are able and willing to live in a wide range of areas throughout a city, then the gains associated with the more spatially flexible voucher-type programs will be greater.

In considering these issues, in this chapter I pay special attention to four mechanisms that drive the location of the poor within individual cities. First, "standard" urban economic theory describes a tension between commuting costs, on the one hand, and housing demand, on the other. The argument is that housing demand rises more quickly than commuting costs with an increase in income. In a monocentric city framework—with all employment in the downtown area—the rich derive more net benefit from suburban locations with lower housing prices and longer commutes than do the poor. As a result, the rich outbid the poor for space in the suburbs, and the poor occupy the central cities.[3] For many years, this was the textbook explanation for why the poor are disproportionately concentrated in the central cities. More recently, however, Edward Glaeser, Matthew Kahn, and Jordan Rappaport (forthcoming) have argued convincingly that empirical estimates of the sensitivity of housing demand and commuting costs to changes in income do not support the standard story. Instead, they argue, housing demand is relatively insensitive to increasing income, but commuting costs are likely very sensitive—at least to the extent that individuals value their time at a rate approximately equal to their wage. Under these conditions, the poor should occupy the suburbs and the rich should locate in the central cities.

Glaeser, Kahn, and Rappaport (forthcoming) resolve this seeming discrepancy by taking the role of public transit into account. They note that public transit is more cost effective in densely populated areas that allow for economies of scale in the provision of transit services. For that reason, public transit is naturally and disproportionately concentrated in the central cities. The poor, meanwhile, lack the resources to own cars and must live in neighborhoods with good access to public transit—irrespective of housing demand. For this reason, the poor are disproportionately drawn to areas that provide access to public transit, including and especially the central cities.[4]

Aging of the housing stock is another factor that affects where the poor live. As a stylized fact, apart from subsidized housing, the poor occupy older homes originally built for higher-income families (see, for example, Rosenthal, forthcoming; Brueckner and Rosenthal 2006). As those homes age, they tend to deteriorate despite maintenance efforts (for example, Harding, Sirmans, and Rosenthal

3. The standard monocentric city model is often attributed to separate works by William Alonso (1964), Edwin Mills (1967), and Richard Muth (1969) and is therefore sometimes referred to as the AMM model.

4. Stephen Leroy and Jon Sonstelie (1983) make a similar argument.

2007) and are eventually passed down to families of lower-income status. This is the filtering model of housing markets, and filtering has long been recognized as the dominant manner in which the private market supplies housing to the poor. This model predicts that the poor will live where older homes are found.[5]

A third mechanism arises from social dynamics and related externalities. Families' concerns about the attributes of their neighbors, such as race-ethnicity and income, can lead to a "tipping" phenomenon (Schelling 1971). For example, if some white families in a community harbor discriminatory preferences for neighbors, in-migration of minority families could cause such families to relocate, further increasing the minority share in the neighborhood. That, in turn, could cause white families with more mild discriminatory preferences to move, reinforcing the trend. Because minority incomes are lower, on average, than those of white families, this suggests that racial segregation in the housing market will tend to concentrate poverty in select areas of a city. This tendency may be further reinforced by behavior of individuals that generates social capital or costs. Suppose, for example, that low-income families commit more crimes and criminal activity causes higher-income families to flee. The presence of low-income families will thereby lower rents. That, in turn, will attract a greater concentration of low-income families to the area, further reducing the economic status of the community. This suggests that poverty may itself attract more poverty.

The fourth and final mechanism considered here is the location of place-based subsidized rental housing—more precisely, public and LIHTC housing. Both of these programs mandate that low-income families occupy the units (or at least a portion of the units, in the case of the LIHTC program). The presence of these projects, therefore, has the potential to affect where the poor will be found.

These mechanisms differ in the degree to which they imply systematic patterns regarding where the poor live. Social interactions, for example, clearly affect who may want to live in a neighborhood but have little direct implication for where poor neighborhoods will be found. Similarly, although public and LIHTC housing is generally restricted to low-income families, that in itself does not dictate where those units will be sited. This differs from the role of filtering, which says that the poor will move to different neighborhoods over extended periods of time as they follow older and lower-valued housing stock. Similarly, the need to access public transit suggests that the poor will be disproportionately concentrated in densely developed areas, and especially in the central cities.

A primary goal of this chapter is to provide empirical evidence that each of these mechanisms affects where the poor are found and to shed further light on the nature

---

5. Moreover, because cities develop and redevelop from the center outward over time, this model implies that long-running (decades long) cycles govern where the poor live as they follow slow-moving waves of aging housing across a metropolitan area.

of these effects. To do so, I draw upon census-tract data from 1970, 1980, 1990, and 2000. These data have all been coded to year 2000 census-tract boundaries and can be used, therefore, to follow neighborhoods over time.[6] Throughout the chapter, a census tract is treated as a neighborhood.

For the purpose of describing the location of poor rental neighborhoods, both in the present and over time, it is helpful to define at the outset what constitutes a poor household. This is not entirely straightforward because poverty depends not only on a family's level of income but also on other household factors that affect a family's needs. Bearing this in mind, I use the census-tract poverty rate as defined by the U.S. Census Bureau as the measure of poor families in a given neighborhood—specifically, the number of families in a tract deemed below the poverty line divided by the total number of families in the tract.

In focusing on the U.S. Census Bureau definition of poverty, two considerations should be noted. First, an important goal of this chapter is to shed light not just on where low-income families and neighborhoods are found but also on where low-income rental housing is needed. In this regard, an implicit assumption is that where poverty rates are high, the need for adequate rental housing is also high. Data from the 2000 census provide direct evidence on this point.

Based on data in the 2000 decennial census, the rental rate among U.S. households living in poverty, excluding those living in mobile homes, was 68.67 percent. As would be anticipated, that rate was lower outside of metropolitan statistical areas (MSAs) (55.25 percent) and in the more rural portions of identified MSAs (63.88 percent). Among central city residents, the rate was much higher, 80.82 percent.[7] Partly for that reason, in the empirical work throughout this chapter, I focus on neighborhoods in metropolitan statistical areas. As the foregoing measures suggest, for these regions poverty is closely associated with the need for adequate rental housing.

Second, much of the analysis here includes comparisons of local poverty rates across decades. Comparability in the definition of poverty over time is therefore important. In that regard, the Census Bureau definition of poverty is based on an absolute poverty line.[8] The intent in defining that absolute measure is to identify a threshold below which families are believed to lack sufficient resources to meet the minimum requirements of food, shelter, and clothing necessary for a healthy

6. A detailed description of the data is provided in Rosenthal (forthcoming), Brueckner and Rosenthal (2006), and Eriksen and Rosenthal (2007).

7. Estimates are based on household-level data from the 2000 decennial census. These data were obtained from the Integrated Public Use Micro Sample (IPUMS), available over the web (www.ipums.org). The sample used to measure rental rates was restricted to households that do not live in mobile homes and was weighted to ensure that the rental rates are representative of the entire country.

8. See the U.S. Census Bureau website on poverty (www.census.gov/hhes/www/poverty/poverty.html).

Table 2-1. *Census Bureau–Defined Poverty Limit, United States,*
Various Regions, 2005
U.S. dollars

Number of persons in family unit	Forty-eight contiguous states and D.C.	Alaska	Hawaii
1	9,570	11,950	11,010
2	12,830	16,030	14,760
3	16,090	20,110	18,510
4	19,350	24,190	22,260
For each additional person, add	3,260	4,080	3,750

Source: "Poverty Guidelines, Research, and Measurement," *Federal Register* 70, no.33 (2005): 8373–375. See also Wikipedia, "Poverty in the United States" (en.wikipedia.org/wiki/Poverty_in_the_United_States); U.S. Census Bureau, *Historical Poverty Tables,* table 2, "Poverty Status of People by Family Relationship, Race, and Hispanic Origin: 1959 to 2005" (www.census.gov/hhes/www/poverty/histpov/hstpov2.html).

existence. For this reason, the Census Bureau varies the definition of the poverty line across households depending on family size, number of children under the age of eighteen, and, in earlier decades, the gender of the head of household. The Census Bureau definition of poverty has remained largely unchanged since 1970, except for adjustments to the relevant thresholds for inflation.[9] This facilitates comparisons of the location of poor families across time, families that depend disproportionately on rental housing.

The 2005 family income thresholds that define poverty are outlined in table 2-1, and figure 2-1 graphs the poverty rate in the United States from 1973 until 2005. Poverty rates varied over the period: in 1973 roughly 11 percent of the U.S. population was living in poverty; that figure rose to 13 percent in 1980, 13.5 percent in 1990, and then dropped back to 11 percent in 2000 following the economic boom of the 1990s.

Using the Census Bureau definition of poverty, I examine the propensity of neighborhoods to transition to higher or lower poverty status between 1970 and 2000. Several stylized facts emerge. Most striking is the high degree of persistence in poverty rates across low-poverty neighborhoods, and this holds regardless of city size and also regardless of whether tract poverty is measured relative to overall poverty rates in the MSA or in absolute terms. Among other communities, however, there is much less persistence, although very high poverty

9. In addition, in 1981 separate thresholds for farm and female-headed families were eliminated, and the largest family size was set to nine or more. These changes create some differences in the definition of poverty for the 1990 and 2000 tract data relative to 1970 and 1980 data. But especially given the focus in this study on urban areas (which largely preclude farm-based families), the differences are small.

Figure 2-1. *Poverty Rate in the United States, 1973–2004*

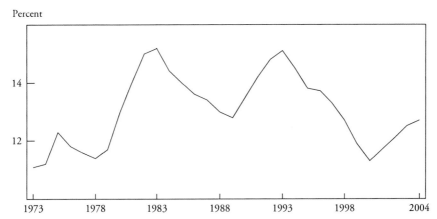

Source: Data from Wikipedia, "Poverty in the United States (http://en.wikipedia.org/wiki/Poverty_in_the_United_States) and U.S. Census Bureau, *Historical Poverty Tables*, table 2, "Poverty Status of People by Family Relationship, Race, and Hispanic Origin, 1959 to 2006" (www.census.gov/hhes/www/poverty/histpov/hstpov2.html).

neighborhoods in large metropolitan areas do tend to remain high poverty over the thirty-year period, from 1970 to 2000, during which these neighborhoods were studied.

Results from a variety of regressions confirm that there is no one single factor governing where the poor are found. In fact, just the opposite appears to be the case: all four of the mechanisms described above contribute, and in the anticipated ways. Thus the location of the poor tends to shift over time as they follow the aging housing stock. The poor are drawn to areas with access to public transit. Socioeconomic attributes create spillover effects that further influence where poor families are found. The poor are attracted to locations with public and LIHTC housing, as would be anticipated.

Persistence in Poverty at the Neighborhood Level

Is poverty persistent at the neighborhood level, or do local poverty rates change widely from one decade to the next? The answer to this question could influence perceptions of the viability of place-based versus tenant-based rental housing support programs. To address this question, I sort neighborhoods within each metropolitan area into four groups based on communities with the lowest to the highest rates of poverty. This is done twice using two different criteria. In the first instance, neighborhoods are sorted based on the first, second, third, and fourth quartiles associated with relative poverty rates within a given metropolitan area. In the second instance, neighborhoods are sorted based on absolute levels of poverty: below 15 percent, 15 to 30 percent, 30 to 45 percent, and above 45 percent. An advantage of focusing on relative measures of poverty is that the number of census tracts in each of the four quartiles is both and numerous and largely the same. In contrast, in absolute terms, there are relatively few very high poverty tracts but many neighborhoods with low poverty rates.[10] An advantage of focusing on absolute measures of poverty is that low-income housing policy is predominantly driven by concerns about absolute levels of economic well-being, although certainly relative differences across society also contribute to policy initiatives.

For both sets of poverty measures, I document the movement into or out of poverty—that is, the degree to which high-poverty neighborhoods in 1970 still had high poverty levels in 2000. A similar exercise is performed for the low-poverty neighborhoods in 1970 and for the two categories in between. These measures are reported in tables 2-2 through 2-6 for all metropolitan areas, very small cities, small cities, medium-sized cities, and large cities.[11] Each of these tables also includes two panels. In the top panel, the focus is on shifts in the relative level of poverty within communities; the bottom panel focuses on changes in the absolute level of poverty. These alternative ways of characterizing neighborhoods provide complementary perspectives on the persistence of local poverty rates.

For all metropolitan areas (table 2-2), 61.64 percent of tracts with relatively high poverty rates in 1970 were still of relatively high poverty status in 2000. Roughly 44 percent of relatively low poverty tracts in 1970 retain their status in 2000, but only about 33 percent of those tracts with "intermediate" levels of relative poverty in 1970 display similar poverty levels thirty years later. Interestingly, the persistence of low relative poverty tracts and high relative poverty tracts is more pronounced among the nation's largest cities—cities with 1,000 or more census tracts. In these metropolitan areas (table 2-3), roughly 51 percent of low relative poverty tracts in 1970 were still low in 2000, and roughly 68 percent of relatively high poverty tracts were still of high-poverty status.

In the lower panels of tables 2-2 to 2-6, neighborhoods are characterized based on absolute levels of poverty. Close review of the summary measures indicates that based on absolute measures of poverty, neighborhood poverty status is even more persistent than when poverty relative to the MSA is considered. According to this measure, 80.75 percent of neighborhoods (in all cities) with low-poverty status in 1970 still had low levels of poverty thirty years later.

10. Among all MSAs in the United States, there were 35,210 census tracts in 1990 with poverty rates below 15 percent, 8,540 tracts with poverty rates from 15 to 30 percent, 3,279 tracts with poverty rates from 30 to 45 percent, and only 1,535 tracts with poverty rates above 45 percent.

11. For these purposes, the definitions of city size are metropolitan areas with fewer than 100 census tracts, 100 to 500 census tracts, 500 to 1,000 census tracts, and more than 1,000 census tracts.

Table 2-2. *All Cities: Transition Rates of Census Tract Poverty Rate, 1970–2000*[a]

Poverty level in 2000	1st quartile: Low poverty in 1970	2nd quartile: Moderate-low poverty in 1970	3rd quartile: Moderate-high poverty in 1970	4th quartile: High poverty in 1970
Based on relative poverty rates within the MSA[b]				
Low poverty	43.86	31.64	19.22	5.71
Moderate-low poverty	29.67	32.20	27.12	10.55
Moderate-high poverty	19.83	25.54	33.11	22.10
High poverty	6.64	10.62	20.55	61.64
	1st tier: Low poverty in 1970	2nd tier: Moderate-low poverty in 1970	3rd tier: Moderate-high poverty in 1970	4th tier: High poverty in 1970
Based on absolute poverty rates[c]				
Low poverty	80.75	34.79	13.95	4.21
Moderate-low poverty	16.49	38.96	27.79	18.01
Moderate-high poverty	2.48	22.60	41.80	34.87
High poverty	0.28	3.66	16.45	42.92

a. Estimates are based on 43,896 census tracts from a balanced panel of 270 MSAs.

b. Tracts with poverty rates less than the MSA's 25th percentile in the given year are defined as *1st quartile*. Tracts with poverty rates from the 25th up to but not including the 50th percentile are *2nd quartile*; tracts with poverty rates from the 50th up to but not including the 75th percentile are *3rd quartile*; and tracts with poverty rates at or above the 75th percentile are *4th quartile*.

c. Tracts with absolute poverty rates less than 15 percent in the given year are defined as *1st tier*. Tracts with poverty rates from 15 percent up to but not including 30 percent are *2nd tier*; tracts with poverty rates from 30 percent up to but not including 45 percent are *3rd tier*; and tracts with poverty rates at or above 45 percent are *4th tier*.

The same degree of persistence among low-poverty neighborhoods is evident in tables 2-3, 2-4, 2-5, and 2-6 for moderate, small, and very small cities. Among large metropolitan areas (table 2-3), the corresponding level of persistence of low poverty was slightly lower, at 76.12 percent, though still very high. Together, these patterns indicate that low-poverty neighborhoods remain so for extended periods of time.

In contrast, higher-poverty neighborhoods exhibit considerable change in their absolute level of poverty between 1970 and 2000. In table 2-2, for example, the main diagonal values for neighborhoods in 1970 with moderate-low poverty, moderate-high poverty, and high poverty are 38.96 percent, 41.80 percent, and 42.92 percent, respectively. Thus although roughly 40 percent of these neighborhoods retained their 1970 absolute poverty status in 2000, approximately 60 percent did not. On the other hand, if neighborhood poverty levels in cities of different sizes are examined, once again, poverty is found to be more persistent in larger cities, especially among high-poverty tracts. In the largest MSAs, for example (table 2-3), the main diagonal values for moderate to high poverty

Table 2-3. *Large Cities: Transition Rates of Census Tract Poverty Rate, 1970–2000*[a]

Poverty level in 2000	1st quartile: Low poverty in 1970	2nd quartile: Moderate-low poverty in 1970	3rd quartile: Moderate-high poverty in 1970	4th quartile: High poverty in 1970
Based on relative poverty rates within the MSA[b]				
Low poverty	51.20	31.26	11.53	2.26
Moderate-low poverty	29.04	33.97	27.51	6.90
Moderate-high poverty	15.05	25.61	37.02	23.02
High poverty	4.71	9.16	23.93	67.82
	1st tier: Low poverty in 1970	2nd tier: Moderate-low poverty in 1970	3rd tier: Moderate-high poverty in 1970	4th tier: High poverty in 1970
Based on absolute poverty rates[c]				
Low poverty	76.12	16.65	6.22	0.00
Moderate-low poverty	19.83	39.50	17.62	3.85
Moderate-high poverty	3.64	38.97	57.51	34.62
High poverty	0.41	5.88	18.65	61.54

a. Estimates are based on 1,855 census tracts from a balanced panel of MSAs. Large cities are defined as those with 1,000 or more census tracts.

b. Tracts with poverty rates less than the MSA's 25th percentile in the given year are defined as *1st quartile*. Tracts with poverty rates from the 25th up to but not including the 50th percentile are *2nd quartile*; tracts with poverty rates from the 50th up to but not including the 75th percentile are *3rd quartile*; and tracts with poverty rates at or above the 75th percentile are *4th quartile*.

c. Tracts with absolute poverty rates less than 15 percent in the given year are defined as *1st tier*. Tracts with poverty rates from 15 percent up to but not including 30 percent are *2nd tier*; tracts with poverty rates from 30 percent up to but not including 45 percent are *3rd tier*; and tracts with poverty rates at or above 45 percent are *4th tier*.

status communities (in absolute terms) are 39.50 percent, 57.51 percent, and 61.54 percent.

Overall, by how much do absolute neighborhood poverty levels change with each passing decade? The data provide evidence on this point. For all MSAs, absolute poverty rates within individual census tracts changed by roughly 4 percentage points in absolute value in each decade from 1970 to 2000 (1970–80, 4.17; 1980–90, 4.09; 1990–2000, 3.96). Thus the amount of variability in poverty rates from one decade to the next has remained steady, on average, over the thirty-year horizon from 1970 to 2000. That similarity, of course, does not do justice to the more complicated patterns of change suggested in tables 2-2 to 2-6.

The patterns in tables 2-2 through 2-6 provide several stylized facts. First, high-poverty tracts display considerable persistence in their poverty status over the 1970 to 2000 period. This is especially true when one considers the absolute level of poverty in the neighborhood. Second, among tracts with low and moderate

Table 2-4. *Medium-Sized Cities: Transition Rates of Census Tract Poverty Rate,*
1970–2000[a]

Poverty level in 2000	1st quartile: Low poverty in 1970	2nd quartile: Moderate-low poverty in 1970	3rd quartile: Moderate-high poverty in 1970	4th quartile: High poverty in 1970
Based on relative poverty rates within the MSA[b]				
Low poverty	40.32	32.21	21.98	6.41
Moderate-low poverty	29.06	31.47	27.14	12.58
Moderate-high poverty	22.11	23.60	30.83	23.77
High poverty	8.51	12.73	20.05	57.23
	1st tier: Low poverty in 1970	2nd tier: Moderate-low poverty in 1970	3rd tier: Moderate-high poverty in 1970	4th tier: High poverty in 1970
Based on absolute poverty rates[c]				
Low poverty	82.59	36.52	7.41	7.94
Moderate-low poverty	15.16	38.24	24.54	14.29
Moderate-high poverty	2.04	22.22	47.69	28.57
High poverty	0.20	3.02	20.37	49.21

a. Estimates are based on 9,621 census tracts from a balanced panel of MSAs. Medium-sized cities are defined as those with 500 to 999 census tracts.

b. Tracts with poverty rates less than the MSA's 25th percentile in the given year are defined as *1st quartile*. Tracts with poverty rates from the 25th up to but not including the 50th percentile are *2nd quartile*; tracts with poverty rates from the 50th up to but not including the 75th percentile are *3rd quartile*; and tracts with poverty rates at or above the 75th percentile are *4th quartile*.

c. Tracts with absolute poverty rates less than 15 percent in the given year are defined as *1st tier*. Tracts with poverty rates from 15 percent up to but not including 30 percent are *2nd tier*; tracts with poverty rates from 30 percent up to but not including 45 percent are *3rd tier*; and tracts with poverty rates at or above 45 percent are *4th tier*.

levels of poverty, there is considerable change in both the relative and absolute poverty measures between 1970 and 2000. Third, persistence in neighborhood poverty rates is most pronounced in the largest MSAs. What drives these different patterns?

Why the Poor Live Where They Do

Further analysis of the data supports the significance of four mechanisms—filtering, access to public transit, spillover effects from social interactions, and location of subsidized housing—in the location of neighborhoods in which the poor live. Table 2-7 reports census-tract average attributes in 1970 by change in poverty level. Column 1 presents the 1970 attributes of all identified census tracts. The next two columns report tract attributes for neighborhoods that were of low-poverty status in 1970. Of these, sample means for those neighborhoods that still retained

Table 2-5. *Small Cities: Transition Rates of Census Tract Poverty Rate, 1970–2000*[a]

Poverty level in 2000	1st quartile: Low poverty in 1970	2nd quartile: Moderate-low poverty in 1970	3rd quartile: Moderate-high poverty in 1970	4th quartile: High poverty in 1970
Based on relative poverty rates within the MSA[b]				
Low poverty	41.52	32.05	21.02	6.39
Moderate-low poverty	31.06	32.51	26.88	9.72
Moderate-high poverty	20.71	26.30	32.68	20.79
High poverty	6.71	9.15	19.42	63.10
	1st tier: Low poverty in 1970	2nd tier: Moderate-low poverty in 1970	3rd tier: Moderate-high poverty in 1970	4th tier: High poverty in 1970
Based on absolute poverty rates[c]				
Low poverty	82.20	35.43	15.22	6.37
Moderate-low poverty	15.35	38.77	27.58	16.18
Moderate-high poverty	2.25	21.85	40.63	29.41
High poverty	0.19	3.95	16.58	48.04

a. Estimates are based on 17,571 census tracts from a balanced panel of MSAs. Small cities are defined as those with 100 to 499 census tracts.

b. Tracts with poverty rates less than the MSA's 25th percentile in the given year are defined as *1st quartile*. Tracts with poverty rates from the 25th up to but not including the 50th percentile are *2nd quartile*; tracts with poverty rates from the 50th up to but not including the 75th percentile are *3rd quartile*; and tracts with poverty rates at or above the 75th percentile are *4th quartile*.

c. Tracts with absolute poverty rates less than 15 percent in the given year are defined as *1st tier*. Tracts with poverty rates from 15 percent up to but not including 30 percent are *2nd tier*; tracts with poverty rates from 30 percent up to but not including 45 percent are *3rd tier*; and tracts with poverty rates at or above 45 percent are *4th tier*.

their low-poverty status in 2000 are reported in column 2, and sample means for neighborhoods that transitioned to high-poverty status by 2000 are reported in column 3. The differences in these two columns (low in 2000 minus high in 2000) are reported in column 4. Columns 5, 6, and 7 in the table repeat the exercise, focusing on census tracts that were of high poverty status in 1970. In this instance, the last column in the table reports the difference between tracts that retained their poverty status in 2000 and those that moved to lower poverty rates.

Several patterns in this table are worth highlighting. Consider first those tracts that were of low-poverty status in 1970. The difference in mean tract attributes between those low-poverty tracts that remained of low-poverty status and those that transitioned to high-poverty status (shown in column 4) is relatively small, at least when one compares sample means. In contrast, when one views tracts that were of high poverty status in 1970, sharp differences, shown in column 7, are evident between those communities that remained of high-poverty status (column 5) and those that transitioned to low-poverty rates (column 6).

Table 2-6. *Very Small Cities: Transition Rates of Census Tract Poverty Rate,
1970–2000*[a]

Poverty level in 2000	1st quartile: Low poverty in 1970	2nd quartile: Moderate-low poverty in 1970	3rd quartile: Moderate-high poverty in 1970	4th quartile: High poverty in 1970
Based on relative poverty rates within the MSA[b]				
Low poverty	45.40	30.60	20.86	6.26
Moderate-low poverty	27.51	31.03	27.38	13.01
Moderate-high poverty	20.49	25.78	32.41	22.27
High poverty	6.60	12.59	19.36	58.46
	1st tier: Low poverty in 1970	2nd tier: Moderate-low poverty in 1970	3rd tier: Moderate-high poverty in 1970	4th tier: High poverty in 1970
Based on absolute poverty rates[c]				
Low poverty	80.69	41.17	18.24	1.90
Moderate-low poverty	16.68	39.16	31.31	21.43
Moderate-high poverty	2.16	16.86	35.59	40.48
High poverty	0.47	2.81	14.86	36.19

a. Estimates are based on 7,488 census tracts from a balanced panel of MSAs. Very small cities are defined as those with fewer than 100 census tracts.

b. Tracts with poverty rates less than the MSA's 25th percentile in the given year are defined as *1st quartile*. Tracts with poverty rates from the 25th up to but not including the 50th percentile are *2nd quartile*; tracts with poverty rates from the 50th up to but not including the 75th percentile are *3rd quartile*; and tracts with poverty rates at or above the 75th percentile are *4th quartile*.

c. Tracts with absolute poverty rates less than 15 percent in the given year are defined as *1st tier*. Tracts with poverty rates from 15 percent up to but not including 30 percent are *2nd tier*; tracts with poverty rates from 30 percent up to but not including 45 percent are *3rd tier*; and tracts with poverty rates at or above 45 percent are *4th tier*.

Of the high-poverty tracts in 1970, those that remained of high-poverty status in 2000 were 45.88 percentage points more likely to have good access to public transit. The persistently high-poverty tracts also had 16.49 percent fewer newly built homes, 18.96 percent more old homes, and 46.6 more public housing units. Most of the socioeconomic indicators are more positive for those neighborhoods that transitioned to low-poverty status. For example, the homeownership rate in such neighborhoods was 24.94 percentage points higher than in neighborhoods that still had high poverty in 1970. The presence of African American families is also much higher in the still-high-poverty tracts: 33.98 percent versus 11.34 percent for tracts that transitioned to low-poverty status. In part, these differences appear to be indicative of the different locations in which the two groups of neighborhoods are situated: high-poverty tracts in 1970 that transitioned to low-poverty status are 10.88 miles further away from the central business district (CBD), on average.

Table 2-7. Census Tract Attributes, by Change in Tract-Level Poverty, 1970–2000

Year 1970 tract attribute	All tracts in 1970 (1)	Low-poverty tracts in 1970[a]			High-poverty tracts in 1970[b]		
		Low in 2000 (2)	High in 2000 (3)	Low—high (4)	High in 2000 (5)	Low in 2000 (6)	High—low (7)
Tract average income / MSA average income	0.9986	1.3520	1.1250	0.2270	0.6973	0.8511	-0.1537
Poverty rate	0.1055	0.0351	0.0415	-0.0065	0.2326	0.1805	0.0521
Access to public transit	0.2340	0.1420	0.0983	0.0437	0.5715	0.1127	0.4588
Percent homes 0–9 years old	0.3322	0.4655	0.4892	-0.0237	0.1417	0.3066	-0.1649
Percent homes 10–19 years old	0.2357	0.2840	0.2943	-0.0103	0.1472	0.1927	-0.0455
Percent homes 20–29 years old	0.1217	0.0890	0.0925	-0.0035	0.1518	0.1311	0.0208
Percent homes 30 or more years old	0.3104	0.1615	0.1240	0.0376	0.5592	0.3696	0.1896
Density (1,000 units / mile)	1.9590	0.8380	1.2447	-0.4067	4.2585	1.1180	3.1405
Number of public housing units	9.9025	1.1020	3.7820	-2.6800	47.4301	0.7829	46.6472
Homeownership rate	0.6749	0.8358	0.7404	0.0955	0.4241	0.6735	-0.2494
Percent high school diploma (household head)	0.4405	0.5151	0.5123	0.0028	0.3172	0.3848	-0.0677
Percent college degree or more (household head)	0.1204	0.2152	0.1545	0.0607	0.0619	0.0807	-0.0187
Percent married (men aged 18 or older)	0.6642	0.7198	0.7077	0.0121	0.5428	0.6479	-0.1051
Percent population under age 15	0.2936	0.3142	0.3024	0.0119	0.2834	0.3048	-0.0214
Percent population aged 15–29	0.2356	0.2089	0.2453	-0.0364	0.2583	0.2324	0.0259
Percent population aged 30–54	0.2940	0.3342	0.3133	0.0209	0.2521	0.2780	-0.0259
Percent population aged 55 and older	0.1772	0.1427	0.1390	0.0037	0.2063	0.1849	0.0214
Percent African American (household head)	0.0903	0.0097	0.0210	-0.0113	0.3398	0.1134	0.2264
Percent Hispanic (household head)	0.0571	0.0296	0.0372	-0.0076	0.1002	0.0719	0.0283
IQR log inc (year 2000 $)	37.1623	46.5077	38.3973	8.1104	29.4160	34.3861	-4.9701
Distance to 2000 CBD (miles)	12.6583	11.9742	9.2185	2.7557	7.6522	18.5381	-10.8860
Observations: Distance variable	43,896	4,922	2,706	…	6,640	1,916	…
Observations: Other variables	50,511	4,827	2,674	…	6,544	1,847	…

a. Low poverty in 1970 and 2000 is defined as tract poverty rates in the first quartile in the MSA in that year. High poverty in 2000 is defined as tract poverty rates in the third and fourth quartiles in the MSA in that year.

b. High poverty in 1970 and 2000 is defined as tract poverty rates in the fourth quartile in the MSA in that year. Low poverty in 2000 is defined as tract poverty rates in the first and second quartiles in the MSA in that year.

These patterns suggest that several mechanisms most likely account for where the poor are found in our cities. Public transit, age of the housing stock, the presence of public (and by implication, LIHTC) housing, and spillover effects arising from socioeconomic factors and related dynamics all may have a role to play. In addition, given the geographic expansion of many cities over the 1970–2000 period and the well-known movement of the middle class to the suburbs, it is perhaps not surprising to discover that many of the poorest tracts in 1970 that experienced significant declines in poverty were, on average, 18.53 miles from the CBD, based on values indicated in table 2-7. With these summary measures as background, I consider now each of the four mechanisms that might contribute to where the poor live.

Public Transit

Glaeser, Kahn, and Rappaport (forthcoming) provide compelling evidence that poor households are attracted to central cities in part because of their need for public transit. Table 2-8 provides further perspective on this point. The table presents regressions in which the dependent variable is the percentage of occupied housing units in a census tract whose inhabitants own a car. The control measures are the distance to the central business district—a proxy for the density of the development in the community—and the census-tract poverty rate. The first three columns in table 2-8 present results for 1980, 1990, and 2000 separately. Each of these regressions also controls for MSA fixed effects that capture MSA-wide unobserved factors that might influence the tendency to own a vehicle.

In each regression, the coefficient on the distance variable is positive and highly significant, indicating that families living in less densely developed areas are more

Table 2-8. *Car Ownership and Poverty*[a]

	Decade			Balanced panel
Attribute	*1980*	*1990*	*2000*	*1980–2000*
Tract poverty rate	−1.0432	−0.8692	−0.8001	−0.8867
	(−300.36)	(−301.42)	(−265.77)	(−265.07)
Distance to CBD	0.0022	0.0019	0.0015	0.0019
	(61.51)	(57.49)	(47.62)	(75.35)
Constant	0.9711	0.9647	0.9657	0.9679
	(1,340.51)	(1,396.17)	(1,374.65)	(1,855.94)
Observations[b]	48,950	50,312	50,511	145,590
Adjusted R^2	0.7573	0.7510	0.7242	0.7380
MSA fixed effects[c]	325	331	331	. . .
MSA*year fixed effects[c]	. . .	. . .	. . .	975

a. The dependent variable is the percentage of census tract–occupied housing units that own a car; numbers in parentheses are *t* ratios based on robust standard errors.

b. Samples are restricted to census tracts in MSAs.

c. Fixed-effect values reflect deviations from the samplewide constant.

likely to own a car. That result is anticipated, since lightly developed areas provide limited public transit opportunities.

Consider next the coefficients on tract poverty rates. If the coefficient on tract poverty rate equaled −1.0, that would imply that a tract in which everyone is below the poverty line would have zero car ownership—consistent with the idea that families in poverty do not own cars. Relative to that benchmark, the coefficient on the tract poverty rate (−1.04 in 1980, −0.87 in 1990, and −0.80 in 2000) is highly significant in each year. In the last column, data are pooled in a balanced panel of tracts from 1980 to 2000 and MSA*year fixed effects included in the model. The coefficient on tract poverty rate in this model is −0.89. On balance, these results strongly confirm that the lowest-income families do not own cars, although the declining pattern of coefficients over time suggests that this is less so today than it was in 1970. Overall, however, the results confirm that the great majority of families living in poverty must live within walking distance of public transportation. Because public transit is most cost effective in the central cities, this implies that the poor will be disproportionately concentrated in the city center as well. This is the predominant thesis of the work by Glaeser, Kahn, and Rappaport (forthcoming).[12] Additional evidence on the influence of proximity to public transit on the location of poor neighborhoods is provided shortly.

Filtering

The argument that filtering influences where the poor are found is based on several core principles. The first of these is that, on average, homes tend to deteriorate over time. Evidence on this point is found throughout the hedonic literature on house prices: a standard result is that, controlling for other factors, older homes sell and rent for less. More recently, Harding, Sirmans, and Rosenthal (2007) examined depreciation of housing capital, controlling for the influence of maintenance. Results from the study indicate that in the absence of maintenance efforts, single-family homes would depreciate at roughly 2.49 percent a year and that net of maintenance, the annual rate of depreciation is roughly 1.94 percent a year. Traditional hedonic price studies that do not strip out the influence of maintenance often estimate somewhat lower housing depreciation rates of between 0.5 and 1 percent a year (for example, Margolis 1982). Again, these studies all confirm that the typical home deteriorates over time, even allowing for maintenance and home improvement efforts.

A second principle underlying the filtering story is that housing demand increases with income. This too has been well documented (for example, Rosen 1979, 1985; Olsen 1987). As homes age, therefore, they are passed down to

---

12. I also estimated the car ownership model using the balanced panel from 1980 to 2000 including census-tract fixed effects. The coefficient on tract poverty rate in that model equaled −0.2936 with a *t* ratio of 53.65. However, this estimate understates the overall relationship between poverty and car ownership because it does not take into account the attraction of low-income families to locations close to public transit facilities.

Table 2-9. *Standard Deviation of Age of the Housing Stock in 2000*[a]
Years

Percentile	Within census tracts	Within census tract's MSA	Individual tract – tract's MSA
1	5.37	13.78	−13.70
10	9.87	17.06	−9.47
25	13.28	18.87	−6.69
50	16.99	21.02	−3.65
75	20.35	22.86	−0.79
90	22.98	22.86	1.38
99	25.99	23.78	4.67

a. The average age of the housing stock in 2000 was 33.09 years. Sample restricted to census tracts in MSAs.

families of progressively lower economic status. This is the standard filtering story.[13] Other studies (Rosenthal, forthcoming; Brueckner and Rosenthal 2006) emphasize that cities tend to develop—and subsequently redevelop—from the center outward over time. In large measure, this is because the oldest and most economically obsolete housing stock is most ripe for redevelopment.[14]

Combining these assumptions implies that the location of older, lower-valued housing stock will cycle in waves emanating from the city center outward over extended periods of time. This has clear implications for where low-income families will live and also implies that the location of the poor will shift systematically over time as the location of older, lower-valued housing stock shifts. Table 2-9 provides indirect evidence consistent with this view. Notice that the standard deviation of the age of the housing stock in 2000 is smaller within individual census tracts than in the cities in which those tracts are located.[15] This is what would be expected to the extent there is a link between the timing and location of development. Additional support for the role that filtering plays in driving where poor neighborhoods are found is provided later in the paper.

Social Dynamics and Externalities

As discussed earlier, social dynamics create spillover (externality) effects on the neighborhood for two different reasons: some families may care about attri-

13. The seminal theoretical work is often attributed to James Sweeney (1974). Additional important theoretical papers on filtering include Ohls (1975), Brueckner (1977, 1980), Sands (1979), Bond and Coulson (1989), and Arnott and Braid (1997). Important empirical studies include Jones (1978), Weicher and Thibodeau (1988), Baer (1986), Coulson and Bond (1990), Rothenberg and others (1991), and Aaronson (2001). George Galster (1996) provides a nice review of several of these papers, along with a number of additional studies in this area.

14. See Rosenthal and Helsley (1994) and Dye and McMillen (forthcoming) for empirical evidence on urban redevelopment.

15. Observe that at the median, $\sigma_{tract}^{HouseAge}$ is 3.65 years less than $\sigma_{MSA}^{HouseAge}$ and at the 10th percentile, the differential is 9.47 years. To put that in perspective, the average age of the U.S. housing stock in 2000 was 33.09 years. Thus homes within a given neighborhood tend to be of more similar age than the homes throughout the neighborhood's broader MSA.

butes of their neighbors, such as race, and some families may behave in ways that generate negative spillovers, such as crime, or positive spillovers, such as gardening. In the empirical work that follows, controls are provided for a large number of census-tract socioeconomic factors that proxy for spillover effects. Here, I highlight a couple of guiding principles.

Consider the tendency to behave in ways that provide social capital for the community. Suppose also that such behavior is positively related to the financial and human capital resources a family brings to the neighborhood. As such, the presence of prime-age workers and college-educated people are expected to attract higher-income families to the neighborhood, reducing a census tract's poverty rate. This argument most likely applies to homeownership, as well. Indeed, recent literature has argued that homeowners make better citizens (DiPasquale and Glaeser 1999; Rohe 2000). Denise DiPasquale and Glaeser (1999), for example, provide evidence that homeowners are more likely to behave in civic-minded ways, including knowing their congressional representative, voting, and the like.[16] One argument for why homeowners behave in this manner is that they are financially invested in their neighborhoods. This is another example in which individuals bring resources to the community. It is partly for this reason that policymakers continue to advocate homeownership, even in low-income areas.[17]

Crime, in contrast, clearly imposes a negative social cost on a community. To the extent that certain types of families commit more crimes, the presence of such households will discourage investment in the community, lower property values, and shift the composition of the population more toward low-income families. Recent work by DiPasquale and Glaeser (1999) and Glaeser and Bruce Sacerdote (1999) suggest that cities are subject to higher crime rates because criminals are more difficult to apprehend in populous areas. This implies that densely developed neighborhoods may be more subject to crime and related adverse negative social spillovers.

If families choose to migrate into or out of a neighborhood because they care about a neighborhood's social status, this could further affect the future economic standing of the neighborhood. A prominent example of this concerns the racial composition of the community. The term *white flight* was first used to describe

16. DiPasquale and Glaeser (1999) recognize that homeowners stay in their homes and neighborhoods longer than renters and that length of stay, rather than homeownership, could actually be the salient factor. However, when they control for length of stay, they still find evidence that homeowners pay more attention to their local communities than do renters.

17. Jean Cummings, DiPasquale, and Matthew Kahn (2002), for example, note that the City of Philadelphia has "long encouraged homeownership as part of its overall community development strategy." Furthermore, a primary goal stated in the strategic plan of the Office of Housing and Community Development of the City of Philadelphia is "promoting homeownership and housing preservation. . . . To more effectively support economic development and reinvestment in Philadelphia, the City will continue to emphasize homeownership and preservation of the existing occupied housing stock" (City of Philadelphia 1997, p. 9; Cummings, DiPasquale, and Kahn 2002, p. 332).

the huge numbers of white central city households that moved to the suburbs following the race riots of the 1960s. Implicit in the phrase is the idea that white families do not want to live in close proximity to African Americans. Because minorities tend to be of lower economic status than whites, sorting by race and ethnicity has an indirect effect on neighborhood economic status. To allow for such effects, in the regressions that follow, controls are provided for the racial-ethnic composition of the neighborhood, specifically, the percent of the neighborhood's population that is African American and the percent that is Hispanic.

Public and LIHTC Housing

Place-based subsidized rental housing targets low-income families and has the potential to influence where poor families live. The most prominent of these programs is public housing, under which housing projects were built from 1937 to the early 1980s. These projects were fully funded by the federal government. The location of these projects was therefore determined through the political process rather than in response to economic incentives. In most instances, public housing units were located in lower-income neighborhoods.

The siting of LIHTC units is quite different. Under the LIHTC program, the federal government deeply subsidizes the construction of LIHTC projects in partnership with for-profit developers.[18] Developers own and manage the units and receive the construction subsidy in exchange for commitments to lease out a minimum of 40 percent of the units to low-income families. In practice, 85 percent of LIHTC units are filled with low-income families. Although half of these units are situated in census tracts in the bottom third of the income distribution, the rest are split roughly equally between census tracts in the top two thirds of the income distribution (see Eriksen and Rosenthal 2007). This program seemingly provides opportunities for lower-income families to live in higher-income communities, although some of that effect is most likely offset by crowding out of projects that the private market would otherwise have built.[19]

Although the public and LIHTC housing programs have different features, they share two overriding common traits. First, both programs, by virtue of their mandates, accommodate low-income families; second, because of the durability of housing, these units are fixed to their existing locations. For that reason, the poor are expected to be attracted to neighborhoods in which public and LIHTC housing is present.

18. It should also be noted that Cummings and DiPasquale (1999) emphasize that many LIHTC units are in fact of high quality compared to other low-income housing.

19. Todd Sinai and Joel Waldfogel (2005) estimate that for every 100 place-based units built, the private market reduces construction by roughly 50 units. Using different methods and taking both stigma and interactions across neighborhoods into account, Michael Eriksen and I estimate, over a region broad enough for stigma effects to dissipate, the remaining crowd-out effect is close to 50 percent (Eriksen and Rosenthal 2007).

Empirical Model

In the empirical exercises that follow, the primary dependent variable is the change in a census tract's poverty rate between decades. The primary control variables are selected to address the influence of each of the four mechanisms described above. Although various specifications of the empirical model will be presented, they are all variants of the same basic structure. That structure is as follows:

$$\Delta y_{it} = \delta_{t,MSA} + b_1 PublicTransit_{i,t-1} + b_2 HouseAge_{i,t-1} + b_3 PublicHousing_{i,t-1}$$

$$+ b_4 LIHTC_{i,t-1} + b_5 SES_{i,t-1} + b_6 Distance_i + \theta_1 y_{i,t-1} + \theta_2 y_{i,t-1} + e_{it}, \qquad (2\text{-}1)$$

where i denotes the census tract and t is the "current" decade. The dependent variable, $\Delta y_{it} \equiv y_{it} - y_{i,t-1}$, is the change in census-tract poverty rate between periods t and $t-1$. The lagged level of neighborhood economic status, $y_{i,t-1}$, is included to allow for mean reversion, while one lag of the dependent variable is included to soak up serial correlation in the error term.

PublicTransit is a dummy variable that equals 1 if 10 percent or more of the census-tract population takes public transit. The idea here is that if at least 10 percent of the community uses public transit, then the census tract must have access to such services, and it is access that is being highlighted. *HouseAge* is a vector that describes the age distribution of the housing stock. *PublicHousing* and *LIHTC* are the number of public housing and LIHTC housing units present in the census tract. It is worth noting that because the LIHTC program only began in 1986, this variable equals zero for decades before 1990. *SES* is a vector of one-decade lagged-level socioeconomic attributes of the neighborhood that control for local externalities. All of these variables just mentioned (*PublicTransit, HouseAge, PublicHousing,* and *SES*) are entered with lags in equation 2-1.

To complete the model, *Distance* is included in equation 2-1 to allow for correlation in the location and timing of development, where distance measures the number of miles to the census tract with the highest population density in year 2000. The model also includes a set of MSA fixed effects, $\delta_{t,MSA}$. These fixed effects strip away unobserved factors common to tracts in a given MSA and given decade.[20] Identification, therefore, is based on within-MSA variation across census tracts for a given decade.

In the discussion that follows, some of the empirical models adhere closely to the specification described in equation 2-1. Others, however, employ different levels of fixed effects (for example, no fixed effects, MSA*year fixed effects). Other models use more deeply lagged regressors, in some cases up to thirty years

---

20. This would include the citywide level of income, racial segregation, fiscal policies, and broader macroeconomic conditions specific to the city that affect immigration, job turnover, and so on.

in the past. These different specifications are used to highlight various factors pertinent to the location of the poor.

One further consideration warrants special attention. It is possible that one-decade lagged covariates could be endogenous to the future change in a census tract's poverty rate. On this point, it is worth noting that few families remain in their homes and neighborhoods longer than ten years. For this reason, the one-decade change in a census tract's poverty rate and its socioeconomic attributes (the *SES* measures) are driven primarily by the influence of turnover in the neighborhood's population (in- and out-migration) as opposed to change in the economic status of existing residents. This helps to reduce the degree to which the one-decade lagged *SES* variables might be endogenous. Similarly, the one-decade lagged *HouseAge* variables reflect the legacy of past construction decisions. This also helps to reduce the degree to which the *HouseAge* variables might be endogenous.

Nevertheless, one cannot rule out the possibility that unobserved factors might cause some one-decade lagged covariates to be endogenous. Suppose, for example, that in 1988 the future construction of a noxious facility is announced, such as a landfill, a noisy rail line, or some other facility that is unappealing to local residents. Forward-looking investors might then build LIHTC housing projects in the area in anticipation that market forces will tend to push low-income families into such neighborhoods. Similarly, prospective middle-income homeowners might choose not to invest in such neighborhoods, lowering the current homeownership rate. Analogous arguments could be given for many of the other covariates in the model as well. Under these conditions, the one-decade lagged control variables may themselves reflect the influence of anticipated change in the census-tract poverty rate. This would bias estimates of the causal effects of the control variables, potentially obscuring both the magnitude and even the direction of their effects.

These examples illustrate the potential endogeneity problem but also suggest an appealing solution. Lagging the covariates two or even three decades, instead of one, most likely eliminates much of the remaining correlation with the model error term: it seems unlikely that investors in 1970, for example, would have made decisions based on the anticipated change in poverty rates between 1990 and 2000. While appealing, use of deeply lagged regressors does not come without cost. The major drawback is that the more deeply lagged the regressors, the weaker their direct influence on the change in future poverty rates. Partly because of that trade-off, several different modifications of the specification outlined in equation 2-1 are presented below.

Results

Results from various specifications of equation 2-1 are presented in tables 2-10 and 2-11. Table 2-10 presents estimates for three versions of the equation. For each of the three models, the dependent variable is the one-decade change in tract

Table 2-10. *One-Decade Change in Tract-Level Poverty from 1980 to 2000,
by Level of Location Fixed Effects*[a]

Attribute	No fixed effects	MSA fixed effects	MSA*year fixed effects
Access to public transit	−0.0072	0.0048	0.0059
	(−10.87)	(6.35)	(8.00)
Percent homes 0–9 years old	−0.0083	−0.0226	−0.0246
	(−7.06)	(−16.86)	(−18.24)
Percent homes 10–19 years old	0.00685	−0.00157	0.00739
	(5.43)	(−1.20)	(5.61)
Percent homes 20–29 years old	0.00412	0.00365	0.00102
	(2.47)	(2.22)	(0.61)
Number of public housing units	3.500E-05	4.720E-05	4.360E-05
	(7.17)	(8.81)	(8.44)
Number of LIHTC units	1.210E-05	1.380E-05	1.260E-05
	(0.85)	(1.01)	(0.90)
Density (1,000 units/mile)	−4.420E-06	5.731E-04	4.425E-04
	(−0.07)	(7.39)	(5.90)
Homeownership rate	−0.05600	−0.06635	−0.06691
	(−30.05)	(−34.75)	(−35.63)
Percent high school degree (household head)	−0.09079	−0.13157	−0.13670
	(−25.09)	(−30.73)	(−29.87)
Percent college degree or more (household head)	−0.04350	−0.05795	−0.05798
	(−14.79)	(−16.90)	(−16.85)
Percent married (men aged 18 or older)	−0.04598	−0.07631	−0.05179
	(−9.76)	(−15.01)	(−9.76)
Percent population under age 15	0.32081	0.36527	0.34937
	(28.71)	(28.37)	(26.32)
Percent population aged 15–29	0.23415	0.23106	0.23470
	(34.72)	(32.92)	(26.99)
Percent population aged 55 or older	0.20573	0.18598	0.18576
	(34.44)	(27.62)	(25.94)
Percent African American (household head)	0.03598	0.03641	0.03504
	(23.07)	(21.87)	(21.56)
Percent Hispanic (household head)	0.02743	−0.00485	−0.01437
	(13.56)	(−1.79)	(−5.12)
IQR log inc (year 2000 $)	−0.00005	0.00000	−0.00015
	(−2.78)	(−0.16)	(−8.49)
Distance to 2000 CBD (miles)	−3.096E-04	−8.090E-05	−1.158E-04
	(−15.72)	(−3.59)	(−5.16)
Tract poverty rate in 1990	−0.35935	−0.46985	−0.45564
	(−52.30)	(−57.23)	(−54.64)
Difference in tract poverty rate: 1990−1980	−0.11122	−0.09488	−0.05287
	(−17.29)	(−14.39)	(−7.74)
Constant	−0.00214	0.05350	0.04946
	(−0.37)	(8.03)	(6.90)
Observations	91,780	91,780	91,780
Fixed effects	. . .	325	595
Adjusted R^2	0.1967	0.2576	0.3008

a. Sample includes all census tracts in identified MSAs; numbers in parentheses are *t* ratios based on robust standard errors.

poverty rate as outlined in equation 2-1. Note, however, that data are pooled for changes in tract poverty from 1980 to 2000. The first column omits the MSA fixed effects, the second column includes MSA fixed effects, and the third column includes MSA*year fixed effects. Controlling for MSA fixed effects captures unobserved features of the MSAs that were time invariant between 1980 and 2000. Controlling for MSA*year fixed effects allows those MSA-wide factors to change between decades.

Consider first the adjusted R squared values at the bottom of the table. Not surprisingly, including additional fixed effects explains a greater share of the variation in change in poverty rates across tracts over time. The magnitudes of these R squared values are important, though. In the no-fixed-effect model, the adjusted R squared is just shy of 20 percent. This indicates that the various control measures account for roughly 20 percent of the variation in change in tract poverty rates. Adding in MSA-wide fixed effects improves that mark to 25.76 percent, while controlling further for MSA*year fixed effects increases the adjusted R squared value to 30 percent. These patterns indicate that while MSA-wide factors are important, tract-specific attributes account for the great majority of the change in census-tract poverty rates between decades; this includes the 20 percent accounted for through the model's observable covariates and the residual 70 percent that is unobserved.[21]

Consider next the public transit variable. In the no-fixed-effect model, this term has a negative and significant effect. But upon controlling for MSA and MSA*year fixed effects, the influence of proximity to public transit becomes positive and, again, highly significant. This difference implies that cities with little public transit tend to have higher poverty rates. Because the wealthy also use public transit, this is plausible, although it need not be the case. Regardless, the MSA and MSA*year fixed-effects models are more robust and are favored for that reason. These models also yield the anticipated result: access to public transit is positively associated with an increase in a census tract's poverty rate, all else being equal. Concern remains, however, as to whether estimates in these models may suffer from endogeneity bias.

Table 2-11 addresses that issue. The table presents four specifications of the model. The dependent variable in the first three columns is always the one-decade change in census-tract poverty rate from 1990 to 2000. The dependent variable in the fourth column is the two-decade change from 1980 to 2000. Apart from these

21. To further explore this issue, the model was also estimated using census-tract fixed effects. In this specification, each census tract contributes effectively only one observation—the change in poverty rate from 1980 to 1990 as compared to the change in poverty rate from 1990 to 2000. The corresponding adjusted R squared was 64.78 percent, considerably higher than in the other models. This seemingly reinforces the idea that changes in census-tract poverty rates are driven predominantly by changes in within-MSA census-tract-specific conditions. However, a family's choice of census tract may be endogenous to anticipated future change in the tract poverty rate, for reasons outlined earlier. Thus results from the tract fixed-effects model are not emphasized above.

Table 2-11. *One- and Two-Decade Change in Tract-Level Poverty from 1980 to 2000, Using Lagged Covariates*[a]

Attribute	Change from 1990 to 2000			Change from 1980 to 2000
	1990 controls	*1980 controls*	*1970 controls*	*1970 controls*
Access to public	0.00401	0.00465	0.00573	0.01049
transit	(3.84)	(4.66)	(6.04)	(8.90)
Percent homes	−0.01340	0.00171	0.00673	0.00680
0–9 years old	(−7.13)	(0.89)	(3.38)	(2.76)
Percent homes	0.00163	0.01432	0.01236	0.01761
10–19 years old	(0.93)	(6.98)	(6.04)	(7.02)
Percent homes	0.00832	0.01168	−0.00652	−0.00740
20–29 years old	(3.53)	(4.64)	(−1.86)	(−1.70)
Number of public	2.210E-05	1.850E-05	1.020E-05	4.050E-05
housing units	(4.26)	(3.48)	(1.49)	(4.73)
Number of	4.720E-05	. . .	. . .	. . .
LIHTC units	(3.29)	. . .	. . .	. . .
Density	7.315E-04	7.967E-04	1.129E-03	4.970E-04
(1,000 units/	(6.82)	(6.18)	(8.04)	(2.99)
mile)				
Homeownership	−0.05626	−0.04962	−0.02258	−0.03320
rate	(−21.74)	(−16.91)	(−8.39)	(−10.61)
Percent high school	−0.09861	−0.06083	−0.00749	−0.03649
diploma	(−12.58)	(−9.53)	(−1.73)	(−6.64)
(household head)				
Percent college	−0.05852	−0.03438	−0.03253	−0.04716
degree or more	(−10.01)	(−8.61)	(−10.10)	(−11.96)
(household head)				
Percent married	−0.05617	−0.00904	0.04139	0.05763
(men aged 18	(−7.43)	(−1.18)	(7.37)	(7.88)
or older)				
Percent population	0.29759	0.17204	−0.05883	−0.06921
under age 15	(15.73)	(8.46)	(−4.80)	(−4.52)
Percent population	0.21288	0.17599	0.08317	0.11138
aged 15–29	(17.15)	(12.97)	(8.01)	(9.20)
Percent population	0.16042	0.11382	−0.01768	0.00391
aged 55 or older	(16.23)	(9.40)	(−1.95)	(0.34)
Percent African	0.02374	0.02011	0.00392	0.00038
American	(10.67)	(8.18)	(1.63)	(0.13)
(household head)				
Percent Hispanic	−0.01823	−0.00923	−0.00911	−0.00284
(household head)	(−4.50)	(−2.24)	(−2.00)	(−0.51)
IQR log inc	−0.00015	−0.00013	−0.00009	−0.00011
(year 2000 $)	(−6.78)	(−4.24)	(−5.42)	(−6.03)
Distance to 2000	−2.598E-04	−4.367E-04	−5.146E-04	−6.304E-04
CBD (miles)	(−8.56)	(−13.64)	(−15.05)	(−14.07)

(continued)

Table 2-11. *One- and Two-Decade Change in Tract-Level Poverty from 1980 to 2000, Using Lagged Covariates*[a] (*continued*)

| Attribute | Change from 1990 to 2000 | | | Change from 1980 to 2000 |
	1990 controls	1980 controls	1970 controls	1970 controls
Tract poverty	−0.45330	−0.35300	−0.17067	. . .
rate in 1990	(−38.62)	(−26.90)	(−22.07)	. . .
Tract poverty	. . .	. . .	. . .	−0.16675
rate in 1980	. . .	. . .	. . .	(−14.67)
Difference in tract	−0.09286	−0.05146	−0.16798	. . .
poverty rate:	(−8.55)	(−3.82)	(−15.98)	. . .
1990 − 1980				
$F(1, DF)$ for	14.73	21.68	36.46	79.18
PublicTransit				
$F(3, DF)$ for	18.17	12.11	2.21	22.34
HouseAge				
variables				
$F(1, DF)$ for	36.88	27.98	15.30	19.25
PublicHousing				
$F(11, DF)$ for	261.06	153.07	102.41	130.77
SES variables				
Observations	48,566	48,564	43,153	43,153
MSA fixed effects	325	325	270	270
Adjusted R^2	0.3337	0.2833	0.2544	0.1403

a. Numbers in parentheses are *t* ratios based on robust standard errors.

differences, the specifications further differ in the year from which the covariates are drawn. The first column uses 1990 control measures, the second uses 1980 controls, and the remaining two columns use control variables drawn from 1970. Relative to the dependent variables, the lags implicit in this modeling strategy differ in a corresponding manner. The more deeply lagged the regressors, the more clearly exogenous the control measures. This helps to ensure that the estimated qualitative effect (that is, the sign) of these controls is robust.

Consider again the public transit variable. In each of the models, proximity to public transit increases the future tract poverty rate. This is true even in the third model 3, which uses 1970 attributes to explain change in tract poverty rates in the 1990s. These patterns, therefore, confirm that the poor are indeed attracted to neighborhoods that provide access to public transit.

Interpreting results based on the age distribution of the housing stock requires some further explanation. First, for each of the models, the omitted category is the percentage of the housing stock thirty or more years in age. Consider now estimates from the first column. Relative to that omitted category, the presence of newly built homes (zero to nine years in age) reduces the one-decade-ahead

Figure 2-2. *Effects of Dwelling Age on Poverty Rate, 1990–2000*

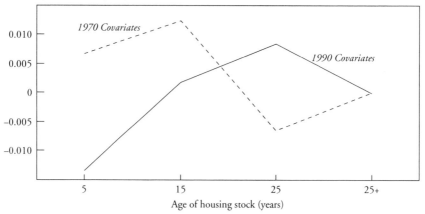

Influence of 1 percentage point increase
in housing stock on change in poverty rate

Source: Table 2-11.

census-tract poverty rate. The presence of housing aged ten to nineteen years has a small positive (and insignificant) effect, while housing age of twenty to twenty-nine years has a more positive (and significant) influence. Comparing these results to those based on 1970 covariates shows that the signs on the age zero- to nine- and age twenty- to twenty-nine-year-old housing stock are reversed.

Figure 2-2 helps in interpreting the patterns for the house age coefficients. The figure plots the coefficients for the house age variables, with age of the housing stock oriented along the horizontal axis and the corresponding coefficient value on the vertical axis. The implicit coefficient for the omitted category, age thirty and over, is set to 1 in each instance. Moreover, to facilitate review, only estimates for the first and third models from table 2-11 are plotted, those with 1990 covariates and 1970 covariates, respectively. As noted earlier, the dependent variable for both of these models is the change in tract poverty rate from 1990 to 2000. A further point to bear in mind is that, absent demolitions, housing from 1970 will be twenty years older in 1990. For example, age twenty to twenty-nine housing in 1970 is age forty to forty-nine years old in 1990.

In figure 2-2, observe that, with respect to the 1990 covariates, young housing reduces tract poverty rates from 1990 to 2000 relative to age thirty and older housing. Housing age ten to nineteen and twenty to twenty-nine have positive effects, with the latter of larger magnitude. This is consistent with the idea that very old (age thirty and over) housing stock is increasingly ripe for redevelopment. When such housing is replaced, gentrification often occurs (see, for example, Brueckner and Rosenthal 2006). Very old housing stock, therefore, forecasts future renovation in the community and a reduction in tract poverty rates.

Compare these results now to those based on the 1970 covariates. Relative to homes age thirty and over, the presence of housing age twenty to twenty-nine does the most to reduce tract poverty rates in the 1990s. That housing, of course, is age forty to forty-nine as of 1990 and as such is increasingly ripe for renovation or demolition. Young housing in 1970, in contrast, is of middle age in 1990. Such housing would not ordinarily be candidates for demolition but would have aged enough to be subject to filtering effects. This could account for the positive and rising effects associated with newer 1970 homes, aged zero to nine and ten to nineteen years. On balance, these results are exactly the patterns one would anticipate to the extent that filtering and periodic redevelopment and gentrification influence where the poor are found.

Returning to table 2-11, the institutional structure of public and LIHTC housing provides compelling reasons to anticipate that the presence of such housing will attract the poor. Consistent with that view, the coefficients on these variables are positive and (with one exception), always significant in each of the models. In the first model, with 1990 controls, observe also that the coefficient on LIHTC housing is roughly twice the size of the coefficient on public housing. On the surface, this could be interpreted as suggesting that LIHTC housing holds a greater appeal to the poor than public housing. An alternative possibility that cannot be ruled out, however, is that for-profit developers may site LIHTC housing in neighborhoods that are expected to experience an increase in the concentration of the poor.[22] This is the endogeneity issue, discussed earlier, arising again. Regardless, and not surprisingly, the positive coefficient on the public housing variable in the other models provides clear support for the idea that the poor are attracted to neighborhoods in which such housing is present.

The socioeconomic variables in table 2-11 proxy for the influence of spillover effects arising from social dynamics. These variables also perform as anticipated. High-density development always has a positive (that is, increasing) and significant effect on the future change in tract poverty rate. This is consistent with the idea that high-density development is associated with high crime rates, congestion, and other disamenities, all else being equal.

Evidence also supports the idea that individuals who bring human capital and financial resources to a community lower future tract poverty rates. Relative to the presence of individuals with less than a high school diploma (the omitted education category), the presence of individuals with high school or college education always reduces the future tract poverty rate. This is in keeping with the idea that

22. A feature of the tax-credit program is that developers promise to rent a minimum share of units to low-income families. Under some provisions of the program, developers can offer to charge lower rents and house larger shares of project units with low-income families in exchange for considerably more generous subsidies. For such projects, it is possible that developers could favor development in areas expected to retain high concentrations of poor families in order to meet their promised low-income occupancy levels.

educated individuals behave in more socially productive ways and that, in turn, attracts higher-income families to the neighborhood, lowering the future tract poverty rate.

An analogous pattern is found with respect to the age distribution of individuals residing in the tract. Prime-age potential workers—individuals aged twenty-nine to fifty-four—bring financial resources to a community and possibly word-of-mouth job networks. The presence of such individuals should, in principle, also strengthen a community, attracting higher-income families and lowering future poverty rates. Results in table 2-11 are largely consistent with that idea. When 1990 or 1980 control measures are used, for example, the coefficients on the included age categories—less than age fifteen, age fifteen to twenty-nine, and age fifty-five and over—all are positive and highly significant. As an example, increasing the share of the population in 1980 that is aged fifteen to twenty-nine would increase the change in tract poverty rate from 1990 to 2000 by 1.76 percent.

Higher tract homeownership also reduces poverty rates. Based on 1980 controls (the second column), raising the tract homeownership rate from 0 to 100 percent would reduce the tract poverty rate by 4.96 percentage points in the 1990s. This too is indicative of the positive spillovers generated by individuals who bring resources to a community. In this case, those additional resources are manifested in the wealth and time homeowners invest in their neighborhoods.

Race and ethnicity also appear to play a role. In all of the models, a higher initial concentration of African Americans is associated with an increase in the future tract poverty rate. This effect, however, is sizable and significant only in the first two columns, which use one- and two-decade lagged attributes to explain change in the 1990s: an increase in the African American population from 0 to 100 percent in 1980 would add 2 percentage points to the tract poverty rate in the 1990s. On the other hand, the presence of Hispanic families has a negative and significant effect on change in tract poverty rates in the 1990s: shifting from 0 to 100 percent Hispanic status in 1980 would reduce the 1990s tract poverty rate by just under 1 percentage point. For two reasons these results regarding the influence of African Americans and Hispanic families should be viewed with caution. The first is that norms change over time, and especially perhaps with respect to perceptions of race and ethnicity. The results noted above, therefore, could be quite different in a different era. The second consideration is that Hispanic immigration into the United States has been operating on a massive scale since 1980. As a result, the composition and character of the Hispanic population in 1980 was different from the current Hispanic population.

Results also indicate that income mixing reduces future tract poverty rates. This is clear from the interquartile range of the tract log income level—the IQR variable. Greater spread in this variable implies the presence of individuals with incomes substantially above the tract median. To the extent that such individuals serve as role models, or possibly sources of information about job networks, their presence would be expected to create spillover effects that reduce future tract poverty rates. It is partly for that reason that policymakers have increasingly sought opportunities to foster mixed-income development and communities.[23]

F statistics at the bottom of table 2-11 gauge the joint significance of the four groups of variables that proxy for the four highlighted mechanisms: the role of public transit, the role of filtering as related to the age distribution of the housing stock, the presence of public housing (and LIHTC housing), and the influence of socioeconomic factors. Regardless of how many decades the covariates are lagged, each of these four factors has a significant (or nearly significant, in a few instances) influence on change in the census-tract poverty rate in the 1990s. These patterns underscore the broader point that all four mechanisms contribute to the location of the poor.

Finally, distance from the central business district (CBD) is always associated with a future decline in tract poverty rates. Since we have controlled for other factors, this could reflect the attraction of higher-income families to more lightly developed areas, suitable for single-family housing. However, this variable may also proxy for other unobserved factors characteristic of suburban areas, including better schools, parks, and other attractive local public services.

Table 2-12 repeats the regression from the second column of table 2-11 (1980 controls) but stratifies the sample by 1990 absolute poverty levels. Specifically, table 2-12 uses 1980 census-tract attributes as the control variables and examines the one-decade change in tract poverty rate from 1990 to 2000. This regression is run separately for census tracts with four levels of poverty as of 1990. Comparisons across columns enable one to assess whether the four mechanisms driving the location of the poor have different effects depending on the initial poverty status of the community.

The sample sizes for the different regressions in table 2-12 are reported at the bottom of the table. Observe that there are 35,210 low-poverty census tracts but much lower numbers for moderate-low (8,540), moderate-high (3,279), and high-poverty (1,535) communities. Given the relatively small sample sizes for the moderate- and high-poverty tracts, larger standard errors and noisier coefficient estimates should be expected, in comparison with those obtained from the low-poverty sample. For this reason, the discussion below focuses on comparisons of the qualitative effects of the covariates across columns rather than the point estimates.

---

23. The LIHTC program, for example, stipulates that developers must rent at least 40 percent of their project units to lower-income families, leaving 60 percent for higher-income renters. Similarly, the Moving to Opportunity demonstrations conducted by the Department of Housing and Urban Development in five cities in the 1990s required low-income housing voucher beneficiaries to locate in middle-income neighborhoods. Nehemiah experiments, such as the ones in New York and Philadelphia, also foster mixed-income development by placing middle-class homeowners in low-income neighborhoods. All of these programs have been developed in part with the hope that mixed-income development will alleviate poverty traps.

Table 2-12. *One-Decade Change in Tract-Level Poverty from 1990 to 2000, Using 1980 Covariates*[a]

Attribute	Low poverty in 1990: Poverty < 15 percent	Moderate-low poverty in 1990: Poverty 15 to 30 percent	Moderate-high poverty in 1990: Poverty 30 to 45 percent	High poverty in 1990: Poverty ≥ 45 percent
Access to public transit	0.00356 (4.20)	0.00640 (2.42)	0.00732 (1.49)	0.01649 (1.66)
Percent homes 0–9 years old	0.00259 (1.63)	−0.00273 (−0.45)	0.00885 (0.60)	−0.00015 (−0.01)
Percent homes 10–19 years old	0.01097 (6.39)	0.02134 (2.62)	0.04060 (2.11)	0.06529 (1.66)
Percent homes 20–29 years old	0.00783 (3.77)	0.03273 (3.80)	0.06703 (3.29)	−0.00553 (−0.13)
Number of public housing units	3.690E-05 (2.26)	7.110E-06 (1.32)	2.730E-05 (2.11)	3.020E-05 (2.14)
Density (1,000 units/mile)	2.157E-04 (1.90)	1.120E-03 (4.25)	1.656E-03 (3.59)	1.965E-03 (2.48)
Homeownership rate	−0.04547 (−17.14)	−0.06791 (−9.16)	−0.05774 (−3.54)	−0.18000 (−4.15)
Percent high school diploma (household head)	−0.04104 (−8.53)	−0.05016 (−3.82)	−0.09547 (−3.47)	−0.14012 (−1.84)
Percent college degree or more (household head)	−0.03679 (−10.17)	−0.05851 (−4.01)	−0.08622 (−2.45)	0.05120 (0.63)
Percent married (men aged 18 or older)	−0.00246 (−0.41)	−0.02945 (−1.77)	−0.05972 (−1.82)	−0.00669 (−0.10)
Percent population under age 15	0.06081 (3.70)	0.33300 (7.70)	0.16385 (1.78)	0.64501 (3.74)
Percent population aged 15–29	0.06749 (5.49)	0.26172 (8.65)	0.14017 (2.04)	0.41513 (3.51)
Percent population aged 55 or older	0.05449 (5.46)	0.21103 (7.14)	0.06633 (0.92)	0.39585 (2.71)
Percent African American (household head)	0.03154 (11.29)	0.01594 (3.50)	−0.01298 (−1.39)	−0.01247 (−0.67)
Percent Hispanic (household head)	0.03751 (6.27)	−0.03246 (−4.23)	−0.07402 (−4.88)	−0.09693 (−2.67)
IQR log inc (year 2000 $)	−0.00014 (−6.71)	−0.00011 (−0.74)	−0.00029 (−0.77)	0.00031 (0.39)
Distance to 2000 CBD (miles)	−3.781E-04 (−13.02)	−5.711E-04 (−7.06)	−7.347E-04 (−3.86)	7.631E-04 (0.96)
Tract poverty rate in 1990	−0.32324 (−20.15)	−0.34331 (−13.61)	−0.54490 (−11.74)	−0.62697 (−6.52)

(continued)

Table 2-12. *One-Decade Change in Tract-Level Poverty from 1990 to 2000, Using 1980 Covariates*[a] *(continued)*

Attribute	Low poverty in 1990: Poverty < 15 percent	Moderate-low poverty in 1990: Poverty 15 to 30 percent	Moderate-high poverty in 1990: Poverty 30 to 45 percent	High poverty in 1990: Poverty ≥ 45 percent
Difference in tract poverty rate: 1990–1980	−0.05083 (−3.06)	−0.02767 (−1.56)	−0.03545 (−1.12)	0.00926 (0.11)
$F(1, DF)$ for *PublicTransit*	17.66	5.83	2.21	2.77
$F(3, DF)$ for *HouseAge* variables	17.48	11.19	5.60	0.99
$F(1, DF)$ for *PublicHousing*	5.11	1.75	4.44	4.59
$F(11, DF)$ for SES variables	129.74	29.59	8.13	6.62
Observations	35,210	8,540	3,279	1,535
MSA fixed effects	325	325	290	220
Adjusted R^2	0.1859	0.2167	0.2095	0.2637

a. Numbers in parentheses are t ratios based on robust standard errors.

What is most striking is that coefficients on the different control measures are often of the same sign regardless of the initial level of poverty in 1990. For example, access to public transit attracts poverty to a neighborhood in each of the samples. The same is true for the impact of public housing (positive coefficients) and density (positive coefficients). For homeownership and high school or college education, the coefficients are always negative.

One of the sharpest differences in qualitative effects across columns appears to pertain to the presence of minorities. Broadly speaking, the presence of African American and Hispanic families reduces poverty rates in the high-poverty neighborhoods.[24] In contrast, among low-poverty neighborhoods the coefficients on African American and Hispanic presence are both positive and clearly significant. On balance, it appears that the presence of African Americans and Hispanic households attracts poverty in low-poverty neighborhoods but not in higher-poverty communities. Although these differences are important, the dominant pattern in table 2-12 is that the qualitative impact of the mechanisms driving local poverty rates are broadly similar across communities with different initial levels of poverty.

24. It should also be noted that estimates of the coefficients on African American presence are insignificant even based on a one-tailed test.

Conclusions

Where the poor live affects their access to jobs, schools, and other local attributes that influence their ability to rise up out of poverty. For that reason, and because housing support programs influence where the poor can live, it is important to take into account the broad set of factors that determine the location of poor neighborhoods when rental housing support programs are developed. This is especially relevant when one considers the advantages of the location flexibility afforded by tenant-based voucher-type programs as compared with place-based subsidized rental housing programs.

Summary measures demonstrate that low-poverty census tracts display a high degree of persistence. On average, roughly 80 percent of low-poverty tracts in 1970 are still of low-poverty status in 2000. When one focuses on high-poverty tracts, however, the patterns are more variable. Across all cities in the United States, roughly 43 percent of census tracts with poverty rates in excess of 40 percent in 1970 retained such status in 2000; among the largest metropolitan areas, the corresponding number is 62 percent. Thus though poverty rates are very persistent in some communities, they are subject to considerably more change in other neighborhoods.

Additional analysis provides compelling evidence that several mechanisms contribute to change in where poor neighborhoods are found. It is clear that the poor are drawn to neighborhoods filled with older housing and to locales that provide good access to public transit. This suggests that when developing place-based subsidized rental housing programs, policymakers should seek to anticipate where access to public housing and older housing stock are likely to be found decades ahead in the future. That task is complicated, however, by local spillover effects arising from social interactions that affect in- and out-migration at the neighborhood level. This includes how existing communities respond to the presence of minorities, families of different socioeconomic status, the presence of homeowners, and more. Evidence presented in this chapter indicates that such spillovers also drive change in local poverty rates.

On balance, these mechanisms explain 20 to 30 percent of the change in neighborhood poverty rates from 1990 to 2000 and roughly 14 percent of the change from 1980 to 2000. This confirms the importance of the mechanisms noted above. But the large unexplained share of change in local poverty rates presents a challenge to policymakers. In part, that is because evidence presented here also confirms that public and LIHTC housing attract the poor, consistent with both programs' mandates to cater to low-income families. The risk exists, then, that place-based subsidized rental housing projects may be sited in areas that will not meet the needs of the future poor. Of course, spatial flexibility is just one dimension of housing support programs, and other programmatic factors need to be considered when the relative merits of different housing support strategies are evaluated. Nevertheless, with regard to location opportunities, these results provide support for the idea that location-flexible tenant-based programs offer advantages over placed-based subsidized rental housing.

References

Aaronson, Daniel. 2001. "Neighborhood Dynamics." *Journal of Urban Economics* 49, no. 1: 1–31.

Alonso, William. 1964. *Location and Land Use.* Harvard University Press.

Arnott, Richard, and Ralph Braid. 1997. "A Filtering Model with Steady-State Housing." *Regional Science and Urban Economics* 27, no. 4: 515–46.

Baer, William. 1986. "The Shadow Market in Housing." *Scientific American* (November) pp. 29–35.

Bond, Eric, and Edward Coulson. 1989. "Externalities, Filtering, and Neighborhood Change." *Journal of Urban Economics* 26, no. 2: 231–49.

Brueckner, Jan. 1977. "The Determinants of Residential Succession." *Journal of Urban Economics* 4, no. 1: 45–59.

———. 1980. "Residential Succession and Land-Use Dynamics in a Vintage Model of Urban Housing." *Regional Science and Urban Economics* 10, no. 2: 225–40.

Brueckner, Jan, and Stuart Rosenthal. 2006. "Gentrification and Neighborhood Cycles: Will America's Future Downtowns Be Rich?" *Mimeograph.* Syracuse University.

City of Philadelphia. 1997. Office of Housing and Community Development. "Year 23 Consolidated Plan (Fiscal Year 1998)." Report 9.

Coulson, Edward, and Eric Bond. 1990. "A Hedonic Approach to Residential Succession." *Review of Economics and Statistics* 72, no. 3: 433–44.

Cummings, Jean L., and Denise DiPasquale. 1999. "The Low-Income Housing Tax Credit: The First Ten Years." *Housing Policy Debate* 10, no. 2: 257–67.

Cummings, Jean L., Denise DiPasquale, and Matthew Kahn. 2002. "Measuring the Consequences of Promoting Inner City Homeownership." *Journal of Housing Economics* 11, no. 4: 330–59.

DiPasquale, Denise, and Edward Glaeser. 1999. "Incentives and Social Capital: Are Homeowners Better Citizens?" *Journal of Urban Economics* 45, no. 2: 354–84.

Dye, Richard F., and Daniel P. McMillen. Forthcoming. "Teardowns and Land Values in the Chicago Metropolitan Area." *Journal of Urban Economics.*

Eriksen, Michael, and Stuart Rosenthal. 2007. "Crowd-Out, Stigma, and the Dynamic Effects of Place-Based Subsidized Rental Housing." Mimeograph. Syracuse University.

Galster, George. 1996. "William Grigsby and the Analysis of Housing Sub-Markets and Filtering." *Urban Studies* 33, no. 10: 1797–805.

Glaeser, Edward L., Matthew E. Kahn, and Jordan Rappaport. Forthcoming. "Why Do the Poor Live in Cities? The Role of Public Transportation." *Journal of Urban Economics.*

Glaeser, Edward L., and Bruce Sacerdote. 1999. "Why Is There More Crime in Cities?" *Journal of Political Economy* 107, no. 6: 225–58.

Harding, John, C. F. Sirmans, and Stuart S. Rosenthal. 2007. "Depreciation of Housing Capital, Maintenance, and House Price Inflation: Estimates from a Repeat Sales Model." *Journal of Urban Economics* 61, no. 2: 193–217.

Jones, Colin. 1978. "Household Movement, Filtering, and Trading Up within the Owner Occupied Sector." *Regional Studies* 12: 551–61.

Leroy, Stephen F., and Jon Sonstelie. 1983. "Paradise Lost and Regained: Transportation Innovation, Income, and Residential Location." *Journal of Urban Economics* 13, no. 1: 67–89.

Margolis, Stephen E. 1982. "Depreciation of Housing: An Empirical Consideration of the Filtering Hypothesis." *Review of Economics and Statistics* 64, no. 1: 90–96.

Mills, Edwin S. 1967. "An Aggregative Model of Resource Allocation in a Metropolitan Area." *American Economic Review* 57, no. 2: 197–210.

Murray, Michael P. 1983. "Subsidized and Unsubsidized Housing Stocks, 1961 to 1977." *Review of Economics and Statistics* 65, no. 4: 590–97.

———. 1999. "Subsidized and Unsubsidized Housing Stocks, 1935 to 1987: Crowding Out and Cointegration." *Journal of Real Estate Finance and Economics* 18, no. 1: 107–24.

Muth, Richard F. 1969. *Cities and Housing.* University of Chicago Press.

Ohls, James C. 1975. "Public Policy toward Low Income Housing and Filtering in Housing Markets." *Journal of Urban Economics* 2, no. 2: 144–71.

Olsen, Edgar. 1987. "The Demand and Supply of Housing Services: A Critical Survey of the Empirical Literature." In *Handbook of Regional and Urban Economics,* edited by Edwin Mills, pp. 989–1022. Amsterdam: North-Holland.

Rohe, William, George McCarthy, and Shannon Van Zandt. 2000. "The Social Benefits and Costs of Homeownership: A Critical Assessment of the Research." Working Paper 00-01. Washington: Research Institute for Housing America (May).

Rosen, Harvey. 1979. "Housing Decisions and the U.S. Income Tax: An Econometric Analysis." *Journal of Public Economics* 11, no. 1: 1–23.

———. 1985. "Housing Subsidies: Effects on Housing Decisions, Efficiency and Equity." In *Handbook of Public Economics,* edited by Alan Auerbach and Martin Feldstein. Amsterdam: North-Holland.

Rosenthal, Stuart. Forthcoming. "Old Homes, Externalities, and Poor Neighborhoods: A Dynamic Model of Urban Decline and Renewal." *Journal of Urban Economics.*

Rosenthal, Stuart, and Robert Helsley. 1994. "Redevelopment and the Urban Land Price Gradient." *Journal of Urban Economics* 35, no. 2: 182–200.

Rothenberg, Jerome, and others. 1991. *The Maze of Urban Housing Markets: Theory and Evidence.* University of Chicago Press.

Sands, Gary. 1979. "A Model for the Evaluation of Filtering." *Growth and Change* 10, no. 4: 20–24.

Schelling, Thomas. 1971. "Dynamic Models of Segregation." *Journal of Mathematical Sociology* 1: 143–86.

Sinai, Todd, and Joel Waldfogel. 2005. "Do Low-Income Housing Subsidies Increase the Occupied Housing Stock?" *Journal of Public Economics* 89, no. 11: 2137–164.

Susin, Scott. 2002. "Rent Vouchers and the Price of Low-Income Housing." *Journal of Public Economics* 83, no. 1: 109–52.

Sweeney, James L. 1974. "A Commodity Hierarchy Model of the Rental Housing Market." *Journal of Urban Economics* 1, no. 3: 288–323.

Weicher, John, and Thomas Thibodeau. 1988. "Filtering and Housing Markets: An Empirical Analysis." *Journal of Urban Economics* 23, no. 1: 21–40.

3

The Costs of Concentrated Poverty: Neighborhood Property Markets and the Dynamics of Decline

GEORGE C. GALSTER, JACKIE M. CUTSINGER, AND RON MALEGA

Researchers and policymakers have long harbored concerns over the location of low-income ("poor," hereafter) households, expressing fears that the concentration of poverty contributes to a variety of social maladies (Wilson 1987, 1996; Jargowsky 1997). More recently, the issues related to the spatial distribution of the poor have been framed in more positive way. Housing subsidy programs, it has been argued, should be structured to give poor households wider residential options. This enrichment of spatial alternatives would serve to improve not only the well-being of housing subsidy recipients in the short run but also their families' prospects for economic self-sufficiency in the long run by enhancing their access to employment and job information networks, better-quality education, and community social norms more supportive of education and employment (Polikoff 1994; Cisneros 1995; Rosenbaum 1995). The arguments have almost entirely been framed in terms of reputed benefits gained by poor households that move from high- to lower-poverty neighborhoods, not in terms of the consequences for households residing in the places from which and to which the poor move.

Nevertheless, this set of arguments has been sufficiently persuasive to generate an array of federal legislative and judicial initiatives. These include replacing deteriorated, high-rise public housing complexes with smaller-scale, mixed-income complexes through the Housing Opportunities for People Everywhere (HOPE VI) program, court-ordered dispersal programs for minority tenants as a remedy to past discrimination by public housing authorities, and the encouragement of spatial mobility by housing choice voucher (formerly Section 8) rental subsidy recipients through the Moving to Opportunity (MTO) demonstration and the Regional Opportunity Counseling program (Goering and others 1995; Burchell, Listokin, and Pashman 1994; Ludwig and Stolzberg 1995; Peterson and Williams 1996; HUD 1996; Hogan 1996).

This chapter analyzes theoretically and empirically whether the current housing policy emphasis on deconcentrating poor populations can be justified on the grounds of economic efficiency—that is, does society as a whole gain from switching from a more- to a less-concentrated poverty regime, without recourse to claims of distributional equity (that is, what's good for the poor)? The emphasis on efficiency in this chapter should not be taken as an implicit claim that distributional equity concerns are of less importance. On the contrary, distributional concerns are omitted purely for the purpose of isolating efficiency impacts. Nevertheless, we would argue that in the current political context of "performance measurement" of federal programs, the salience of efficiency impacts is large indeed.

The Effect of Concentrated Poverty on Households

What role does living in a neighborhood of concentrated poverty play in shaping an individual's behavior? A rapidly expanding body of empirical research has emerged during the past decade assessing with multivariate statistical techniques the degree to which neighborhood environments affect the social and economic outcomes of low-income minority families and their children (see reviews by Haveman and Wolfe 1994; Brooks-Gunn, Duncan, and Aber 1997; Ellen and Turner 1997, 2003; Furstenberg and others 1999; Leventhal and Brooks-Gunn 2000; Sampson, Morenoff, and Earls 2002; Dietz 2002; Lupton 2003). Although findings have been the subject of considerable methodological debate (Duncan and Raudenbush 1999; Manski 1995, 2000; Galster 2003a; Ellen and Turner 2003; McLanahan and others 2003), they consistently suggest that those living in disadvantaged, inner-city neighborhoods characterized by high levels of poverty and social disorganization have poorer health outcomes, lower levels of academic achievement, fewer employment opportunities, heightened vulnerability to gang recruitment, and greater exposure to violence relative to otherwise-comparable people living in more advantaged neighborhoods. The neighborhood scale thus appears to be an important element of what Galster and Sean Killen (1995, p. 9) term one's "opportunity structure."

The Mechanisms of Neighborhood Effects

What are the mechanisms through which these effects transpire? Six deserve particular mention: socialization, collective socialization, social networks, exposure to crime and violence, the weakness of local institutional and public resources, and stigmatization. There have been several comprehensive reviews of the potential links between neighborhood processes and individual behaviors and outcomes (see especially Jencks and Mayer 1990; Duncan, Connell, and Klebanov 1997; Gephart 1997; Friedrichs 1998; Atkinson and Kintrea 2001; Dietz 2002; Sampson, Morenoff, and Gannon-Rowley 2002; and Ioannides and Loury 2004). We therefore outline these mechanisms with some brevity.

Behaviors and attitudes may be changed (for the worse) by contact with neighboring peers, especially in the absence of more positive role models provided by middle-class neighbors (Sullivan 1989; Anderson 1990, 1991; Case and Katz 1991; Diehr and others 1993; South and Baumer 2000). This mechanism has been most famously articulated in the concept of social isolation (Wilson 1987, 1996). A nonlinear, threshold-like relationship is implied in this perspective. In William Julius Wilson's words, "Poverty concentration effects should result in an exponential increase in . . . forms of social dislocation" (1987, p. 57).

A special subset of socialization effects is characterized by a minimum threshold's being achieved before noticeable consequences arise. The tenet of this approach, known as collective socialization, is that a social group can influence others to conform to its customs, norms, and behaviors to the degree that the group can exert relatively more powerful inducements or threats on an individual to conform to its positions than other, competing groups. These two preconditions imply the existence of a threshold-type relationship. If the individuals making up the group in question are scattered thinly over urban space, they are less likely to be able to either convey their positions effectively to others with whom they might come in contact or to exert much pressure to conform. It is only as a given group approaches some critical mass over a predefined area that it is likely to become a potentially effective vehicle for shaping others. Past this threshold, as more members are recruited to the group the power of the group to reward and sanction those outside it most likely grows nonlinearly. This effect is especially likely when the position of the group becomes so dominant as to become normative in the area; at this point its social norms can be described as epidemic.

Although one may say that socialization proceeds through social networks, this is a distinct process involving the interpersonal communication of information and resources. One local group may intensify the density and multinodal structure of its social networks (create "strong ties") by clustering, thereby increasing the sources of assistance in times of need. On the other hand, such situations may lack the "weak ties" that offer the prospect of bringing new information and resources into the community, thereby increasing social isolation. Wilson (1996), for example, argues that living among unemployed neighbors reduces one's ability to acquire information about prospective jobs.

Heightened exposure to crime and violence in disadvantaged neighborhoods has been associated with an array of physical and mental health problems, as well as poorer educational outcomes among children (Martinez and Richters 1993;

Aneshensel and Sucoff 1996). Another indirect effect is possible: parents who perceive that the neighborhood is too dangerous are more likely to limit their children's activities outside the home, thereby potentially retarding the development of interpersonal skills.

Poverty-stricken neighborhoods typically have access to fewer private, nonprofit, or public institutions and organizations that work to improve the quality of life and opportunities (Kozol 1991; Wolman, Lichtman, and Barnes 1991; Card and Krueger 1992). Moreover, the internal workings of institutions serving poor communities shape expectations and life chances of their clientele in repressive ways (Rasmussen 1994; Bauder 2001). This institutional decay transpires because of withering financial support and leadership associated with the out-migration of local residents with higher education and disposable incomes. In addition, delivery of public services to the neighborhood may decline as fewer residents have the political savvy and clout to effectively lobby for it.

Stigmatization of a neighborhood transpires when important institutional, governmental, or market actors negatively stereotype all those residing there or reduce the quantity or quality of resources flowing into the place (Atkinson and Kintrea 2004). It is reasonable to posit that such stigmatization can occur when the neighborhood's share of residents living in poverty exceeds a threshold amount (Wacquant 1993; Wilson 1996).

The Importance of Nonlinear Effects

The foregoing theoretical description of various mechanisms through which neighborhood poverty might influence the behaviors of residents echoes the theme of nonlinear effects. Unfortunately, relatively few econometric studies have taken these theoretical foundations seriously and investigated potential nonlinear relationships in their models. However, all consistently find that opportunities for individuals are disproportionately limited in higher-poverty neighborhoods. Tom Vartanian (1999) has undertaken a comprehensive investigation of the neighborhood conditions experienced by children that may influence their economic well-being when they reach young adulthood, using data from the Panel Study of Income Dynamics. He finds that, compared with otherwise similar children growing up in low-poverty neighborhoods (the least-poor tercile, that is, roughly under 5 percent poverty rate), children growing up in neighborhoods with poverty rates of roughly 5 to 15 percent (that is, from the 34th to 66th percentiles) evinced 13 percent lower annual labor incomes and 16 percent longer periods of poverty when they were young adults.

In a similar comparison, those growing up in neighborhoods with poverty rates of 15 to 30 percent (that is, the poorest 11 to 33 percent of all neighborhoods) had 12 percent lower hourly wages, 18 percent lower annual labor income, and 21 percent longer periods of poverty. Finally, those growing up in neighborhoods having poverty rates in excess of 30 percent (the poorest 10 percent of neighborhoods) experienced 18 percent lower hourly wages, 21 percent lower annual labor income, and 25 percent longer periods of poverty. Bruce Weinberg, Patricia Reagan, and Jeffrey Yankow (2004) used the 1979 National Longitudinal Survey of Youth to analyze the impact of various neighborhood characteristics on residents' hours of work. Controlling for individual characteristics and neighborhood selection effects, they find a growing marginal decrement in hours worked associated with increases in neighborhood poverty. Finally, Nick Buck's (2001) analysis of British Household Panel Study data identifies substantial nonlinearities between unemployment rate in the neighborhood and both the probability of not starting work and the probability of not escaping from poverty, which suggests that the worst results for individuals occurred when the share of neighborhood residents unemployed exceeded 23–24 percent (that is, the most-deprived 5 percent of all neighborhoods). All these results are consistent with the notion of a threshold of neighborhood poverty past which the socioeconomic harms to residents become substantially greater; we call this the "social problem threshold" for residents.

Property Crime Behaviors in Disadvantaged Neighborhoods

In the model of residential property maintenance developed in the next section, we emphasize the impact of local property crimes. We therefore discuss this particular behavior in more detail here. Fortunately, much criminological literature can be applied to understanding the relationship between neighborhood poverty rates and property crime rates.

The most established is the "social strain" perspective (Kornhauser 1978). It argues that individuals who have low and unstable sources of income face powerful social strains when confronting their personal lack of resources in the midst of a society that places inordinate value on such. Personal poverty thus creates the motivator for crime as a vehicle for economic gain. The "social disorganization" perspective argues that whether an individual acts on a criminal motivation depends upon the social order and cohesion of the surrounding community (Aneshensel and Sucoff 1996). The effects of disadvantaged neighborhoods on criminality primarily operate through the context of weakened community norms, values, and structures enveloping residents' behaviors, what has been labeled "collective efficacy."[1] The "criminal opportunity" perspective argues that even a motivated, unrestrained individual will not engage in property crime if there is a dearth of suitable (that is, relatively vulnerable, high-value) potential victims (Cohen, Felson, and Land 1980; Cook 1986; Robinson 1999).

---

1. Sampson (1992, 1997); Sampson and Groves (1989); Robert Sampson, Stephen Raudenbush, and Felton Earls, "Neighborhoods and Violent Crime: A Multilevel Study of Collective Efficacy," *Science,* August 15, 1997, pp. 918–24; Sampson, Morenoff, and Earls (1999); Morenoff, Sampson, and Raudenbush (2001).

These multiple perspectives collectively suggest that neighborhood poverty may have an unpredictable relationship with property crime (van Dijk 1994; Hannon 2002). On the one hand, poor neighborhoods are expected to have a higher incidence of more socially strained individuals and a weakened social organization. On the other hand, there may be fewer prospective personal and property targets of high value. Empirically, the evidence suggests that the former elements dominate, producing positive correlations between neighborhood poverty and property crime rates (Neapolitan 1994; Krivo and Peterson 1996; Hannon and Defronzo 1998; Hannon 2002).

This relationship is further complicated by potential nonlinearities. Lance Hannon (2002) argues that motivation (social stress) rises linearly with neighborhood poverty but opportunities for property crime decrease exponentially, producing a net concave function. Kevin Murphy, Andrei Shleifer, and Robert Vishny (1993) argue that as the number of criminals in an area grows, three things may happen simultaneously. First, returns from noncriminal activities will be reduced as crime siphons a portion away, thus increasing social stress for neighbors. Second, the number of individuals who monitor, report, or directly sanction criminal behavior (collective efficacy) will fall (relatively and perhaps absolutely). Finally, the stigma associated with criminal activity will be eroded as crime becomes normative. In concert, these three factors quite likely interact to alter in a nonlinear (convex) fashion the relative economic and social payoffs from crime relative to noncriminal activities, and rates of crime will escalate dramatically in poorer neighborhoods.

Unfortunately, the scant empirical evidence on this point of nonlinearity is inconsistent. Lauren Krivo and Ruth Peterson (1996), investigating property crime rates in various neighborhoods of Columbus, Ohio, find no relationship between crime and neighborhood poverty until the latter exceeds 20 percent. Compared with neighborhoods with poverty rates of less than 20 percent, aggregate property crime rates were 20 percent higher in those with poverty rates of 20 to 39 percent and 25 percent higher in neighborhoods with poverty rates of more than 39 percent. Hannon's (2002) analysis of property crimes in Seattle, Washington, and Austin, Texas, finds, on the contrary, that increases in neighborhood poverty had a decreasing (though positive) marginal impact on crime, even at low poverty levels. Krivo and Peterson's result is consistent with the existence of a social problem threshold at 20 percent poverty, but the Hannon result is not.

The Effect of Concentrated Poverty on Residential Property Owners

From the neighborhood's perspective, the key decision that owners of residential property make involves the extent to which they will invest in the repair, maintenance, and improvement of their properties, because these activities involve significant externalities for proximate households and owners.[2] There have been many, long-standing theoretical models and empirical studies of how owners make these decisions (Asmus and Iglarsh 1975; Boehm and Ihlanfeldt 1986; Chinloy 1980; Galster 1987, chap. 3; Shear 1983; Stewart and Hyclak 1986; Taub, Taylor, and Dunham 1984; Varady 1986). However, none have focused on the potential role of concentrated poverty in this process. We therefore develop from this literature a conceptual model of residential maintenance decisionmaking that posits dual roles for neighborhood poverty rates: influences on housing depreciation and influences on residential values (or rental streams).

Received theory suggests that the rate at which the capital embodied in a residential structure depreciates in real terms (that is, the degree to which resources must be sunk back into it in the form of maintenance and repair expenditures to hold it capital stock constant)[3] is determined by the following:

—Quality of construction and building materials (for example, solidly built brick homes will depreciate more slowly than shoddily built frame units)

—Vintage (older dwellings depreciate more quickly)

—Climate (meteorological conditions affect structural material aging and probabilities of weather-related damages)

—Intensity of usage (dwellings with higher occupation density or more tenants with behavioral problems that lead to dwelling damage depreciate more quickly)

—Neighborhood environment (buildings that are more frequently exposed to property crime—breaking-and-entering burglaries, vandalism, and graffiti—depreciate more quickly)

We would argue that the poverty concentration in a neighborhood may affect dwelling depreciation through both of the last two of these mechanisms. Insofar as poverty-stricken individuals are more likely to commit and be victimized by property crime and to be involved in more unstable, violent social subcultures, their increasing presence in and around the dwelling in question should be associated with its higher rate of depreciation.

The market value of the residential property (or, equivalently, the discounted present value of net rental revenues) is determined by the capital embodied in the structure and parcel and in its immediate environs and surrounding political jurisdiction (often termed the "hedonic value" of this bundle of attributes) and the degree to which this bundle is in a relatively strong competitive position in the metropolitan area market (typically measured by vacancy rates). The competitive position of a dwelling possessing a particular hedonic value is determined by the

---

2. It is beyond the scope of this chapter to deal with the effects transpiring through owners of nonresidential property in the neighborhood.

3. In this sense, *depreciation* as used here is distinct from its usage in financial or taxable income circles.

aggregate supply and demand functions operative in the relevant housing sub-market (Rothenberg and others 1991).

Neighborhood poverty rates potentially come to bear on market values and rents both directly and indirectly. Directly, the socioeconomic status of the households making up the surrounding neighborhood is one component of the hedonic value of the dwelling package. Thus, given that most Americans prefer not to live among poor neighbors, the value of a dwelling and the rents it can command will tauto-logically be lower the higher the poverty concentration, all else equal. Moreover, to the extent that poverty spawns other sorts of socially problematic behaviors among neighbors (such as crime, as explained in the prior section), these compo-nents of hedonic value will be eroded as well. Indirectly, poverty concentration accelerates property depreciation, as outlined above, and thus should be inversely related to the capital embodied in the dwelling.

In arriving at a decision regarding maintenance, owners not only assess the current rates of depreciation and rental streams or assessed value, they also form expectations of their future estimates. This provides yet another potential means through which neighborhood poverty can have an effect. Inasmuch as increases in poverty in the neighborhood provide a signal that the neighbor-hood quality of life is likely to decline significantly in the future, owners' esti-mates of the present value of future revenue streams from the property will be attenuated (Taub, Taylor, and Dunham 1984; Galster 1987; Grigsby and others 1987).

How these elements of depreciation, revenues, and expectations come together to shape maintenance decisions can be explained heuristically with the aid of figure 3-1. The vertical axis in figure 3-1 shows the discounted present value of both future revenues and costs associated with maintaining a particular dwelling structure, as assessed through the expectations of the owner of the self-selected future planning horizon. The horizontal axis measures the current rate of poverty in the neighborhood where the dwelling in question is located. For the purposes of this exposition, the only variable costs (VC) that are subject to volitional choice of the owner involve various maintenance regimes: high (which holds the capital in the dwelling constant by offsetting depreciation exactly); low (which is greater than zero but insufficient to hold the capital in the dwelling constant); and none.[4] All other costs associated with owning the unit (taxes, insurance, and so on) and hav-ing it occupied (utilities, management, and so on) are considered fixed (FC) for the purposes of this exposition. Total costs are given as TC. The total rental revenue (implicit in the case of owner-occupants) associated with different maintenance

4. It is assumed that the owner wishes to have all units occupied in the structure at all times and seeks to maximize the discounted present value of net financial gains. Because owner-occupants have consumption as well as investment motives, the figure for them needs to be modified by inclusion of some monetarized consumption value. For one such formulation, see Galster (1987).

Figure 3-1. *A Graphic Model of Housing Maintenance Behavior and Neighborhood Poverty*[a]

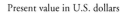

Present value in U.S. dollars

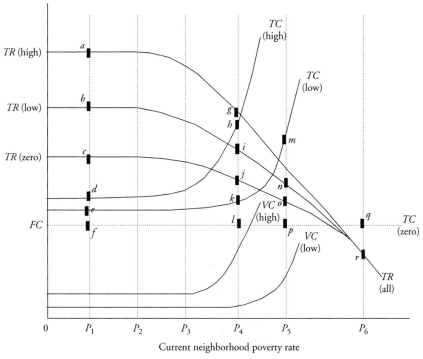

Current neighborhood poverty rate

a. *TR* = total revenue from rental; *VC* = variable costs; *FC* = fixed costs; *TC* = total costs.

regimes is shown by a family of *TR* functions; higher maintenance is associated with a higher revenue profile since there is more hedonic value in the dwelling. The owner is assumed to take the neighborhood's poverty rate as exogenous and therefore to adopt the maintenance regime that maximizes the difference between present values of revenue and cost streams in the future (that is, maximum *TR* − *TC*, where *TC* = *FC* + *VC*).[5]

It is reasonable to posit that both *TR* and *TC* functions manifest threshold points and nonlinearities of consequence, although there is, to our knowledge, no direct evidence regarding this question. It is known from the evidence summarized in the prior section, however, that many problematic behaviors associated with poverty (and inversely with dwelling hedonic value) only start to rise noticeably when rates exceed a threshold of around 10–15 percent, which suggests that threshold P_2 lies in this range for the *TR* function family (see figure 3-1). Given that these behaviors

5. None of the functions portrayed in this figure are assumed to be at the correct scale.

will be increasingly likely to affect the depreciation rates of the dwelling (through problems arising from tenants or neighbors), the threshold for the VC (and thus for TC) functions is likely to be in the same range. For generality, we portray threshold P_3 as slightly greater than P_2.

Consider what maintenance regime will be chosen under different scenarios of neighborhood poverty. At very low levels of poverty (such as P_1), the high mainte-nance regime will be chosen because the net gain associated with it $(a - d)$ is larger than for either the low maintenance $(b - e)$ or no maintenance $(c - f)$. At moder-ate poverty levels (point P_4, for example), the owner will choose the low-maintenance regime, because net gain from this option $(i - k)$ is superior to the gain from either high $(g - h)$ or zero $(j - 1)$ maintenance. At high poverty levels (point P_5, for example), the owner will find that only the zero-maintenance option yields a positive gain $(0 - p)$. In contexts of extreme poverty concentration (point P_6, for example), the owner may find that even withholding all maintenance cannot produce a net gain; should such persist for a considerable period, the owner will eventually abandon the unit if no buyer can be found.

The upshot of the foregoing analysis is that the relationship between changes in a neighborhood's poverty rate and maintenance choices by local residential property owners will be lumpy and nonlinear. Substantial variations in poverty rates in the low-to-moderate range yield no deviations in the owner's decision to maintain the building at a high level, offsetting depreciation. Past some percentage of poverty, however, the owner will switch to an undermaintenance mode, whereby net depreciation will occur. We call this point the owner's disinvestment threshold. Subsequent increases in neighborhood poverty rates will trigger even more radical disinvestment choices, eventually including abandonment.

Concentrated Poverty, Individual Responses, and the Dynamics of Decline

Now we switch the scale of analysis from the micro- to the meso-level: from individ-ual actors to their aggregation over the neighborhood. The point here is to show how individual behaviors related to socially problematic behavior (especially prop-erty crime) and residential property maintenance, which are influenced directly and indirectly in nonlinear ways by the overall poverty rate in the neighborhood, in aggregate produce neighborhood-wide changes that erode the competitive posi-tion of the neighborhood over time and thereby tend to encourage further increases in poverty concentrations there. As such, concentrated poverty, social problems, and housing upkeep should be viewed as endogenous or mutually causal attributes of neighborhoods. This view complicates empirical analyses of these relationships, as explained below.

These relationships are shown in figure 3-2. In most American neighborhoods, an increase in the poverty rate is a consequence, rather than cause, of a decline in

Figure 3-2. *Neighborhood-Level Relationships between Concentrated Poverty, Dwelling Upkeep, and Crime*

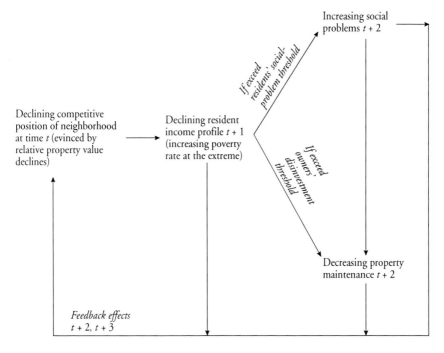

the relative competitive position of the neighborhood in the metropolitan area.[6] In the absence of housing subsidies, the only financially feasible way that a poor household can move into a neighborhood is if the rents and property values there have declined to the point where it has become affordable to them.[7] But such declines in market valuation can only occur if the housing submarket that this neighborhood's dwellings constitute has witnessed a reduction in its aggregate demand or an increase in its aggregate supply (Rothenberg and others 1991).

This typically occurs as part of the well-known "filtering" process (Galster and Rothenberg 1991). From the perspective of a particular neighborhood, filtering typically means that there has been a net out-migration of the households in the income range typically represented in the neighborhood in the previous period and a corresponding net in-migration of households with a somewhat lower income

---

6. Two exceptions would be neighborhoods in which current homeowners suffer a decline in their incomes but retain sufficient resources to remain in their homes, and neighborhoods into which poor households are able to move with the aid of subsidized housing.

7. We use *affordability* advisedly, recognizing that most low-income renters must pay more than the federally specified affordability limit of 30 percent of income to occupy private apartments.

profile than the previous group. As a neighborhood approaches the least competitive ranks of the metropolitan hierarchy, the in-moving group will increasingly
include those who fall below the poverty line. This transition to a lower-income
group may involve not only a fall in the real price of the given housing stock but
also some physical transformations of that stock to make it more affordable, such
as subdivision of large dwellings into several smaller units, postponement of maintenance and repairs, and removal of expensive amenities.

Once the poverty rate is increasing in a neighborhood, both residents and
dwelling owners make behavioral adjustments, as described in the prior two
sections. These adjustments will be most noticeable when the poverty rate exceeds
the social problem threshold of residents and the disinvestment threshold of
owners. (These two thresholds are not necessarily defined by the same poverty
rate.) As residents engage in more problematic behaviors in the neighborhood, like
committing more property crimes, two results follow. First, dwelling owners are
ever-more-quickly encouraged to switch to a more extreme disinvestment regime,
thereby hastening the physical decay of the neighborhood's housing stock. Second,
increases in crime and other problematic behaviors directly reduce the hedonic
value of the neighborhood's housing stock.[8] In concert, declines in the neighborhood's resident income profile, quality of housing stock, and safety combine to
further erode its competitive position, manifesting itself as a decline in the values
of its properties (perhaps in nonlinear ways) relative to others in the metropolitan
area. The spiral of decline is thus completed.

Considerable scholarship supports this formulation of relationships embodied
in figure 3-2. The two predominant early theories of neighborhood socioeconomic
change were the invasion-succession model advanced by the Chicago School of
Sociology (Park 1952; Duncan and Duncan 1957; Taeuber and Taeuber 1965)
and the life-cycle model (Hoover and Vernon 1959).[9] Subsequently, more-or-
less comprehensive theories of neighborhood change have been forwarded (see
Maclennan 1982; Taub, Taylor, and Dunham 1984; Grigsby and others 1987;
Galster 1987; Rothenberg and others 1991; Temkin and Rohe 1996; Lauria 1998;
and Galster 2003b). Notable efforts in empirically modeling neighborhood socio-
economic changes have been undertaken (Guest 1974; Vandell 1981; Coulson and
Bond 1990; Galster and Mincy 1993; Galster, Mincy, and Tobin 1997; Carter,
Schill, and Wachter 1998; and Galster, Cutsinger, and Lim 2007).

8. There may be additional feedbacks, not shown in figure 3-2, between the decay of the physical environment and increases in crime, as through the well-known "broken windows" theory. One
other interesting feedback not shown is how the tenure composition of the neighborhood may be
influenced by demographic changes and physical decay.

9. Other early theories of neighborhood socioeconomic change include the demographic-
ecological model, the sociocultural-organizational model, the stage model, the political economy
model, and the social movements model (Downs 1981; Bradbury, Downs, and Small 1982;
Schwirian 1983).

Recent work by Geoffrey Meen (2004, 2006) has provided important theoretical and empirical support for the notion of nonlinear response mechanisms that rest at the core of these neighborhood dynamic processes. Meen finds a (negative) logit-shaped relationship between mean housing prices across neighborhoods and their level of deprivation (a multi-item index of economic, social, and physical problems in a political ward) across the United Kingdom. The ratio of mean housing prices in a ward to those of the highest-priced ward in that same metropolitan area changes little across areas with low levels of deprivation but begins to decline rapidly within one standard deviation of the mean deprivation. Once a neighborhood becomes extremely disadvantaged (moving, say, to the highest decile), there are few subsequent declines in relative value; it has reached the bottom of the hierarchy.

A Model of Concentrated Poverty, Crime, Property Maintenance, and Housing Values

Model Specification

The discussion in the prior sections informs the specification of an empirical model of the neighborhood-level relationship between housing values, concentrated poverty, crime, and housing upkeep levels. We focus on modeling housing values because of their ability to capitalize neighborhood attributes of interest and thus allow the aggregate costs of concentrated poverty to be estimated in dollar terms. We specify for some neighborhood observed at time t that the natural logarithm of its mean price of specified owner-occupied homes ($VALUE_t$) will be determined by the following equation:

$$
\begin{aligned}
\text{Ln}(\text{VALUE})_t = {} & b_0 + b_1[\text{STRUCTURE}]_t + b_2[\text{CONDITION}]_t + b_3\text{CRIME}_t \\
& + b_4\%\text{POOR}_t + b_5[\text{OTHER NEIGH'D}]_t \\
& + b_6[\text{JURISDICTION}]_t + b_7[\text{MSA FIXED}]_t \\
& + b_8[\text{MSA VARYING}]_t + \varepsilon,
\end{aligned}
$$

where

$[\text{STRUCTURE}]_t$ = the vector of distributions of quantitative characteristics of the dwellings (numbers of rooms, age, structure type, and so on),

$[\text{CONDITION}]_t$ = the vector of distributions of qualitative characteristics of the dwellings (state of repair and maintenance, operability and reliability of systems, and so on),

CRIME_t = the population-adjusted rate of property crime,

%POOR$_t$ = the percentage of population living below the poverty line,

[OTHER NEIGH'D]$_t$ = the vector of other, time-varying characteristics of neighborhood (demographics like race and age distributions, homeownership rates, and so on),

[JURISDICTION]$_t$ = the vector of (assumed to be time-invariant) characteristics of the jurisdictions in which the neighborhood is located (the tax-service quality package offered by various levels of government serving that locale),

[MSA FIXED]$_t$ = the vector of time-invariant characteristics of the metropolitan area in which the neighborhood is located that affect both housing demand and elasticity of housing supply (climate, historical developmental idiosyncrasies, regional natural amenities, and so on),

[MSA VARYING]$_t$ = the vector of time-varying characteristics of the metropolitan area in which the neighborhood is located that affect aggregate housing demand (job opportunities, incomes, population changes, and so on),

ε is a random error term with statistical properties we discuss below, and

all lower case b are parameters to be estimated.

Many of the elements of [JURISDICTION]$_t$ and [MSA FIXED]$_t$ are difficult if not impossible to measure, yet their omission from the model could well bias the coefficients of %POOR, were they to be correlated. However, these vectors of variables do not vary appreciably over a decade, permitting them to be differenced away. An analogous equation can be written for another time ten years later, $t + 1$; the difference between the two equations would yield a decadal change equation:

$$\Delta \text{Ln}(\text{VALUE})_{t \text{ to } t+1} = b_0' + b_1 \Delta [\text{STRUCTURE}]_{t \text{ to } t+1}$$

$$+ b_2 \Delta [\text{CONDITION}]_{t \text{ to } t+1} + b_3 \Delta \text{CRIME}_{t \text{ to } t+1}$$

$$+ b_4 \Delta \% \text{POOR}_{t \text{ to } t+1} + b_5 \Delta [\text{OTHER NEIGH'D}]_{t \text{ to } t+1}$$

$$+ b_8 \Delta [\text{MSA VARYING}]_{t \text{ to } t+1} + \varepsilon, \tag{3-1}$$

where $b_0' = b_{0t+1} - b_{0t}$.

Based on the earlier discussion, a further equation can be written, indicating that a change over time in the condition of a dwelling is related to the degree of maintenance invested in it during the period. Upkeep, in turn, is a (nonlinear) function of neighborhood crime, poverty rates, and other conditions and structural attributes of the dwelling (age, construction materials, and so on):

$$\Delta[\text{CONDITION}]_{t\text{ to }t+1} = c_0' + c_1 \Delta \text{CRIME}_{t\text{ to }t+1} + c_2 \Delta \%\text{POOR}_{t\text{ to }t+1}$$

$$+ c_3 \Delta \%\text{POOR}_{t\text{ to }t+1}^2 + c_4 \Delta \%\text{POOR}_{t\text{ to }t+1}^3$$

$$+ c_5 \Delta[\text{OTHER NEIGH'D}]_{t\text{ to }t+1}$$

$$+ c_6 \Delta[\text{STRUCTURE}]_{t\text{ to }t+1} + \varepsilon. \tag{3-2}$$

Based on the discussion in prior sections, a change over time in the neighborhood's crime rate can be expressed:

$$\Delta \text{CRIME}_{t\text{ to }t+1} = d_0' + d_1 \Delta \%\text{POOR}_{t\text{ to }t+1} + d_2 \Delta \%\text{POOR}_{t\text{ to }t+1}^2$$

$$+ d_3 \Delta \%\text{POOR}_{t\text{ to }t+1}^3 + d_4 \Delta[\text{OTHER NEIGH'D}]_{t\text{ to }t+1} + \varepsilon. \tag{3-3}$$

Equations (3-2) and (3-3) can be substituted into equation (3-1), expressing the reduced form:

$$\text{Ln}(\text{VALUE})_{t\text{ to }t+1} = g + (b_1 + b_2 c_6)\Delta[\text{STRUCTURE}]_{t\text{ to }t+1}$$

$$+ b_8 \Delta[\text{MSA VARYING}]_{t\text{ to }t+1}$$

$$+ (b_5 + b_2 c_5 + b_3 d_4)\Delta[\text{OTHER NEIGH'D}]_{t\text{ to }t+1}$$

$$+ (b_4 + b_2 c_2 + b_2 c_1 d_1 + b_3 d_1)\Delta \%\text{POOR}_{t\text{ to }t+1}$$

$$+ (b_2 c_3 + b_2 c_1 d_2 + b_3 d_2)\Delta \%\text{POOR}_{t\text{ to }t+1}^2$$

$$+ (b_2 c_4 + b_2 c_1 d_3 + b_3 d_3)\Delta \%\text{POOR}_{t\text{ to }t+1}^3 + \varepsilon, \tag{3-4}$$

where $g = b_0' + b_2 c_1 d_0' + b_3 d_0'$.

Equation 3-4 conveniently distills the determinants of changes in neighborhood housing values into net changes in four categories: the aggregate structural characteristics represented by the dwellings there (owing to home demolitions, structural modifications, and new construction or rehabilitation); housing-demand-related characteristics of the metropolitan area; changes in neighborhood demographic and other attributes; and poverty rates.[10] The impact of poverty rates is a joint measure of both direct (hedonic value) effects and indirect effects through housing upkeep conditions and crime rates. Equation 3-4 thus provides the vehicle for assessing the aggregate costs of concentrated poverty, as capitalized into housing values.

---

10. For a more formal derivation that yields a virtually identical estimating equation, see Meen (2004).

Econometric Issues

Unfortunately, obtaining unbiased, consistent estimates of the coefficients for neighborhood poverty in equation 3-4 runs afoul of two potential issues: endogeneity and spatial autocorrelation. As the analysis surrounding figure 3-2 makes clear, over time the changes observed in a neighborhood's poverty rate and housing prices and rents are likely to be mutually causal in varied degrees. Failure to account for this would produce a biased estimate of the independent effect of concentrated neighborhood poverty.[11]

We try to meet this challenge with two versions of instrumental variables (IV) techniques. In the cross-metropolitan model embodied in equation 3-4 we instrument for census-tract poverty rate using the encompassing county's poverty rate, the analog of an instrumentation strategy advanced by William Evans, Wallace Oates, and Robert Schwab (1992) and E. M. Foster and Sarah McLanahan (1996).[12] We would argue for the validity of this instrument as follows (following Murray 2006). First, because changes in the county's poverty rate can occur only when poverty in its constituent tracts changes, the two will be correlated. Second, because changes in an individual tract's housing values will not affect the county's poverty rate, the latter should not be correlated with ε in equation 3-4. Finally, though the overall health of the regional economy may be reflected in both the county's poverty rate and the overall housing price level, we believe that such potential influence is controlled by use of metro-level fixed effects; thus county poverty rate is not an explanatory variable in equation 3-4. We would further argue that the instrument is reasonably strong: changes in census-tract and county poverty rates from 1990 to 2000 are statistically significantly correlated ($\rho = .28$). We recognize, however, that county-level changes have much more limited variation (standard deviation of 2.1 versus 5.9 for tract level) and few observations at the extremes of both levels of poverty and changes in poverty. Thus we urge caution in interpreting nonlinear functions estimated with this IV at the extremes of the distribution.

In the other application of IV we use individual observations of Cleveland home sales over the early 1990s and relate them to prior-year poverty rates in the neigh-

11. One way to circumvent this issue is to examine the impacts on property values resulting from an exogenous change in the neighborhood's poverty rate associated with the introduction of households holding rental vouchers or subsidized housing sites (Galster, Tatian, and Smith 1999; Galster, Tatian, and others 2003). However, given that we want to estimate equation 3-4 across the nation, the extraction of subsidized housing information from HUD databases at such a scale is infeasible here.

12. Evans, Oates, and Schwab (1992) use metropolitan-level variables for unemployment rate, median family income, poverty rate, and percentage of adults completing college as identifying variables predicting the "neighborhood variable" in their study: proportion of students in the local school who are economically disadvantaged. Foster and McLanahan (1996) use citywide labor market conditions as identifying variables predicting neighborhood high school dropout rates. In a few instances (for example, Baltimore City) we substitute the independent municipality's poverty rate for the county's, since the latter is not defined.

borhood where the sale occurred. Again, we would argue that contemporaneous and lagged values of neighborhood poverty are highly correlated, but it is more difficult to make the case that lagged values are uncorrelated with ε in equation 3-4. Indeed, instrumentation using temporal lags is caught in a dilemma: shortening the lag increases the power of the instrument but at a likely cost of increasing correlation with the disturbance term in the original equation (Murray 2006).

Unfortunately, at this stage of the research we are unable to adjust for the consequences of spatial autocorrelation by using a spatial lag specification. Again, given the nationwide breadth of this analysis, it is infeasible to gather all the geographic information necessary to implement the estimation of a spatial lag for each metropolitan area.

An Exploration Using Sales Values of Individual Homes in Cleveland

Data and Variables

In the first of two empirical explorations of the relationship between the spatial distribution of poverty and property values, we analyze data from Cleveland, Ohio. Cleveland is used because it offers unusually rich, publicly accessible data on neighborhood (census-tract) conditions culled from a variety of administrative databases, measured annually since the early 1990s. Administrative data from the City of Cleveland were obtained from the Urban Institute through its National Neighborhood Indicators Partnership.[13] This unusual database assembles demographic, public assistance, crime, and housing data tabulated at the census-tract level by several administrative agencies and combines them into a consistent annual series for the period 1993–99. Indicators from this database that we used for time-varying neighborhood characteristics include percentage of births of low-weight babies, percentage of birth mothers who are not married, birthrate of women under the age of twenty, percentage of parcels that are nonresidential, percentage of residential and commercial parcels that are vacant, percentage of parcels that are tax delinquent, percentage of parcels that are single-family dwellings, percentage of commercial properties that are vacant, percentage of residential properties that are vacant, and welfare receipt rate. Descriptive statistics of these variables are presented in appendix table 3A-1. To operationalize time-invariant neighborhood characteristics we specified a set of census-tract dummy variables as fixed effects.

Of particular relevance for the current work, Cleveland has recorded census-tract rates of receipt of public assistance since 1992, which we use as a proxy for poverty rates, at least until welfare reforms that were operationalized in the field after 1997 disrupted the relationship between the two. As evidence of the close relationship

13. Thanks to Peter Tatian, Jennifer Johnson, and Chris Hayes of the Urban Institute for their help in obtaining the data.

between public assistance receipt rates and poverty rates in the era before Temporary Assistance for Needy Families, we regressed the former (measured in 1992) on the latter variable (measured in 1990) for all census tracts in the City of Cleveland. The resultant coefficients (and associated t statistics) are as follows:

$$\text{Public assistance rate} = 4.21 + .583 \text{ Poverty rate}$$
$$(3.62) \ (18.42) \quad r \text{ squared} = .663$$

As for characteristics of the individual single-family homes that form the unit of observation in this analysis, the most complete and accurate source of home sales data available is the property tax rolls maintained by local property tax assessment offices. We used the property tax roll records for the City of Cleveland provided by the private data vendor Experian. The Experian data contain all the information available from the tax rolls on the property itself (including address, number of rooms, square footage, type of construction, and numerous other measures) as well as the dates and amounts of the past two sales for each property.[14] Descriptive statistics of these variables are presented in appendix table 3A-1. Files were geographically coded to match street addresses with latitude and longitude coordinates and census-tract identifiers.[15]

Our main purpose in employing this particular database is that public assistance receipt rates are available at the census-tract level on an annual basis for an extended period. This permits us to deal with the endogeneity problem here by specifying the lagged neighborhood rate of public assistance receipt as an instrumental variable predicting individual home values in the following year.

Results

The hedonic home price equation is estimated for sales in all 200 neighborhoods (census tracts) within Cleveland. Because the estimation sample varies both cross-sectionally and over time, econometric procedures appropriate for pooled samples were employed to obtain robust standard errors (Kmenta 1986, pp. 616–25). The specification of tract fixed effects serves not only as a way to measure unobserved, time-invariant characteristics but also as a means of correcting for any heteroskedasticity and serial correlation associated with a combined cross-sectional and

14. The tax roll data may not be sufficient to obtain a complete sales history for each property, however. If a property was sold more than two times during the period of interest, then the sales record will not be complete, as only the two most recent sales will be recorded. Therefore, these tax roll data were supplemented with a sales history data file, also obtained from Experian, which lists the dates and amounts of every sale of the properties in the city, though no property characteristics. This sales history file permitted the creation of a complete record of sales back to 1993.

15. To help ensure that we were dealing only with single-family homes conveyed in arm's-length transactions, we eliminated all sales of less than $2,500.

panel dataset such as ours (Hsiao 1986, pp. 29–32). The estimated home-price equation also includes latitude and longitude variables to control for spatial heterogeneity, as suggested by Ayse Can (1997).[16]

Results of our hedonic model, regressing the natural logarithm of sales prices of the 12,650 single-family homes sold in Cleveland from 1993 to 1997, are presented in table 3-1. The model also includes 199 dummies for census-tract fixed effects, but for brevity their coefficients are not presented. Results correspond to what is conventionally found with hedonic regressions: homes that are newer, larger, on larger lots, and with garages and more bathrooms sell for more. Houses located in census tracts with lower percentages of nonresidential parcels and lower residential vacancy rates also sell for more. Independent of characteristics of the dwelling and neighborhood, prices rose steadily in Cleveland throughout the period and were systematically higher in seasons other than winter.

Of central interest are the results for the lagged neighborhood public assistance rate variable. We experimented with many versions of quadratic, cubic, and spline specifications in an attempt to capture nuances of potential nonlinearities. Ultimately, we settled on a simple specification that produced a robust finding: the percentage of neighborhood residents receiving public assistance only begins to have a negative impact on the following year's individual home sales prices when it exceeds 15 percent. None of the spline specification trials produced evidence of statistically significant decrements in home values in neighborhoods with public assistance percentages below 15 percent. Given the aforementioned regression relating public assistance and poverty rates, this threshold translates into an approximately 19 percent rate of poverty in the census tract. Above this threshold, an additional 1 percentage point increase in the neighborhood public assistance rate (corresponding to a 1.72 percentage point increase in its poverty rate) yields a 1.78 percent decline in single-family home value during the next year.

This result is remarkable because it suggests that, in low spatial concentrations, changes in neighborhood poverty rates have no noticeable consequence for property values, suggesting that there are no visible neighborhood externalities associated with such variations or that the market fails to capitalize them. We deem the latter less plausible, given the long-standing literature on local amenity capitalization. Moreover, this result closely corresponds to the thresholds identified in several prior studies of the relationship between various social externalities associated with concentrated poverty, such as crime and dropping out of school (see Galster 2002).

16. Previous work with this sort of price equation suggests that a spatial lag variable not only is computationally burdensome but also adds little explanatory power once neighborhood time-invariant and time-varying characteristics are controlled, so we do not use it here (Galster, Tatian, and Smith 1999).

Table 3-1. *Regression Results for Determinants of Cleveland Home Prices*[a]

Variable	Coefficient	t statistic
Intercept	9.95226	22.42***
Dwelling characteristics at time t		
Number of baths / number of bedrooms	−0.12002	−2.35*
1.5 baths (vs. 1)	0.05202	2.78**
2+ baths (vs. 1)	0.04741	1.74*
Garage	0.23854	18.59****
Building 1 story (vs. more)	−0.03896	−3.40**
Built 1900–19 (vs. pre-1900)	0.11189	5.55***
Built 1920–39 (vs. pre-1900)	0.23613	10.38***
Built 1940–49 (vs. pre-1900)	0.36312	12.98***
Built 1950–59 (vs. pre-1900)	0.34779	12.33***
Built 1960–69 (vs. pre-1900)	0.46763	12.15***
Built 1970–79 (vs. pre-1900)	0.31302	3.45**
Built 1980–1989 (vs. pre-1900)	0.54527	4.59***
Built 1990 or later (vs. pre-1900)	0.98107	24.11***
Lot size (square feet)	0.00002037	8.82***
Square of lot size	−9.79E-11	−7.92***
Lot width (feet)	0.00002632	0.32
Pool	−0.00152	−0.01
Square feet / number of rooms	0.0003214	1.85*
Square feet	0.0003718	7.52***
Square of square feet	−2.85E-08	−2.48*
Census-tract characteristics during year t		
Percent nonresidential parcels at time *t*	−0.01782	−2.49*
Percent all units that are single family at time *t*	−0.0039	−0.76
Percent all parcels tax delinquent at time *t*	−0.00679	−1.17
Percent all commercial parcels vacant at time *t*	0.00209	1.05
Percent all residential parcels vacant at time *t*	−0.01317	−2.50*
Percent of population receiving public assistance *t* − 1	0.01273	1.68
15 percent or more public assistance rate spline at time *t* − 1	−0.01777	−2.29*
Temporal characteristics		
Sale April–June (vs. January–March)	0.02758	2.06*
Sale July–September (vs. January–March)	0.0328	2.47*
Sale October–December (vs. January–March)	0.04496	3.36**
Sale year 1993 (vs. 1997)	−0.24911	−13.47***
Sale year 1994 (vs. 1997)	−0.16645	−9.90***
Sale year 1995 (vs. 1997)	−0.11271	−6.83***
Sale year 1996 (vs. 1997)	−0.05255	−3.83**
Spatial characteristics (heterogeneity corrections)		
Latitude	0.50899	0.38
Longitude	−5.23404	−2.93**
Latitude*Latitude	49.35535	5.74***
Longitude*Longitude	23.27268	0.82
Latitude*Longitude	−111.79858	−5.05***
Adjusted R^2	0.4993	
F statistic (DF = 212, 12438)	59.78***	

a. Regression includes tract fixed-effect dummies; results not shown. Dependent variable = ln (individual single-family dwelling sales price at time *t*).

*$p < .05$, **$p < .01$, ***$p < .001$; one-tailed test if expected sign (two-tailed otherwise).

An Exploration Using Median Tract Values
in Large Metropolitan Areas

Our second empirical exploration tries to discern whether there are any common patterns between changes in census-tract poverty rates in 1990–2000 and corresponding changes in values of owner-occupied dwellings and rents of renter-occupied dwellings in the nation's 100 largest metropolitan areas. This exploration has the advantage of a more general sample across the country than Cleveland, but it lacks the intradecade dynamic detail and the ability to carefully control for dwelling characteristics. We also employ a different vehicle here—instrumental variables instead of intertemporal lags—for dealing with simultaneity.

Data

The primary units of analysis are the 100 largest metropolitan areas—statistical areas (MSAs) and primary metropolitan statistical areas (PMSAs)—in the United States, according to the 2000 census. We limit the analysis to them because they are the locales of virtually all instances of concentrated urban poverty (Jargowsky 1997). In keeping with virtually all other quantitative studies that involve analysis of concentrated poverty and neighborhood dynamics, we use census tracts as the secondary unit of analysis. Based upon our review of previous research (Lee and Wood 1991; Ellen 2000), we specified that census tracts had to meet the following criteria to be included in the study:

—A total population of 500 persons or more
—A group-quarters population that is not more than 50 percent of the total population
—A reported population for whom poverty status was determined[17]

Population greater than 500 individuals provides a threshold that helps ensure a robust sample size from each tract contributing to the long-form census surveys from which the key data are derived. In addition, tracts with large group-quarters populations (prisons, college dorms, nursing homes) are irrelevant to this study and are excluded to prevent them from skewing the poverty concentration results. Finally and most important, tracts without income data were eliminated from this study.

The primary data source used in the study is the Neighborhood Change Database (NCDB), which was created by GeoLytics in conjunction with the Urban Institute. We used the NCDB census long-form database, which contains sample data from the 1990 and 2000 censuses. A major benefit of using the NCDB is that it adjusts (if necessary, owing to changes in tract boundaries) 1990 data to correspond with 2000 census-tract boundaries, which is essential to our econometric

17. Because of respondent confidentiality, certain demographic measures like income are suppressed under certain circumstances. Thus in several cases the data include total population and racial characteristics but no income statistics.

modeling. We also obtained metropolitan- and county-level poverty rates from the U.S. Census Bureau's Factfinder website.[18]

Variable Definitions

We employed the NCDB to operationalize the concepts in the model shown in equation (3-4) as follows:

—ΔLn(VALUE)$_{t \text{ to } t+1}$ = the difference between 2000 and 1990 in the median value of specified owner-occupied dwellings in the tract (in a variant of this model we substitute the median contract rent)

—Δ[STRUCTURE]$_{t \text{ to } t+1}$ = a set of variables showing the differences between 2000 and 1990 values of characteristics of housing units in the tract; these are distinguished by tenure and used in the appropriate value or rent models (unless indicated by *):

—Proportion of dwelling units aged ten years or less; eleven to twenty years; twenty-one to thirty years; thirty-one to forty years; forty-one to fifty years (excluded category: fifty years or more)
—Proportion of dwelling units that lack complete plumbing facilities*
—Proportion of dwelling units that lack complete kitchen*
—Proportion of units in structures with one attached unit; two units; three or four units; five or more units; mobile home units; other types of units (excluded category: single-unit detached)
—Proportion of units with no bedrooms; one bedroom; two bedrooms; four, five, or more bedrooms (excluded category: three bedrooms)

—Δ[MSA VARYING]$_{t \text{ to } t+1}$ = a set of ninety-nine dummy variables, one for each metro area (excluded category: Los Angeles PMSA); serves as a summary proxy for all metro-wide decadal changes

—Δ[OTHER NEIGH'D]$_{t \text{ to } t+1}$ = a set of variables showing the differences between 2000 and 1990 values of tract characteristics:

—Proportion of dwelling units that are owner occupied
—Proportion of units that are vacant and not available for sale or rent
—Proportion of population that is non-Hispanic white; non-Hispanic African American; non-Hispanic Asian; Hispanic; (excluded category: Native American and other)
—Proportion of the population that is aged under fifteen; fifteen to nineteen; twenty to twenty-four; twenty-five to twenty-nine; thirty to thirty-four; thirty-five to forty-four; forty-five to fifty-four; fifty-five to sixty-four; sixty-five to seventy-four (excluded category = older than seventy-four)

—Δ%POOR$_{t \text{ to } t+1}$ = differences between 2000 and 1990 percentages of population (for whom poverty status has been determined) living below the poverty line during prior year in the census tract

18. The URL is factfinder.census.gov.

Table 3-2. *Distribution of Census Tracts in 100 Largest Metropolitan Areas, by Poverty Rate, 1990 and 2000*[a]

	Frequency	
Poverty rate (percent)	1990	2000
0–4.99	12,966	11,632
5–9.99	10,099	10,007
10–14.99	4,997	5,261
15–19.99	3,026	3,454
20–24.99	1,949	2,339
25–29.99	1,420	1,795
30–34.99	1,045	1,332
35–39.99	883	928
40–44.99	690	688
45–49.99	454	367
50–54.99	328	258
55–59.99	195	126
60–64.99	113	79
65–69.99	78	44
70–74.99	46	30
75–79.99	33	18
80–84.99	23	6
85–89.99	18	3
90–94.99	7	3
95–100	4	4
Total	38,374	38,374

a. All data are adjusted to constant tract boundaries 1990 and 2000.

Descriptive statistics for all these variables are shown in appendix table 3A-2. Of particular note is the change in the spatial distribution of poverty during the 1990s. Since these changes previously have been the subject of considerable analysis and controversy (Jargowsky 2003; Kingsley and Pettit 2003; Galster 2005), suffice it to present the basic contours. Table 3-2 shows how the distribution of census tracts (defined by 2000 boundaries, with 1990 figures adjusted as necessary) in the largest metropolitan areas has changed from 1990 to 2000. Overall, there were fewer tracts both with more than 40 percent poverty and with less than 10 percent poverty, with gains in all the intermediate categories.

Results

Overall, the results robustly show a strong, highly statistically significant correlation between decadal changes in poverty rates and highly nonlinear changes in the natural logarithm of median home prices and rents in census tracts. Both models of median home values and rents produce remarkably similar results in this regard, which is gratifying; the value models evince higher explanatory power, however

(R^2 of about .75, compared with .55 for rents). After considerable exploration we also found that this relationship differs according to whether the neighborhood in 1990 had a poverty rate above or below 20 percent and whether the change in poverty during the ensuing decade was positive or negative.[19] The former was observed by stratifying the sample, the latter by adding a set of linear, quadratic, and cubic poverty-change interaction terms to the model that assume the value of the poverty change only when that change was negative. The estimated parameters for these key variables are shown in table 3-3; comparative estimates using county-level poverty rates as instruments are presented in table 3-4, and parameters for the control variables are presented in appendix table 3A-3. Virtually all the poverty-change variables—in all their nonlinear and interactive incarnations—prove highly statistically significant, whether or not instrumental variables estimation is used.

The highly nonlinear and asymmetric nature of the relationships shown in tables 3-3 and 3-4 makes them difficult to interpret on their face, so we graph them for a hypothetical census tract with a median home price of $100,000 and a median monthly rent of $1,000 (both of which are approximately the 2000 sample means) and various assumed 1990 poverty rates. The results for the poverty concentration variables in table 3-3 are portrayed graphically in figure 3-3 (for values) and figure 3-4 (for rents). The corresponding graphs with relationships estimated with IV estimates are shown in figures 3-5 and 3-6.

RESPONSES OF VALUES AND RENTS TO INCREASING NEIGHBORHOOD POVERTY. First, consider how neighborhood property values and rents respond as the poverty rate in the area increases. The first core observation is that the response depends crucially on the poverty rate in the neighborhood at the beginning of the decade. Both low- and high-poverty strata of neighborhoods evince a common pattern, regardless of estimation technique employed: declines in values and rents occur after a smaller increment in poverty and thereafter drop more rapidly the higher the beginning level of poverty. As illustration, the IV-estimated parameters for the low-poverty stratum indicate that a 10 percentage point decadal increase in neighborhood poverty would trigger a decadal decline in rent of only 3 percent if the hypothetical $1,000 rental unit were located in a neighborhood that began with a poverty rate of 5 percent. By contrast, this decline grows to 42 percent if the neighborhood began at 10 percent poverty and 68 percent if it began at 15 percent poverty (see bottom panel of figure 3-6).

The second core observation is that the evidence is consistent with a threshold of response in the range of 10–20 percent poverty rates, regardless of whether IV estimates are used. A neighborhood with no poor individuals in 1990 does not appear to experience any declines in values until its poverty rate exceeds 11 percent

19. This asymmetric effect of neighborhood poverty change on home prices also has been observed with descriptive statistics by Chenoa Flippen (2004).

Table 3-3. Estimated Parameters of Poverty Variables in Housing Price and Rent Change Models[a]

Variable	Housing price model[b]			Rent model[c]		
	Full sample	< 20% poor	≥ 20% poor	Full sample	< 20% poor	≥ 20% poor
Change in poverty rate, 1990–2000	.039	.051	.059	0.028	.020	.062
	(.002)***	(.002)***	(.013)***	(.01)***	(.001)***	(.006)***
Change in square of poverty rates (/100)	-.169	-.374	-.126	-.122	-.148	-.112
	(.007)***	(.013)***	(.034)***	(.004)***	(.005)***	(.015)***
Change in cube of poverty rates (/10,000)	.141	.601	.086	.090	.159	.054
	(.008)***	(.024)***	(.027)***	(.005)***	(.007)***	(.012)***
Change in poverty rate, 1990–2000 (when change < 0; zero otherwise)	-.083	-.181	-.116	-.049	-.138	-.089
	(.003)***	(.006)***	(.014)***	(.002)***	(.004)***	(.007)***
Change in square of poverty rates (when change < 0; zero otherwise) (/100)	.344	1.521	.244	.198	1.297	.139
	(.009)***	(.056)***	(.035)***	(.006)***	(.044)***	(.016)***
Change in cube of poverty rates (when change < 0; zero otherwise) (/10,000)	-.276	-3.214	-.158	-.125	-3.039	-.044
	(.010)***	(.184)***	(.028)***	(.006)***	(.144)***	(.012)***
R^2	0.749	0.756	0.759	0.556	0.549	0.582
F	786.7***	667.8***	148.1***	336.2***	264.7***	70.1***
N of census tracts	36,795	30,121	6,674	37,480	30,355	7,145

a. All regressions include 1990 value of dependent variable on right-hand side; parameters for control variables in appendix table 3A-3. Standard errors are in parentheses.
b. Dependent variable = 2000 ln(median price).
c. Dependent variable = 2000 ln(median rent).
***$p < .01$; **$p < .05$; *$p < .10$ (two-tailed tests).

Table 3-4. *Estimated Parameters of Poverty Variables in Housing Price and Rent Change Models, Using Instrumental Variables*[a]

Variable[b]	Housing price model[c]			Rent model[d]		
	Full sample	< 20% poor	≥ 20% poor	Full sample	< 20% poor	≥ 20% poor
Change in poverty rate, 1990–2000	.007	.035	-.082	.074	.081	-.036
	(.010)	(.010)***	(.031)***	(.006)***	(.006)***	(.014)*
Change in square of poverty rates (/100)	-.070	-.303	.233	-.257	-.349	.288
	(.053)	(.056)***	(.141)*	(.038)***	(.042)***	(.080)***
Change in cube of poverty rates (/10,000)	-.573	.100	-.693	.255	.442	-.534
	(.104)***	(.112)	(.246)***	(.076)***	(.086)***	(.144)***
Change in poverty rate, 1990–2000 (when change < 0; zero otherwise)	-.082	-.011	-.008	-.022	-.118	-.026
	(.009)***	(.009)	(.024)	(.001)***	(.004)***	(.002)***
Change in square of poverty rates (when change < 0; zero otherwise) (/100)	.553	.276	.232	.075	1.123	.027
	(.024)***	(.026)***	(.058)***	(.004)***	(.044)***	(.005)***
Change in cube of poverty rates (when change < 0; zero otherwise) (/10,000)	.113	.139	.034	-.035	-2.823	.009
	(.019)***	(.276)***	(.026)	(.003)***	(.147)***	(.004)**
R^2	0.731	0.738	0.748	0.534	0.531	0.568
F	717.2***	607.8***	139.7***	308.2***	245.8***	66.2***
N of census tracts	36,795	30,121	6,674	37,480	30,355	7,145

a. All regressions include 1990 value of dependent variable on right-hand side; parameters for control variables in appendix table 3A-3. Standard errors are in parentheses.

b. Instrumented by county value.

c. Dependent variable = 2000 ln(median price).

d. Dependent variable = 2000 ln(median rent).

***$p < .01$; **$p < .05$; *$p < .10$ (two-tailed tests).

Figure 3-3. *Estimated Relationships between Changes in Neighborhood Poverty Rate and Property Values*[a]

Neighborhoods with 20 percent or more poor

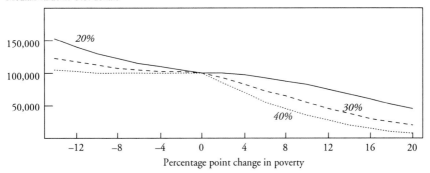

Neighborhoods with less than 20 percent poor

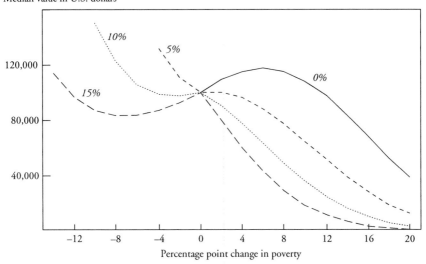

a. Estimates based on change in poverty rate from 1990 to 2000.

nor any decline in rents until its poverty rate exceeds 18 percent (IV estimate).[20] Similarly, IV estimates show that neighborhoods starting at 5 percent poverty must exceed 10 percent poverty before any noticeable decline in values occurs and even higher for rents to decline. Finally, all estimates show that neighborhoods starting at 10 percent poverty begin suffering value and rent declines with any subsequent increase in poverty (see the bottom panel of figure 3-6). All this is

20. The rental decline threshold is estimated at 12 percent if no IV is used.

Figure 3-4. *Estimated Relationships between Changes in Neighborhood Poverty Rate and Median Rent*[a]

Neighborhoods with 20 percent or more poor

Median rent in U.S. dollars

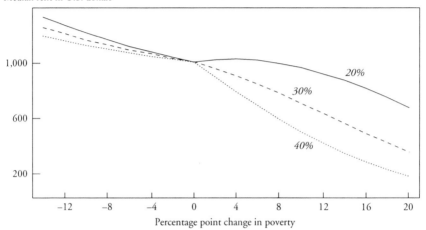

Percentage point change in poverty

Neighborhoods with less than 20 percent poor

Median rent in U.S. dollars

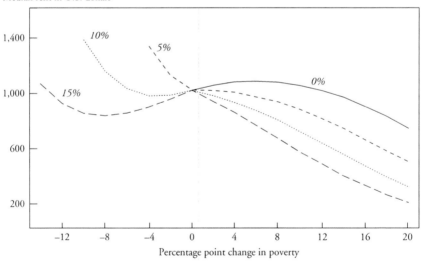

Percentage point change in poverty

a. Estimates based on change in poverty rate from 1990 to 2000.

Figure 3-5. *IV-Estimated Relationships between Changes in Neighborhood Poverty Rate and Property Values*[a]

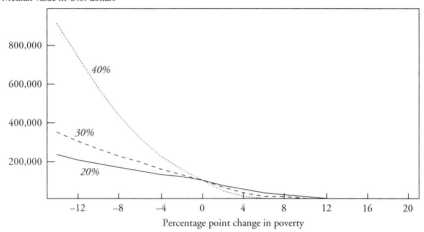

Neighborhoods with 20 percent or more poor

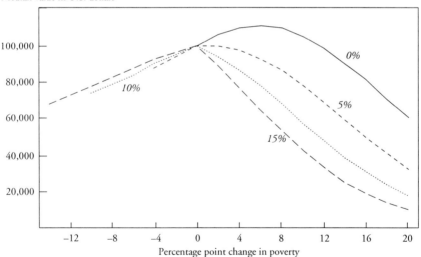

Neighborhoods with less than 20 percent poor

a. Estimates based on change in poverty rate from 1990 to 2000.

Figure 3-6. *IV-Estimated Relationships between Changes in Neighborhood Poverty Rate and Median Rent*[a]

Neighborhoods with 20 percent or more poor

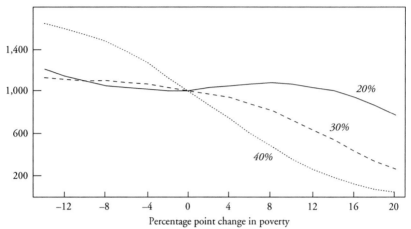

Neighborhoods with less than 20 percent poor

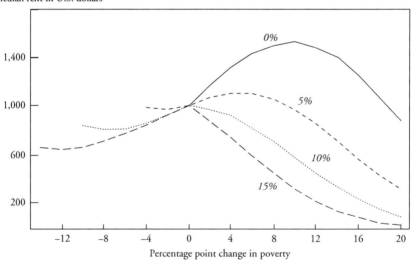

a. Estimates based on change in poverty rate from 1990 to 2000.

consistent with the theoretical predictions of the threshold model of dwelling owners' maintenance behavior presented above.

The evidence further shows, however, that this housing market response to rising neighborhood poverty past the threshold is subject to diminishing returns. In the neighborhoods that already had poverty rates of at least 20 percent by 1990 (top panel of figure 3-6), the relationship of increases in poverty to values and rents is concave from below, suggesting that the market declines triggered by the threshold before 20 percent poverty continue to accelerate with further poverty increases. This starts to abate as the poverty concentration solidifies, though, as indicated by the 40 percent poverty neighborhood, which shows a value-rent and poverty increase function that has become convex from below.

The third core observation is that, regardless of estimation technique employed, values of the owner-occupied stock are more sensitive to poverty rate increases than rents appear to be, especially in neighborhoods with 5 percent of poverty or less. As illustrated by the IV estimates, a 10 percentage point decadal increase in poverty for a neighborhood starting the decade with a 5 percent poverty rate yields a decline of 23 percent in owner-occupied median home values but only a 3 percent decline in median rents (see bottom panel in figure 3-5).

Why might it be the case that the owner-occupied market apparently has a lower threshold of response to rising neighborhood poverty? Four possibilities, not mutually exclusive, come to mind. First, it may be that the disinvestment threshold is lower for owner-occupiers than for absentee owners. This is unlikely, however, given evidence that owner-occupiers maintain their dwellings to a higher standard than absentee owners and often respond to perceived declines in the quality of neighborhood life by increasing their home investments in a compensatory manner (Galster 1987). Second, consumers in the owner-occupied market may react more strongly and negatively to neighborhood poverty increases than consumers in the rental market, because they typically have less residential mobility and thus are more vulnerable to such increases, especially if these are coupled with increases in the minority composition of the neighborhood (Ellen 2000). Third, owner-occupiers may become more quickly aware of the upsurge in social externalities associated with increasing poverty because absentee owners are less frequently on the scene to experience them. Fourth, increasing neighborhood poverty may endogenously lower the overall rate of homeownership in the neighborhood. This neighborhood attribute may be valued more highly by current owner-occupants because it proxies for stability in quality of life and property values through enhanced social participation, home upkeep efforts, and collective efficacy (Dietz and Haurin 2003). As shown in appendix table 3A-3, the coefficient of the percentage of homeowners in the census tract is three times larger in the median value equation than in the median rent equation.

RESPONSES OF VALUES AND RENTS TO DECREASING NEIGHBORHOOD POVERTY. The focus of this chapter is how increasing concentrations of poverty may spur a variety of socially problematic responses (such as crime and property disinvestment) that are reflected in the loss of home values and rents. However, the estimates do permit an exploration into the dynamics of reducing neighborhood poverty rates. Unfortunately, few firm conclusions emerge.

For high-poverty neighborhoods, both estimating procedures find that reductions in poverty result in increases in values and rents, as would be expected. Moreover, it is clear that the housing market response function in these neighborhoods is asymmetric in increasing and decreasing directions. Increases in poverty yield a decline in values and rents that is larger absolutely than an identical decline in poverty from the same starting poverty rate. Beyond this, however, the instrumented and noninstrumented estimates are quite dissimilar regarding the magnitude of marginal response and whether the owner or renter markets or the higher- or lower-poverty neighborhoods are more responsive.

For low-poverty neighborhoods, it appears that marginal effects of reducing poverty are inversely related to initial poverty level. However, inconsistent results again emerge regarding whether these effects are positive or negative and whether they are larger or smaller than comparable responses to increases in poverty, depending on the estimation technique. We believe that this sensitivity of results can partly be traced to the necessarily circumscribed variation in this set of neighborhoods in the direction of decreased poverty, as has been observed in prior work (Galster, Quercia, and others 2003). But we also believe that it bespeaks a reality in which low-poverty neighborhoods—especially those below 5 percent—have virtually no sensitivity to changes in neighborhood poverty rates in either direction.

Here again there are important differences in the high-poverty neighborhood stratum in terms of how values and rents respond to a decline in poverty. Comparison of the top panels of figure 3-5 and 3-6 reveals a much higher marginal increment in median values than median rents associated with decreases in neighborhood poverty rates during the decade, especially when neighborhoods with higher initial poverty are considered. As potential rationale we offer the same causal hypotheses as above. The practical import of these findings is that rental levels seem to be less responsive than values to changes in neighborhood poverty in either direction. This implies that deconcentrating poverty will have a larger impact on aggregate values than on rents both in neighborhoods experiencing increasing poverty and in those experiencing decreasing poverty. This difference is substantial.

Estimation of the Aggregate Neighborhood Property Costs of Concentrated Poverty

What do the foregoing estimates of the relationship between neighborhood poverty and property values and rents imply for the aggregate costs to the United States of a distribution of neighborhoods that (as shown in table 3-2) includes thousands that manifest concentrations of poverty (which we operationalize as greater than 20 percent poverty rates)? There are several potential ways in which this question may be addressed. In this section we employ the instrumental variable estimates of the causal impact of concentrated poverty presented in table 3-4 to parameterize a thought experiment involving a hypothetical distribution of poverty across metropolitan space in the United States. Specifically, we examine a counterfactual situation in which no changes in neighborhood poverty rates occur from 1990 to 2000 except one: a hypothetical reallocation of poor and nonpoor populations such that all 1990 census tracts with poverty rates above 20 percent have their rates reduced to 20 percent by 2000, and all their erstwhile poor populations reallocated to accomplish this are relocated in the lowest-poverty neighborhoods in 1990, with none of these low-poverty neighborhoods increasing their poverty rate by more than 5 percentage points over the decade as a consequence.

For the simulation of this counterfactual we use the simplifying assumption that all census tracts are of equal populations, so that switching an equal number of poor and nonpoor populations between two neighborhoods will produce equal percentage point changes in poverty in both. We first calculate that reducing poverty rates to 20 percent in all 7,286 tracts that exceeded this figure in 1990 would require that 21,045 census tracts serve as destinations for the poor if each tract were to have no more than a 5 percentage point increase as a consequence. If we start with the lowest-poverty census tracts for this exercise, we end up using all tracts with 1990 poverty rates of less than 8.64 percent for these hypothetical destinations. We thus can compute a hypothetical change from 1990 to 2000 for a specific number of census tracts that will increase or decrease their poverty rates according to this scenario, then multiply them by their respective coefficients to produce a predicted value for change in the log of value or rent.[21]

We add this change to the log of the actual 1990 median value or rent, exponentiate this predicted value, and then multiply it by the 1990 total number of specified owner-occupied (or renter-occupied, as appropriate) dwellings in that tract to give the aggregate dollar valuation of that tract's property values and rents that

21. For tracts with poverty rates of less than 20 percent in 1990 we allow no simulated increase in value or rent associated with increased poverty. This produces a conservative estimate of the net social cost of concentrated poverty because the actual coefficients would have produced (unrealistically, as argued above) an increase in value and rent associated with increasing poverty in very low poverty tracts. In this simulation we specify that poverty rates of all tracts with 1990 poverty rates greater than 40 percent are set equal to 40 percent (thus simulating a decrease in their poverty rates by 20 percentage points). We do this because of the extreme nonlinearity in the estimated function for values increases associated with decreases in poverty in tracts with greater than 20 percent poverty and because of the aforementioned reliability issues of the IV parameter estimates at the extremes of the distribution. This specification produces a more conservative estimate of the gains from reducing concentrated poverty.

Table 3-5. *Estimated Change in Property Values and Monthly Rents, Actual and Simulated, by Neighborhood Change in Poverty, 1990*
Billions of dollars, except as indicated

	Poverty change			
Item	Decrease	Increase	No change	Total
Value				
Actual	134.9	2,517.8	490.2	3,142.9
Simulated	556.3	2,517.6	490.2	3,564.1
Difference	421.4	−0.2	0	421.2
Change (%)	312.38	−0.01	0	13.40
Rent				
Actual	2.0	5.0	3.0	10.0
Simulated	2.7	4.7	3.0	10.4
Difference	0.7	−0.3	0	0.4
Change (%)	35.00	−6.00	0.00	4.00
N of tracts	7,286	21,045	9,149	37,480

would ensue from this hypothetical redistribution of the poor.[22] Summing these values and rents across all tracts, the 100 largest metropolitan areas produce the aggregate dollar figure of how much aggregate property values (or rents) of owner- (or renter-) occupied homes would have been had the population been redistributed in the 1990s to eliminate concentrated poverty. A similar procedure can be used to measure the actual aggregate values and rents in these metropolitan areas in 1990, as a benchmark for comparison.

The results of these simulations are presented in table 3-5. As for the owner-occupied stock, the 21,045 low-poverty tracts that would experience an increase in poverty would suffer only a small loss in aggregate value: $200 million, or .01 percent of their 1990 aggregate value. By contrast, the 7,286 high-poverty neighborhoods that would see their poverty rates reduced to 20 percent would have their values more than triple in the aggregate, gaining more than $421 billion. The net gain overall ($421.2 billion) represents a 13.4 percent increase in the aggregate value of the owner-occupied stock in the 100 largest metropolitan areas in 1990.

22. The simulation uses the 1990 counts of dwelling units. The actual change in units during the decade was undoubtedly causally related to the actual changes in poverty, with low-poverty tracts typically gaining units through new construction and high-poverty tracts losing units through abandonment and demolition. By contrast, our counterfactual imagines a world where the dwelling counts remain the same for a decade and all that need be done is reallocate populations, other things being equal. This procedure assumes that the median is approximately the mean, which, unfortunately, is not available from the census.

A comparable result is obtained for renter-occupied stock, though the increases in the reduced-poverty tracts are less dramatic: a $700 million gain (35 percent) in aggregate monthly rents. This is offset by the $300 million (6 percent) aggregate loss in monthly rents in neighborhoods where poverty rates hypothetically rose. The net gain in aggregate monthly rents overall is estimated as $400 million, or 4 percent.

If we capitalize this figure for rents using the conventional yardstick of the ratio of monthly rent to value equals 1/100, the equivalent net property value gain for the absentee-owned stock in this scenario is $40 billion.[23] Thus the net gain in residential property values (regardless of ownership status) associated with this hypothetical redistribution of poverty populations is $461 billion.

Conclusion and Implications

In this chapter we have established the micro foundations of how concentrated poverty affects the antisocial behaviors of households and the dwelling investment behaviors of property owners. In both behavioral areas there are strong a priori reasons to believe that major behavioral responses ensue only when neighborhood poverty rates exceed a particular threshold. We have also demonstrated conceptually how these sorts of behaviors jointly affect property values and rents in a neighborhood and, in turn, spawn subsequent changes in neighborhood poverty rates, behavioral adjustments, and so on, in a circular pattern of causation.

Our empirical explorations use two techniques for dealing with the simultaneity bias that this circular pattern of causation can often cause. The first is a hedonic model of individual home sales in Cleveland from 1993 to 1997, which uses lagged annual observations of public assistance rates in the surrounding census tracts. The second models median values and rents in all census tracts in the 100 largest metropolitan areas from 1990 to 2000 and instruments for neighborhood poverty rates with county-level poverty rates. Both empirical models specify in reduced form the changes in property values and rents that transpired from changes in neighborhood poverty rates, both directly and indirectly through impacts on housing upkeep and crime. Results from both models are remarkably similar and show that there is no substantial relationship between neighborhood poverty changes and property values or rents when poverty rates stay below 10 percent. By contrast, marginal increases in poverty when neighborhood poverty rates are in the range of 10–20 percent result in dramatic declines in value and rent, strongly suggesting a threshold corresponding to the theoretical prediction.

Using IV-estimated parameters from the second model, we simulated how property values and rents would have changed in the aggregate for the 100 largest

---

23. The figure 1/100 is virtually equivalent to the ratio of the observed mean net annual operating income to value observed for nonmortgaged multifamily properties of .09 (Galster, Tatian, and Wilson 1999).

Figure 3-7. *Summary Relationship between Aggregate Value or Rent and Increasing Poverty Rate in a Neighborhood*

U.S. dollars value or rent

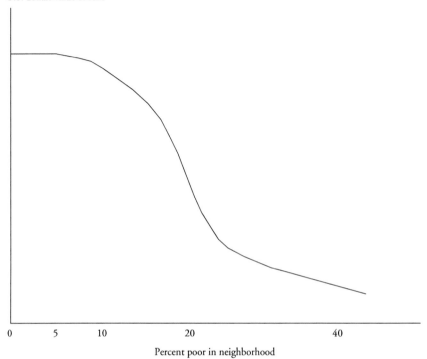

Percent poor in neighborhood

metropolitan areas had populations been redistributed such that all census tracts in 1990 exceeding 20 percent poverty had their rate reduced to 20 percent by 2000, and only the lowest-poverty tracts were allocated additional poor populations, with each increasing their poverty rate by 5 percentage points. In this thought experiment. owner-occupied property values rise $421 billion (13 percent) and monthly rents rise $400 million (4 percent) in aggregate, other things being equal. These figures are anything but trivial and, if they even roughly approximate the social costs of concentrated poverty, suggest that policymakers cannot ignore this issue.

The empirical estimates from both the Cleveland and cross-metropolitan models point to a relationship between increasing neighborhood poverty and aggregate social costs (both direct and indirect, as measured by property values and rents in the neighborhood) that is best described by a (negative) logistic function with characteristics as portrayed in figure 3-7.[24] Such a relationship holds three

24. This is consistent with the finding of Meen (2004, 2006) using U.K. data.

powerful implications for policymakers, as amplified elsewhere (Galster, Quercia, and Cortes 2000; Galster 2002, 2005). First, preventing neighborhoods from sliding past their threshold into a state of concentrated poverty would result in avoiding substantial social harms, as capitalized in dramatic losses of property values. Second, reducing poverty in extremely high poverty neighborhoods is unlikely to yield substantial increments in property values without major and sustained investments. Third, if concentrated poverty is prevented or undone, the alternative destination neighborhoods for the poor should primarily be those of low poverty, not moderate poverty. Upsurges in poverty in neighborhoods already near their thresholds are likely to produce such dramatic losses in property values that they will overwhelm the gains in value in neighborhoods that experience declines in poverty.

In the current policy environment, these goals are difficult to pursue. Moreover, it is obvious that although a deconcentration of poverty will result in potential Pareto improvements, there will be redistributional consequences (away from property owners in low-poverty neighborhoods and toward those in high-poverty neighborhoods) unless actual compensation is provided. Nevertheless, the mounting evidence to which this chapter contributes demonstrates that major gains in net social well-being would ensue were policymakers to enact programs that fought exclusionary zoning, concentrations of subsidized housing, and "not in my backyard" responses to proposed developments of assisted housing (Galster, Tatian, and others 2003) and instead promoted inclusionary zoning, mixed-income developments, and mobility counseling for recipients of rental vouchers.

Table 3A-1. *Descriptive Statistics of All Variables in Cleveland Home Sales Price Regression*

Variable	Mean	SD
Number of baths / number of bedrooms	0.39822	0.13932
1.5 Baths (versus 1)	0.08412	0.27757
2+ Baths (versus 1)	0.07306	0.26024
Garage	0.81088	0.39162
Building 1 story (vs. more)	0.49991	0.50002
Built 1900–19 (vs. pre-1900)	0.38796	0.48730
Built 1920–39 (vs. pre-1900)	0.28055	0.44928
Built 1940–49 (vs. pre-1900)	0.10359	0.30474
Built 1950–59 (vs. pre-1900)	0.10163	0.30217
Built 1960–69 (vs. pre-1900)	0.02249	0.14827
Built 1970–79 (vs. pre-1900)	0.00289	0.05366
Built 1980–89 (vs. pre-1900)	0.00141	0.03757
Built 1990 or later (vs. pre-1900)	0.01782	0.13230
Lot size (square feet)	5,081.91041	4,399.74944
Square of lot size	45,182,419	769,378,678

(continued)

Table 3A-1. *Descriptive Statistics of All Variables in Cleveland Home Sales Price Regression (continued)*

Variable	Mean	SD
Lot width (feet)	41.07588	52.69925
Pool	0.00111	0.03324
Square feet / number of rooms	203.54621	39.92127
Square feet	1,266.74931	369.53291
Square of square feet	1,741,200	1,290,385
Latitude	−0.00493	0.07741
Longitude	−0.00428	0.04034
Latitude*Latitude	0.00602	0.00482
Longitude*Longitude	0.00165	0.00224
Latitude*Longitude	0.00173	0.00319
Census-tract characteristics		
Percent births that are low birth weight	10.82849	6.43689
Percent nonresidential parcels	10.48299	7.23579
Births to unmarried moms/1,000 live births	610.40819	206.38484
Percent all homes single family	48.58403	22.96892
Percent all parcels tax delinquent	12.32671	7.0618
Births to teens/1,000 teen females 19 yrs. or younger	104.80560	50.47510
Percent all commercial parcels vacant	22.84646	11.42141
Percent all residential parcels vacant	7.42196	7.77063
Percent of population receiving public assistance	11.29291	7.64126
Timing of sale characteristics		
Sale April–June	0.27373	0.44589
Sale July–September	0.27459	0.44632
Sale October–December	0.25143	0.43385
Sale year 1996	0.16430	0.37056
Sale year 1997	0.18986	0.39220
Sale year 1998	0.23748	0.42555
Sale year 1999	0.26108	0.43923

Table 3A-2. *Descriptive Statistics for Model of 100 Metropolitan Areas*[a]

Variable	N	Mean	SD
1990–2000 change in log of median housing value	37,454	0.518	0.558
1990–2000 change in log of median rent	38,194	0.490	0.516
Change in proportion own-occ HUs built 10 yrs ago or less	38,276	−0.053	0.167
Change in proportion own-occ HUs built 11 to 20 yrs ago	38,276	−0.047	0.175
Change in proportion own-occ HUs built 21 to 30 yrs ago	38,276	−0.004	0.183
Change in proportion own-occ HUs built 31 to 40 yrs ago	38,276	−0.029	0.186
Change in proportion own-occ HUs built 41 to 50 yrs ago	38,276	0.065	0.155
Change in proportion rent-occ HUs built 10 yrs ago or less	38,240	−0.105	0.208
Change in proportion rent-occ HUs built 11 to 20 yrs ago	38,240	−0.060	0.207
Change in proportion rent-occ HUs built 21 to 30 yrs ago	38,240	0.028	0.189

(continued)

Table 3A-2. *Descriptive Statistics for Model of 100 Metropolitan Areas* [a] (*continued*)

Variable	N	Mean	SD
Change in proportion rent-occ HUs built 31 to 40 yrs ago	38,240	0.023	0.153
Change in proportion rent-occ HUs built 41 to 50 yrs ago	38,240	0.047	0.124
Change in proportion HUs w/o complete plumbing	38,322	0.000	0.013
Change in proportion HUs w/o complete kitchen	38,326	0.003	0.021
Change in proportion own-occ HUs that are 1 unit, attached	38,276	0.006	0.062
Change in proportion own-occ HUs that are 2 units	38,276	−0.002	0.042
Change in proportion own-occ HUs that are 3 or 4 units	38,276	0.001	0.044
Change in proportion own-occ HUs that are 5 or more units	38,276	−0.006	0.080
Change in proportion own-occ mobile homes	38,276	−0.006	0.055
Change in proportion own-occ "other" types of HUs	38,276	−0.008	0.021
Change in proportion rent-occ HUs that are 1 unit, attached	38,240	0.002	0.078
Change in proportion rent-occ HUs that are 2 units	38,240	−0.005	0.073
Change in proportion rent-occ HUs that are 3 or 4 units	38,240	0.002	0.071
Change in proportion rent-occ HUs that are 5 or more units	38,240	0.002	0.147
Change in proportion rent-occ mobile homes	38,240	0.003	0.061
Change in proportion rent-occ "other" types of HUs	38,240	−0.014	0.028
Change in proportion own-occ HUs w/ no bedroom	38,276	0.004	0.041
Change in proportion own-occ HUs w/ 1 bedroom	38,276	0.000	0.067
Change in proportion own-occ HUs w/ 2 bedrooms	38,276	−0.011	0.092
Change in proportion own-occ HUs w/ 4 bedrooms	38,276	0.014	0.068
Change in proportion own-occ HUs w/ 5 or more bedrooms	38,276	0.004	0.039
Change in proportion rent-occ HUs w/ no bedroom	38,240	0.018	0.053
Change in proportion rent-occ HUs w/ 1 bedroom	38,240	0.004	0.112
Change in proportion rent-occ HUs w/ 2 bedrooms	38,240	−0.027	0.131
Change in proportion rent-occ HUs w/ 4 bedrooms	38,240	0.006	0.084
Change in proportion rent-occ HUs w/ 5 or more bedrooms	38,240	0.001	0.040
Change in proportion own-occ HUs	38,322	0.018	0.085
Change in proportion vacant HUs not for sale or rent	37,569	−0.046	0.286
Change in proportion population that is non-Hispanic white	38,374	−0.080	0.101
Change in proportion population that is non-Hispanic African American	38,374	0.022	0.075
Change in proportion population that is non-Hispanic Asian	38,374	0.016	0.039
Change in proportion population that is Hispanic	38,374	0.039	0.072
Change in proportion population under the age of 15	38,374	0.002	0.036
Change in proportion population age 15 to 19	38,374	0.000	0.022
Change in proportion population age 20 to 24	38,374	−0.008	0.026
Change in proportion population age 25 to 29	38,374	−0.019	0.026
Change in proportion population age 30 to 34	38,374	−0.018	0.023
Change in proportion population age 35 to 44	38,374	0.011	0.033
Change in proportion population age 45 to 54	38,374	0.030	0.030
Change in proportion population age 55 to 64	38,374	0.000	0.026
Change in proportion population age 65 to 74	38,374	−0.008	0.027

a. HU = housing unit.

Table 3A-3. *Estimated Parameters for Control Variables, Full Sample of Census Tracts* [a]

Variable	B	Std. error	Sig.
Dependent variable: ln (2000 median value of owner-occupied home in census tract)			
(Constant)	7.999	0.038	0.000
Natural log of own-occ housing value, 1990	0.375	0.003	0.000
Change in proportion own-occ HUs built 10 yrs ago or less	0.701	0.023	0.000
Change in proportion own-occ HUs built 11 to 20 yrs ago	0.775	0.021	0.000
Change in proportion own-occ HUs built 21 to 30 yrs ago	0.598	0.019	0.000
Change in proportion own-occ HUs built 31 to 40 yrs ago	0.567	0.016	0.000
Change in proportion own-occ HUs built 41 to 50 yrs ago	0.413	0.018	0.000
Change in proportion HUs w/o complete plumbing	0.045	0.150	0.764
Change in proportion HUs w/o complete kitchen	−1.469	0.097	0.000
Change in proportion own-occ HUs that are 1 unit, attached	0.033	0.031	0.295
Change in proportion own-occ HUs that are 2 units	0.411	0.047	0.000
Change in proportion own-occ HUs that are 3 or 4 units	0.127	0.049	0.009
Change in proportion own-occ HUs that are 5 or more units	0.203	0.033	0.000
Change in proportion own-occ mobile homes	0.061	0.038	0.111
Change in proportion own-occ "other" types of HUs	1.179	0.099	0.000
Change in proportion own-occ HUs w/ no bedroom	−0.435	0.060	0.000
Change in proportion own-occ HUs w/ 1 bedroom	−0.153	0.036	0.000
Change in proportion own-occ HUs w/ 2 bedrooms	0.056	0.026	0.030
Change in proportion own-occ HUs w/ 4 bedrooms	0.609	0.029	0.000
Change in proportion own-occ HUs w/ 5 or more bedrooms	1.011	0.047	0.000
Akron fixed effects	−0.387	0.026	0.000
Ann Arbor fixed effects	−0.114	0.026	0.000
Baltimore fixed effects	−0.481	0.015	0.000
Bergen-Passaic fixed effects	−0.157	0.021	0.000
Boston fixed effects	−0.109	0.014	0.000
Chicago fixed effects	−0.134	0.011	0.000
Cincinnati fixed effects	−0.429	0.018	0.000
Cleveland fixed effects	−0.405	0.015	0.000
Dallas fixed effects	−0.463	0.015	0.000
Denver fixed effects	0.042	0.017	0.012
Detroit fixed effects	−0.262	0.012	0.000
Ft. Lauderdale fixed effects	−0.080	0.021	0.000
Ft. Worth–Arlington fixed effects	−0.611	0.019	0.000
Gary fixed effects	−0.380	0.028	0.000
Houston fixed effects	−0.523	0.014	0.000
Jersey City fixed effects	−0.396	0.027	0.000
Miami fixed effects	−0.123	0.019	0.000
Middlesex fixed effects	−0.287	0.021	0.000
Milwaukee fixed effects	−0.415	0.018	0.000
Monmouth-Ocean fixed effects	−0.330	0.021	0.000
Nassau-Suffolk fixed effects	−0.114	0.015	0.000
New Haven fixed effects	−0.503	0.029	0.000
New York fixed effects	−0.025	0.011	0.018

(continued)

Table 3A-3. *Estimated Parameters for Control Variables, Full Sample of Census Tracts (continued)*

Variable	B	Std. error	Sig.
Dependent variable: ln (2000 median value of owner-occupied home in census tract)			
Newark fixed effects	−0.269	0.016	0.000
Oakland fixed effects	0.040	0.016	0.013
Orange County fixed effects	0.026	0.015	0.093
Philadelphia fixed effects	−0.540	0.012	0.000
Portland fixed effects	0.007	0.018	0.713
Riverside–San Bernardino fixed effects	−0.092	0.016	0.000
Sacramento fixed effects	−0.268	0.019	0.000
San Francisco fixed effects	0.421	0.018	0.000
San Jose fixed effects	0.431	0.019	0.000
Seattle fixed effects	0.047	0.016	0.003
Tacoma fixed effects	−0.075	0.027	0.005
Vallejo fixed effects	−0.078	0.032	0.013
Ventura fixed effects	−0.071	0.027	0.008
Washington, D.C., fixed effects	−0.262	0.012	0.000
Wilmington fixed effects	−0.446	0.027	0.000
Albany fixed effects	−0.675	0.022	0.000
Albuquerque fixed effects	−0.253	0.025	0.000
Atlanta fixed effects	−0.267	0.015	0.000
Austin fixed effects	−0.299	0.022	0.000
Bakersfield fixed effects	−0.461	0.029	0.000
Baton Rouge fixed effects	−0.502	0.030	0.000
Birmingham fixed effects	−0.534	0.024	0.000
Buffalo fixed effects	−0.702	0.020	0.000
Charleston fixed effects	−0.414	0.031	0.000
Charlotte fixed effects	−0.373	0.020	0.000
Columbia fixed effects	−0.487	0.030	0.000
Columbus fixed effects	−0.396	0.018	0.000
Dayton fixed effects	−0.562	0.022	0.000
El Paso fixed effects	−0.584	0.030	0.000
Fresno fixed effects	−0.389	0.026	0.000
Grand Rapids fixed effects	−0.416	0.022	0.000
Greensboro fixed effects	−0.516	0.021	0.000
Greenville fixed effects	−0.590	0.023	0.000
Harrisburg fixed effects	−0.533	0.028	0.000
Hartford fixed effects	−0.537	0.020	0.000
Honolulu fixed effects	0.073	0.028	0.011
Indianapolis fixed effects	−0.493	0.019	0.000
Jacksonville fixed effects	−0.550	0.024	0.000
Kansas City fixed effects	−0.565	0.017	0.000
Knoxville fixed effects	−0.582	0.028	0.000
Las Vegas fixed effects	−0.103	0.021	0.000
Little Rock fixed effects	−0.541	0.028	0.000
Louisville fixed effects	−0.473	0.022	0.000

(continued)

Table 3A-3. *Estimated Parameters for Control Variables, Full Sample of Census Tracts (continued)*

Variable	B	Std. error	Sig.
Dependent variable: ln (2000 median value of owner-occupied home in census tract)			
McAllen fixed effects	−0.700	0.037	0.000
Memphis fixed effects	−0.534	0.021	0.000
Minneapolis–St. Paul fixed effects	−0.276	0.014	0.000
Mobile fixed effects	−0.622	0.028	0.000
Nashville fixed effects	−0.330	0.022	0.000
New Orleans fixed effects	−0.482	0.018	0.000
Norfolk–Virginia Beach fixed effects	−0.471	0.019	0.000
Oklahoma City fixed effects	−0.713	0.020	0.000
Omaha fixed effects	−0.405	0.024	0.000
Orlando fixed effects	−0.327	0.019	0.000
Phoenix fixed effects	−0.289	0.015	0.000
Pittsburgh fixed effects	−0.686	0.015	0.000
Providence fixed effects	−0.509	0.021	0.000
Raleigh fixed effects	−0.302	0.023	0.000
Richmond fixed effects	−0.507	0.022	0.000
Rochester fixed effects	−0.742	0.021	0.000
St. Louis fixed effects	−0.525	0.016	0.000
Salt Lake City fixed effects	−0.027	0.021	0.205
San Antonio fixed effects	−0.618	0.020	0.000
San Diego fixed effects	0.056	0.015	0.000
Sarasota fixed effects	−0.250	0.028	0.000
Scranton fixed effects	−0.690	0.025	0.000
Springfield fixed effects	−0.545	0.030	0.000
Stockton-Lodi fixed effects	−0.346	0.030	0.000
Syracuse fixed effects	−0.832	0.023	0.000
Tampa fixed effects	−0.474	0.016	0.000
Toledo fixed effects	−0.577	0.026	0.000
Tucson fixed effects	−0.173	0.024	0.000
Tulsa fixed effects	−0.606	0.022	0.000
West Palm Beach fixed effects	−0.311	0.021	0.000
Wichita fixed effects	−0.637	0.028	0.000
Youngstown fixed effects	−0.716	0.027	0.000
Allentown fixed effects	−0.637	0.028	0.000
Change in proportion own-occ HUs	0.419	0.027	0.000
Change in proportion vacant HUs not for sale or rent	−0.009	0.006	0.136
Change in proportion population that is non-Hispanic white	0.500	0.122	0.000
Change in proportion population that is non-Hispanic African American	−0.213	0.123	0.084
Change in proportion population that is non-Hispanic Asian	0.728	0.127	0.000
Change in proportion population that is Hispanic	−0.516	0.123	0.000
Change in proportion population under the age of 15	0.462	0.083	0.000
Change in proportion population age 15 to 19	0.040	0.107	0.706
Change in proportion population age 20 to 24	−0.982	0.095	0.000

(continued)

Table 3A-3. *Estimated Parameters for Control Variables, Full Sample of Census Tracts (continued)*

Variable	B	Std. error	Sig.
Dependent variable: ln (2000 median value of owner-occupied home in census tract)			
Change in proportion population age 25 to 29	0.095	0.095	0.316
Change in proportion population age 30 to 34	−0.006	0.100	0.950
Change in proportion population age 35 to 44	−2.192	0.083	0.000
Change in proportion population age 45 to 54	−0.052	0.087	0.548
Change in proportion population age 55 to 64	0.801	0.096	0.000
Change in proportion population age 65 to 74	−0.255	0.104	0.014
Dependent variable: ln (2000 median value of renter-occupied home in census tract)			
(Constant)	5.709	0.018	0.000
Natural log of median rent, 1990	0.165	0.003	0.000
Change in proportion rent-occ HUs built 10 yrs ago or less	0.388	0.013	0.000
Change in proportion rent-occ HUs built 11 to 20 yrs ago	0.432	0.012	0.000
Change in proportion rent-occ HUs built 21 to 30 yrs ago	0.342	0.012	0.000
Change in proportion rent-occ HUs built 31 to 40 yrs ago	0.194	0.012	0.000
Change in proportion rent-occ HUs built 41 to 50 yrs ago	0.237	0.013	0.000
Change in proportion HUs w/o complete plumbing	0.236	0.106	0.026
Change in proportion HUs w/o complete kitchen	−0.390	0.067	0.000
Change in proportion rent-occ HUs that are 1-unit, attached	−0.221	0.018	0.000
Change in proportion rent-occ HUs that are 2-units	−0.107	0.019	0.000
Change in proportion rent-occ HUs that are 3 or 4 units	−0.208	0.020	0.000
Change in proportion rent-occ HUs that are 5 or more units	−0.146	0.014	0.000
Change in proportion rent-occ mobile homes	−0.421	0.022	0.000
Change in proportion rent-occ "other" types of HUs	0.105	0.050	0.034
Change in proportion rent-occ HUs w/ no bedrooms	−0.461	0.027	0.000
Change in proportion rent-occ HUs w/ 1 bedroom	−0.212	0.016	0.000
Change in proportion rent-occ HUs w/ 2 bedrooms	−0.043	0.013	0.001
Change in proportion rent-occ HUs w/ 4 bedrooms	0.123	0.017	0.000
Change in proportion rent-occ HUs w/ 5 or more bedrooms	0.136	0.033	0.000
Akron fixed effects	−0.260	0.020	0.000
Ann Arbor fixed effects	−0.160	0.020	0.000
Baltimore fixed effects	−0.216	0.011	0.000
Bergen-Passaic fixed effects	0.072	0.016	0.000
Boston fixed effects	−0.057	0.011	0.000
Chicago fixed effects	−0.111	0.008	0.000
Cincinnati fixed effects	−0.326	0.013	0.000
Cleveland fixed effects	−0.282	0.011	0.000
Dallas fixed effects	−0.097	0.011	0.000
Denver fixed effects	0.017	0.012	0.165
Detroit fixed effects	−0.209	0.009	0.000
Ft. Lauderdale fixed effects	0.094	0.016	0.000
Ft. Worth-Arlington fixed effects	−0.186	0.014	0.000
Gary fixed effects	−0.286	0.021	0.000
Houston fixed effects	−0.178	0.010	0.000
Jersey City fixed effects	−0.114	0.020	0.000

(continued)

Table 3A-3. *Estimated Parameters for Control Variables, Full Sample of Census Tracts* (*continued*)

Variable	B	Std. error	Sig.
Dependent variable: ln (2000 median value of renter-occupied home in census tract)			
Miami fixed effects	−0.034	0.014	0.016
Middlesex fixed effects	0.005	0.016	0.759
Milwaukee fixed effects	−0.249	0.013	0.000
Monmouth-Ocean fixed effects	0.034	0.016	0.035
Nassau-Suffolk fixed effects	0.127	0.012	0.000
New Haven fixed effects	−0.150	0.022	0.000
New York fixed effects	−0.047	0.008	0.000
Newark fixed effects	−0.030	0.012	0.016
Oakland fixed effects	0.091	0.012	0.000
Orange County fixed effects	0.164	0.012	0.000
Philadelphia fixed effects	−0.155	0.009	0.000
Portland fixed effects	−0.124	0.013	0.000
Riverside-San Bernardino fixed effects	−0.010	0.012	0.397
Sacramento fixed effects	−0.120	0.014	0.000
San Francisco fixed effects	0.223	0.014	0.000
San Jose fixed effects	0.320	0.015	0.000
Seattle fixed effects	−0.012	0.012	0.330
Tacoma fixed effects	−0.092	0.020	0.000
Vallejo fixed effects	0.000	0.024	0.984
Ventura fixed effects	0.154	0.021	0.000
Washington DC fixed effects	−0.010	0.009	0.285
Wilmington fixed effects	−0.146	0.021	0.000
Albany fixed effects	−0.294	0.017	0.000
Albuquerque fixed effects	−0.222	0.019	0.000
Atlanta fixed effects	−0.085	0.011	0.000
Austin fixed effects	−0.003	0.016	0.837
Bakersfield fixed effects	−0.269	0.022	0.000
Baton Rouge fixed effects	−0.364	0.023	0.000
Birmingham fixed effects	−0.396	0.018	0.000
Buffalo fixed effects	−0.364	0.015	0.000
Charleston fixed effects	−0.275	0.023	0.000
Charlotte fixed effects	−0.248	0.015	0.000
Columbia fixed effects	−0.323	0.023	0.000
Columbus fixed effects	−0.279	0.014	0.000
Dayton fixed effects	−0.377	0.017	0.000
El Paso fixed effects	−0.337	0.023	0.000
Fresno fixed effects	−0.244	0.019	0.000
Grand Rapids fixed effects	−0.315	0.017	0.000
Greensboro fixed effects	−0.370	0.016	0.000
Greenville fixed effects	−0.445	0.018	0.000
Harrisburg fixed effects	−0.362	0.021	0.000
Hartford fixed effects	−0.199	0.015	0.000
Honolulu fixed effects	0.097	0.020	0.000
Indianapolis fixed effects	−0.293	0.014	0.000

(continued)

Table 3A-3. *Estimated Parameters for Control Variables, Full Sample of Census Tracts (continued)*

Variable	B	Std. error	Sig.
Dependent variable: ln (2000 median value of renter-occupied home in census tract)			
Jacksonville fixed effects	−0.262	0.018	0.000
Kansas City fixed effects	−0.262	0.013	0.000
Knoxville fixed effects	−0.463	0.021	0.000
Las Vegas fixed effects	−0.016	0.016	0.307
Little Rock fixed effects	−0.332	0.021	0.000
Louisville fixed effects	−0.399	0.017	0.000
McAllen fixed effects	−0.401	0.028	0.000
Memphis fixed effects	−0.276	0.016	0.000
Minneapolis-St. Paul fixed effects	−0.189	0.011	0.000
Mobile fixed effects	−0.429	0.021	0.000
Nashville fixed effects	−0.228	0.017	0.000
New Orleans fixed effects	−0.347	0.014	0.000
Norfolk-Virginia Beach fixed effects	−0.223	0.014	0.000
Oklahoma City fixed effects	−0.387	0.015	0.000
Omaha fixed effects	−0.265	0.018	0.000
Orlando fixed effects	−0.074	0.015	0.000
Phoenix fixed effects	−0.056	0.011	0.000
Pittsburgh fixed effects	−0.436	0.011	0.000
Providence fixed effects	−0.323	0.016	0.000
Raleigh fixed effects	−0.162	0.018	0.000
Richmond fixed effects	−0.237	0.016	0.000
Rochester fixed effects	−0.260	0.016	0.000
St. Louis fixed effects	−0.328	0.012	0.000
Salt Lake City fixed effects	−0.076	0.016	0.000
San Antonio fixed effects	−0.231	0.015	0.000
San Diego fixed effects	0.064	0.012	0.000
Sarasota fixed effects	−0.062	0.021	0.003
Scranton fixed effects	−0.521	0.019	0.000
Springfield fixed effects	−0.319	0.023	0.000
Stockton-Lodi fixed effects	−0.165	0.023	0.000
Syracuse fixed effects	−0.359	0.018	0.000
Tampa fixed effects	−0.184	0.012	0.000
Toledo fixed effects	−0.418	0.020	0.000
Tucson fixed effects	−0.133	0.018	0.000
Tulsa fixed effects	−0.350	0.016	0.000
West Palm Beach fixed effects	0.016	0.016	0.333
Wichita fixed effects	−0.327	0.022	0.000
Youngstown fixed effects	−0.488	0.020	0.000
Allentown fixed effects	−0.279	0.021	0.000
Change in proportion own-occ HUs	0.143	0.018	0.000
Change in proportion vacant HUs not for sale or rent	0.002	0.004	0.734
Change in proportion population that is non-Hispanic white	−0.098	0.090	0.277
Change in proportion population that is non-Hispanic black	−0.043	0.091	0.636

(continued)

Table 3A-3. *Estimated Parameters for Control Variables, Full Sample of Census Tracts (continued)*

Variable	B	Std. error	Sig.
Dependent variable: ln (2000 median value of renter-occupied home in census tract)			
Change in proportion population that is non-Hispanic Asian	0.833	0.093	0.000
Change in proportion population that is Hispanic	−0.317	0.090	0.000
Change in proportion population under the age of 15	−0.510	0.061	0.000
Change in proportion population age 15 to 19	−0.637	0.079	0.000
Change in proportion population age 20 to 24	−1.053	0.069	0.000
Change in proportion population age 25 to 29	−0.774	0.070	0.000
Change in proportion population age 30 to 34	−1.181	0.074	0.000
Change in proportion population age 35 to 44	−1.979	0.061	0.000
Change in proportion population age 45 to 54	−0.715	0.064	0.000
Change in proportion population age 55 to 64	−0.146	0.070	0.036
Change in proportion population age 65 to 74	−0.351	0.078	0.000

a. HU = housing unit.

References

Anderson, Elijah. 1990. *Streetwise: Race, Class, and Change in an Urban Community.* University of Chicago Press.

———. 1991. "Neighborhood Effects on Teenage Pregnancy." In *The Urban Underclass,* edited by Christopher Jencks and Paul Peterson, pp. 375–98. Brookings.

Aneshensel, C. S., and C. A. Sucoff. 1996. "The Neighborhood Context and Adolescent Mental Health." *Journal of Health and Social Behavior* 37, no. 4: 293–310.

Asmus, Karl, and Harvey Iglarsh. 1975. "Dynamic Model of Private Incentives to Housing Maintenance: Comment." *Southern Economic Journal* 42, no. 4: 326–29.

Atkinson, Rowland and Keith Kintrea. 2001. "Area Effects: What Do They Mean for British Housing and Regeneration Policy?" *European Journal of Housing Policy* 2, no. 2: 147–66.

———. 2004. "Opportunities and Despair, It's All in There: Practitioner Experiences and Explanations of Area Effects and Life Chances." *Sociology* 38, no. 3: 437–55.

Bauder, Harald. 2001. "You're Good with Your Hands, Why Don't You Become an Auto Mechanic: Neighborhood Context, Institutions, and Career Development." *International Journal of Urban and Regional Research* 25, no. 3: 593–608.

Boehm, Thomas, and Keith Ihlanfeldt. 1986. "The Improvement Expenditures of Urban Homeowners." *American Real Estate and Urban Economics Association Journal* 14, no. 2: 48–60.

Bradbury, Katherine, Anthony Downs, and Kenneth Small. 1982. *Urban Decline and the Future of American Cities.* Brookings.

Brooks-Gunn, Jeanne, Gregory J. Duncan, and J. Lawrence Aber, eds. 1997. *Context and Consequences for Children.* Vol. 1 of *Neighborhood Poverty.* New York: Russell Sage Foundation.

Buck, Nick. 2001. "Identifying Neighborhood Effects on Social Exclusion." *Urban Studies* 38, no. 12: 2251–275.

Burchell, Robert, David Listokin, and Arlene Pashman. 1994. *Regional Opportunities for Low Income Households: A Resource Guide to Affordable Housing and Regional Strategies.* U.S. Department of Housing and Urban Development, Office of Policy Development and Research.

Can, Ayse. 1997. "Spatial Segmentation in Urban House Prices: Alternative Approaches." Working Paper. Washington: Fannie Mae Foundation, Policy, Research, Evaluation, and Training Division.

Card, David, and Anne Krueger. 1992. "Does School Quality Matter?" *Journal of Political Economy* 100, no. 1: 1–40.

Carter, William, Michael Schill, and Susan Wachter. 1998. "Polarization, Public Housing, and Racial Minorities in U.S. Cities." *Urban Studies* 35, no. 10: 1889–911.

Case, Anne, and Lawrence Katz. 1991. *The Company You Keep: The Effects of Family and Neighborhood on Disadvantaged Youth.* Working Paper 3705. Cambridge, Mass.: National Bureau of Economic Research.

Chinloy, Peter. 1980. "The Effect of Maintenance Expenditures on the Measurement of Depreciation in Housing." *Journal of Urban Economics* 8, no. 1: 86–107.

Cisneros, Henry. 1995. *Regionalism: The New Geography of Opportunity.* U.S. Department of Housing and Urban Development.

Cohen, L. E., Marcus Felson, and Kenneth Land. 1980. "Property Crime Rates in the United States: A Macrodynamic Analysis, 1947–1977, with Ex Ante Forecasts for the Mid-1980s." *American Journal of Sociology* 86, no. 1: 90–118.

Cook, Phillip. 1986. "The Demand and Supply of Criminal Opportunities." In *Crime and Justice: An Annual Review of Research,* vol. 7, edited by Michael Tonry and Morris Norval, pp. 1–28. University of Chicago Press.

Coulson, N. Edward, and Eric Bond. 1990. "A Hedonic Approach to Residential Succession." *Review of Economics and Statistics* 72, no. 3: 433–44.

Diehr, Paula, and others. 1993. "Do Communities Differ in Health Behaviors?" *Journal of Clinical Epidemiology* 46, no. 10: 1141–149.

Dietz, Robert. 2002. "The Estimation of Neighborhood Effects in the Social Sciences." *Social Science Research* 31, no. 4: 539–75.

Dietz, Robert, and Donald Haurin. 2003. "The Social and Private Micro-Level Consequences of Homeownership." *Journal of Urban Economics* 54, no. 3: 401–50.

Downs, Anthony. 1981. *Neighborhoods and Urban Development.* Brookings.

Duncan, Gregory J., James Connell, and Pamela Klebanov. 1997. "Conceptual and Methodological Issues in Estimating Causal Effects of Neighborhoods and Family Conditions on Individual Development." In *Context and Consequences for Children,* vol. 1 of *Neighborhood Poverty,* edited by Jeanne Brooks-Gunn, Gregory J. Duncan, and J. Lawrence Aber, pp. 219–50. New York: Russell Sage Foundation.

Duncan, Gregory J., and Stephen Raudenbush. 1999. "Assessing the Effects of Context in Studies of Child and Youth Development." *Educational Psychologist* 34, no. 1: 29–41.

Duncan, Otis D., and Beverly Duncan. 1957. *The Negro Population of Chicago.* University of Chicago Press.

Ellen, Ingrid Gould. 2000. *Sharing America's Neighborhoods: The Prospects for Stable Racial Integration.* Harvard University Press.

Ellen, Ingrid Gould, and Margery Austin Turner. 1997. "Does Neighborhood Matter? Assessing Recent Evidence." *Housing Policy Debate* 8, no. 4: 833–66.

———. 2003. "Do Neighborhoods Matter and Why?" In *Choosing a Better Life? Evaluating the Moving to Opportunity Experiment,* edited by John Goering and Judith Feins, pp. 313–38. Washington: Urban Institute Press.

Evans, William, Wallace Oates, and Robert Schwab. 1992. "Measuring Peer Group Effects." *Journal of Political Economy* 100, no. 5: 966–91.

Flippen, Chenoa. 2004. "Unequal Returns to Housing Investment?" *Social Forces* 82, no. 4: 1523–551.

Foster, E. M., and Sarah McLanahan. 1996. "An Illustration of the Use of Instrumental Variables: Do Neighborhood Conditions Affect a Young Person's Chance of Finishing High School?" *Psychological Methods* 1, no. 3: 249–60.

Friedrichs, Jurgen. 1998. "Do Poor Neighborhoods Make Their Residents Poorer? Context Effects of Poverty Neighborhoods on Their Residents." In *Empirical Poverty Research in a Comparative Perspective,* edited by H. Andress, pp. 77–99. Aldershot, U.K.: Ashgate.

Furstenburg, Frank, and others. 1999. *Managing to Make It: Urban Families and Adolescent Success.* University of Chicago Press.

Galster, George. 1987. *Homeowners and Neighborhood Reinvestment.* Duke University Press.

———. 2002. "An Economic Efficiency Analysis of Deconcentrating Poverty Populations." *Journal of Housing Economics* 11, no. 4: 303–29.

———. 2003a. "Investigating Behavioral Impacts of Poor Neighborhoods: Towards New Data and Analytical Strategies." *Housing Studies* 18, no. 6: 893–914.

———. 2003b. "Neighbourhood Dynamics and Housing Markets." In *Housing Economics and Public Policy,* edited by Tony O'Sullivan and Kenneth Gibb, pp. 153–71. Oxford, U.K.: Blackwell.

———. 2005. *Neighborhood Mix, Social Opportunities, and the Policy Challenges of an Increasingly Diverse Amsterdam.* Amsterdam, Neth.: University of Amsterdam, Department of Geography, Planning, and International Development Studies.

Galster, George, Jackie Cutsinger, and Up Lim. 2007. "Are Neighbourhoods Self-Stabilizing? Exploring Endogenous Dynamics." *Urban Studies* 44, no. 1: 1–14.

Galster, George, and Sean Killen. 1995. "The Geography of Metropolitan Opportunity: A Recent Reconnaissance and Conceptual Framework." *Housing Policy Debate* 6, no. 1: 7–43.

Galster, George, and Ron Mincy. 1993. "Understanding the Changing Fortunes of Metropolitan Neighbourhoods." *Housing Policy Debate* 4, no. 3: 303–52.

Galster, George, Ron Mincy, and Mitchell Tobin. 1997. "The Disparate Racial Neighborhood Impacts of Metropolitan Restructuring." *Urban Affairs Review* 36, no. 6: 797–824.

Galster, George, Roberto Quercia, and Alvaro Cortes. 2000. "Identifying Neighborhood Thresholds: An Empirical Exploration." *Housing Policy Debate* 11, no. 3: 701–32.

Galster, George, Roberto Quercia, and others. 2003. "The Fortunes of Poor Neighborhoods." *Urban Affairs Review* 39, no. 2: 205–27.

Galster, George, and Jerome Rothenberg. 1991. "Filtering in a Segmented Model of Urban Housing Markets." *Journal of Planning Education and Research* 11, no. 1: 37–50.

Galster, George, Peter Tatian, and Robin Smith. 1999. "The Impact of Neighbors Who Use Section 8 Certificates on Property Values." *Housing Policy Debate* 10, no. 4: 879–917.

Galster, George, Peter Tatian, and Charlene Wilson. 1999. "Alternative Measures of the Financial Condition of the Multifamily Housing Stock." *Housing Policy Debate* 10, no. 1: 59–73.

Galster, George, Peter Tatian, and others. 2003. *Why NOT In My Back Yard? Neighborhood Impacts of Deconcentrating Assisted Housing.* New Brunswick, N.J.: Center for Urban Policy Research Press.

Gephart, Martha. 1997. "Neighborhoods and Communities as Contexts for Development." In *Context and Consequences for Children,* vol. 1 of *Neighborhood Poverty,* edited by Jeanne Brooks-Gunn, Gregory J. Duncan, and J. Lawrence Aber, pp. 1–43. New York: Russell Sage Foundation.

Goering, John, and others. 1995. *Promoting Housing Choice in HUD's Rental Assistance Programs.* U.S. Department of Housing and Urban Development, Office of Policy Development and Research.

Grigsby, William, and others. 1987. *The Dynamics of Neighbourhood Change and Decline.* Progress in Planning Series 28. London, U.K.: Pergamon.

Guest, Avery M. 1974. "Neighborhood Life Cycles and Social Status." *Economic Geography* 50, no. 3: 228–43.

Hannon, Lance. 2002. "Criminal Opportunity Theory and the Relationship between Poverty and Property Crime." *Sociological Spectrum* 22, no. 3: 363–81.

Hannon, Lance E., and James Defronzo. 1998. "Welfare and Property Crime." *Justice Quarterly* 15, no. 2: 273–88.

Haveman, Robert, and Barbara Wolfe. 1994. *Succeeding Generations: On the Effects of Investments in Children.* New York: Russell Sage Foundation.

Hogan, James. 1996. *Scattered-Site Housing: Characteristics and Consequences.* U.S. Department of Housing and Urban Development, Office of Policy Development and Research.

Hoover, Edgar M., and Raymond Vernon. 1959. *Anatomy of a Metropolis.* Harvard University Press.

Hsiao, Cheng. 1986. *Analysis of Panel Data.* Cambridge University Press.

Ioannides, Yannis M., and Linda Datcher Loury. 2004. "Job Information Networks, Neighborhood Effects, and Inequality." *Journal of Economic Literature* 42, no. 2: 1056–093.

Jargowsky, Paul. 1997. *Poverty and Place.* New York: Russell Sage Foundation.

———. 2003. "Stunning Progress, Hidden Problems: The Dramatic Decline of Concentrated Poverty in the 1990s." Living Cities Census Series. Brookings Institution Center on Urban and Metropolitan Policy (May 19) (www.brookings.edu/urban).

Jencks, Christopher, and Susan Mayer. 1990. "The Social Consequences of Growing Up in a Poor Neighborhood." In *Inner-City Poverty in the United States,* edited by Lawrence E. Lynn and M. F. H. McGeary, pp. 111–86. Washington: National Academy Press.

Kingsley, G. Thomas, and Kathryn L. S. Pettit. 2003. "Concentrated Poverty: A Change in Course." Neighborhood Change in Urban America Series. Washington: Urban Institute (www.urban.org/nnip).

Kmenta, Jan. 1986. *Elements of Econometrics.* 2d ed. New York: Macmillan.

Kornhauser, Ruth. 1978. *Social Sources of Delinquency.* University of Chicago Press.

Kozol, Jonathan. 1991. *Savage Inequalities.* New York: Harper.

Krivo, Lauren, and Ruth Peterson. 1996. "Extremely Disadvantaged Neighborhoods and Urban Crime." *Social Forces* 75, no. 2: 619–50.

Lauria, Mickey. 1998. "A New Model of Neighborhood Change: Reconsidering the Role of White Flight." *Housing Policy Debate* 9, no. 2: 395–424.

Lee, Barrett, and Peter Wood. 1991. "Is Neighbourhood Succession Place-Specific?" *Demography* 28, no. 1: 21–40.

Leventhal, Tama, and Jeanne Brooks-Gunn. 2000. "The Neighborhoods They Live In." *Psychological Bulletin* 126, no. 2: 309–37.

Ludwig, Jens, and Simeon Stolzberg. 1995. "HUD's Moving to Opportunity Demonstration: Uncertain Benefits, Unlikely Costs, Unfortunate Politics." *Georgetown Public Policy Review* 1, no. 1: 25–37.

Lupton, Ruth. 2003. " 'Neighbourhood Effects': Can We Measure Them and Does It Matter?" CASE Paper 73. London School of Economics, Centre for Analysis of Social Exclusion (September).

Maclennan, Duncan. 1982. *Housing Economics: An Applied Approach.* London, U.K.: Longmans.

Manski, Charles. 1995. *Identification Problems in the Social Sciences.* Harvard University Press.

———. 2000. "Economic Analysis of Social Interactions." *Journal of Economic Perspectives* 14, no. 3: 115–36.

Martinez, Pedro., and John E. Richters. 1993. "Children's Distress Symptoms Associated with Violence Exposure." Part 2 of "The NIMH Community Violence Project." *Psychiatry* 56, no. 1: 22–35.

McLanahan, Sarah, and others. 2003. "The Fragile Families and Child Well-Being Study: Baseline National Report." Princeton University, Bendheim-Thomen Center for Research on Child Well-Being.

Meen, Geoffrey. 2004. "Non-Linear Behaviour in Local Housing Markets and the Implications for Sustainable Mixed-Income Communities in England." University of Reading, United Kingdom.

———. 2006. "Modelling Local Deprivation and Segregation in England." University of Reading, United Kingdom.

Morenoff, Jeffrey, Robert Sampson, and Stephen Raudenbush. 2001. "Neighborhood Inequality, Collective Efficacy, and the Spatial Dynamics of Homicide." *Criminology* 39, no. 3: 517–60.

Murphy, Kevin, Andrei Shleifer, and Robert Vishny. 1993. "Why Is Rent Seeking So Costly to Growth?" *American Economic Review* 83, no. 2: 409–14.

Murray, Michael. 2006. "Avoiding Invalid Instruments and Coping with Weak Instruments." *Journal of Economic Perspectives* 20, no. 4: 111–32.

Neopolitan, Jerome. 1994. "Poverty and Property Crime: The Moderating Effects of Population Size and Concentration." *Sociological Spectrum* 14, no. 2: 181–91.

Park, Robert. 1952. *Human Communities*. Glencoe, Ill.: Free Press.

Peterson, George, and Kale Williams. 1996. *Housing Mobility: What Has It Accomplished and What Is Its Promise?* Washington: Urban Institute Press.

Polikoff, Alexander. 1994. *Housing Policy and Urban Poverty*. Washington: Center for Housing Policy.

Rasmussen, David. 1994. "Spatial Economic Development, Education, and the New Poverty." *International Regional Science Review* 16, no. 1–2: 107–17.

Robinson, Matthew. 1999. "Lifestyles, Routine Activities, and Residential Burglary Victimization." *Journal of Crime and Justice* 22, no. 1: 27–56.

Rosenbaum, James. 1995. "Changing the Geography of Opportunity by Expanding Residential Choice: Lessons from the Gautreaux Program." *Housing Policy Debate* 6, no. 1: 231–69.

Rothenberg, Jerome, and others. 1991. *The Maze of Urban Housing Markets*. University of Chicago Press.

Sampson, Robert. 1992. "Family Management and Child Development." In *Facts, Frameworks, and Forecasts: Advances in Criminological Theory*, vol. 3, edited by Joan McCord, pp. 63–93. New Brunswick, N.J.: Transaction Books.

———. 1997. "Collective Regulation of Adolescent Misbehavior: Validation Results for Eighty Chicago Neighborhoods." *Journal of Adolescent Research* 12, no. 2: 227–44.

Sampson, Robert, and W. Byron Groves. 1989. "Community Structure and Crime: Testing Social Disorganization Theory." *American Journal of Sociology* 94, no. 4: 774–802.

Sampson, Robert, Jeffrey Morenoff, and Felton Earls. 1999. "Beyond Social Capital: Spatial Dynamics of Collective Efficacy for Children." *American Sociological Review* 64 (October): 633–60.

Sampson, Robert, Jeffrey Morenoff, and Thomas Gannon-Rowley. 2002. "Assessing 'Neighborhood Effects': Social Processes and New Directions in Research." *Annual Review of Sociology* 28: 443–78.

Schwirian, Kent. 1983. "Models of Neighbourhood Change." *Annual Review of Sociology* 9: 83–102.

Shear, William. 1983. "Urban Housing Rehabilitation and Move Decisions." *Southern Economic Journal* 49, no. 2: 1030–052.

South, Scott, and Eric Baumer. 2000. "Deciphering Community and Race Effects on Adolescent Pre-Marital Childbearing." *Social Forces* 78, no. 4: 1379–407.

Stewart, James, and Thomas Hyclak. 1986. "Determinants of Household Expenditures for Additions, Alterations, Replacements, and Repairs to Owner-Occupied Residences." Pennsylvania State University, Department of Economics.

Sullivan, Mercer. 1989. *Getting Paid: Youth Crime and Work in the Inner City.* Cornell University Press.

Taeuber, Karl, and Alma Taeuber. 1965. *Negroes in Cities.* Chicago: Aldine.

Taub, Richard, D. Garth Taylor, and Jan Dunham. 1984. *Paths of Neighborhood Change.* University of Chicago Press.

Temkin, Kenneth, and William Rohe. 1996. "Neighborhood Change and Urban Policy." *Journal of Planning Education and Research* 15, no. 3: 159–70.

U.S. Department of Housing and Urban Development (HUD). 1996. *Expanding Housing Choices for HUD-Assisted Families.* Office of Policy Development and Research.

Vandell, Kerry. 1981. "The Effects of Racial Composition on Neighbourhood Succession." *Urban Studies* 18, no. 3: 315–33.

van Dijk, Jan J. M. 1994. "Understanding Crime Rates: On the Interactions between the Rational Choices of Victims and Offenders." *British Journal of Criminology* 34, no. 2: 105–20.

Varady, David. 1986. *Neighborhood Upgrading: A Realistic Assessment.* State University of New York Press.

Vartanian, Tom. 1999. "Adolescent Neighborhood Effects on Labor Market and Economic Outcomes." *Social Service Review* 73, no. 2: 142–67.

Wacquant, Loic. 1993. "Urban Outcasts: Stigma and Division in the Black American Ghetto and the French Periphery." *International Journal of Urban and Regional Research* 17, no. 3: 366–83.

Weinberg, Bruce, Patricia Reagan, and Jeffrey Yankow. 2004. "Do Neighborhoods Affect Work Behavior? Evidence from the NLSY79." *Journal of Labor Economics* 22, no. 4: 891–924.

Wilson, William J. 1987. *The Truly Disadvantaged.* University of Chicago Press.

———. 1996. *When Work Disappears.* New York: Alfred A. Knopf.

Wolman, Harold, Cary Lichtman, and Suzie Barnes. 1991. "The Impact of Credentials, Skill Levels, Worker Training, and Motivation on Employment Outcomes." *Economic Development Quarterly* 5, no. 2: 140–51.

4

Spillovers and Subsidized Housing: The Impact of Subsidized Rental Housing on Neighborhoods

INGRID GOULD ELLEN

At a congressional hearing in 1948, Rep. A. S. Mike Monroney argued that the construction of new, subsidized rental housing improves the surrounding neighborhood and in so doing raises property tax revenues. "One of the principal arguments, with which I go along," he stated, "is that the establishment of a housing project in a city raises the assessed valuation for blocks around it and puts back onto the municipal tax rolls a great deal more money than is taken off by the land that is occupied by these public housing projects" (quoted in Fisher 1959, p. 159). Monroney was not alone in his beliefs; when the federal public housing program was first established in the late 1930s, neighborhood benefits were a key justification.

Yet it is hard to imagine a member of Congress making a similar argument today. The current assumption is that the production of subsidized rental housing, if anything, accelerates neighborhood decline—"There goes the neighborhood" is the common refrain. Partially as a result, the United States has seen the policy pendulum swing away from place-based housing investment toward demand-side housing programs, such as housing vouchers.

Despite this policy shift, many of the local developers and nonprofits that build and manage subsidized rental housing continue to believe that their efforts not only provide shelter but help to revitalize communities as well, which raises the obvious question: Who is right? This chapter revisits this critical policy issue, exploring how and why investments in subsidized rental housing might affect surrounding neighborhoods. Unlike most of the existing research, which simply asks whether subsidized housing has a negative or positive impact, my aim is to explore the factors that shape the direction and size of the effect. For though recent research on this topic suggests that subsidized rental housing can have positive impacts on communities, that has not been the case for all housing developments. The aim here is to look across a variety of empirical papers on the topic to glean lessons for policymakers about the types of investments in subsidized rental housing most likely to generate positive spillovers to the surrounding community.

The Spillover Effects of Subsidized Rental Housing

Although the impacts of subsidized rental housing developments on communities may be smaller than those of their market-rate counterparts, theory does not offer clear guidance about the direction of the effects, which are likely to vary with the housing and the circumstances. Amy Ellen Schwartz and others (2006) identify five general mechanisms through which subsidized housing might affect the value of neighboring properties: the removal effect, the physical structure effect, market effects, the population growth effect, and population mix effects. This framework can also be used to understand how subsidized rental housing might affect neighborhood demographics, services, and quality of life.

Removal Effect

The construction of subsidized rental housing can affect a community simply because of what it removes. In urban areas, subsidized housing often replaces abandoned, boarded-up buildings or littered, vacant lots, disamenities that can signal that the community is disorganized and that criminal activity will go largely unchecked.[1] The removal of such blight can help to make a neighborhood more attractive and safe and thereby catalyze neighborhood revitalization. Of course, subsidized rental housing may also replace a desirable use, like a park, an attractive set of older buildings, or simply open space. In these cases, removal effects would most likely be negative.

Physical Structure Effect

The construction or rehabilitation of a building or set of buildings may also have an independent effect, over and above the removal of the prior use. In particular, a new subsidized project that is viewed as unattractive or not fitting with the existing character of a community, or a project that is not cared for over time, may detract from the appeal of a community. Alternatively, an attractive, high-quality, well-maintained building that fits in nicely with the existing properties can enhance the overall design and appearance of a community.

1. Skogan (1990); James Q. Wilson and George Kelling, "Broken Windows: The Police and Neighborhood Safety," *Atlantic Monthly,* March 1982, pp. 29–38.

Market Effects

Developers sometimes avoid blighted neighborhoods because they fear that investments there will not be profitable. By ensuring a certain level of activity, subsidized housing developments may help to allay such fears. Moreover, if subsidized developments include market-rate units, they may signal to developers that an area is viable and thereby attract additional investment. On the other hand, the creation of new subsidized housing may also have a depressing effect on the neighborhood by glutting the local market with low-rent housing and crowding out unsubsidized, private investment (see Murray 1999; Sinai and Waldfogel 2005; Malpezzi and Vandell 2002).

Population Growth Effect

The construction of new housing is likely to bring in new residents and thus increase population.[2] On the one hand, this population increase might make local streets safer, promote new commercial activity, and thereby make the neighborhood more desirable, especially in areas that have been depopulated in the past. On the other hand, such growth might be detrimental to a community, resulting in congested streets, overcrowded schools, and strains on local police and infrastructure.

Population Mix Effects

The impacts of new housing may depend not only on how many people move into a neighborhood but also who moves into it and how their incomes and ethnicity compare with those of existing residents. Such changes may not be linear—lower-income in-movers may make little difference in high-income areas, but they may risk destabilizing neighborhoods that already have high concentrations of poverty and joblessness (see Ellen and Turner 1997).[3] The racial or ethnic composition of occupants may be relevant, as well. Research has shown that after increases in the African American population in a community, white households—and white homeowners, in particular—tend to report lower neighborhood satisfaction and are more likely to move (Ellen 2000). Other research suggests that during the 1970s and 1980s, housing prices were typically lower in neighborhoods with greater shares of nonwhites (Kiel and Zabel 1996). The construction of subsidized rental housing may also lead to a more stable population, and a more stable community, in turn, since households living in subsidized housing tend to live in their units for longer periods of time.

---

2. Of course, if the subsidized construction fully crowds out private construction, then the population will remain steady. But while most research on this topic finds evidence of crowding out, no paper has found it to be complete (see Murray 1999; Sinai and Waldfogel 2005).

3. Children growing up in communities characterized by high rates of poverty and joblessness will be disadvantaged by their lack of exposure to role models of successful working adults. Crime may increase as alternatives are less apparent, and local schools may struggle, perhaps because they face difficulties in recruiting strong teachers or because local parents are typically less educated (see Ellen and Turner 1997).

Naturally, the size and direction of all these effects are likely to vary across programs and even particular projects, depending on what the housing replaces, the size, design, and upkeep of the development, the characteristics of the tenants, housing market conditions, and the characteristics of the surrounding neighborhood. In general, investments in housing—the rehabilitation of old housing or the construction of new housing—can be expected to have positive spillover effects on the surrounding community, especially when that housing replaces an abandoned or otherwise blighted site. Those positive impacts might be tempered to some degree, however, by poor or incongruous design, deficient management and upkeep, or the perception that tenants—either because of their lower relative incomes or different ethnic compositions—will make undesirable neighbors.

Existing Evidence of the Spillover Effects on Property Values

Identifying and quantifying the neighborhood spillover effects generated by housing investment is quite difficult. The first challenge lies in measuring any neighborhood improvements. Sources of data are hard to come by, and many of the outcomes one might wish to capture (for example, social capital and collective efficacy) are difficult to quantify.[4] However, because land is immobile, to the extent that any of these outcomes occur they should be capitalized into, or reflected in, higher property values. Put simply, if a neighborhood becomes a better place to live, people will be willing to pay more to live there. Thus much of the existing research measures neighborhood benefits by increases in the value of surrounding properties.[5]

Given the conventional view that the likely effect of subsidized rental housing developments is to accelerate neighborhood decline, it is perhaps not surprising that the literature on this subject has virtually all been framed to ask whether these subsidized housing developments reduce surrounding property values.[6] Yet contrary to the conventional wisdom, empirical research yields inconclusive evidence about the nature of spillover effects generated by subsidized rental housing. Most

4. *Collective efficacy* is defined as the willingness of local residents to intervene for the common good. For more on the concept, see Robert J. Sampson, Stephen W. Raudenbush, and Felton Earls, "Neighborhoods and Violent Crime: A Multilevel Study of Collective Efficacy," *Science,* August 15, 1997, pp. 918–24.

5. Of course, it may be true that neighborhood changes occur even when little change in property values is apparent, perhaps because these underlying changes in services and conditions cancel one another out. Consider the effects of an increase in population resulting from new housing. On the one hand, this increase is likely to make a neighborhood safer; on the other hand, it may lead to unwanted noise and congestion.

6. One exception is Hugh Nourse (1963), who considers whether federally subsidized housing might deliver benefits to the surrounding neighborhood. But this paper was published more than forty years ago, almost ten years before the demolition of Pruitt Igoe, the infamous St. Louis public housing development that was beset by crime, vandalism, and disrepair and ultimately torn down by the local housing authority in 1972, just sixteen years after its completion. This was clearly a time when attitudes about subsidized rental housing differed.

of these past studies either rely on cross-sectional data or do not have access to project completion dates and therefore cannot determine whether subsidized housing is systematically located in weak or strong neighborhoods or whether subsidized housing leads to neighborhood decline or improvement (see, for example, Green, Malpezzi, and Seah 2003; Lee, Culhane, and Wachter 1999; Lyons and Loveridge 1993).[7]

Several studies have attempted to disentangle the causality problem by estimating impacts based on a comparison of price changes of properties within the vicinity of new housing with price changes citywide, while controlling for idiosyncratic features of the neighborhood (typically through census-tract fixed effects). Xavier de Souza Briggs, Joe Darden, and Angela Aidala (1999), for instance, use a census-tract fixed-effects model to examine price changes surrounding seven scattered-site public housing developments on property values in neighborhoods in Yonkers, New York. They find little effect on the surrounding area. Anna Santiago, George Galster, and Peter Tatian (2001) use a similar model to estimate the impact of the Denver Housing Authority's scattered-site public housing program on the sales prices of surrounding single-family homes. Testing for both changes in price levels and trends after completion, they find that proximity to dispersed public housing units is associated with an increase, if anything, in the prices of single-family homes.

Although these two studies go a long way to challenge the common belief that scattered-site public housing reduces the value of surrounding properties, neither reveals anything about possible differences in impacts across different types of programs. To address this gap, my colleagues at New York University and I have written a series of papers investigating the impacts of subsidized rental housing in New York City.[8] Although limited to a single city, these studies offer more opportunities to compare impacts across programs, in part because of the sheer scale of the activity in New York. From 1986 to roughly 2000, New York City engaged in a massive effort to rebuild its housing stock, funded with a mix of city, state, and federal dollars. Much of the effort was focused on the large stock of dilapidated housing and vacant land that the city had acquired through tax foreclosure proceedings during the 1970s.

During this roughly fifteen-year period, city officials used close to 100 different programs to build or rehabilitate nearly 200,000 units of housing, most of it rental. (Specific program features differed, but in general, the city gave land or buildings

7. Richard Green, Stephen Malpezzi, and Kiat-Ying Seah (2003) estimate a repeat sales model and use an interesting gravity measure of distance to LIHTC development sites. Nonetheless, they do not have access to project completion dates, which makes it impossible to interpret their coefficients on distance as impact measures. To do so, one has to assume that the coefficient on distance to LIHTC sites was zero before project completion.

8. See Ellen and others (2007); Ellen and Voicu (2006); Schwartz and others (2006); Schill and others (2002). The latter two papers also explore neighborhood impacts of owner-occupied housing, but the bulk of the housing studied is rental.

or both, together with low-interest financing, to nonprofit and for-profit developers who would then undertake the rehabilitation or construction and ultimately own and manage the buildings.) Another 58,000 units of federally subsidized rental housing were also built in New York City from 1977 to 2000, through the Section 8, Section 202, and public housing programs.[9] The unique scale of the efforts gives us statistical power to identify impacts, and the diversity of the city's neighborhoods as well as its programs allows us to compare and contrast the impacts of different programs (both federal and local) in different circumstances.

Although the specifications differ across individual papers, the core model used is a hedonic regression model with a difference-in-difference specification. Intuitively, the estimated impacts are the difference between the change in property values in the vicinity of subsidized housing investment before and after the investment and price changes of comparable properties farther away but still in the same neighborhood. We include census-tract fixed effects to control for idiosyncratic neighborhood characteristics and neighborhood*time interaction variables to control for idiosyncratic price trends in the local neighborhood. We also include variables that allow us to investigate the extent to which impact estimates vary with project size, housing characteristics, and submarkets in the city.

In general, our papers find that the city-assisted programs have had significant, positive effects, far larger than those estimated for subsidized housing in other cities. Before rehabilitation or construction, these city-assisted housing sites—typically, abandoned properties or vacant lots that the city had taken over in the 1970s—appear to have significantly depressed the value of neighboring properties.

As shown in figure 4-1, properties located right next door to the typical city-assisted project (distance = 0) sold for almost 30 percent less than comparable properties located farther away but still in the same neighborhood. As expected, the price discount declines with distance from the site. Nonetheless, as the figure also shows, prices remained significantly lower 1,000 feet away from assisted housing sites. Specifically, the prices of properties located 1,000 feet from assisted housing sites were almost 15 percent lower than the prices of comparable properties selling at the exact same time in the surrounding neighborhood. It cannot be said for certain that these blighted, city-owned sites fully explained the lower property values in the 1,000-foot rings surrounding them, but it is likely that they were a contributor.

A second, and perhaps more critical, result is that New York City's investment in these abandoned, tax-foreclosed properties appears to have yielded significant positive benefits. Figure 4-2 shows the extent to which the gap between prices of properties near assisted housing sites and those in the surrounding neighborhood

9. There were also roughly twenty thousand units built through the LIHTC program, but most of these units also received city assistance through the city's ten-year plan for housing and are thus counted in the total number of units assisted by the city (Schill and others 2002).

Figure 4-1. *Baseline Difference in Sale Prices between Properties Located Close to City-Assisted Rental Housing and Comparable Properties in Surrounding Neighborhood, New York City, 1980–99*[a]

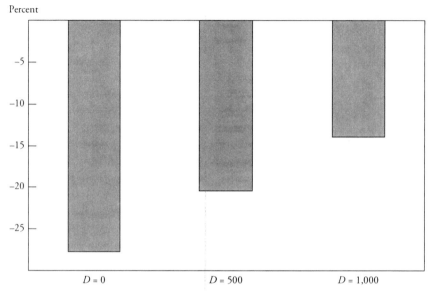

Percent

D = 0   D = 500   D = 1,000

Source: Data from New York City Department of Finance (property transactions); New York City Department of Finance, Real Property Assessment Data file (property characteristics); New York City Department of Housing Preservation and Development (subsidized housing completions).

a. Estimates are for the "average" city-assisted rental project, defined as the rental project in the vicinity of the average sale within 2,000 feet of a city-assisted rental housing unit. This is a project of 127 units. D = distance in feet from the assisted property.

fell after completion—in other words, how much prices rose in the vicinity of the completed subsidized housing relative to other comparable properties in the same neighborhood. Immediately after completion, prices of properties right next to city-assisted housing rose by 8.9 percentage points more than the prices of properties in the surrounding neighborhood. Moreover, these impacts grow over time, perhaps as families move into the housing and the population rises. Five years after completion, properties next to city-assisted housing had appreciated 11.4 percentage points more than other comparable properties in the neighborhood.

Impacts shrink with distance from the city-assisted housing, as one would expect, but the figure shows significant positive effects at 1,000 feet from subsidized housing investment as well. Building more units appears to bring a greater benefit, though this marginal effect declines as the number of units increases.

Our analyses suggest that these relationships are causal, that is, the investments that New York City made during the 1980s and 1990s to build new subsidized housing and rebuild dilapidated properties as affordable housing actually generated

Figure 4-2. *Impact of Proximity to Assisted Housing on Neighborhood Property Values, Change over Time, New York City, 1980–99*[a]

Ring-tract price gap reduction, percent

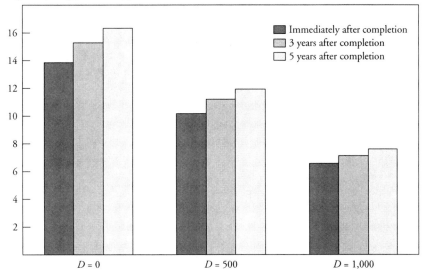

Source: Data from New York City Department of Finance (property transactions); New York City Department of Finance, Real Property Assessment Data file (property characteristics); New York City Department of Housing Preservation and Development (subsidized housing completions).

a. The figure presents the reduction over time in the gap between prices of properties near assisted rental housing and those in the surrounding neighborhood. Estimates are for the "average" city-assisted project, defined as the project in the vicinity of the average sale in a 2,000-foot ring. This is a project of 250 units, of which 55.5 percent are multifamily rental units. D = distance in feet from the assisted property.

improvements in the surrounding neighborhoods. Although there are plausible alternative explanations for these price patterns, the evidence does not support them. For example, though city officials may have hoped to pick "winning" sites, where prices were going to appreciate anyway, even in the absence of investment, they had little latitude in their selection. By the end of our study period, virtually all available sites in New York City had been developed. Moreover, the results are robust to various different specifications and statistical techniques.

The magnitude of these neighborhood benefits appears to be substantial. Our analysis of costs and benefits suggests that New York City's housing investments delivered a tax benefit to the city that exceeded the cost of the city's subsidies and amounted to some 75 percent of total public investment, which includes both state and federal dollars.[10] It is worth emphasizing that in these calculations we did

10. For more detail on these tax benefit estimates, see Schwartz and others (2006).

not consider the benefits enjoyed by the households that actually reside in the new subsidized housing. Adding such individual benefits would yield even more favorable estimates.

Our research on federally assisted rental housing in New York City yields more-mixed conclusions (see Ellen and others 2007). We find evidence that housing produced through the Section 202 and Low Income Housing Tax Credit (LIHTC) programs generates sustained increases in property values in the surrounding community. By contrast, Section 8 and public housing appear to lead to reductions in property values, although these initially negative effects diminish over time and, in the case of public housing, dissipate within three years of completion. Furthermore, impacts are very sensitive to scale, with larger Section 8 and public housing projects generating more negative impacts. Interestingly, however, these marginal impacts diminish with scale, at least in the case of public housing. In other words, whereas larger projects generally result in larger initial declines, adding another unit to a 500-unit public housing development has a less negative effect than adding another unit to a 100-unit development.

In summary, the New York City research suggests that subsidized rental housing created through the Section 202 program, the LIHTC program, and New York City's many local housing programs has delivered significant neighborhood benefits. (Since many of the city programs make use of tax credits, there is, in fact, considerable overlap between the latter two categories.) By contrast, the research finds that housing built through the Section 8 and public housing programs is associated with reductions in property values, at least initially.

Exploring the Heterogeneity of Impacts

The foregoing discussion makes clear that impacts differ across programs and circumstances. A key question for policymakers is why. Why, for instance, did the tax-credit developments and the city-sponsored housing in New York City appear to generate more positive impacts than housing built through the Section 8 and public housing programs? This section aims to summarize what the existing research can tell us about the types of rental housing investments most likely to generate positive community spillovers. I focus mostly on the differences in impacts across housing programs in New York City (both federal and local), since most of the other empirical studies on this topic examine the impacts of housing built through just a single program. Where possible, however, I also speculate about the root causes of differences between findings in New York City and those in other cities, as well as impact differences found within studies examining assisted housing built outside of New York City.[11]

---

11. I turn mostly to the two studies employing data and methods closest to the New York City studies: Briggs, Darden, and Aidala (1999) and Santiago, Galster, and Tatian (2001).

Siting

Existing research offers some lessons about where to site new rental housing. The experience of New York City suggests that focusing on blighted sites can lead to greater spillovers. Compared with federal efforts in the city and most housing programs elsewhere, the New York City programs focused more explicitly on neighborhood revitalization. One of the key aims of the city's housing efforts—evident from speeches and documents describing the programs—was to revitalize the neighborhoods that had suffered from disinvestment and arson during the 1970s (Schill and others 2002). As a result, city officials in New York chose sites (either buildings or vacant land) that were extremely blighted. This focus on improving blighted sites may help to explain the greater benefits delivered by city-assisted housing.

The evidence is more mixed about what neighborhoods to build in. On the one hand, the research in New York suggests that average-sized projects generate more positive impacts in neighborhoods that are more distressed (Schwartz and others 2006). On the other hand, the spillover benefits of very small projects developed in New York appear to be weaker in more distressed or blighted neighborhoods, perhaps because building just a few new housing units in a highly blighted area may simply not be enough to make a difference.[12] Moreover, the research on federally subsidized rental housing suggests that adding significantly more subsidized housing and low-income households to already vulnerable, low-income communities can be detrimental. Elsewhere, for instance, my colleagues and I (Ellen and others 2007) find that the effects of Section 8 housing are more negative in lower-income areas. Similarly, Santiago, Galster, and Tatian (2001) find that while scattered-site public housing generates positive effects in affluent, white areas, it leads to consistently negative spillover effects in substantially African American, low-income communities.

Scale

In general, larger projects are expected to have more dramatic effects (either positive or negative) on a community, and this is typically what the research finds. Robert Lyons and Scott Loveridge (1993) find, for instance, that greater numbers of subsidized units are associated with larger reductions in property values. Similarly, my colleagues and I have found that larger public housing and Section 8 projects generate more negative impacts (Ellen and others 2007). Meanwhile, studies finding positive impacts tend to find that impacts of larger projects are more positive (Schwartz and others 2006; Santiago, Galster, and Tatian 2001).

That said, the studies examining subsidized housing in New York find evidence that scale effects are nonlinear. Specifically, the marginal effects of additional sub-

---

12. In general, city officials were fairly systematic about the sequence of investment, staging their efforts so that investments were clustered and full blocks and groups of blocks were rehabilitated at the same time, which may have helped to enhance neighborhood benefits (Schill and others 2002).

sidized housing units—whether positive or negative—tend to diminish in magnitude with the number of units (Schwartz and others 2006; Ellen and others 2007). In other words, contrary to what many believe, the impact of adding additional housing units will actually be progressively smaller in larger developments.

Type of Housing

Few clear lessons emerge about different types of housing. Structure type is surprisingly irrelevant in the New York City studies; the magnitude of the spillover effect is unchanged whether the subsidized housing consists of single-family homes, two- to four-unit buildings, or multifamily apartment buildings (Schwartz and others 2006). Of course, it is possible that neighbors are more sensitive to structure type in other, lower-density cities. Among studies outside of New York City, the two that find the most positive impacts are those that examine scattered-site public housing, which is typically made up of in-fill, single-family, and two-family houses (Santiago, Galster, and Tatian 2001; Briggs, Darden, and Aidala 1999). As for type of construction, the New York City studies also fail to find any difference between the neighborhood spillover effects of units created through the rehabilitation of vacant buildings and those generated by in-fill, new construction projects, suggesting perhaps that the presence of an untended vacant lot can be as destructive to the surrounding community as a vacant, dilapidated building (Schwartz and others 2006).

Tenant Characteristics

Unfortunately, no study has had access to project-specific information about tenant characteristics. However, assumptions about tenant characteristics can be made, given the rules of the programs governing the developments. For example, in our analysis of federal rental housing programs, my colleagues and I have found that housing programs targeted to the elderly typically have more positive impacts than those aimed at families (Ellen and others 2007), suggesting that low-income elderly tenants are typically more welcomed, or less feared, than low-income families. In addition, among the programs targeted to families, those that house the lowest-income tenants (Section 8 and public housing) have the most negative effects. These initially negative impacts appear to dissipate fairly quickly, however, at least in the case of public housing.

Significantly, in examining the impact of the New York City programs, we did not find any evidence that the share of homeless tenants in a project depressed benefits (Schill and others 2002). This may be because the programs in New York City all aimed to achieve some mix of incomes, so formerly homeless families were housed together with working families.

Indeed, one reason why the city-sponsored efforts in New York City appear to have yielded more positive impacts than the traditional federal programs may be just this focus on income mixing. As compared with federal programs, the city-run programs in New York placed a fair amount of emphasis on mixing incomes within projects. Rather than concentrating the very poorest households in particular neighborhoods or projects, the city programs generally aimed to house a mixture of low- and moderate-income tenants (Salama, Schill, and Roberts 2003).

Management and Ownership

No studies to date evaluate the impact of the quality or style of management. We can, however, draw some inferences about ownership. Ioan Voicu and I (Ellen and Voicu 2006), for instance, find some differences between the impacts of housing developed by nonprofit and for-profit organizations. In particular, neighborhood spillover benefits appear to be somewhat more sustained over time when rehabilitation projects are undertaken by nonprofit developers. This finding is consistent with theoretical predictions. In the presence of information asymmetries with respect to housing quality, nonprofits are likely to invest more in developing and maintaining features that benefit the broader community than their for-profit counterparts.

However, in the case of small projects, nonprofit organizations appear to deliver significantly smaller neighborhood benefits than their for-profit counterparts. That scale makes such a difference to nonprofit impacts may be explained by the capacity issues that often challenge smaller nonprofits. It might also reflect the fact that projects developed by smaller nonprofits typically lack community amenities.

That the public housing developed in New York City appears to have yielded lesser positive neighborhood impacts than the projects owned and managed by private developers may also be rooted, at least in part, in the different incentives, resources, and constraints faced by public and private actors. (That said, the housing program that appears to deliver the most negative spillover effects is Section 8 housing, which is also privately owned.)

Finally, the most important distinction may be between federal and local programs. The housing built through city-assisted programs in New York appears to have generated significantly greater neighborhood benefits than housing built through federal programs. (One of the two federal programs that appeared to generate positive impacts, the LIHTC, was administered locally, in partnership with private developers, while the other was aimed at the elderly.) Perhaps local policymakers and developers simply have a greater motivation, as well as greater capacity owing to their local knowledge, to build housing that will benefit the surrounding community.

Context

Given that the housing delivering the greatest benefits is found in New York City, exploring the New York context is instructive. Many of the features that appear to have worked so well in New York City—the focus on income mixing and neighborhood revitalization—could surely be transplanted to other cities and to other times. But it is also possible that New York City is simply different, as we hear all the time. Certainly, it is hard to imagine other cities replicating New York's efforts at the same tremendous scale.

Moreover, while additional housing might trigger the removal of buildings from the housing stock in weak markets, public subsidies for housing production and rehabilitation may serve as far more effective spurs to neighborhood revitalization in tighter housing markets such as New York City. During the 1990s, the city's population was growing rapidly, and structural barriers inhibited the construction of affordable private housing. The result was a tight housing market. New York's extraordinarily high density may also magnify spillover effects, since the city's buildings tend to have many more close neighbors than buildings in other cities. So some caution is warranted in extrapolating the conclusions here to other cities, especially those that are economically weaker.

Conclusions

The evidence clearly fails to support the notion that subsidized rental housing will, as a general matter, depress neighborhood property values or otherwise undermine communities. Both theory and existing evidence suggest that the neighborhood impacts of subsidized rental housing will differ depending on where it is built, the scale of the development, the characteristics of its tenants, and the nature of ownership and management. Reading across these studies, it is possible to identify a few guidelines for policymakers who wish to make the types of rental housing investments most likely to deliver neighborhood benefits.

First, in siting housing, policymakers should pay attention to what is being replaced. Housing that replaces an existing disamenity will naturally benefit a community more than housing that replaces an otherwise desirable use. Even in affluent communities, there are often unattractive and underused sites that depress the value of surrounding properties. Attention should also be paid to the larger neighborhood context. Renovating a single home on an otherwise abandoned block is likely to do little. Concentrating too much lower-income housing in already low-income and vulnerable neighborhoods, however, may be harmful. And of course, policymakers should consider impacts on tenants, who are likely to do better when living in more economically integrated communities.

Second, tenants matter, but perhaps not in the ways people think. The experience of city-assisted housing in New York suggests that the share of formerly homeless families in a development makes little difference to neighborhood impacts. On the other hand, there is at least suggestive evidence that developments that have some mix of incomes (such as those developed through New York City's programs) may yield greater benefits to the surrounding area than those that house only low-income tenants.

Third, scale matters. Projects need to be large enough, especially in distressed areas, to overcome the blight around them. But they need not be too large. In New York City, we find that the marginal effect of an additional unit appears to diminish with overall size. Thus for housing that delivers neighborhood benefits, total benefits will be maximized through building a set of moderate-sized developments in several neighborhoods, rather than a single, very large development.

Finally, research in New York suggests that housing created through local government programs has done more to benefit surrounding neighborhoods than that created through federal programs, owing to differing incentives or knowledge (or both). And local governments will be well-served by providing housing subsidies to either nonprofit or for-profit organizations, though there appears to be greater heterogeneity within the nonprofit sector (Ellen and Voicu 2006).

Other factors that researchers have yet to explore also may matter. The extent of ongoing maintenance is likely to be important, for instance. The nature of the design and the extent to which it fits into the existing character of the community are also likely to make a difference. Indeed, one of the unique features of the subsidized housing produced in New York City is that much of it was created through the gut rehabilitation of vacant, uninhabitable buildings. Although these buildings were no more than shells, the city chose not to demolish them and instead used the existing structures for new housing units. By definition, this meant that the design of the new housing built by the city fit in with the existing neighborhood context.

In future work, researchers should explore these critical policy issues. Clearly, the notion that all subsidized rental housing depresses property values and undermines a neighborhood is simply wrong. The experience of New York City suggests that well-designed, well-managed projects built on distressed sites can play an important role in revitalizing a community. But it behooves us to move further on this research, to give clearer guidance to policymakers about the particular features that make housing investments more effective in different markets and communities.

References

de Souza Briggs, Xavier, Joe T. Darden, and Angela Aidala. 1999. "In the Wake of Desegregation: Early Impacts of Scattered-Site Public Housing on Neighborhoods in Yonkers, New York." *Journal of the American Planning Association* 65, no. 1: 27–49.

Ellen, Ingrid Gould. 2000. *Sharing America's Neighborhoods: The Prospects for Stable, Racial Integration*. Harvard University Press.

Ellen, Ingrid Gould, and Margery Austin Turner. 1997. "Does Neighborhood Matter? Assessing Recent Evidence." *Housing Policy Debate* 8, no. 4: 833–66.

Ellen, Ingrid Gould, and Ioan Voicu. 2006. "Non-Profit Housing and Neighborhood Spillovers." *Journal of Policy Analysis and Management* 25, no. 1: 31–52.

Ellen, Ingrid Gould, and others. 2007. "Does Federally Subsidized Rental Housing Depress Property Values?" *Journal of Policy Analysis and Management* 26, no. 2: 257–80.

Fisher, Robert Moore. 1959. *Twenty Years of Public Housing*. New York: Harper and Brothers.

Green, Richard K., Stephen Malpezzi, and Kiat-Ying Seah. 2003. "Low-Income Housing Tax Credit Housing Developments and Property Values." Paper prepared for the midyear conference of the American Real Estate and Urban Economics Association. Washington, May 27–28.

Kiel, Katherine A., and Jeffrey E. Zabel. 1996. "House Price Differentials in U.S. Cities: Household and Neighborhood Racial Effects." *Journal of Housing Economics* 5, no. 2: 143–65.

Lee, Chang-Moo, Dennis P. Culhane, and Susan M. Wachter. 1999. "The Differential Impacts of Federally Assisted Housing Programs on Nearby Property Values: A Philadelphia Case Study." *Housing Policy Debate* 10, no. 1: 75–93.

Lyons, Robert F., and Scott Loveridge. 1993. "An Hedonic Estimation of the Effect of Federally Subsidized Housing on Nearby Residential Property Values." Staff Paper P93-6. University of Minnesota, Department of Agriculture and Applied Economics.

Malpezzi, Stephen, and Kerry Vandell. 2002. "Does the Low-Income Housing Tax Credit Increase the Supply of Housing?" *Journal of Housing Economics* 11, no. 4: 330–59.

Murray, M. P. 1999. "Subsidized and Unsubsidized Housing Stocks, 1935–1987: Crowding Out and Cointegration." *Journal of Real Estate Economics and Finance* 18, no. 1: 107–24.

Nourse, Hugh O. 1963. "The Effects of Public Housing on Property Values in St. Louis." *Land Economics* 39, no. 4: 433–41.

Salama, Jerry, Michael H. Schill, and Richard Roberts. 2003. "This Works: Expanding Urban Housing." *Civic Bulletin* 35 (February). New York: Manhattan Institute.

Santiago, Anna M., George C. Galster, and Peter Tatian. 2001. "Assessing the Property Value Impacts of the Dispersed Housing Subsidy Program in Denver." *Journal of Policy Analysis and Management* 20, no. 1: 65–88.

Schill, Michael H., and others. 2002. "Revitalizing Inner-City Neighborhoods: New York City's Ten-Year Plan for Housing." *Housing Policy Debate* 13, no. 3: 529–66.

Schwartz, Amy Ellen, and others. 2006. "The External Effects of Subsidized Housing." *Regional Science and Urban Economics* 36, no. 6: 679–707.

Sinai, Todd, and Joel Waldfogel. 2005. "Do Low-Income Housing Subsidies Increase the Occupied Housing Stock?" *Journal of Public Economics* 89, nos. 11–12: 2136–64.

Skogan, Wesley. 1990. *Disorder and Decline: Crime and the Spiral of Decay in American Cities.* University of California Press.

PART II

What Happened? Current Rental Housing Policy

5

Designing Subsidized Rental Housing Programs: What Have We Learned?

JILL KHADDURI AND CHARLES WILKINS

For more than half a century, the federal government has provided subsidies under numerous programs to build, rehabilitate, and preserve affordable rental housing. In total, some 5 million units have been created using direct federal subsidies, block grants, and tax credits.[1] Subsidizing housing presents special challenges because making housing affordable to those who most need it requires administrative rules that govern how the rents are set and who may live in the housing. Typically, this disconnects the housing from the market for two specific reasons: First, owners of the housing are not able to finance cost increases by raising rents or to tap into the appreciated value of their properties to finance capital improvements. Instead, they must apply for additional subsidies, which may or may not be forthcoming. Second, owners are relieved of the discipline of a competitive market. Up to a point, tenants will stay even if the housing is not well managed and maintained, because they cannot find equally affordable rents elsewhere. Properties that have become obsolete in design or are in undesirable locations (because the neighborhood has changed or because the original decision to build there was misguided) are not allowed to fail financially. The flow of subsidies continues and, in many cases, is augmented by a well-intentioned preservation decision.

---

1. Including roughly 2 million U.S. Department of Housing and Urban Development–assisted privately owned units, 1.5 million units financed by the low-income housing tax credit, and 1.5 million units of public housing (public housing is largely outside the scope of this chapter).

The central dilemma of project-based subsidized rental housing is this: the more the housing serves the neediest households (without whose needs there is no rationale for rental subsidies in the first place), the more it is disconnected from the market by rent-setting policies and other administrative constraints. The public housing program is the extreme case, but developments using project-based Section 8 subsidies also operate at a distance from the market, despite recent efforts to reset their total rents (tenant payment plus subsidy amount) to market levels.[2] The Low Income Housing Tax Credit (LIHTC) program operates much closer to the market. The maximum rents permitted by law—and the rents permitted by state implementation of the tax credit program—often are indistinguishable from market rents or only slightly below market. These rents, as has often been pointed out, are not affordable for the neediest households.

This chapter examines the lessons learned from decades of experience with the several programs under which project-based affordable rental housing has been developed. These lessons can guide future policies and programs aimed at developing and preserving affordable rental housing.

Purposes of Project-Based Assistance

Rental housing assistance is necessary because the private market will not produce housing at rents low enough to be affordable for the lowest-income individuals and families. Over time, rents of some older housing "filter down," but owners of rental property must charge rents that are high enough to support a basic level of operating costs. Minimum standards for housing quality established by building, housing, and other codes prevent the widespread creation of low-rent housing through subdivision of larger units, construction of ancillary rental units on existing single-family lots, intensive occupancy of dwelling space, or placement of mobile homes.

The result is a housing stock that is largely of good quality, which affordable housing created by the filtering-down process often would not be. However, this good-quality housing stock has relatively few units affordable to people with incomes below the poverty line (or a proxy that varies by geography). Severe housing cost burdens among very low-income renters dominate housing needs in most of the United States.[3] Many households pay more than half of their income for rent;[4] few are overcrowded or live in substandard housing units (HUD 2007; Joint Center for Housing Studies 2006).

2. An important distinction is that the worst Section 8 properties have been allowed to fail financially, while that principle only recently has been applied to public housing.

3. Exceptions—housing conditions dominated by substandard and overcrowded housing—are found on or near Indian reservations and in Alaskan Native villages.

4. Affordability is typically measured as the percentage of adjusted income (gross income minus certain adjustments, for example, for high medical and child-care expenses) required for rent and tenant-paid utilities. In this chapter we use *rent* as shorthand for "rent and tenant-paid utilities" and *income* as shorthand for "adjusted income."

Renters with extremely low incomes—below 30 percent of area median income—have a much greater incidence of severe cost burdens than even renters in the next-highest income group—between 30 and 50 percent of area median income. Severe rent burdens virtually disappear among renters with incomes greater than 50 percent of area median. Elderly households and people with disabilities are particularly likely to have severe rent burdens or other worst-case needs for housing assistance (HUD 2007).

Because most needy renters have severe rent burdens in standard-quality, uncrowded housing, federal housing policy turned in the mid-1970s to demand-side subsidies—housing vouchers—that accept private market rents as a given but provide a subsidy to cover the difference between market rents and 30 percent of a household's actual income. The shift to vouchers began with a "moratorium" on the Department of Housing and Urban Development's rental production programs in 1973, followed by a high-profile federal study that detailed the high costs of current rental production programs and the conceptual case against them based on economic theory. Major legislation in 1974 created a dual system that included both vouchers and rental production—the Section 8 New Construction and Substantial Rehabilitation programs—and also revived production of public housing. Large numbers of units were produced under the project-based Section 8 programs in the late 1970s and early 1980s.

Most supply-side subsidies were discontinued in 1983, following further review of the relative costs and benefits of demand- and supply-side programs, and the 1980s saw major growth in the numbers of households subsidized through vouchers. However, there has never been a consensus that demand-side subsidies alone can meet the needs of poor renters, and accordingly some amount of subsidized production of rental housing continued during the mid-1980s.[5] The enactment of the LIHTC in 1986 and the HOME Investment Partnerships program in 1990 marked a return to substantial reliance on the production of affordable rental housing through new construction and substantial rehabilitation.

The rationale for rental production programs (supply-side subsidies) is that relying on private rental housing produced through market dynamics and incentives does not always work. Some of the reasons are as follows:

—In housing markets with unresponsive supply, production of additional affordable housing is needed to prevent the additional demand for rental housing (created by vouchers) from inflating rents for both subsidized and unsubsidized households.

—Some households have difficulty using vouchers because the private market does not produce enough of the type of rental housing they need. Research on the

---

5. For example, the Section 8 Moderate Rehabilitation program, the interesting but short-lived Housing Development Action Grants program, and the addition of project-based Section 8 subsidies to some previously unassisted Federal Housing Administration–insured properties.

voucher program suggests that this argument has the greatest merit for large families (those who need three or more bedrooms) and elderly people (who may need or want on-site services linked to their housing) (Finkel and Buron 2001).

—Production of rental housing can expand the opportunities for poor people and minorities to live in relatively high-cost neighborhoods, counteracting the tendency of housing market dynamics—and historic patterns of racial segregation—to create concentrations of households by income and race.

—Production of rental housing can support efforts to revitalize distressed neighborhoods.

The intellectual debate surrounding the first point—the need to subsidize the expansion of the rental housing stock to prevent rent inflation created by vouchers—has never been resolved. Recent work by Scott Susin suggests that vouchers may inflate rents at the low end of the housing market, but his results are not conclusive (Susin 2002; Khadduri, Burnett, and Rodda 2003). It is likely that in some metropolitan areas—those with expanding demand from population and income growth and with supply constraints caused by regulation or geography—subsidized expansion of the rental stock is warranted.

A further complication is the issue of substitution. Instead of expanding the rental stock, subsidized rental housing may simply replace housing that would have been built without a subsidy. The degree to which this happens has been investigated empirically (Murray 1983, 1999; Malpezzi and Vandell 2002), with the conclusion that at least some substitution occurs, and the substitution is likely to be greater for subsidized rental housing that is most like private rental housing—that is, not intended for the lowest-income renters and not intended for specific types of households with special needs.

Thus the most effective use of subsidized rental production may be housing for large families and for people with special needs. However, production of such housing faces other dilemmas. The history of family public housing suggests that clustering large numbers of children in close residential concentration is a bad idea, especially if their families are poor and have weak social supports and even more so in high-density urban surroundings. There is a similar issue of "ghettoization" for people with some types of special needs. The strong preference of many people with disabilities (for example, those with severe mental illness) is to live in regular private market housing and not in specialized developments (Schutt, Goldfinger, and Penk 1992). For both large families and special-needs populations, the issue of scale might be addressed by limiting the size of a development or by integrating large units or units designated for special-needs populations into a larger housing complex.

Using subsidized rental housing to support economic and racial integration also faces the issue of scale, but the perils of creating new concentrations of poor people and minorities should not be exaggerated. The scale of subsidized rental developments need not be so large as to create a new concentration of low-income families. Developments can be located with a sensitivity to the pattern of change in a neighborhood, avoiding places that have relatively low but increasing shares of minorities and poor people. When subsidized rental housing is built in the same low-poverty parts of metropolitan areas where other new construction is taking place—that is, on the urban fringe—it may well substitute for unsubsidized rental housing that would have been built on the same sites. However, the unsubsidized housing would not have been affordable for low-income renters and might not have been available to families attempting to use housing vouchers.[6]

Neighborhood revitalization is often given as the reason for developing subsidized rental housing in a particular location. However, there is little evidence that adding subsidized rental housing to a distressed neighborhood has a positive effect on that neighborhood. It certainly can have the opposite effect, drawing households away from the existing rental stock in the neighborhood and leading to increased deterioration and abandonment (Rothenberg and others 1991). Recent careful empirical work by researchers at New York University finds that the production of subsidized rental housing can have a positive effect on neighborhoods (Schwartz and others 2005; Ellen and others 2005). However, this may only work when the overall housing market is strong (as it was in New York City in the 1990s) and when redeveloped housing replaces deteriorated housing on a large scale. The case for using production of subsidized rental housing as a revitalization tool remains weak.

The policy goals that should be pursued by subsidized rental housing production are clear:

—Avoiding rent escalation in housing markets in which response to the private market supply is not adequate to meet increasing demand for rental housing

—Serving types of households that cannot access the housing they need through a demand-side subsidy because the private housing market does not provide such housing

—Providing opportunities for poor people to live in neighborhoods in which they would otherwise have difficulty using a demand-side subsidy

—Supporting comprehensive—and adequately funded—neighborhood revitalization efforts

Fiscal prudence implies that subsidies should not benefit households with sufficient income to afford housing on their own and should not be used to create rental housing that the private, unsubsidized market would supply. However, it is difficult in practice to serve the neediest households and avoid substitution while at the same time meeting the other policy objectives of subsidized rental housing. The housing markets where subsidized increases in supply are most warranted are also the most expensive, and the gap between the costs of developing and operating

6. Some jurisdictions have laws that require owners of rental housing to accept a voucher as a source of income that can be used for rent, but most do not. In addition, the rent of the "substituted" housing could be beyond the reach of a voucher subsidy.

the housing and the rents that households with extremely low incomes can afford is wide in those locations. Housing for people with special needs implies additional on-site staff and associated operating costs. Units of the size needed by large families can be expensive to develop. (For example, units with multiple bedrooms usually do not exist in buildings that can be rehabilitated or preserved rather than newly built.) For many poor households and households with special needs, the right kind of housing is integrated into larger developments, which implies that some of the subsidy will go to households that do not need it.[7] Cross-subsidization works only in highly specialized market conditions.[8]

Neighborhoods that cannot easily be accessed with a voucher are, by definition, places where the costs of land or existing structures are high. And the type of housing production that can help turn around a distressed neighborhood has proved to be expensive, despite low land costs.

It may be impossible to avoid some of the high costs and inefficiencies associated with meeting the policy goals of subsidized rental production. Some of the production subsidy in a mixed-income or mixed-population development will benefit less needy households or units that substitute for housing that would have been developed without a subsidy. In addition, it may be necessary to use both production subsidies and voucher rental assistance to reach the neediest households, leading to relatively high total subsidy costs for each unit.

The history of privately owned, property-based subsidized rental housing has gone through several phases over the past fifty years.[9] What has come to be called "older assisted" housing was produced during the late 1960s and early 1970s under the Section 236 and Section 221(d)(3) below-market interest rate programs and through the later addition of a rent subsidy to properties that started out as market-rate housing with Federal Housing Administration (FHA) insurance. "Newer assisted" housing was produced under the property-based Section 8 programs between the mid-1970s and the early 1980s. The programs that preceded the LIHTC produced close to 2 million units of privately owned housing subsidized by the U.S. Department of Housing and Urban Development (HUD). As these properties aged and reached the end of their long-term commitments to provide affordable housing, there have also been, essentially, two phases of "preservation" of these properties: older assisted housing, during the early and middle 1990s, and newer assisted housing, starting in the late 1990s and continuing today.

Finally, the early 1990s ushered in the "devolution" era in the production of affordable rental housing, with the enactment of the LIHTC and HOME programs.

---

7. Without such subsidy, there would be no economic incentive for a developer to produce mixed-income housing rather than a 100 percent market-rate unsubsidized development.

8. Cross-subsidization is the use of profits from market-rate units to support low-income units.

9. We do not include the public housing program, which began almost seventy years ago and is outside the scope of this chapter.

These programs have many features that make them similar to block grants. Key decisions are made by state (and, in the case of HOME, also local) officials rather than by the federal government. The rent rules are much simpler: instead of setting maximum rents at 30 percent of income, these programs cap the flat rents (rents that do not vary with actual tenant incomes) that owners may charge. Another simplification compared with earlier programs is that there is no ongoing operating subsidy built into the design of the program. The Low Income Housing Tax Credit program (and HOME, which often is used together with the LIHTC for the same development) provides capital subsidies only. The lack of an ongoing operating or rent subsidy both simplifies the administration of these programs and makes them popular candidates for congressional funding. Unlike the programs that rely on ongoing subsidies (both project-based Section 8 subsidies and vouchers), these programs do not create an overhang of annual obligations for fresh appropriations of funds that must be fitted into a constrained budgetary envelope.[10]

Problems with Early Property-Based Programs

The privately owned assisted housing programs that preceded the LIHTC have exhibited a variety of problems, most of which—ironically—are associated with their major achievement. These programs enabled the neediest families, generally those with extremely low incomes, to live in structurally sound and (usually) well-maintained housing at a cost of no more than 30 percent of their income. The programs either were designed at the outset with rents set at 30 percent of the actual income of the housing unit's occupants or came to have that design as project-based Section 8 subsidies were added. Thus these housing developments were far removed from the market, and the problems detailed below mostly result from the weak incentive structure for property owners and managers. Federal officials were unable to replace missing incentives with successful administrative controls on owner and manager decisions. A related set of problems stems from administrative attempts to impose cost control on properties that were inherently expensive to subsidize, given a subsidy structure that fills the gap between costs and the rents affordable to the programs' target households.

Many of the design features of these programs were stipulated in statute. This made them difficult to change, both because the process for enacting federal housing legislation is slow and because changing design features required lawmakers to take sides on issues that were difficult philosophically (to what extent to target assistance to the neediest) or had powerful stakeholders in the housing industry (how to set limits on costs or profits).

---

10. The LIHTC creates ongoing annual costs to the federal budget in terms of tax revenue forgone from equity investors in rental housing who use the tax credit, but lawmakers are not forced by the federal budget process to confront these costs in the same way as annual appropriations.

We are quick to point out that not all properties exhibited each problem, that most properties survived, and that many properties can be judged successful at their basic mission of providing structurally sound housing, affordable to needy renters. Some properties provided housing in neighborhoods that were or have become difficult for low-income, minority families to access. Many properties provided housing enriched with essential services for frail elderly people or for people with disabilities.

Weak Incentives

The production and operation of rental housing is an inherently risky business, requiring judgments about property design and location based on a careful assessment of demand as well as ongoing property management decisions in response to changing circumstances. The isolation of pre-LIHTC subsidized properties from the rental housing market weakened the incentives that lead private market investors, owners, and managers to make good decisions.

Because most of the properties were financed with FHA mortgage insurance (or direct loans from HUD or the U.S. Department of Agriculture), default risk was transferred from lender to government, severely weakening the incentives for the private mortgage lender to underwrite the project carefully. Typically, the private mortgage lender bore little if any risk.

To make the projects appear feasible, operating costs frequently were underestimated, and unrealistic assumptions were made about the time period required to lease a sufficient number of units to reach the level of rental income needed to sustain the property. The worst problems resulted from a combination of intense competition among developers for limited subsidies and the ability to access additional subsidies later if projects ran into difficulty. In these conditions, developers had little to lose and much to gain from overstating achievable occupancy rates, understating expected operating expenses, and understating the costs of the initial lease-up of units.

Given government guarantees for debt and a guaranteed stream of income, typical financial structures included a high ratio of debt to total development cost, to the extent that often the owner had no substantial equity in the property. Because owners had "no skin in the game," the asset management function of a property owner often was weak or absent. This sometimes led to poor decisions about how to use operating budgets and inattention to growing capital needs. Department of Housing and Urban Development staff responsible for monitoring the properties (because they had Section 8 contracts or FHA-insured mortgages or both) were not able to substitute for the self-interest of an owner with an equity stake.

Financial incentives consisted disproportionately of tax losses, with the bulk of losses expected in the first five to seven years. By contrast, there were relatively few long-term incentives for proper maintenance and good ownership. Typically, after the developer had pocketed the development fee and the investors had received their front-loaded tax losses, the property represented an economic liability rather than an economic asset. Properties were excessively vulnerable to increased operating costs—for example, from sudden spikes in utilities or insurance costs. Properties generally could not—or owners would not—self-fund their ongoing capital needs.

Because Section 8 rents were often at above-market rates—in the case of the Section 8 New Construction program, this was created by the program design—owners' and managers' decisions were not based on preserving and enhancing the value of the property in a competitive market. Instead, the subsidized rents at 30 percent of the renter household's income gave them an automatic market, and the above-market contract rents disconnected owners from market discipline on costs and quality. An additional perverse outcome was that owners and managers correctly perceived HUD (rather than residents) as the primary customer.

Owners and managers typically had few if any ongoing incentives for efficiency in operations. Causes included rents that were based on operating costs or formulas, rather than on market factors, and restrictions on profit. Rent levels for many properties were negotiated with federal officials, which reduced or removed the incentive for the owner and manager to make the cost-effective management choices that would have been necessitated by market-based rents. For other properties, automatic adjustment of rents based on inflation factors provided larger-than-needed operating budgets and exacerbated pressures on the federal budget caused by subsidized rents' exceeding market rates. Restrictions on profits taken from cash flow for many properties (typically allowing no profits at all for nonprofit owners) further dampened incentives for efficiency.

Because of the low risk of financial loss through front-loaded profits, a guaranteed subsidy stream, and government guarantees of debt, inexperienced owners (both for-profit and nonprofit) were willing to invest in subsidized rental housing and to take on the responsibility of managing it, and the housing finance industry was willing to lend to them. Federal program administrators could not replace self-selection into the programs of the most skilled and experienced owners and managers with project selection criteria or subsequent administrative controls.

Projects often were located on sites where, if forced to rely on market rents to cover costs, investors would not have built or rehabilitated rental housing. Many properties were located in neighborhoods with high rates of poverty. This tended to make the properties "housing of last resort," and some of the larger properties came to have sufficient numbers of families with multiple social problems to themselves constitute dysfunctional concentrations of poverty. Neither of these problems is as common in subsidized rental programs as in the public housing program. Conversely, many privately owned, assisted projects were located in relatively low-poverty neighborhoods, including projects occupied by families with children. It is clear, however, that many properties were developed in areas with an over-concentration of poverty and lack of access to jobs, compared with the places where market-motivated investors would have built or rehabilitated housing (Newman and Schnare 1997; Khadduri, Shroder, and Steffan 2003).

Perverse Effects of Controlling Costs

Recognizing weak incentives for efficiency and sensitive to the high costs of programs that built or substantially rehabilitated housing and made it affordable for people with the lowest incomes, policymakers and administrators attempted to impose bureaucratic cost controls that had further perverse effects on program design. In order to be competitive in terms of total development costs, developers had a powerful incentive to prefer low-cost sites. This had at least two effects: First, it largely prevented developments from being located consistent with what are now called smart-growth principles. Second, it tended to concentrate affordable housing opportunities inside traditional low-income (low-land-cost) areas.

Cost limits typically were stated in terms of initial costs only, which created a powerful incentive to use materials with low initial costs without regard to potential adverse impacts on ongoing maintenance, energy, and replacement costs. To make projects appear feasible at lower costs, development budgets and rent structures were approved with inadequate provision for replacement reserves. It is now universally recognized that rules of thumb that are appropriate for market-rate apartments result in insufficient reserves for replacement when imported to budgets for subsidized apartments (Millennial Housing Commission 2002). Unsubsidized properties have high cash flow and ready access to capital markets, so they are able to make fluid decisions about capital improvement programs. Regulated properties lack discretionary cash and often are locked out of refinancing (by mortgage contract, economic infeasibility from soft debt, or regulatory prohibition), so capital for rehabilitation must be accumulated within the regulatory restrictions before it is needed.

In an attempt to control costs, programmatic requirements to house the elderly in efficiency units were added in the mid-1980s. Experience has shown that these units are difficult to market, even with deep subsidies.

Other cost limits resulted in a tendency to underinvest in community space relative to in-unit space. At the same time, the budgets did not adequately provide for "mission costs" (nonhousing services). Attempting to provide for such costs within the property's operating budget has several problems. It creates a moral obligation to continue the services program even if the property can no longer afford to do so; it increases the property's operating costs and gives the impression that the management is inefficient even when it is not; and it shifts costs from other public and private systems to budgets for housing subsidies. Finally, attempts to achieve cost-efficiency—by providing preferences for occupancy by the neediest households and by increasing the tenant portion of the rent from 25 to 30 percent of income—exacerbated the image, and sometimes the reality, of these housing developments as concentrations of the poor.

Preserving Project-Based Rental Housing

As the end of the restrictive-use period approached, first for older assisted properties and then for newer assisted properties, the best properties were at high risk of conversion to market-rate operation, and the worst needed large governmental investments to avoid physical or financial collapse. The era of preservation of the already-subsidized stock of privately owned rental housing began.

The Prepayment Crisis

In the late 1980s older HUD-assisted properties (those that had been developed with below-market FHA-insured financing under the Section 236 and Section 221(d)(3) programs) began to reach the dates at which their owners were eligible to prepay their mortgages and thus end the restrictions on incomes and rents that ran with the mortgage documents rather than being included in a separate use agreement. The programs had not been designed with a formal option that the federal government could exercise to keep these properties within the affordable housing stock.

The first response to this problem was to restrict the prepayments to which owners had an apparent contractual right. The Emergency Low Income Housing Preservation Act of 1987 (ELIHPA) made prepayment requests subject to a significant set of new requirements. Owners contended that these new requirements amounted to a repudiation of the owners' contractual rights to prepay their mortgage loans. A few years later, the Low Income Housing Preservation and Resident Homeownership Act of 1990 (LIHPRHA), while continuing to restrict prepayments, provided incentives to owners not to prepay. Ultimately, prepayment was again allowed beginning in 1996, and residents were protected with what have come to be known as enhanced vouchers. Many of these properties already had Section 8 rent subsidies attached to some or all of the units, and these were replaced with vouchers set at the market value of the units as long as the original tenant used the voucher within the property rather than moving elsewhere. Voucher subsidies were provided also to the residents of some units that did not have Section 8 subsidies to make the rents charged after prepayment affordable.

After repeal of the ELIHPA and LIHPRHA restrictions on prepayment, at-risk properties were preserved whenever an existing owner or a purchaser— and, often, local and state governments that used resources under their control to supplement federal incentives—decided that the property was worthy of preservation.[11] Otherwise, the property exited the use-restricted stock, but residents received vouchers that provided continuing housing affordability (on a tenant-based rather than project-based model, in that the tenant could move out, carrying the voucher subsidy to a different property).

---

11. Preservation purchasers could be nonprofit or for-profit and in any event were willing to own and operate the property subject to a new long-term use and affordability agreement.

Later in the LIHPRHA program, capital-grant financing was used, whereby
HUD made a grant to the nonprofit purchaser to cover the selling owner's equity
and pay for needed repairs, eliminating the need to increase rents. Because rents did
not increase as a result of a capital-grant transaction, the preservation package
typically did not require additional Section 8 units. Similarly, capital-grant transactions retained the ability to adjust rents higher as needed to cover unexpected
cost increases and were less dependent on Section 8 generally. Some 700 properties were preserved under ELIHPA and LIHPRHA, mostly with existing owners
but with a significant number (roughly one-third) transferred to new—generally
nonprofit—owners.

Under the LIHPRHA program, the cost to preserve each unit may have
been higher than was necessary. The incentive program sometimes led to a "war
of the appraisers" through which some owners were overcompensated relative
to the contemporary market value of the properties. In addition, it is widely
believed that some nonprofit purchasers, as a result of HUD's willingness to
bear 100 percent of rehabilitation costs, made unnecessary improvements to their
properties.

After passage of the LIHPRHA, the sales price demanded by some existing
owners who sold properties to be preserved—for example, in an attempt to cover
the "exit taxes" of current investors[12]—made it difficult to structure the financing
of some properties in a way that made them sustainable in the long term. Furthermore, the enhanced voucher approach, by focusing on protecting the sitting tenants,
took attention away from assessing the role of the properties within their rental
housing markets. That is, a particular property may be important for providing
affordable housing in the long term, and that role may be lost unless a supply-side
preservation approach is used.

The Opt-Out Crisis

In the late 1990s, attention shifted to the newer assisted stock, for several reasons.
First, the properties built or redeveloped in the late 1970s and early 1980s began to
reach the end of the multiyear contracts under which their owners agreed to accept
tenants qualifying for Section 8 rent subsidies. At the end of those contract terms,
owners would be able to opt out of the Section 8 program. Second, Congress was
concerned about the implications for federal budgetary outlays associated with
Section 8 contracts that had automatic adjustments for inflation. In the early
1990s Congress began to impose upper limits on contract rents based loosely on
the fair market rents used for the voucher program. Some properties were able to

---

12. After fifteen to twenty years, owners of investment real estate often have a "negative capital
account"—that is, their remaining eligible basis is less than their share of nonrecourse indebtedness,
so that upon sale, when they are relieved of contingent liability (the mortgage), the negative capital
account represents gain (taxable income) even in the absence of any cash price.

operate within those constraints, while others were squeezed. Finally, the newer assisted properties were beginning to show their age and usually had not built up replacement reserves sufficient to meet their looming capital needs, for the reasons we have detailed already.

Ultimately, the response of the federal government to this new preservation crisis was a comprehensive program to restructure the financing and subsidies of the newer assisted stock. This program included new Mark to Market statutory authorities (for properties with above-market rents) and a new HUD initiative (Mark Up to Market) for properties with below-market rents that were at risk of being removed from the subsidized rental market by owner opt-out. These policies applied as well to older assisted properties that had not already been restructured and had not left the assisted housing stock.

Enacted in 1997 and extended through 2011, Mark to Market was conceived as the response to the phenomenon that the rents for many project-based Section 8 properties, particularly for properties produced under the Section 8 New Construction program, were higher than market-comparable rents. In return for reducing the monthly payments on the FHA-insured debt, and for the owner's acceptance of a new thirty-year use and affordability agreement, the Section 8 rents were reset at market level. A certain number of above-market "exception" rents are permitted. Mark to Market is also a preservation program because of the new thirty-year affordability commitment and because the underwriting of the properties is designed for sustainability—taking into account their current and future capital needs and their operating expenses.

The Mark to Market program has become a laboratory for preserving properties in a way that pays attention to their long-term sustainability. Significant sustainability initiatives include especially careful underwriting of revenues and expenses; underwriting an "expense cushion" of 7–10 percent of operating expenses; providing for a replacement reserve deposit sized to cover 100 percent of expected twenty-year capital needs; offering an incentive fee based on performance; and splitting excess cash between the owner and the government. By comparison with LIHPRHA, much more attention was paid to accurately assessing ongoing revenues and expenses, an adequate margin of cash flow after debt service, accurately assessing twenty-year capital needs, and stronger incentives for performance.

Mark to Market avoids the "war of appraisers" by being a voluntary program; owners are free to opt out of the Section 8 program and set rents at market levels, and therefore the government can set the rules. This enables HUD to commission a single private appraisal in a transparent process that gives the owner the ability to participate in the process of determining comparable market rents. The program also discourages overrehabilitating of properties through underwriting that covers only the work needed to restore the property to original condition and by requiring owners to invest 20 percent of repair costs.

Through fiscal year 2005, the Mark to Market program had completed assessments of 2,751 properties, 1,377 of which underwent a restructuring of debt in connection with a new long-term use agreement. Another 823 properties had their rents reduced to market levels without debt restructuring. These transactions produced almost $3 billion of savings in Section 8 costs (net present value, measured over twenty years), and $1.8 billion of net savings (taking into account FHA mortgage insurance claim payments and expected recoveries from future cash flow).

Although most Mark to Market properties are performing well, some are experiencing financial stress. It seems safe to say that future preservation programs should regard the Mark to Market approach as a floor rather than as a ceiling. This, of course, has implications for costs.

An evaluation of the Mark to Market program suggests that the process has been effective overall in preserving affordable housing. Underwriting decisions have been based on careful assessments of individual projects' financial strengths and weaknesses and on the need to provide for the properties' ongoing capital needs. However, the process has been less effective in assessing the need to preserve a property within the broader community context, including the feasibility of alternative ways of meeting the community's housing needs (such as housing vouchers) or of the property's potentially important role in providing housing opportunities where they otherwise might not exist. Overcoming concentrations of poverty by income and race—by preserving affordable housing in places that do not have such concentrations—was not a strong mandate for the program, either in legislation or in the guidance through which the program has been implemented (Hilton and others 2004).

Just as many properties with project-based Section 8 contracts had above-market rents, many had rents below the comparable market rent. This was especially common for the older HUD-assisted stock, properties produced between the late 1960s and the mid-1970s. Under its Mark Up to Market policy, HUD permits those rents to be reset at appraised market values, in an attempt to obtain owners' agreements to retain expiring-use properties within the affordable housing stock. The implicit assumption is that if a property has current rents below comparable market rents, the government is well served by increasing rents at the margin through an increase in Section 8 subsidies rather than allowing opt-outs and replacing the project-based subsidies with vouchers. Unlike Mark to Market, Mark Up to Market does not involve comprehensive underwriting of the property's long-term finances.

Selecting Properties to Be Preserved

Both hard evidence and anecdotal evidence indicate that properties that have been preserved are more likely to be in low-market-rent, high-poverty, low-growth areas. Similarly, properties that opt out of Section 8 are more likely to be in high-market-rent, low-poverty, high-growth areas (Finkel and others 2006). Accordingly, there is reason to fear that preservation-worthy properties are not being preserved. It is also reasonable to ask whether properties not worthy of preservation are being preserved.

A recent analysis that compares multifamily assisted properties that opted out of the assisted housing stock between 1998 and 2004 with properties whose owners chose to keep their Section 8 contracts in force shows that opt-out properties are in neighborhoods with higher median incomes, higher median rents, and lower poverty and vacancy rates. Opt-out properties also are more likely to be family housing—that is, to have two and three-bedroom units and to have smaller numbers of units in the development (Finkel and others 2006).

Positive Attributes of the LIHTC Program

Enacted as part of 1987 tax reform legislation that removed other incentives for investment in affordable rental housing, the low-income housing tax credit is unusual among tax provisions in that it is not an entitlement that can be claimed by any taxpayer who meets certain qualifications. Rather, a fixed quota of tax credit authority is assigned to each state on a per capita basis and then allocated by the state to individual rental housing developments through a competitive process. Although it is based on federal law and regulations, the LIHTC is administered by state officials who make both policy-level decisions on goals and priorities for the use of the resource and retail decisions about which developers and housing projects receive the subsidy.

The LIHTC represents a return to major federal support of rental housing production. The program created an estimated 1.5 million units between 1987 and 2005 (Khadduri, Buron, and Climaco 2006), roughly the same number of units produced since 1937 by the public housing program. The LIHTC and the other contemporary block grant–like program, HOME, also have moved away from the rents used in the Section 8 programs—that is, rents charged as a percentage of the tenant's actual income—to flat rents—that is, rents that must be less than an established maximum related to local affordability but are the same regardless of the actual income of the occupant of the housing unit.

Competition for the Subsidy

Although competition was a feature of many low-income housing programs, the level of competition for the LIHTC subsidies exceeds that of any of the earlier programs. State allocating agencies can design their qualified allocation plans so as to emphasize the factors on which they desire competition and select from among competing developers and projects accordingly. Developers can be sensitive to small numbers of points awarded in LIHTC competitions and design or redesign their properties accordingly. Although there will always be some inefficiency in a tax incentive, the market for the LIHTC among investors has become sufficiently competitive that the loss of efficiency has been much reduced.[13]

Strong Incentives

Because most American markets have rents that roughly approximate current LIHTC ceilings (that is, 30 percent of 60 percent of area median income), LIHTC properties can face competition from older conventional housing. Households that would rent LIHTC units often have other choices at similar (if not identical) rents. This avoids the guaranteed market and the weak incentives to manage the property well that characterized earlier programs that based rents on a percentage of income. Tenants with other alternatives will leave a badly managed and maintained LIHTC property.

The relatively high LIHTC rents also limit the magnitude of a potential LIHTC preservation crisis created by the lure of higher unregulated rents. Changing market circumstances will create that pressure for some properties in some places, but in many other cases LIHTC rents will be every bit as attractive to owners as unrestricted rents. Some owners have agreed to set LIHTC rents considerably below the regulated maximum, but this is most common for mission-driven nonprofits, who are unlikely to leave the program because of economic incentives.

All LIHTC properties have private investors who have purchased the tax credits. Most first-mortgage debt for LIHTC properties is also private, with no government guarantee. As a result, properties have one or two additional stakeholders who are knowledgeable and who have a financial stake in the property's success. Many LIHTC properties have debt in excess of economic value—especially properties that have significant "soft debt."[14] This leads to the same "no skin in the game" problem that was typical of pre-LIHTC programs. However, the problem is mitigated by the LIHTC compliance period, when syndicators (and developers, who typically guarantee LIHTC compliance) have a powerful asset management interest.

The maximum allowable rents rise in step with area median income. In effect, this is a factor-based rent increase mechanism, allowing owners to increase rents modestly each year without the need for property-specific government approval. Regardless of one's views about the best way of creating the limit on rent increases—area median income, market rents, or operating costs—it seems clear that a factor-based approach, in which actual rents are the lower of the factor-based limit or

13. Inefficiencies include the transaction costs of packaging and selling the tax benefit and the return investors must receive in order to be encouraged to invest. In the case of the LIHTC, tax benefits include the value of the income tax credits over the ten-year credit period, the value of "tax losses" driven by depreciation deductions, and the residual value (if any) of the property. Although the tax reform legislation that created the LIHTC ended the rules for rapidly accelerated depreciation available to earlier subsidized rental properties, depreciation still has some value to investors.

14. "Soft" debt has deferred payments, or payments that are contingent on availability of funds.

what the local market will bear, is superior to the budget-based approach followed in some pre-LIHTC programs.[15]

Unlike tax-shelter syndication, which created the near certainty of exit-tax and phantom-income problems, LIHTC investors typically can leave the program after fifteen years without incurring a "recapture tax." This increases the owner's incentive to continue to invest in the property during the compliance period.

Outcome-Based Compliance

The tax credit can be claimed based primarily on two simple objective outcomes: units occupied by eligible households and rents within program limits.[16] This contrasts sharply with the highly complex process-oriented compliance requirements of pre-LIHTC programs. Because the annual LIHTCs can be claimed only as long as the property remains in compliance, the risk of future noncompliance—and the function of monitoring compliance—is borne primarily by the private sector. In the event of noncompliance, the government simply recaptures the LIHTCs rather than having to take protracted enforcement actions against owners or arrange for a transfer of the property to another owner, actions the federal government has found exceedingly difficult.

Combining Stability and Flexibility

The LIHTC has permanent status and resides in the Internal Revenue Code. Because the code is not subject to annual appropriations, is difficult to change, and is in the custody of congressional committees other than those normally concerned with housing issues, the LIHTC does not experience the year-to-year fluctuations characteristic of other affordable housing programs. An ancillary benefit is that the LIHTC does not face direct annual competition with other housing programs. Perhaps the LIHTC program's most significant positive attribute is its resilience during the current era of decreased funding for other housing programs for low-income renters.

Because the state allocating agencies have great flexibility in designing their qualified allocation plans, more than fifty program administrators are trying new approaches each year. There are few barriers to innovation, and communication among states is good. Accordingly, worthy ideas spread quickly. For example,

15. By statute, LIHTC rents are tied to HUD's estimates of local median incomes, which usually rise over time but can fall in some areas in low-inflation environments. In response to concerns about potential rent decreases, the IRS and HUD instituted a "hold harmless" policy under which the estimates of local median incomes that control LIHTC rents would remain flat until data indicate that they should increase. In cases in which such estimates otherwise would show a significant reduction—for example, because of a geographic change in metropolitan area definitions—LIHTC rents might remain unchanged for many years. Failure of rents to grow in concert with expenses under these circumstances could jeopardize project viability.

16. There are other requirements as well—in particular, physical condition standards and compliance with the Fair Housing Act.

some states determined early on that the minimum fifteen-year compliance period was inadequate and changed their allocation plans accordingly. No statutory change was required, and other states followed suit when and as they agreed, adding their own innovations.

Shortcomings of the LIHTC Program

Underfunding of Operating Costs and Capital Needs

The LIHTC has not entirely overcome the financial problems associated with earlier programs. Despite the stronger incentives for equity investors and lenders to underwrite properties carefully, operating costs and capital needs often are understated. With regard to operating costs, LIHTC underwriting standards often do not fully recognize the extent to which LIHTC operating budgets need to include nontraditional expenses such as computer learning centers, after-school programs, and service coordination. Although rent adjustments are pegged to increases in local incomes and are automatic, they may not be sufficient to cover such increases in operating costs as utilities and insurance, which could easily exceed growth in local household income. Real estate is a risky business, and no program—including the LIHTC—has managed both to control rents (inherent in property-based subsidized rental housing) and to provide the full measure of flexibility needed to respond to changing market circumstances. The LIHTC controls rents with a lighter hand, so this problem is less severe than it was for some of the earlier programs, but it is still there. At the same time, while returns to investors are not nearly as front-loaded as they were for earlier programs, typically future capital needs are not adequately provided for when the properties are underwritten.

There is limited information about the capital needs of the early LIHTC properties that now are reaching or passing their fifteen-year mark, but anecdotal evidence indicates that most properties have significant capital needs that cannot be funded from reserves. Whether refinancing alone—that is, refinancing that takes advantage of a reduced mortgage balance or a lower interest rate or both—will be sufficient to meet these capital needs varies from property to property. Whether the owner has the potential to raise rents beyond the LIHTC-regulated levels also varies. Thus though the LIHTC may not have a preservation crisis in the sense that many owners will see opportunities to charge higher rents at the end of their compliance period, many LIHTC properties will need a fresh infusion of subsidy to remain viable.

Figure 5-1 shows a financial simulation for a "plain vanilla" LIHTC property with all units restricted at 60 percent of area median income.[17] The financial

17. That is, the total of rent and tenant-paid utilities is limited to no more than 30 percent of 60 percent of area median income, and occupants may not have incomes higher than 60 percent of area median income.

Figure 5-1. *Financial Simulation of Capital Needs Backlog, 2007–25*[a]

Per unit backlog, in U.S. dollars

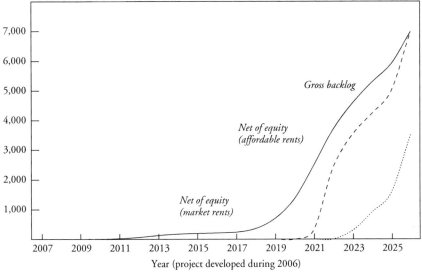

Year (project developed during 2006)

a. Key economic assumptions as follows: small positive cash flow at affordable rents, all years; market rents 5 percent higher than affordable rents, all years; reserve deposit of $300 a month for each unit, increased annually with inflation; "must pay" capital needs (averaging $275 a month for each unit in constant dollars over the first twenty years and $391 a month for each unit over the first sixty years) are funded from the reserve; remaining (deferrable) capital needs (averaging $166 a year for each unit in constant dollars over the first twenty years and $449 a month for each unit over the first sixty years) are deferred until sale or refinance; market and affordable rents grow at 3.0 percent a year; expenses and capital needs grow at 4.0 percent a year.

simulation uses assumptions we consider reasonable for moderate-cost areas: monthly rents averaging $588 a unit, monthly operating expenses averaging $350 a unit, and a replacement reserve deposit of $25 a month for each unit. Total development costs of $100,000 for each unit were financed as follows: 72 percent through LIHTC equity, 25 percent through private mortgage debt (at 7 percent for thirty years), and 3 percent through government-funded "soft debt" (accruing interest at 5 percent but not requiring any payments until maturity at thirty years).

The property has a small but positive cash flow (its debt-service coverage ratio varies between 1.05 and 1.10); properties are usually underwritten to have more cash flow than this, but experience suggests that actual performance is more typically at or close to the break-even point. The simulation assumes that rents grow at 3 percent a year and expenses grow at 4 percent a year.

The simulation's estimated capital needs (for example, roof replacement; heating, ventilation, and air conditioning replacement; appliance replacement) include estimates for each building system (for example, kitchen cabinets, siding).[18] For purposes of this analysis, capital needs were divided into must-pay items (for example, appliances) that must be replaced when they wear out and deferrable items (for example, siding replacement) that can be and often are postponed by making piecemeal repairs. The simulation assumes that must-pay items are funded from the reserve for replacements and that deferrable items are deferred until the end of the twenty-year analysis period (the fifteen-year basic LIHTC compliance period plus five years).

The simulation shows the following:

—There is no capital-needs backlog of any size until after year 10.

—The backlog rises sharply after year 10.

—If market rents are 5 percent higher than affordable rents, the increased equity from a potential conversion to market rents will be sufficient to fund around half of the backlog as of year 20. If market rents are 10 percent higher than affordable rents, the increased equity will be sufficient to erase the full backlog as of year 20.

—There is unlikely to be enough equity, if operations continue at affordable rents, to erase any significant portion of the capital-needs backlog, unless the then-current interest rates are materially lower than the actual interest rate on the first mortgage loan.

—The capital-needs backlog roughly triples between years 20 and 30 (not graphed on figure 5-1).

Thus a typical LIHTC property will need a capital infusion between years 15 and 20 in order to maintain physical and financial viability while continuing to provide affordable housing at LIHTC rents. Of course, results will vary considerably from property to property.

Restrictive Financing Structures

Nor have LIHTC properties avoided entirely the issue of long-term tax side effects. Since the vast majority of LIHTC investors are businesses and therefore exempt from passive loss rules, they are allowed to book the excess depreciation losses of their LIHTC investments. Such owners may run into exit-tax issues at the end of the LIHTC compliance period, and this may complicate the property's future sale or recapitalization either as continued well-maintained affordable housing or as market-rate housing.

In addition, many LIHTC properties have been financed with large "soft" debt, typically obtained from state and local governments, for which payments are wholly or largely deferred. Localities and states may be reluctant to forgive or roll

---

18. Estimates were developed for the Millennial Housing Commission by Charles Wilkins, "Financial Modeling Summaries," "Long-Term Sustainability and Affordability," and "Pre-LIHTC Affordable Housing: Historical Context" (2002) (govinfo.library.unt.edu/mhc/papers.html), with invaluable advice from David Whiston of On-Site Insight.

over their position at the end of the compliance period or when the property needs recapitalization.

Reaching Extremely Low-Income Households

Compared with the earlier subsidized rental production programs, the LIHTC has a major shortcoming as an instrument of public policy. Because it mandates flat rents rather than percent-of-income rents, it does not easily reach households with extremely low incomes or incomes below the poverty line. Fortunately, there are ways of overcoming this problem without introducing the disadvantages of the earlier programs. The LIHTC subsidy can be made more explicitly part of a "split subsidy," whereby extremely low-income families are given housing vouchers and LIHTC developments are among the rental housing options available to these families.

This does not mean that all LIHTC units should be occupied by extremely low-income families using vouchers. An important virtue of the LIHTC program is that it lends itself to the creation of mixed-income housing, in which families with extremely low incomes live in the same development as families with incomes close to the 60 percent-of-median maximum that applies to most LIHTC developments.

This dual approach to rental housing assistance has the drawback that some subsidy dollars are spent on relatively less needy households. This is unavoidable, if mixed-income housing is to be achieved within LIHTC developments and if LIHTC developments are to avoid the stigma (and the community resistance) that makes it hard to locate subsidized rental housing in places with low absolute rates of poverty and low minority rates relative to the metropolitan area.

Limited Information on Program Performance

On-budget subsidy programs are now squarely in the world of performance measurement and reporting. The LIHTC program, in contrast, as a tax provision, has no mandate to report periodically (or ever) on its achievement of those public policy purposes that go beyond narrow compliance with the rules for household eligibility and maximum rents.

For example, LIHTC units that are large enough to house families with children have been located in low-poverty areas in numbers that compare favorably with earlier property-based programs and, indeed, with the voucher program (Khadduri, Buron, and Climaco 2006). What is not known is the extent to which the program is creating mixed-income housing, because of the paucity of information on who actually lives in the LIHTC units. Little research has been done: an old GAO study and a few case studies, also old (GAO 1997, 1999; Buron and others 2000). Some information can be compiled by matching addresses between LIHTC developments and voucher holders (Climaco and others 2006). But without more information, there is no way to know whether voucher allocations need to be tied explicitly to new LIHTC developments.

Related to the limited information on the program is limited debate about what the program should accomplish. Although the competitive nature of the program and the flexibility of the qualified allocation plans make it possible for states to apply changing priorities, this does not necessarily mean that states have made choices consonant with the basic case for property-based assistance as we have articulated it. There is little evidence that states have favored systematically housing large families or individuals with special needs, or housing in low-poverty, low-minority locations (Climaco and others 2006; Khadduri, Buron, and Climaco 2006). The tendency common to block grant–like programs to spread the money around broadly—in this case, around the state— almost certainly means that a substantial number of LIHTC units have been developed, or that the LIHTC has been used for housing preservation, in areas that have an adequate supply of housing accessible to renters with tenant-based vouchers.

Lessons for the Future

If we were designing a new property-based rental subsidy, it would incorporate the following features: First, the program would permit rents close to market-determined rents, and it would not include financial incentives or selection preferences that favor lower rents. Many of the problems with the pre-LIHTC programs stemmed from the lack of connection between management of the properties and market-based competition for tenants. Rents close to the market both maintain competitive pressures for managing the property well and discourage the development of rental housing in neighborhoods in which people with choices would not choose to live.

Second, it would use a split-subsidy approach, to reach poor people who cannot afford rents close to the market, by combining a supply of new or redeveloped housing at rents around the middle of the market rate with adequate funding of demand-side housing vouchers.

Third, the rules for selecting properties to receive the subsidy would mirror the basic purposes of property-based subsidized rental housing described earlier in this chapter. The rules would

—discourage the development of new affordable rental housing in submarkets that already have an oversupply of housing;

—favor housing for large families, either in small-sized developments or as parts of larger developments;

—favor housing for special-needs populations and encourage (or even require) agreements with other systems (for example, state mental health systems) to provide funding for needed services;

—favor housing in neighborhoods with low rates of poverty and outside areas of minority concentration.

Fourth, the program would provide a built-in way of dealing with the increase in capital needs that will occur from year 10 to around year 30. One mechanism is front-end funding of substantial reserves (which could be held at the property level or by the funder). Another mechanism is debt that amortizes rapidly enough to permit refinancing of the property when needed to meet the property's capital needs.

Fifth, it would require a debt-service coverage ratio (or, more to the point, operating expense cushion) high enough to withstand income and expense shocks—for example, short-term spikes in rent loss (vacancies from supply-demand imbalance in the local market, bad debt loss, concessions) and in operating costs (insurance, utilities).[19]

Sixth, the program would provide a more flexible way of changing ownership and management. Ownership capacity rises and falls, regardless of organizational size and maturity. The same is true of management capacity. The result is that properties need an efficient, low-cost means of swapping out sponsors desiring to exit (or who must exit because of program violations or simple lack of attention) and swapping in better providers, without requiring a real estate transfer or acceleration of financing (whether public or private).

Seventh, the program's affordability restrictions would survive financial failure of the property. The restrictions would be in a covenant running with the land and recorded before any mortgage liens, so that the affordability covenant would continue in force even if there were a foreclosure by the mortgagee.

Finally, the program would include a formal option, held by government, for long-term preservation. This could be structured as a right (assignable to a purchaser) to purchase the property at the time the affordability restrictions expire. For example, a structure that provided for an option price that was not lower than outstanding debt and not higher than the appraised value of the property, assuming continuation of the affordability requirements, would provide incentives for good ownership and management while still keeping the option price reasonable from a public-purpose viewpoint.

Potential LIHTC Policy Changes

The LIHTC program already exists, has been quite successful, and has many positive features, not the least of which is its high level of support from lawmakers in an era of severe budget cuts for on-budget domestic programs. Another attractive feature is the flexibility built into its administration by the states. Keeping in mind

19. The U.S. Department of Housing and Urban Development's Mark to Market program introduced an important conceptual innovation: the operating expense cushion. This measurement is calculated by dividing cash flow after debt service by total operating expenses. The resulting percentage is the increase in operating expenses that the property could sustain without incurring negative cash flow. Compared with the traditional debt-service coverage ratio, the operating expense cushion is a more direct way of measuring the ability of a property to withstand economic shocks and is particularly appropriate in affordable rental housing, which often has minimal debt service.

these positive features, we offer the following proposals for changes to the federal rules governing the LIHTC program.[20]

Presently, LIHTCs are limited to a formula based on the proportion of development costs that are eligible to be depreciated under the Internal Revenue Code. We believe that Congress should allow states to allocate LIHTCs to applicants without regard to "qualified basis," in accordance with the state's determination of the public-purpose benefits of each proposed project. States could choose to allocate LIHTCs based on total development costs or using any other reasonable approach developed with the benefit of public comment under the existing qualified allocation plan process. Under this approach, some developments would receive more tax credits than under the current approach, and others would receive fewer, in accordance with each development's public-purpose benefits.

In addition to the obvious problem of creating enormous complexity, limitation of the LIHTC to qualified basis has at least two additional perverse consequences. First, it creates a powerful incentive to maximize investments in eligible basis (for example, construction and rehabilitation). This is controlled to some extent by the competitive nature of LIHTC allocations, but the extent to which state reviewers of applications have the capacity to question the construction costs needed by a project is not clear.

Second, it creates a powerful disincentive for investments that do not constitute eligible basis: prominently, land. This makes it more difficult to site LIHTC properties on high-value land—for example, along transportation corridors in accord with smart-growth principles or in neighborhoods difficult to reach with vouchers.

Recognizing some of the problems with the current approach, Congress created an additional "basis boost" of up to 30 percent for developments located in qualified census tracts and difficult development areas to allow for more LIHTCs in areas in which development costs are presumed to be higher than normal. Direct allocation would require repeal of the basis boost for both categories. This would have the further advantage of removing an incentive currently in the program for locating LIHTC units in high-poverty areas. (Qualified census tracts are, by definition, high-poverty neighborhoods.)

Basis boosts for qualified census tracts and difficult development areas were intended to make it possible to further write down rents in areas where prospective tenants would not have sufficient income to afford LIHTC maximum rents. Providing tenant-based vouchers that make it possible for households with extremely low incomes to pay LIHTC rents set at the maximum is a superior way of handling

20. Some of these proposals—detaching the tax credit from depreciable basis, repealing the ten-year rule, and removing penalties for using the LIHTC with other federal funds—are adopted from earlier suggestions by David Smith and others in a paper prepared for the Millennial Housing Commission, "The Low Income Housing Tax Credit Effectiveness and Efficiency: A Presentation of the Issues" (govinfo.library.unt.edu/mhc/papers/html).

that issue because it does not lock real estate (and its residents) into high-poverty neighborhoods. We believe that LIHTC developments should be located in high-poverty areas only if the development of subsidized rental housing is part of a comprehensive neighborhood revitalization effort with a realistic chance of success.

One argument against making land costs eligible for the LIHTC is that developers could claim the credit on inflated land prices based on sweetheart deals, especially if repeal of qualified basis were combined with repeal of the "ten-year rule," another change to the federal LIHTC rules worthy of consideration.[21] The ten-year rule is intended to prevent "churning," that is, multiple transactions on a single property. However, it may be desirable to invest LIHTCs in properties that have changed hands in the prior ten years, as these properties may be in locations in which it is difficult for low-income households to use vouchers. If qualified basis and the ten-year rule are repealed, it may be necessary to substitute federal rules that require attention to the land transaction to ensure that it reflects a fair market price.

Removing the link between LIHTCs and basis in the tax credits that are limited in volume and allocated by state agencies should be accompanied by similar changes to the "4 percent" LIHTCs that currently accompany tax-exempt bond financing and are not subject to the LIHTC volume cap.[22] One example of such a change would be to allocate annually to each state a dollar amount of 4 percent LIHTCs that corresponds to the amount of the state's tax-exempt bond authority; a state could then use its existing qualified allocation plan process to develop a method for awarding those LIHTCs to developments financed by tax-exempt bonds. Some such developments would receive more LIHTCs than under the current system, and others would receive less.

We also recommend changes that would make the LIHTC easier to use in combination with other subsidies. The first of these changes would simplify the administration of the program by reducing or eliminating conflicting requirements when the LIHTC is used in conjunction with (in particular) HOME and community development block grants. One approach has been termed "hierarchy of compliance": in this approach, compliance with the rules of the HOME and Community Development Block Grant programs would be deemed to have occurred if LIHTC compliance were maintained. Another is to create a universal set of compliance requirements that would be deemed to satisfy all three programs.

---

21. Internal Revenue Code 42.d.2.B.ii. describes a "ten-year rule" under which the acquisition cost of a building may be included in basis only if no significant rehabilitation or change of ownership has occurred in the past ten years.

22. The amount of tax credit that can be taken by investors in such properties is smaller than the maximum amount permitted for state-allocated tax credits. For convenience, this smaller amount is commonly called a "4 percent" credit, and the higher amount a "9 percent credit," although the actual percentages vary from year to year. The restriction to 4 percent credits applies to some other circumstances as well.

A more far-reaching change would repeal the provisions that penalize the use of the LIHTC in conjunction with other federal funds.[23] The original concept was that the LIHTC alone should be sufficient to cover the gap between the project's development costs and the rents available to retire debt and pay for operations. This clearly is not the case today, when it is normal for LIHTC developments to have as many as six sources of funds. The LIHTC is a finite resource for which there is stiff competition. In keeping with the block grant nature of the program, states should be charged with limiting total subsidies to the level necessary to carry out each project.

The federal LIHTC legislation includes many mandates for the content of qualified allocation plans, some of which operate at cross purposes (Gustafson and Walker 2002). These mandates should be recast to relate more explicitly to the fundamental justification for having property-based subsidized rental housing and to use tenant-based vouchers as a benchmark against which allocating agencies make the choice to invest their limited LIHTC resources in particular properties.

For example, qualified allocation plans should favor those areas within a state that have low rental vacancy rates, high rates of population growth, and housing choice voucher programs with low rates of success for families trying to use tenant-based rental assistance. They should encourage developments in portions of metropolitan areas where market rents are out of reach of families with vouchers— that is, where most rents are higher than the voucher program's payment standards. They also should favor LIHTC developments in which some or all units are combined with services for special-needs populations.

Currently, many LIHTC properties have residents who do not use vouchers (Climaco and others 2006). The federal government—and the states—should learn more about the extent to which vouchers are used in LIHTC properties, the characteristics of the households using them, and the reasons that some LIHTC properties do not have vouchers in use (for example, rents may be low enough that vouchers are not needed, lack of information may prevent voucher holders from learning about LIHTC properties, LIHTC rents may be greater than the local voucher payment standard, or owners may be violating the rule that prohibits discrimination against voucher users). This learning should be part of a more general congressional mandate for states to report on their use of LIHTC and to evaluate whether their LIHTC properties are serving specified public purposes.

Finally, the federal rules that govern the LIHTC should require the land-use restriction agreement to be a covenant running with the land that will survive foreclosure. Consistent with the general principle that private lenders and equity providers (and not the government) should take all economic risks in

---

23. Internal Revenue Code 42.b.1.B.i.

the LIHTC program, Congress should require that the LIHTC agreement face no risk of cancellation in the event of a foreclosure.

Making Preservation Decisions

We recommend that the following factors be taken into account when a decision is made whether to preserve an expiring-use property for an additional (say) twenty years: the degree to which the property provides housing opportunities not likely to be available to families trying to use household-based housing vouchers; the current level of demand for the particular type of rental unit or property; the quality of the current or proposed new owner-manager team; the level of poverty in the neighborhood in which the property is located; the cost to make the property sustainable compared to alternative uses of the same funds; and the length of time for which the property can be made truly sustainable. These factors should be taken into account both by state officials deciding on the use of the LIHTC and by federal officials considering whether to sustain (or increase) subsidies for pre-LIHTC subsidized rental properties.

UNIQUE HOUSING OPPORTUNITY. Given the difficulty of preserving affordable housing in the long term and the costs that must be incurred to do so, there is some threshold—when market units available to those using housing vouchers are plentiful and likely to remain so—below which it makes no sense to preserve properties as rent-restricted affordable housing. This is particularly the case when the resources that can be devoted to preservation are scarce, as they almost always are. Resources should instead be prioritized as suggested earlier in this chapter—for example, to areas in which prevailing market rates exceed the voucher payment standard and areas experiencing high growth rates.

Even housing occupied by the elderly or by persons with disabilities may not need to be preserved as rent-restricted housing if alternatives exist that are affordable to the same types of individuals when they use vouchers. Such properties may need to continue to have use restrictions only if they have specific physical features or nonhousing services that are not present in other housing these populations might occupy.

The success rate of the local voucher program is a good indicator of whether the property is needed.[24] When recipients of housing choice vouchers have difficulty securing housing, preservation of existing successful affordable rental housing is indicated. The voucher success rate should be examined for rental units of different sizes. Large low-income families typically have more difficulty securing affordable housing than smaller families; thus a property with three-bedroom and larger units usually is more worthy of preservation.

---

24. Voucher administrators are required to maintain data for reporting to HUD that make it possible to measure the rate at which families to whom vouchers have been issued are able to use them.

LEVEL OF DEMAND. There may be little demand for third-floor walk-up units or for efficiency apartments, even with affordable rents, suggesting that these units should not be preserved over the long term as affordable housing. The history of rent loss for the property under consideration often is an indicator of the importance of preserving particular property-based subsidized rental housing in a particular neighborhood.

Prevailing vacancy rates are one indication of the extent to which the local housing market already provides adequate opportunities for renters to use household-based assistance without the preservation of property-based subsidized rental housing. However, current high vacancy rates in a jurisdiction or a neighborhood may reflect the absorption of newly developed rental housing in high-growth areas (Belsky and Goodman 1996). The assessment of need for preservation of the property should take into account the 1990, 2000, and most recent population data for the city, the county, and the neighborhood.

QUALITY OF OWNERSHIP AND MANAGEMENT. In assessing the quality of a proposed new owner-manager team for a property under consideration for preservation funding, compliance with program rules and operating performance should be examined in comparison with peer properties. If other factors make a property with a weak owner-manager team preservation worthy, a transfer of ownership or management should be sought.

NEIGHBORHOOD POVERTY. A potential indicator that a property is in a location that makes it worth preserving is the level of poverty in the census tract.[25] Another possible indicator is the ratio between the median income of the census tract and the median income of the metro area. If the property is in a neighborhood with a low poverty rate, the preservation decision also should assess the degree to which the property is (or, as improved, can become) a positive resource for the community.

If the property is in a neighborhood with a high poverty rate, the property might still be worthy of preservation if it is part of a comprehensive neighborhood revitalization plan that has realistic expectations of being funded at sufficient scale to change fundamentally the character of the neighborhood.

COST TO PRESERVE. Commonly, the public costs to produce additional affordable rental housing via new construction are three to five times higher than those needed to preserve an existing affordable property. For example, work that one of the authors is performing for a state indicates that a typical expiring-use LIHTC property (for which the nonprofit general partner has an option to purchase at a favorable price) can be preserved at a public cost of roughly $10,000 for each unit, while the level of public investment necessary to produce a single new LIHTC unit significantly exceeds $100,000.

---

25. Most multifamily assisted properties do not by themselves dominate their census tracts, which typically have 3,000 to 5,000 people. Only 7.4 percent of multifamily assisted developments have more than two hundred units, and 40.4 percent have fewer than fifty units.

However, the cost trade-off must be assessed for each individual property, because some preservation efforts are much more expensive than others and because the choice may be not between preserving and building new but between preserving one existing property and another.

PERIOD OF SUSTAINABILITY. Given how difficult it is to create new affordable rental housing, there is much interest in providing for very long-term preservation. However, a "set it and forget it" strategy (under which government would fund a property once, with the expectation of more or less permanent sustainability) has powerful practical drawbacks:

—the difficulty of anticipating evolving markets: A property worth preserving today may not be worthy of continued preservation twenty years from now. Unit sizes, features and amenities will become sufficiently outdated that the property may no longer be worthy of preservation. The history of the public housing program—which, in effect, assumed permanent preservation—is instructive.

—the difficulty of anticipating capital needs past about twenty years: As a property's age approaches or exceeds 50 years since construction, ongoing capital needs will start to include very long-lived systems (for example, the need to tuck-point brick walls, to replace utility pipes inside the walls and under the ground, and to replace electrical wiring).

—the substantial cost of providing up-front funding for very long-term capital needs.

Experience demonstrates that properties benefit from a financing event—sale, refinancing, recapitalization, intra-partner transfer—roughly every fifteen to twenty years. Building financial flexibility into longer-term affordability schemes remains an ongoing policy challenge.

That said, a preservation structure that included a series of twenty-year governmental options to extend preservation, coupled with a "twenty-year check up" (and new subsidies) as each option matures, would be a good framework for long-term preservation.

References

Belsky, Eric, and John L. Goodman Jr. 1996. "Explaining the Vacancy Rate Paradox of the 1980s." *Journal of Real Estate Research* 11, no. 3: 309–23.

Buron, Larry, and others. 2000. *Assessment of the Social and Economic Characteristics of LIHTC Residents and Their Neighborhoods.* Cambridge, Mass.: Abt Associates.

Climaco, Carissa, and others. 2006. *Updating the Low Income Housing Tax Credit (LIHTC) Database: Projects Placed in Service through 2003.* Cambridge, Mass.: Abt Associates.

Ellen, Ingrid Gould, and others. 2005. "Does Federally Subsidized Rental Housing Depress Neighborhood Housing Values?" Working Paper 05-03. New York: New York University, Furman Center for Real Estate and Social Policy.

Finkel, Meryl, and Larry Buron. 2001. *Quantitative Study of Success Rates in Metropolitan Areas.* Cambridge, Mass.: Abt Associates.

Finkel, Meryl, and others. 2006. *Multifamily Properties: Opting In, Opting Out, and Remaining Affordable.* Report prepared for the U.S. Department of Housing and Urban Development. Bethesda, Md.: Econometrica; Cambridge, Mass.: Abt Associates.

Gustafson, Jeremy, and Christopher J. Walker. 2002. *Analysis of State Qualified Allocation Plans for the Low-Income Housing Tax Credit Program.* Washington: Urban Institute.

Hilton, Richard, and others. 2004. *Evaluation of the Mark to Market Program.* Bethesda, Md.: Econometrica; Cambridge, Mass.: Abt Associates.

Joint Center for Housing Studies. 2006. *The State of the Nation's Housing 2006.* Cambridge, Mass.: Harvard University, Joint Center for Housing Studies.

Khadduri, Jill, Kimberly Burnett, and David Rodda. 2003. *Targeting Housing Production Subsidies: Literature Review.* Cambridge, Mass.: Abt Associates.

Khadduri, Jill, Larry Buron, and Carissa Climaco. 2006. "Are States Using the Low Income Housing Tax Credit to Enable Families with Children to Live in Low Poverty and Racially Integrated Neighborhoods?" Washington: Poverty and Race Research Action Council.

Khadduri, Jill, Mark Shroder, and Barry Steffen. 2003. "Can Housing Assistance Support Welfare Reform." In *A Place to Live, a Means to Work: How Housing Assistance Can Strengthen Welfare Policy,* edited by Barbara Sard and Amy S. Bogdon. Washington: Fannie Mae Foundation.

Malpezzi, Stephen, and Kerry Vandell. 2002. "Does the Low-Income Housing Tax Credit Increase the Supply of Housing?" Working Paper. Madison: University of Wisconsin, Center for Urban Land Economics Research (October).

Millennial Housing Commission. 2002. *Meeting Our Nation's Housing Challenges: Report of the Bipartisan Millennial Housing Commission Appointed by the Congress of the United States.* Washington.

Murray, Michael P. 1983. "Subsidized and Unsubsidized Housing Starts: 1961–1977." *Review of Economics and Statistics* 65: 590–97.

Newman, Sandra, and Ann B. Schnare. 1997. ". . . And a Suitable Living Environment: The Failure of Housing Programs to Deliver on Neighborhood Quality." *Housing Policy Debate* 8, no. 4: 703–41.

Rothenberg, Jerome, and others. 1991. *The Maze of Urban Housing Markets: Theory, Evidence, and Policy.* University of Chicago Press.

Schutt, Russell K., Stephen M. Goldfinger, and Walter E. Penk. 1992. "The Structure and Sources of Residential Preferences among Seriously Mentally Ill Homeless Adults." *Sociological Practice Review* 3, no. 3: 148–56.

Schwartz, Amy Ellen, and others. 2005. "The External Effects of Place-Based Subsidized Housing." Working Paper 05-02. New York: New York University, Furman Center for Real Estate and Social Policy.

Susin, Scott. 2002. "Rent Vouchers and the Price of Low-Income Housing." *Journal of Public Economics* 83, no. 1: 109–52.

U.S. Department of Housing and Urban Development (HUD). 2007. *Affordable Housing Needs 2005: Report to Congress.*

U.S. General Accounting Office (GAO). 1997. *Tax Credits: Opportunities to Improve Oversight of the Low-Income Housing Program* (March).

———. 1999. *Tax Credits: The Use of Tenant-Based Assistance in Tax Credit Supported Properties* (September 17).

6

Subsidized Housing and Employment: Building Evidence of What Works

JAMES A. RICCIO

For many years, policymakers have agreed that low-income, working-age people who receive rent subsidies from the government ought to strive for self-sufficiency and that the housing subsidy system should play an actively supportive role—or at least not stand in the way. This intent is clear in the most recent major public housing reform legislation, the Quality Housing and Work Responsibility Act of 1998, which makes promoting residents' self-sufficiency a core objective. At the same time, there is a widely shared belief that government needs to push further in this direction, as reflected in the 2002 recommendation of the Millennial Housing Commission that "more should be done to link housing assistance with economic opportunity, self-sufficiency, and personal responsibility" (Millennial Housing Commission 2002, p. 56).

Reflecting this long-standing interest, a variety of self-sufficiency innovations and housing policy reforms have been tried over the past two decades, and new ones are being proposed all the time. Yet what is striking about innovation in this field—proposed or actual—is that so little of it is based on credible evidence of what works. Rare are the kinds of rigorous impact evaluations based on randomized controlled trials that have become more common in the welfare-to-work and workforce development fields and that are increasingly used in criminal justice and education research.[1] This, of course, makes it difficult to know whether self-sufficiency strategies for assisted housing that sound promising are really a good bet or a bad investment. Given that many work-promoting services and supports exist outside subsidized housing and are already available to assisted residents, do interventions that are explicitly linked to housing subsidies really add value?

A number of descriptive and nonexperimental studies suggest that they might, but most studies are limited by the absence of appropriate control groups or have other data or methodological limitations that make it impossible to know for sure. In addition, many such evaluations do not carefully explore in depth how the programs are administered on the ground, and many do not include even rudimentary benefit-cost assessments.

Also uncertain is whether basic housing assistance in and of itself promotes or impedes residents' progress toward self-sufficiency. Countervailing forces are at play, and theory can be mustered to support competing claims, thus contributing to a need for more convincing evidence.

This chapter argues for building a stronger base of evidence in the housing and employment policy arena through an expanded use of randomized controlled trials. Greater use of this methodology, which involves comparing outcomes of program and control groups to which eligible people have been assigned through a lottery-like process, is technically feasible and practical, and it could substantially improve the body of evidence on what works. With better knowledge in hand, policymakers and others who wish to improve self-sufficiency outcomes could rely less on hunches and hope in deciding how to achieve those aims. Indeed, many experts see more credible evidence as an urgent policy need (see, for example, Newman 1999; Sard and Bogdon 2003; Shroder 2000; Solomon 2006).

Intervening in the Subsidized Housing System to Promote Work

Three main types of programs make up the federal housing assistance system for very low-income families: public housing, tenant-based portable rent vouchers for families to use in seeking private rental housing (known formally as housing choice vouchers), and project-based subsidies, which are attached to privately owned housing units.[2] This system is administered by the U.S. Department of Housing and

1. Mark Shroder (2000) summarizes eight housing-related experiments funded by the U.S. Department of Housing and Urban Development since the 1970s, starting with the Experimental Housing Allowance program. Most focus on housing-specific outcomes—such as take-up of rent subsidies, housing expenditures, and mortgage delinquency—rather than on self-sufficiency results. More recent experiments that do focus more on self-sufficiency outcomes are the Moving to Opportunity and Welfare to Work Voucher demonstrations, which are discussed later in this chapter.

2. Substantial parts of this section were prepared with assistance and written contributions from Sandra Newman and Joseph Harkness of the Institute for Policy Studies at Johns Hopkins University.

Urban Development (HUD) through local public housing authorities.[3] With some variation and exceptions, each of the three main subsidy programs requires tenants to pay 30 percent of their income (after some adjustments) for housing. The Low Income Housing Tax Credit (LIHTC) program is another important federal vehicle for supporting affordable housing, but it operates through the tax system, and its rent subsidies are less generous. Consequently, the lower-income population it serves is considerably less poor and has fewer labor market difficulties than the more deeply subsidized people served by the three HUD-administered programs that are the focus of this chapter.[4]

The tenant-based voucher program is the largest of the three subsidy programs, serving at any given time about 1.8 million households out of a total of about 4.2 million (43 percent) HUD-assisted households. In this program, the government enters into a contract with the landlord of a unit that is identified by the tenant, once the unit passes a quality inspection. Project-based vouchers cover about 1.3 million households (31 percent of HUD-assisted households). In this program, the landlord is identified and funded directly by the housing authority to make units available to eligible residents at reduced rents pegged to residents' incomes. Public housing developments, which are owned by the local housing authorities, are home to about 1.1 million households (26 percent of all HUD-assisted households).[5]

It is also noteworthy that many local housing authorities are replacing severely distressed public housing developments with mixed-income housing complexes. Funded by the federal Housing Opportunities for People Everywhere (HOPE VI) program, they are building HUD-subsidized units within housing developments that also include other rental units subsidized through low-income housing tax credits, market-rate rental units, and owner-occupied units. As of June 2006,

3. The Housing Choice Voucher program was previously called Section 8 Tenant-Based Assistance. In addition to project-based Section 8 subsidies attached to private multifamily housing, the Housing Choice Voucher program allows local public housing authorities to attach up to 20 percent of their tenant-based vouchers to specific housing units in privately owned developments if the landlord meets certain provisions and housing quality standards set by the U.S. Department of Housing and Urban Development.

4. The LIHTC program subsidizes construction of private housing by offering tax breaks to developers who agree to set aside for lower-income families a number of units with below-market rents. Typically, however, these credits are not deep enough to make it feasible for the developer to reduce rents sufficiently far below market rates to make the units affordable for the very low-income renters served through the HUD-administered housing subsidy programs. Thus the rent subsidies offered through this tax credit strategy are generally considered "shallower" than the "deep" subsidies" offered by the three HUD programs that target the poorest tenants. Self-sufficiency among LIHTC tenants has consequently not been as significant a policy concern as it has been with respect to people living in public housing or using vouchers.

5. See U.S. Department of Housing and Urban Development, "Resident Characteristics Report," data as of December 31, 2006 (www.hud.gov); HUD (2006). The total number of funded vouchers and the total number of public housing units are somewhat higher than the numbers cited here. Some vouchers are not redeemed, and some housing units are vacant at any given time (because of rehabilitation or replacement, normal tenant turnover, and other reasons).

HOPE VI funds were sufficient to support construction of 57,100 deeply subsidized units for families that meet the normal income and other requirements for public housing (Popkin and Cove 2007).

The purpose of all these different forms of housing subsidies is, first and foremost, to help poor people afford decent rental housing, and local authorities are, by and large, achieving that mission. So why bother with matters of work and self-sufficiency, which are traditionally the responsibility of other government systems? There are at least three reasons: to reach many of the nation's work-capable poor in need of employment support, to counter possible negative work influences associated with housing assistance, and to increase access to a limited supply of housing assistance by cycling recipients through the system more rapidly.

Reaching the Work-Capable Poor

Although housing subsidies are not an entitlement, they reach a large number of very low-income people. Many of these residents are capable of gainful employment (and many are already working), but they commonly have difficulty securing steady employment or advancing in work, despite whatever other government employment assistance might be available.

Of the approximately 4.2 million low-income households receiving HUD housing assistance at any given time, 46 percent (more than 1.9 million) are headed by working-age, nondisabled people, about 83 percent of whom (1.6 million) are raising children.[6] Taking into consideration the natural turnover of residents, this part of the nation's "housing safety net" actually touches many times more low-income individuals over a period of time. By contrast, the number of families who have children and are receiving cash aid through the Temporary Assistance for Needy Families (TANF) program at any given time (many of whom are also receiving HUD-assisted housing) is only somewhat higher: about 1.8 million in June 2006.[7]

How much do tenants with housing assistance actually work? According to HUD data from 2000, about 57 percent of nonelderly, nondisabled households across the three subsidy programs had some income from earnings at the time they were recertified as eligible for housing assistance that year.[8] Employment levels varied somewhat by subsidy program. Approximately 52 percent of residents of public housing, 57 percent of people with tenant-based vouchers, and 65 percent of those in project-based Section 8 housing reported earned income. Not surpris-

6. The percentage distribution is based on the author's calculations using data from Jeffrey Lubell, Mark Shroder, and Barry Steffen (2003, exhibit 1).

7. U.S. Department of Health and Human Services, "TANF: Total Number of Families, Fiscal Year 2006" (www.acf.hhs.gov).

8. Author's calculations using data from Lubell, Shroder, and Steffen (2003, exhibit 2). There is likely to be some degree of underreporting of earnings by tenants or inaccuracy or lags in reporting by housing authorities.

ingly, substantial numbers also rely on cash welfare. In 2000, for example, about 27 percent of working-age, nondisabled, HUD-assisted households received TANF (in some cases in combination with earnings) or state general assistance.[9]

It is important to note, however, that the amount of earned income of households with workers was quite low (according to housing authority records), with about 30 percent earning less than $8,300 a year, half earning less than $12,000 a year, and about 80 percent earning $18,000 a year or less.[10] This puts most employed recipients of federal housing assistance firmly in the ranks of the working poor or near poor. Moreover, in reviewing data on both nonworking and working residents, HUD emphasizes in a 2005 report to Congress that "public housing and Housing Choice Vouchers continue to serve the poorest segments of the population. . . . By 2004, 77 percent of the families in public housing had incomes less than 30 percent of local median income; the percentage in Housing Choice Vouchers was 79 percent" (HUD 2005, pp. 8–9).[11]

In terms of volume alone, then, the subsidized housing system is a good place to find large numbers of the very kinds of people that policymakers want to help succeed in work. But even if this system is a potentially valuable portal to the working poor or work-capable poor, it is reasonable to ask whether these residents are already being reached and helped through the mainstream jobs programs in their communities, especially those operated by the TANF Welfare to Work and Workforce Investment Act programs. Certainly some are. Yet the majority (about three-quarters) of nondisabled, working-age residents of assisted housing do not receive welfare and, consequently, do not participate in welfare-to-work programs (although many of them undoubtedly have in the past). In addition, those currently receiving welfare may very well exit welfare (and become ineligible for further employment assistance through that system) while still living in HUD-assisted housing because they get (usually low-wage) jobs, reach welfare time limits, or leave for other reasons. Still other working-age residents have older children or no children, or they do not otherwise qualify for welfare.

Evidence on the extent to which assisted housing residents use employment services funded under the Workforce Investment Act is scant, as is evidence on their participation in other job placement programs or education and training, such as those offered by community colleges or nonprofit service organizations. However, it is reasonable to expect that many potentially eligible residents are not aware of such opportunities or do not use them for any number of other reasons.

9. Author's calculations using data from Lubell, Shroder, and Steffen (2003, exhibit 1).

10. Author's calculations using data from Lubell, Shroder, and Steffen (2003, exhibit 4).

11. The report explains, "The predominance in the Housing Choice Voucher program of extremely low income households, those with incomes less than or equal to 30 percent of median income, is not surprising given the current income targeting requirements. In Housing Choice Vouchers, 75 percent of new households must have incomes less than or equal to 30 percent of median income. In public housing, 40 percent of new households must have incomes less than or equal to 30 percent of area median income" (HUD 2005, pp. 9–10).

It is also important to recognize that both the welfare-to-work and the workforce development systems are focused primarily on helping unemployed people find jobs, not on helping the working poor sustain employment and advance.

Even if these other systems are already helping to improve work outcomes for HUD-assisted tenants to some extent, the employment and earnings data cited above suggest that considerable room for improvement remains. Indeed, it is reasonable to speculate that, given proper assistance and incentives, many more assisted residents could enter work, sustain work, and advance in work than now do. Many such residents face substantial personal and situational barriers to employment, including low education and skill levels, health problems, and personal or family problems, and often they have poor knowledge about or skill in finding jobs or navigating their way to better opportunities. Special assistance tailored to assisted tenants that addresses these problems—and that could be supplied in collaboration with existing, nonhousing workforce programs (as is the case with some initiatives, such as the Family Self-Sufficiency and Jobs-Plus programs)—might help improve assisted tenants' success in the labor market.

In sum, these data show that many people with HUD-assisted housing who presumably have some potential to work are not working at a given point in time or that, if they do work, they often have difficulty getting or keeping anything other than low-paying jobs. It also appears that many are not served extensively through employment-related programs operated by other systems. Thus assisted housing offers one important opportunity for government to "do better" in reaching substantial numbers of some of the lowest-income people in the nation and helping them succeed in work.

Countering Negative Work Influences

Given that the main purpose of housing assistance is to provide access to affordable housing, the system's effect on self-sufficiency should, at the very least, be neutral: it should neither penalize nor impede work. Yet in its current incarnation, housing assistance may do just that; like any income transfer benefit program, it may deter many residents from trying to increase their earnings. According to this perspective, housing assistance recipients, on average, work and earn less than they would if they did not have a housing subsidy, because of the way the housing subsidy is structured.

With the tenant's rent contribution set at 30 percent of adjusted gross income, every dollar increase in income is effectively taxed at 30 percent. In other words, as residents' earnings rise, their rent also goes up (and the housing subsidy is reduced), thus substantially offsetting the gain in income through work. Housing assistance benefits phase out entirely when income rises beyond a certain point. Under the voucher program, for example, when 30 percent of income has been greater than or equal to the rent for six months, the tenant is no longer eligible for a subsidy. In public housing, when 30 percent of income equals the "ceiling rent" attached to a particular housing unit—if the ceiling is pegged to the cost of operating the unit or to market rates—the housing subsidy essentially ends, although residents paying the ceiling rent are not required to move out of public housing. Because this income-based-rent rule is equivalent to a tax on earnings, theory says—and many housing experts certainly believe—it will be a disincentive to increasing work effort, other things being equal. Theory also suggests that residents may feel less pressure to work to maintain a given lifestyle when their current living expenses are subsidized.

Of course, the real world is more complicated than this simple economic model assumes. Assisted tenants face a complex environment in which other public benefit and tax systems interact with rent subsidy rules in ways that could deepen the hypothesized negative effects of rent rules for some residents or, for others, could counteract the rules. Moreover, the sheer complexity of this system makes the overall work incentive structure difficult for residents even to comprehend, much less rationally tailor their behavior to. Consequently, how individual tenants view work in response to traditional rent rules may vary dramatically, depending on their personal ambitions, circumstances, and perceptions (right or wrong) about the added economic payoff of increased work effort in low-paying jobs.

The limited supply of housing assistance is another factor that might dampen work effort, especially among voucher holders and those on waiting lists for housing assistance. Unlike most federal safety net programs, housing assistance is not an entitlement; only about a fourth of eligible households receive it, and there are long waiting lists for assistance in many communities. As a consequence, families with vouchers may be more reluctant to increase their earnings to the point of becoming ineligible for housing assistance, because they are not assured of being able to obtain a voucher again if they later lose their job or see their earnings fall for other reasons (Harkness and Newman 2006; Newman 1999). This concern over job loss would seem particularly justified for those who could expect to participate in only the bottom rungs of the labor market, given that low-wage workers change jobs more than other workers and experience turnover that is more likely to be involuntary (because of layoffs, for example) and to be followed by a period of unemployment (Anderson, Holzer, and Lane 2005). One study estimates that only about 60 percent of low-wage workers in their mid-thirties held a job for at least a year (Bernhardt and others 2001).

Beyond the structure of the subsidy itself are possible negative peer and neighborhood effects. One hypothesis is that the large concentration of very low-income tenants in dense public housing and other project-based assisted housing developments, which also tend to be disproportionately located in poorer neighborhoods, discourages work effort (Newman and Schnare 1994, 1997; Kingsley and Tatian 1999).[12] Part of the negative effect, if there is one, might arise from

12. Thomas Kingsley and Peter Tatian (1999) show that the proportion of recipients of HUD housing assistance (including recipients of tenant-based vouchers) who live in high-poverty census tracts is much more extreme in some metropolitan areas than in others.

the more limited information, experience, and contacts through social networks in such settings. Philip Kasinitz and Jan Rosenberg's (1996) qualitative study of the Red Hook neighborhood in Brooklyn, New York, graphically illustrates the second hypothesis. Industrial employers with vacancies in blue-collar jobs located in this neighborhood were much less likely to hire residents of local public housing than other residents. Not being tied into the right networks, many public housing residents were unaware of job openings and did not apply.

An alternative perspective argues that housing assistance may function as a springboard into work (see, for example, Millennial Housing Commission 2002; Newman 2005; Sard and Waller 2002).[13] Because housing assistance provides a decent, stable, and affordable residence, recipients may be in a better position than they otherwise would to focus their energies on looking for employment rather than on housing problems. It may also be that physical adequacy, stability, and affordability might reduce their stress and improve their health, making it easier for them to focus on work. Finally, with regard to portable rent vouchers, it is possible that, by giving participants the ability to live in more advantageous locations relative to work opportunities, vouchers might improve success in finding work and, possibly, better jobs.

Taking account of these alternative perspectives and the numerous countervailing forces at play, it becomes quickly evident that, as some experts stress, theory itself is ambiguous when it comes to understanding the likely link between housing assistance and labor force behavior.[14] Ultimately, the question is an empirical one, making carefully built evidence all the more important.

What does the available evidence indicate? A growing body of nonexperimental research points to conflicting results. Some studies show positive effects of housing assistance on work outcomes; others show negative effects; and still others find little effect either way.[15] Overall, the weight of this evidence suggests that housing assistance may not matter consistently for labor force participation.

---

13. Citing research by Michael Murray (1980) and Barbara Schone (1992), Shroder (2002) notes that housing assistance, because it is not fungible, could be viewed as a "price cut" to a commodity that, under certain assumptions, may increase work effort to consume other goods.

14. Good discussions of the complicated theoretical underpinnings of this issue are provided by Shroder (2002), Jennifer Stoloff (2001), and Edgar Olsen and others (2005).

15. For a comprehensive review, see Shroder (2002). In a more recent review, Sandra Newman (2005) shows that among eleven nonexperimental studies that looked at the effects of housing subsidies—any housing subsidy or certain types—alone (that is, not as part of special employment services or welfare reform initiatives), four find negative effects (Schone 1994; Murray 1980; Fischer 2000; Susin 2005), one finds a positive effect (Ong 1998), and six find no enduring statistically significant effects (Reingold 1997; Ong 1998; Painter 2001; Reingold, Van Ryzin, and Ronda 2001; Berger and Heintze 2004; Joseph Harkness and Newman's analysis, subsequently published in 2006). Another recent study, drawing heavily on HUD data on housing type and income, adds to the negative side of the ledger, finding that vouchers as well as place-based housing subsidies reduce earnings compared with earnings in the absence of housing assistance but that the effects of vouchers are smaller (Olsen and others 2005).

To some extent, the conflicting results may be driven by problems in measuring housing receipt through self-reported survey data (Shroder 2002). But the three studies of this group that use more accurate measures of assisted housing receipt (from HUD administrative data) show more consistency, finding initial negative effects on work and earnings but also finding that these effects lessen over time (Harkness and Newman 2006; Susin 2005; Olsen and others 2005).

The best evidence on this issue comes from the few unusual studies that use experimental (that is, random assignment) research designs and that collect administrative records data to measure receipt of housing assistance as well as employment outcomes. One of these is the evaluation of the Welfare to Work Voucher program (Patterson and others 2004), which tested the effects of awarding tenant-based rent vouchers to recipients of cash welfare in six cities. To enroll in this study, a family had to be eligible to receive, to be receiving, or to have been a recipient of cash aid from federal or state welfare funds within the prior two years. In addition, the housing voucher had to be "critical" to the family's success in obtaining or retaining employment (although this standard was applied only loosely and inconsistently) (Smith and Johnson 2001). The study randomly assigned more than 8,7000 qualifying applicants who were on voucher waiting lists in six cities either to a program group that was offered a voucher or to a control group that was not. Few additional services were provided to the program group, thus making the study a reasonably "pure" test of the vouchers themselves.

The findings reveal no evidence that the program improved participants' labor market outcomes. On the contrary, in a pattern generally consistent with the findings of the three nonexperimental studies highlighted above, the study finds statistically significant declines in work and earnings for five to seven quarters after random assignment, but these declines faded over time. Over three and a half years of follow-up, the differences in employment and earnings between the treatment and control groups were not statistically significant (Mills and others 2006).

The second source of experimental evidence on this question comes from the Moving to Opportunity demonstration. As part of that demonstration, interested residents of public or other project-based housing in high-poverty areas of large central cities were randomly assigned to one of three groups: one that was offered special tenant-based rent vouchers (along with relocation counseling) that could be used only in low-poverty areas (where less than 10 percent of the population were poor), another that was offered the regular Section 8 rental vouchers, or a control group that was offered neither. Within the first four years of follow-up, neither the special Moving to Opportunity vouchers nor the regular Section 8 vouchers produced statistically significant changes in employment or earnings outcomes, relative to what the control group had achieved. It is noteworthy, however, that although the results are not statistically significant, the outcomes for the two voucher groups were worse than those for the control group, though these differences became less negative in the third and fourth years of follow-up.

The third important experimental study in this area examined the effects of offering housing choice vouchers to residents of unsubsidized private housing in Chicago who were on a voucher waiting list maintained by the city's public housing authority. The study took advantage of the fact that the priority on the waiting list was determined through a randomized process, so that the people who were and those who were not offered rental vouchers within a given period of time represented, in effect, naturally occurring experimental and control groups with otherwise similar characteristics. The study finds that receipt of a housing voucher reduced employment by 6 percentage points, or nearly 11 percent, and decreased average quarterly earnings by approximately $367, or 15 percent. The vouchers also increased the likelihood of receiving TANF, by 21 percent (Jacob and Ludwig 2006).

Increasing Access to a Limited Supply of Housing Assistance

Leaving aside the question of whether housing assistance reduces recipients' efforts to become self-sufficient, a different motivation for promoting greater employment and earnings among housing assistance recipients arises from the recognition that the supply of assistance is limited. As a consequence, it is unequally distributed, with some qualified families receiving housing assistance and other, equally qualified families not receiving it. Two obvious solutions would be to increase the size of housing programs and to tighten eligibility standards. A third approach would be to cycle participants through the program more rapidly. Many working-age, nondisabled residents do use housing assistance for only a short period of time. Although longitudinal data that would permit a true picture of the length of residents' spells in assisted housing are unavailable, some insights about tenant turnover can be gleaned from a study that measured tenancy duration for public housing residents and tenant-based voucher recipients as of late 2000. Among the households receiving assistance at this time that were headed by a resident who was neither elderly nor disabled, the median length of stay had so far been about 3.6 years for those in public housing and about 2.8 years among voucher holders. (Note, however, that in neither group did tenants complete their stays.) At the same time, about 20 percent of such tenants had already accumulated about 11.3 years in public housing and 7.0 years in the voucher program.[16]

One controversial way to reduce time spent receiving housing assistance would be to impose time limits on that assistance itself. Another approach that would hold wider appeal would be to accelerate participants' progress toward self-sufficiency so they would have the means to leave assisted housing or could manage with a reduced amount of subsidy, freeing up resources to serve other eligible families. In that way, a given pot of housing assistance dollars could be used to assist more households within a given year.

16. Author's calculations using data from Lubell, Shroder, and Steffen (2003, exhibits 5 and 7).

The Quality Housing and Work Responsibility Act of 1998 manifests this logic. The stated "purpose" in Section 502(b) of the legislation is to "promote homes that are affordable to low-income families in safe and healthy environments, and thereby contribute to the supply of affordable housing." As one of seven "strategies" for achieving this goal, the act lists "creating incentives and economic opportunities for residents of dwelling units assisted by public housing agencies to work, become self-sufficient, and transition out of public housing and federally assisted dwelling units." According to this perspective, the policy problem is not so much that housing assistance discourages work effort but that there is a shortage of affordable housing. Speeding the transition of housing assistance recipients to self-sufficiency so that more families can be assisted is one possible way of addressing this problem.

Reforms and Interventions Already Tried

A number of housing-based interventions to promote work among HUD-assisted tenants have been tried over the past two decades. They have generally involved collaboration between a local housing authority and other public and private agencies to supply employment-related services.

The Family Self-Sufficiency Program and Its Predecessors

The most important of these housing-employment programs have been part of a sequence of initiatives that many housing authorities across the nation have operated: Project Self-Sufficiency, launched in 1984; Operation Bootstrap, launched in 1989; and the Family Self-Sufficiency (FSS) program, which began in 1991 and continues today.[17] The first two of these programs were available exclusively to low-income people who were applying for Section 8 assistance. In addition to receiving that assistance, they were offered help with education, training, and job placement in addition to other assistance. The current FSS program—which also includes a financial incentive to work and save—is open to residents of public housing and recipients of housing choice vouchers but not to residents of project-based Section 8 housing.

Like its predecessors, FSS requires participants to agree to a personalized self-sufficiency plan (generally lasting up to five years) that identifies the steps they will take to become employed, improve their earnings, and become independent of

---

17. The Gateway Transitional Families program—a small-scale initiative operated as a special demonstration project in the late 1980s to early 1990s by the Charlotte, North Carolina, Public Housing Authority—expanded on the Project Self-Sufficiency model by piloting an escrow savings account to promote homeownership, an idea later incorporated into the national Family Self-Sufficiency program. As a further work incentive, it obtained authorization to have participants' welfare and food stamp benefits frozen for a period of time so that earnings gains would not be offset by benefit reductions (Rohe and Kleit 1997).

TANF or state general assistance. The program provides each participant with a case manager who helps arrange job counseling, education, job training, and support services (such as child care and transportation assistance) as called for by the plan. These services are provided by other agencies in the community, through a collaborative arrangement with the housing authority. The program also includes an important work-promoting asset-building component.[18] For participants in good standing who increase their incomes by increasing their earnings, the extra rent they would normally be obligated to pay (up to certain limits) is deposited into an interest-bearing escrow account maintained by the housing authority. Those who complete their self-sufficiency plans get a full disbursement of the escrow accounts, as long as they are employed and are not receiving cash welfare at the time of disbursement.[19]

The FSS program currently serves more than 52,000 participants, of whom approximately 87 percent hold vouchers.[20] Despite the large number of participants, only about 5 percent of working-age, nondisabled housing choice voucher recipients are enrolled in the program at any given time, and roughly 1 percent of similar people living in public housing are enrolled.[21]

Evidence of whether any of these programs actually improved participants' employment, earnings, and other self-sufficiency outcomes is weak. The existing evaluations are largely descriptive in nature, showing outcomes for program participants over time, but they were not able to produce reliable estimates of program effects, or "impacts," because they lacked control groups made up of truly equivalent types of people who did not have access to the program. (A proper control group is essential for establishing a benchmark showing what program participants would have achieved in the absence of the intervention.) Other limitations include the absence of outcome data on employment and receipt of transfer benefits, other than the information reported to the housing authorities. This is a problem not simply as a matter of accurate reporting but also because these data cannot capture program effects on self-sufficiency outcomes that may grow larger or disappear after residents exit the program or leave housing assistance.

18. The U.S. Department of Housing and Urban Development provides housing authorities with funding to hire a case manager and to pay for the escrow savings. Housing authorities may also use other local resources to hire additional staff or provide other service enrichments.

19. Interim disbursements are also available if needed to help continue working (such as to pay for car repairs) or for education and training that can improve job opportunities.

20. The program was optional for housing authorities in 1991 and 1992, but it became mandatory in 1993. Public housing authorities were required to increase the number of FSS participants in accordance with any increase in the number of housing subsidies they offered. Because the number of new tenant-based vouchers far exceeded the number of new public housing units, most FSS slots have been allocated to the voucher program. This rule was rescinded under QHWRA (Ficke and Piesse 2004).

21. Author's calculations using data from Robert Ficke and Andrea Piesse (2004) and from Lubell, Shroder, and Steffen (2003, exhibit 1).

The evaluations also do not provide any information on costs or cost-benefit results.[22]

The Moving to Work Demonstration

The Moving to Work demonstration, launched in 1997 within HUD, has become a laboratory for trying a broader set of reforms intended to promote self-sufficiency among assisted tenants. As part of this initiative, twenty-four competitively selected public housing authorities have been granted far-reaching flexibility to combine their different streams of HUD subsidies and use them in any way they think will encourage tenants to enter the workforce, free of many of the rules and regulations of typical housing programs. Variations in rent reforms that are being tried include delaying rent increases as income increases, reducing the rent-to-income ratio for a period of time, and setting flat rents or ceiling rents so that rents do not continue to increase with income. More recently, some public housing authorities have begun to institute time limits on housing assistance. Although the Moving to Work demonstration has been an impressive source of creative reform, these efforts have not been assessed through rigorous evaluation. Thus whether they have any substantial positive effects on residents' self-sufficiency remains unknown (Newman 1999).[23]

The Jobs-Plus Demonstration

An important exception to this lack of evidence can be found in the Jobs-Plus Community Revitalization Initiative for Public Housing Families, a (now-completed) demonstration project that was authorized under the Moving to Work legislation and involved an additional six public housing authorities.[24] The Jobs-Plus program was one of the most comprehensive employment interventions ever tried in public housing.[25] The program model included the following key elements:

22. For a review and critique of the evaluations of these programs and a recommendation to use random assignment designs in future evaluations, see Bogdon (1999). A recent HUD-sponsored impact assessment of the FSS program for voucher holders is more comprehensive than past evaluations of FSS and uses a comparison group made up of non-FSS voucher recipients. The analysis is limited to single parents aged twenty-five to forty-four. Despite baseline comparability between the FSS and non-FSS groups on several important demographic variables, selection bias cannot be ruled out. As the report itself states, "Although the comparison group was similar to the FSS group in terms of age and family composition, it is possible that the groups differed in other characteristics that may have affected the outcomes discussed here. For example, because the comparison group members were not in the FSS program, they may be less motivated than were FSS participants" (Ficke and Piesse 2004, p. 29).

23. For a summary and assessment of this initiative, see Abravanel and others (2004).

24. The six housing authorities operating Jobs-Plus, added to the twenty-four main Moving to Work sites, brought the total number of demonstration sites to thirty, the maximum number authorized by Congress. Jobs-Plus was jointly sponsored by HUD and the Rockefeller Foundation, with additional support from other public and private funders.

25. Findings on the impacts of this initiative are presented in Bloom, Riccio, and Verma (2005).

—Assistance with job placement and training from job coaches, job developers, and other staff conveniently located on-site at a small job center established within the housing development

—New rent rules that helped make low-wage work pay by allowing working residents to keep more of their earnings, usually in the form of a flat rent, with an income-based rent retained as a safety net option for those who lost jobs and would have had difficulty affording the flat rent

—A community-support-for-work component that involved residents in neighbor-to-neighbor information-sharing about work opportunities, rent incentives, and other program benefits

Jobs-Plus was not a limited-slot program; instead, it targeted all working-age, nondisabled residents of the housing development. It attempted to saturate the social environment within public housing with work-focused encouragement, information, incentives, and active assistance. Jobs-Plus was to be operated in each city through a local interagency partnership that involved the welfare department and the workforce development agency, along with the housing authority, which provided overall leadership. These partnerships also included resident representatives, whose voice and support were considered essential for such a significant intervention into their communities. Other social service, training, and employment agencies and schools also participated.

The evaluation of Jobs-Plus's effectiveness on residents' work outcomes combined a comparative interrupted time-series analysis with a development-level random assignment design. Within each of the six cities, two or three matched housing developments were placed in a pool, and one was then randomly selected to operate Jobs-Plus while the others were allocated to the control group, which did not operate the program. The results of this study show conclusively that, when properly implemented, the program increased public housing residents' earnings, by an average of 14 percent over four years and by 20 percent in the last year. In dollar terms, residents in the Jobs-Plus developments, on average, earned in excess of $1,100 more a year, and $1,543 more in the last year, than they would have earned without the program. For some groups, the annual earnings gains exceeded $3,000.[26] This success was brought about by a close collaboration among local welfare, workforce, and public housing agencies and is especially noteworthy because it was achieved in some of the poorest public housing developments in the nation, in different cities, and for different types of residents—including black single parents in Dayton, Ohio; married Latino men in Los Angeles, California; and Southeast Asian refugee men and women in St. Paul, Minnesota.

---

26. These average earnings estimates are based on all working-age, nondisabled residents, not just those who were employed. Consequently, actual earnings gains accruing to those who worked were larger.

The effectiveness of Jobs-Plus stands in marked contrast to the absence of labor market effects (at least in the short term) from an alternative approach tested by HUD's Moving to Opportunity demonstration (Bloom, Riccio, and Verma 2005).[27] The Moving to Opportunity demonstration, as described above, tested a strategy that sought to improve public housing residents' self-sufficiency not through special services or incentives but rather through residential mobility. Residents were offered special tenant-based rent vouchers to subsidize their rent in the private housing market in low-poverty neighborhoods. The designers of this approach hoped that these vouchers would allow residents to move to areas where more jobs and better jobs would be more accessible to them and where they could become part of community-based social networks that had a better flow of information about job opportunities and were more supportive of work.

The interim results show that, within the first four years of follow-up, the intervention had not improved residents' employment or earnings. Of course, mobility strategies like these may take more time to make a difference on employment, and perhaps the demonstration's longer-term findings will later reveal positive effects. Or it may be that mobility strategies by themselves are unlikely to produce effects on work outcomes for public housing residents. If so, perhaps they would be more likely to produce such effects if, like Jobs-Plus, they included explicit services to help residents find, keep, and advance in work, along with extra financial incentives to provide further encouragement to do so (Bloom, Riccio, and Verma 2005).

Welfare-to-Work Evaluations

A number of random assignment evaluations of welfare reform strategies of the 1990s speak to the question of whether employment-focused interventions—particularly, welfare-to-work services and participation requirements and, in some cases, welfare-based work incentives—can improve the self-sufficiency outcomes of welfare recipients who also receive housing subsidies. The findings are fairly consistent, showing that welfare reform typically produced larger earnings impacts for residents who were receiving HUD-administered housing assistance than it did for those without housing assistance.

This is clear from table 6-1, which summarizes the results of such analyses completed through 2003. (Each earnings impact shown in the table reflects the estimated difference in cumulative average earnings between the program and control group members of the specified housing subgroup.) In fact, of the ten different analyses listed (counting the two Minnesota studies as one), eight show some evidence of substantially larger earnings effects for welfare recipients who

---

27. For a helpful comparison of Jobs-Plus with Moving to Opportunity and another HUD demonstration focusing on transportation to suburban jobs (Bridges to Work), see Turner and Rawlings (2005).

Table 6-1. *Impacts of Welfare Reform Interventions on Average Cumulative Earnings of Welfare Recipients, by Housing Subgroup*[a]
U.S. dollars

Intervention	Follow-up period (years)	Public housing	Vouchers	Combined Section 8[b]	Any housing assistance	No housing assistance
Minnesota Family Investment program						
Interim findings; no HUD data	1.5	...	...	...	2,041***	429
Long-term findings; with HUD data	3	...	...	...	5,473***	603
Indiana Manpower and Comprehensive Training (IMPACT) program						
Early cohort	5	2,209	2,549	...	...	2,003***
Later cohort	2	...	...	...	1,461*	−202
Delaware's A Better Chance	2	...	...	...	591	318
Connecticut Jobs First						
First comparison	4		...	...	3,965**	1,658
Second comparison	4	3,564	3,368	...		1,658
Atlanta NEWWS						
Labor Force Attachment strategy	3	2,115***	...	1,801**	...	1,585*
Human Capital Development strategy	3	1,762***	...	1,471*	...	853
Columbus NEWWS						
Traditional case management strategies	3	2,819*	...	−20	...	140
Integrated case management strategies	3	2,239	...	460	...	992

Source: Adapted from Verma and Riccio (2003, table 6.1). Data are from Miller (1998), Verma and Riccio (2003), Lee and others (2003), and Riccio and Orenstein (2003).

a. Numbers reflect differences in earnings between program and control group members within each housing subgroup category. All results are based on a random assignment research design in which eligible people were randomly allocated across program and control groups for each study. The earnings impacts shown in each cell of this table were regression-adjusted using ordinary least squares, controlling for pre-random assignment characteristics of sample members. "HUD data" refers to HUD administrative records used to determine sample members' housing status at the time of random assignment. "NEWWS" refers to National Evaluation of Welfare-to-Work Strategies.

b. Combined Section 8 category includes project-based Section 8 assistance and Section 8 vouchers.

***$p = .01$; **$p = .05$; *$p = .10$.

were receiving some form of housing assistance at the time of enrollment in the study, compared with recipients who had no housing assistance. Although not all of the estimated impacts for recipients with housing assistance are statistically significant, the overall pattern is striking (Verma and Riccio 2003; see also Riccio and Orenstein 2003).[28]

These welfare reform findings lend credence to the idea that, at least for welfare recipients already receiving housing assistance, providing an employment-focused intervention may improve their earnings outcomes. Taken together with the Jobs-Plus results, they are a reason for encouragement that effective work-focused interventions for recipients of various forms of housing assistance can be designed and operated. Still, many questions remain about how to approach this challenge—and build reliable evidence of effectiveness—from within the housing assistance world.

Elements of a Comprehensive Random Assignment Evaluation

A randomized controlled trial, where feasible, is a highly credible way of determining whether a social intervention is successful in producing its intended effects. In a simple design, individuals (or groups) slated for an intervention are assigned through a lottery to either a program group that is subject to the intervention or a control group that is not. Because this assignment is made purely on the basis of chance, no systematic differences will distinguish the two groups at the beginning of the study (assuming sufficiently large sample sizes). For example, both the intervention group (the "program group") and the control group will have similar proportions of people with measurable traits (for example, age, education, prior work experience) and immeasurable background traits or circumstances (such as ambition to succeed, people skills, technical adeptness, supportive family environments) that might affect future employment, earnings, and other outcomes of interest. Thus if subsequent average differences in outcomes do emerge between the groups, those differences can be attributed with confidence solely to the intervention.

One common first response to the idea of using random assignment to study a social program is that it is unethical. It is true that in many situations random

---

28. The Indiana program's early cohort results and those from the Delaware study run counter to the overall pattern. However, the Delaware program was not very effective for either housing subgroup, and the full study finds that, by the second year of follow-up, its overall earnings effects had faded completely. It may be noted also that, for the Columbus integrated case management study component of the National Evaluation of Welfare-to-Work Strategies, none of the subgroup earnings impacts shown in table 6-1 is statistically significant. However, the impacts for the two subgroups with assisted housing are still much larger than those for the subgroup with no housing assistance. Furthermore, other data show that the program impacts on employment rates and average earnings in the last quarter of the follow-up period are statistically significant for the public housing subgroup but not for the Section 8 or unassisted subgroups.

assignment cannot be defended on ethical grounds. For example, it would not be ethical to use this methodology to assess the labor market effects of the current earned income tax credit, which qualifying individuals are already entitled to under current law. Denying access to this national benefit to a randomly selected subgroup of eligible taxpayers would be considered unfair. However, not all social programs are entitlements funded at levels permitting all who qualify to participate. That is true of assisted housing in general, for which, in many cities, long waiting lists exist, and it is true of many government-funded employment initiatives. In circumstances in which the demand for a service or benefit outstrips the supply, random assignment can be viewed as a fair way of allocating a scarce resource, because all applicants have an equal chance of obtaining it. Indeed, some housing authorities have been known to randomly assign applicants to their placement on a waiting list to determine who has priority for assisted housing.

In many cases, randomly assigning individuals to a program or control group is simply not feasible. For example, because Jobs-Plus was designed as a saturation initiative that targeted all working-age, nondisabled residents and aimed to build a work-promoting social environment within public housing, it was not feasible for the evaluation to isolate from the intervention a subset of households within a public housing development to serve as a control group. Similarly, an education reform agenda may apply to a whole school, so that it is not feasible to isolate some students within the school to serve as a control group that would be untouched by the reforms. In these and other circumstances, however, it may be possible to make the institution or group the unit of randomization. Thus in Jobs-Plus entire housing developments within the selected cities were randomly allocated to the program or control groups. Similarly, in a number of education evaluations, whole schools have been randomly assigned to the program or control group. In some studies, whole communities have been randomly assigned.[29]

Where feasible and implemented correctly, random assignment offers a highly credible means for determining the effectiveness of a social intervention. However, it is only a foundation. Maximizing the learning from such a trial calls for a comprehensive evaluation strategy with several strands of research, such as an impact analysis, an implementation and process analysis, and a cost-benefit analysis. An impact analysis measures the differences made by the program on self-sufficiency and quality-of-life outcomes. In the best impact studies, a wide range of outcomes is measured using data collected from administrative records (such as unemployment insurance wage records and welfare agency records) and surveys of residents. An effect, or impact, is the difference in an outcome—for example, in average earnings after random assignment—between the program and control groups.

---

29. For a discussion of group-level randomization, see Bloom (2005).

Thus an impact analysis would answer such questions as, To what extent does the intervention improve job entry, employment retention, career advancement, and total income for the program group relative to the control group? How much does the intervention reduce the need for welfare and improve various aspects of child and family well-being?[30] Which types of effects emerge in the short term, and which ones take longer to materialize? How long do the observed effects last? Which approaches are most successful in producing positive impacts?

Through carefully specified subgroup analyses, an impact study can determine whether the effectiveness of an intervention is similar for different types of residents (for example, those with different types of barriers to work or different degrees of disadvantage) or whether the effects are much larger for some than for others. This is important, given the great heterogeneity of assisted housing families and the dynamics of their lives (Shroder 2002).

An implementation and process study documents and assesses how—and how well—the intervention model was put into practice, how it functioned "on the ground," and the challenges entailed in transforming the intervention concept into an operational program. This analysis answers such questions as, Was the treatment implemented as planned, permitting a fair test of the underlying concept? Which services were provided, how well were they delivered, and how widely and intensively were they used? Recognizing that members of the control group might find their way to similar alternative services on their own, to what extent did the intended difference in service receipt between the program and control groups actually materialize? Given that the intervention in question may represent a bundle of attributes (say, services of different kinds plus financial incentives), implementation and process analyses are often essential in getting behind the complexity of the model, showing how it functioned in the real world, and producing insights into what may or may not have contributed to the program's effects—or why it did not work. These analyses typically draw on a combination of qualitative field research and quantitative data on service receipt from agency records and surveys of residents.

A cost-benefit study draws on both the impact and the process analyses to estimate the resources used by the program and the overall economic outcomes it generates. It examines such issues as the cost to operate the program and which

---

30. None of the past evaluations of FSS or other housing-based self-sufficiency programs have estimated effects on child outcomes. Moreover, according to Newman (2005), only two studies have examined the effects of assisted housing on children, and both focused on public housing: Janet Currie and Aaron Yelowitz (2000), who studied grade retention; and Newman and Harkness (2002), who analyze a range of long-term outcomes including work, earnings, and educational attainment after the age of twenty. As Newman (2005) notes, both studies yield the unexpected finding that public housing children experienced better outcomes than their unassisted counterparts. Work now under way is examining both short- and long-term effects for children.

factors drive those costs, the added investment above the cost of any relevant alternative services received by the control group, and how the economic outcomes produced by the program stack up against the net investment made in the intervention. In comparing costs and benefits, it is necessary to distinguish from whose perspective the comparison is being made. It is common for such analysis to examine separately the return on investment to government budgets and taxpayers and also the gains and losses to the program's participants. In the case of housing employment initiatives, it would be relevant to extend such an analysis to include the perspective of housing authorities as well.

The overall quality and usefulness of a random assignment study depend on a number of factors. First and foremost, care must be taken to ensure, as much as possible, that the interventions are implemented as designed and that the sites in which the experiment is carried out reflect common conditions. Key, of course, is implementing the random assignment process correctly in the field. This means ensuring not only that the allocation of sample members is truly random but also that the treatment differential between the program and control groups is maintained over time—for example, that the control group members do not inadvertently or deliberately get the treatment reserved for the program group for a specified period of time and that there is no differential attrition in the collection of follow-up data on the program and control groups that could introduce post–random assignment bias. This requires careful monitoring in the field.

Also important is that the sample size must be large enough to make it possible to determine whether observed program effects are statistically significant (that is, not chance outcomes) and to measure the program's effects across a variety of important subgroups. Multisite studies are valuable for assessing whether the intervention can work in a variety of settings and whether some types of practices or implementation conditions make the intervention more effective or less effective.[31]

Randomized Trials within the Housing Choice Voucher Program

It is possible to envision a number of research demonstration projects for building evidence about ways to improve work outcomes for residents of assisted housing.

---

31. All these considerations can add appreciably to the cost of a randomized control trial. At the same time, it is important to recognize that often it is the cost of collecting and cleaning survey and administrative records data that accounts for a large portion of evaluation costs. But these are not costs that are peculiar to randomized trials; they would also be incurred for a nonexperimental evaluation that used comparison groups and required similar types of data. The added cost of the randomization process—and maintaining the integrity of the experimental design in the field—may, depending on the study, be a relatively small or modest share of the overall research costs in a comprehensive evaluation.

These interventions for housing choice voucher recipients would allow evaluation through randomized controlled trials.[32]

There are at least three reasons to focus work-promoting efforts on the voucher program. First, it is the best place to find working-age, able-bodied adults who receive HUD-administered housing assistance vouchers. In fact, able-bodied, working-age residents make up 61 percent of all voucher recipients, compared with 50 percent of public housing residents and 26 percent of residents of private project-based assisted housing (that is, project-based Section 8).[33] Overall, vouchers serve more families headed by an able-bodied, working-age resident than the other two programs combined.

Second, the voucher program is the only program among the three that has grown substantially over the past decade. Except for replacement of some aging units, largely through the HOPE VI program, there has been little new public housing construction. In fact, because of demolition, the total number of public housing units is shrinking. In the face of a strong rental market, project-based Section 8 is seeing increased expirations and nonrenewals of government contracts with private owners. Tenants who are displaced from the latter programs are typically transferred to vouchers.

Third, the Quality Housing and Work Responsibility Act of 1998 requires that 75 percent of vouchers be reserved for families with incomes below 30 percent of the area's median income. In contrast, at least 40 percent of public housing units must be reserved for families at this income level. For privately owned assisted housing subsidized under the Section 8 project-based program, income-targeting requirements are the same as for public housing. This raises at least the possibility that the tenant mix will shift over time, with the most disadvantaged segments of the working-age population being increasingly concentrated in the voucher program.[34]

Evaluating the Family Self-Sufficiency Program

As discussed above, a large federal program designed to increase the self-sufficiency of housing choice voucher recipients already exists: the Family Self-Sufficiency

32. The types of experiments discussed here take the existence of housing assistance for granted. They ask, For those receiving housing assistance, can employment-focused interventions improve various work and life outcomes? In contrast to the Welfare to Work Vouchers experiment, it does not ask, What are the effects of vouchers alone on self-sufficiency outcomes, relative to the control condition of no (or a much lower likelihood of receiving) housing vouchers or other housing assistance? From a methodological standpoint, focusing on recipients of housing vouchers who have already gotten landlords to accept their vouchers would avoid the problem that both the Welfare to Work Vouchers and the Moving to Opportunity evaluations confronted—the fact that a substantial proportion of program group members in each study failed to find an apartment for which they could actually use the voucher.

33. Author's calculations using data from Lubell, Shroder, and Steffen (2003, exhibit 1).

34. Joseph Harkness (personal communication).

program. Although not a place-based intervention, FSS, like the successful Jobs-Plus program for public housing residents, combines employment-related services and financial work incentives. However, the effectiveness of this program remains largely unknown, as do its economic costs and benefits, because of the significant limitations of its prior evaluations. Subjecting FSS to a comprehensive, random assignment test could thus add substantially to the evidence on employment interventions in the assisted housing field.

The random assignment process could be set up in a number of ways, but any of these would require that there be substantially more people who are eligible for the program who want to join it than there are FSS slots available. With a surplus of applicants, random assignment would be a fair way to ration the limited supply of slots.

Assuming that an adequate supply of vacant FSS slots exists (which might require an overall expansion of the program capacity in evaluation sites), one way of setting up random assignment would begin with the housing authority's identifying all eligible working-age residents who are receiving vouchers but are not currently enrolled in FSS (the majority of working-age voucher holders). A recruitment campaign would encourage eligible candidates to apply for a chance—as in a lottery—to secure one of the limited number of new FSS slots. Half of those who volunteer would then be randomly assigned to the program group, and the remainder would be placed in the control group. Members of the control group would be restricted from participating in FSS during the study period.

Because the allocation of people to the program and control groups would be determined randomly, the two groups would be similar, on average, in terms of measurable and immeasurable background characteristics (assuming adequate sample sizes). In this way, the true effect of the intervention itself could be estimated with confidence by comparing the subsequent outcomes that the two groups achieve. This approach is especially important for tests of voluntary programs like FSS because certain difficult-to-measure traits (for example, ambition to succeed) that might lead some housing voucher recipients to volunteer for FSS in the first place are traits that might also affect their success in the labor market.[35]

To assess the effectiveness of FSS nationally, such an experiment would ideally be conducted in a representative and randomly selected subset of housing authorities that operate FSS programs. However, practical and other considerations may rule this out. If so, it would be essential to select at least a variety of locations that broadly capture the diversity of local conditions in which FSS programs operate and the diversity of the tenant populations they serve. Of course,

35. Precisely because they are so difficult to measure, nonexperimental statistical modeling methods cannot adequately control for the effects of these traits on future self-sufficiency outcomes. For a comparison of experimental and nonexperimental impact estimates for various initiatives, see Bloom (2005).

the greater the number of locations and conditions, the more challenging and expensive the study would be in terms of recruiting sites and households to participate, setting up and sustaining a proper trial, and collecting the necessary data. In general, however, the larger and more diverse the set of locations involved, the better would be the evaluation's ability to speak to the possible generalizability of the results beyond the study sites, and the more opportunity it would have to determine whether the intervention worked for different types of people and places served or, in contrast, was effective only under certain conditions or for certain types of residents but not overall.

Evaluating an Enhanced Family Self-Sufficiency Program

Despite the appeal of the FSS program in its current form, it is possible to envision a number of modifications and enhancements that have the potential to make it a more powerful intervention. These would include changes in the program's incentives structure that might broaden its appeal and strengthen its potential to induce bigger changes in residents' efforts and capacities to advance in work.

The current FSS program takes an escrow-based approach to rewarding work. Although clear evidence is lacking, it may be that the long delay in getting access to the escrow savings may limit the appeal of the program and its work incentives to a narrower—and more selective—slice of the potentially eligible population of residents than would other alternatives that offer more immediately accessible incentives. It is possible, for example, that the residents who are most motivated to take advantage of the FSS program are also the ones who need the least assistance in order to work steadily—in other words, they may be just as likely to work (or to work consistently, full time, or to seek better employment) as they would without the program. Although the escrow strategy increases participants' assets— a positive accomplishment—it is not clear that it changes participants' work behavior and opportunities or that as a behavior-changing intervention it is as effective as alternative strategies that might provide more income immediately. It may be that the escrow strategy primarily rewards behavior that would have occurred anyway. (If that were the case, this should not be considered a "failure," particularly if one goal is to transfer more resources to people who are working but who still have quite low incomes.)

Another reason for rethinking the FSS model is that housing authorities vary widely in the scope and intensity of services they offer participants through their partnerships with other agencies and local service providers. There is nothing inherent in the FSS model itself, however, that calls for postemployment support, such as job coaching to promote advancement among working participants and assistance in accessing other financial work supports for which working residents may be eligible (such as food stamps, Medicaid, the State Children's Health Insurance Program, child care subsidies, the earned income tax credit, and the child tax credit). In addition, there are no immediate, direct incentives to build skills.

Although escrow funds can be used to pay for extra education or training, it can take time for these to accumulate income gains through earnings.

With these limitations in mind, an enhanced FSS program—referred to here as FSS-Plus—could incorporate some important features as part of the core program model. A new rent-based work incentive would change how earnings are treated in calculating rent. The main objective would be to provide residents with a more immediate gain from increasing their labor supply and wages than is possible through the FSS escrow strategy. Such a rent policy could be structured in a number of different ways.

Assistance in accessing existing financial work supports would help make low-wage work "pay." As mentioned above, these work supports include the earned income tax credit, the child tax credit, food stamps, child care subsidies, Medicaid, and the State Children's Health Insurance Program. Educating participants on the potential value of these financial work supports when combined with earnings, assessing participants' likely eligibility for them, and assisting participants in getting them would help working residents take full advantage of the current highly complicated patchwork of existing government make-work-pay benefits, which are thought to be substantially underused by eligible low-income workers. Increased use of such benefits could put more money quickly into the pockets of these workers. "Fill-the-gap" child care and transportation subsidies would be included where existing resources for such assistance for low-income workers are inadequate to meet the demand: This assistance would help reduce the cost of working and, in that way, would also help to make low-wage work pay.

An expanded scope of job coaching with a strong focus on employment retention and advancement (included in demonstration projects under way in the United States and the United Kingdom) would aim to help working residents stay employed and also acquire occupational skills, knowledge of the labor market, capacity for identifying better job opportunities, and a vision and confidence to move to better opportunities. The job search guidance would be informed by an understanding of how a particular job's earnings would affect the worker's net income, taking into account the interaction between earnings and the financial work supports described above (which can be aided with a special computerized income calculator).[36]

36. For information on large-scale random assignment tests of the United Kingdom Employment Retention and Advancement project and, in the United States, the Employment Retention and Advancement demonstration and the Work Advancement and Support Center demonstration—all of which target low-income people—see the MDRC website (www.mdrc.org). For examples on the design and use of the income calculator, see Anderson, Kato, and Riccio (2006) and Gardenhire-Crooks (2004). Providing job coaching and case management through a housing-based employment initiative raises the important practical question concerning how to deal with the fact that many residents may already have case managers in other programs in which they are involved, such as welfare-to-work programs. Resolving potentially overlapping services requires careful coordination across agencies. For examples of how this was addressed in Jobs-Plus, see Kato and Riccio (2001).

Financial incentives to encourage participants to take up job-related education and training while employed could help them prepare for better-paying jobs in occupations with strong labor market demand. The incentives could take the form, for example, of tuition assistance and a bonus paid for completing approved courses while also holding a part-time or full-time job.[37]

Finally, a new asset-building component that is not tied to the rent structure could help workers accumulate resources and provide a cushion against possible future spells of unemployment or poverty and be a foundation for continued improvement in their economic security. It might be used, for example, to help residents save for a "rainy day," prepare for a transition into unsubsidized housing or homeownership, pay for future education or training or self-employment opportunities, or even build resources for retirement. Escrow accounts are one type of asset-building strategy, of course, and they were the centerpiece of the FSS program. However, if other types of work-based rent reforms are adopted as an alternative, a program could still encourage residents to save for the future through other mechanisms. For example, asset-building strategies could include individual development accounts or other savings accounts in which savings are rewarded with a small matching contribution. The matched portion of these accounts could be made payable on exiting from the housing assistance program or for expenses relating to education, training, or work. The program could also offer banking services (for example, free checking accounts and check cashing), debt counseling, and other financial planning services.

Taken together, this varied list of features of an enhanced FSS program would seek to address a broad range of conditions that discourage or make it difficult for many residents to become more self-sufficient.[38] As such, it is likely to be a more intensive intervention than the typical FSS program implemented across the country. It might also be more costly. Therefore, it is important to consider how to contain those costs. One way, as noted above, might be to shorten the time that participants have access to the rent-based work incentives—perhaps to three years rather than the current FSS program's five-year maximum. It may also be worth considering shortening the length of eligibility for other services. A shorter period of eligibility for each resident would allow a given number of staff to serve a larger number of people over time.

Evaluating the Individual Components of a Family Self-Sufficiency Program

One evaluation strategy is to evaluate FSS or FSS-Plus in its entirety. This makes sense if it is hypothesized that the program model contains a variety of features

---

37. This strategy is being tested in the United Kingdom's Employment Retention and Advancement project and in New York City's Opportunity NYC demonstrations (at www.mdrc.org).

38. Not all eligible residents would need or benefit from all these features, but having a comprehensive set of features increases the chances that, in a broad group of residents, everyone would be helped by at least something the program has to offer.

that work together to produce positive earnings and other effects. Thus the impact evaluation question would be, Did the program, as a whole, succeed? However, there may also be reason to measure how much, if at all, certain core features of the program contributed to its success. For example, could the program (if it does succeed) be just as effective if it offered only the financial incentives, with no additional services? Or if it offered only the work-related services, with no incentives? A streamlined program would be less costly to operate, so knowing whether the added components of the program actually add value to its effectiveness (and not just to its costs) would be important.

Constructing an evaluation to provide this type of evidence is more complicated because it requires the creation of multiple treatment groups as well as a control group. Ideally, a multiple-group random assignment design would be implemented within each of several sites. For example, eligible applicants could be assigned at random to one of the following four groups: one would receive only the financial incentives, another only the work-related services, a third the comprehensive program offering the full package of services plus incentives, and the fourth, the control group, would be offered no special services or incentives.

This type of test would allow a comparison of each alternative relative to the others. However, practical considerations—such as difficulty generating a large enough sample for all four groups or limited local capacity to operate more than one form of intervention at a time—might rule out this design in many locations. An alternative would be to test each of the three treatment group options separately against the control group in different sets of sites. Comparing the advantages or disadvantages of any given intervention strategy relative to the others would be more complicated and leave more uncertainty, but it could still be highly informative.

Evaluating Alternative Strategies within a Family Self-Sufficiency Program

Another way to build evidence on the effectiveness of FSS or related strategies is to conduct a more limited randomized control trial that focuses only on alternative rent-based work incentive strategies within the current FSS program. For example, one such test would compare a group of housing choice voucher recipients that is offered the current FSS program with the escrow-based incentive plan and a group that is offered FSS with an alternative incentive plan, such as a type of flat-rent strategy, as described above, or some other alternative. This would show whether alternative approaches would convince more residents to enroll in FSS and would improve their employment, earnings, savings, and other outcomes.

Evaluating Other Strategies

As discussed above, evidence available so far from the Moving to Opportunity (MTO) demonstration suggests that simply relocating public housing residents to low-poverty communities with the help of special rent vouchers does not improve their self-sufficiency outcomes. However, this leaves open the question of whether some version of such vouchers combined with employment-focused services could be effective (an approach that might be dubbed MTO-Plus).[39] With these considerations in mind, one can easily envision adapting one of the FSS-related tests outlined above to incorporate such a strategy. For example, eligible public housing or project-based Section 8 tenants would be randomly assigned to a program group that received MTO-Plus (the special rent voucher and relocation assistance combined with special self-sufficiency services) or to a control group that received neither. This would make it possible to learn whether the package of such assistance can boost self-sufficiency in ways that the original program strategy did not and, down the road, could also generate other positive outcomes for families and children.[40]

The ideas presented thus far all focus on people who receive housing subsidies. The intent is to determine whether certain kinds of additional interventions can improve the self-sufficiency outcomes of voucher holders. Another approach would be to test more explicitly for whether—and, if so, by how much—a self-sufficiency intervention packaged with a voucher program would counteract any negative effects on employment outcomes that vouchers alone might have. To answer this question, a random assignment study would focus on low-income people who are not receiving any housing subsidies but who are eligible for housing choice vouchers. These voucher applicants would be assigned randomly to one of three research groups: a group that is offered the full package of a voucher plus the self-sufficiency assistance, a group that is offered only a voucher, and a control group that is offered neither. Such a study may show whether, in order to promote self-sufficiency, a voucher must come with other services and incentives designed specifically with employment-related outcomes in mind.

Randomized Trials for Place-Based Housing Employment Initiatives

Under certain conditions, the effectiveness of employment interventions that are based in and targeted toward residents of assisted housing developments can also be evaluated through randomized controlled trials. These would include interventions for residents of traditional public housing, project-based Section 8 developments, and HOPE VI developments (where subsidized units are mixed together with unsubsidized rental units and privately owned units). Depending

39. Another consideration is whether, to ease the challenge of accessing jobs, special vouchers should be targeted toward neighborhoods that have good access to the kinds of jobs that assisted tenants could fill; not all low-poverty communities have such jobs; see Goering (2005).

40. Considering that fewer than half the Moving to Opportunity program group were able to use the vouchers that were offered to them, any subsequent test of an intervention of this type should also carefully consider how to improve lease-up rates.

on the type of intervention and receptiveness of local housing officials and residents, either individual-level or group-level randomization could be used. For some types of interventions, however, only group-level randomization would be appropriate.

Evaluating Rent Reform

The Jobs-Plus evaluation showed that a comprehensive and saturation-based employment intervention in public housing that includes a change in rent rules to promote work can succeed. That evidence provides an empirical justification for a wider replication of the program, especially in high-need public housing developments. However, the cost of Jobs-Plus makes it unlikely that the federal government would implement the program on more than a limited scale in the current federal fiscal environment. This makes it important to consider whether, in many public housing developments, a less comprehensive intervention can also produce substantial earnings effects and achieve other positive outcomes.

Of particular interest is whether rent reform—a critical component of Jobs-Plus—could, by itself, promote greater employment and earnings among residents than occurs in the absence of such reform (beyond those reforms already enacted under the Quality Housing and Work Responsibility Act).[41] Many experts believe that it may. Indeed, rent reform continues to be the most widely advocated self-sufficiency reform measure for public housing. As mentioned above, it is a core feature of the housing reforms implemented at the Moving to Work sites; it is strongly urged by tenant advocates and industry trade groups (although they may differ substantially on the types of reforms they recommend); and it is an important feature of new legislative proposals for housing assistance reforms.[42]

Yet there is no solid evidence that rent reform by itself would improve residents' employment and earnings. The patterns of results in the Jobs-Plus evaluations suggest that that program's rent-based work incentives were certainly a major contributor to its overall success, but other features of the program appear to have mattered as well. Unfortunately, that evaluation was not able to disentangle defin-

41. Among other things, the law's rent reform provisions require housing authorities, when computing existing residents' rent, to disregard for a period of twelve months—for certain types of residents—any increase in earnings resulting from employment. In such situations, the rent is held constant for a year, despite the increased income. In the next twelve months, the rent increase is to be limited to half the amount it would normally be under traditional rent rules. Qualifying residents include those who have been receiving TANF in the prior six months, those who have been unemployed for at least a year, and those who increase their earnings while participating in a qualifying employment training or self-sufficiency program. Many experts believe that these rent-based work incentives are complex to administer and are unevenly promoted and implemented across housing authorities. Public housing authorities must also establish flat-rent options, which are generally set at market rates. For an in-depth discussion of the implementation of Jobs-Plus rent-based work incentives and residents' use of them, see Gardenhire-Crooks (2004).

42. For example, U.S. House of Representatives (2005, 2006); U.S. Senate (2005). See also PHADA (2005); Solomon (2006).

itively the effects of the rent-based work incentives from the program's other components. Thus the potential independent influence of rent reform on self-sufficiency and other outcomes remains a critical open question. For this reason, it would be valuable to make it the centerpiece of a future, carefully evaluated employment initiative in public housing.

The question of whether rent reform could improve residents' self-sufficiency is also an important one for project-based Section 8 and HOPE VI developments. In both these types of settings, income-based rents, like those used in traditional public housing, are still the norm for tenants who live in subsidized units. Because in many cities the social environment within Section 8 and HOPE VI developments may differ substantially from what is found in many traditional public housing developments, the "added value" of rent reform in promoting self-sufficiency—if there is any—may not be the same across all three forms of place-based housing assistance. Thus evidence about the effectiveness of such reforms should be gathered separately by type of housing development.

It would be challenging, but not impossible, to evaluate such rent reform for place-based housing assistance using a randomized controlled trial. Such an evaluation could be done through either a group-level or an individual-level random assignment design. A group-level design (as used in the Jobs-Plus evaluation) would involve identifying a pool of eligible developments in a given city or set of cities and then randomly allocating some to a program group and some to a control group. All eligible residents of the complexes assigned to the program group would be entitled to have their rents determined according to the new policy being tested (and promotional efforts would be initiated to get the word out about the advantages of the new policy), while those in the comparison developments would continue to be subject to existing rules. A more ambitious study (requiring a larger sample of developments) could adopt a multiple-group design to test the relative merits of alternative rent policies. For example, one group of randomly selected developments might implement a flat-rent strategy (with income-based rents as a safety net feature); a second group might implement a new earnings disregard policy; and the third group could continue under current rules.

In principle, the selection of housing developments for such trials could be made from a pool of qualifying apartment complexes affiliated with a nationally representative sample of public housing authorities. However, this may not be feasible or practical, for the same reasons noted above in regard to evaluations of FSS. In that case, it would be important to pick a set of housing developments that reflects at least to some degree the diversity of local settings and tenant populations found across the country.

A different kind of evaluation strategy would be to use an individual-level random assignment research design to test an alternative rent policy for a limited number of households within a single housing development. Some eligible households would be randomly selected to have their rent determined by the new policy, and the remaining households would continue to be subject to current rules. (Again, though, such a study would ideally include a variety of housing developments operating a similar test but under different local conditions.)

Individual-level random assignment within a given housing development would present special challenges. Indeed, convincing housing authorities and residents to participate in a study in which neighbors in the same complexes are subjected to different rent policies might seem especially daunting. However, this may not be an insurmountable obstacle. Cooperation might be forthcoming if administrators and residents understand that the number of households that could be offered the new and presumably more "favorable" rent options is limited owing to limited HUD funding but that all qualifying households have an equal chance of accessing them. Moreover, those not selected for the program group would be no worse off, because they would continue to be subject to the existing rules. That some residents would be allowed to pay rent under a set of rules different from those their neighbors are subject to might also not be as problematic as it might first appear. As it is, different residents in the same kinds of housing units already pay different rents in accordance with their different personal income levels.

Evaluating a Services-plus-Incentives Strategy

It may be that rent reform, by itself, would not have as large an effect on self-sufficiency outcomes as it would if packaged with employment-related services. As discussed above, this is part of the theory behind the FSS model. Incentives and services make up two of the three core components of the successful Jobs-Plus model. Thus random assignment trials could be usefully deployed to test whether an incentives-plus-services strategy would be effective in the context of project-based Section 8 and HOPE VI developments or in a broader range of public housing developments than were included in the Jobs-Plus trial.

Place-based housing assistance through Section 8 and HOPE VI also creates an opportunity to incorporate some of the place-based elements of a Jobs-Plus program into an employment intervention. This could include, for example, a community-support-for-work component wherein residents reach out to and support their neighbors' efforts to join and improve their standing in the labor market. Moreover, following the Jobs-Plus example, the initiative could adopt a saturation targeting strategy whereby all eligible residents would become the focus of the intervention. It should be noted that, for this type of intervention, individual-level random assignment would be impossible. Because a saturation intervention involving community-support-for-work strategies aims to change the whole environment within public housing and to tap residents' social networks to help promote work, it would be impossible to isolate a control group of residents within the targeted development who would be left untouched by the intervention. In this case, randomly assigning entire developments—instituting the intervention in some and not in others—would be the only appropriate method for a randomized controlled trial.[43]

Assessing Development-Level Effects

In evaluations involving random assignment of whole developments, it becomes possible to assess program effects not only on individual residents—which requires following individuals even if they move away from the place—but also on the places themselves. For example, from the perspective of the place, the evaluation could test (as the Jobs-Plus evaluation did) whether the proportion of working people or the average earnings among tenants increases from year to year, contributing to making the place a more mixed-income development. This result is more likely to occur, of course, when residents who are helped by the employment intervention do not quickly move out of the development, so that their units are not filled by incoming residents with lower employment rates or earnings.[44]

Conclusion

Although the primary mission of government-subsidized housing is to increase access to safe, decent, affordable housing, it may also be an important platform for reaching and helping many low-income people improve their economic self-sufficiency. Whether it really can serve this purpose, however, is far from certain. There is no solid evidence that housing assistance alone improves the labor market outcomes of those who are fortunate enough to obtain it. There is also a dearth of reliable evidence on whether housing assistance that is packaged with work-promoting interventions makes a difference. The Jobs-Plus evaluation shows convincingly that at least one approach to offering self-sufficiency services in combination with rent-based work incentives can substantially improve earnings among public housing residents. However, there is no comparably convincing evidence that other models can succeed and no evidence on the effectiveness of self-sufficiency interventions that are aimed at recipients of housing vouchers or at people receiving private, project-based assistance or at those living in HOPE VI developments.

Despite the vast resources invested in housing vouchers and other subsidies, and even in existing self-sufficiency programs, the gap in reliable evidence of what works leaves policymakers and housing experts having to guess about what new directions to take or to advocate. Fortunately, it is technically feasible to build

43. If only a relatively small number of developments and cities were available for randomization, the Jobs-Plus evaluation strategy, combining group randomization with a comparative interrupted time-series analysis, may be a reasonable alternative.

44. In Jobs-Plus, individual-level earnings yielded larger development-level impacts in those locations where tenant turnover was lower, a condition that appeared to be related to the tightness of the housing market; see Bloom, Riccio, and Verma (2005).

much better evidence through a strategic use of random assignment methods as part of comprehensive implementation, impact, and benefit-cost evaluations. Doing so will cost money. But making policy in the absence of credible evidence can also be quite costly.

References

Abravanel, Martin D., and others. 2004. *A Summary Assessment of HUD's "Moving to Work" Demonstration.* Washington: Urban Institute Press.

Anderson, Fredrik, Harry J. Holzer, and Julia I. Lane. 2005. *Moving Up or Moving On: Who Advances in the Low-Wage Labor Market?* New York: Russell Sage Foundation.

Anderson, Jacquelyn, Linda Yuriko Kato, and James A. Riccio, with Susan Blank. 2006. *A New Approach to Low-Wage Workers and Employers: Launching the Work Advancement and Support Center Demonstration.* New York: MDRC.

Berger, Lawrence, and Theresa Heintze. 2004. "Employment Transitions and Housing Assistance." Paper prepared for the 2004 annual meeting of the Association for Public Policy Analysis and Management. Atlanta, October 28–30.

Bernhardt, Annette, and others. 2001. *Divergent Paths: Economic Mobility in the New American Labor Market.* New York: Russell Sage Foundation.

Bloom, Howard S., ed. 2005. *Learning More from Social Experiments: Evolving Analytic Approaches.* New York: Russell Sage Foundation.

Bloom, Howard S., James A. Riccio, and Nandita Verma. 2005. *Promoting Work in Public Housing: The Effectiveness of Jobs-Plus.* New York: MDRC.

Bogdon, Amy S. 1999. "What Can We Learn from Previous Housing-Based Self-Sufficiency Programs?" In *The Home Front,* edited by Sandra J. Newman, pp. 149–74. Washington: Urban Institute Press.

Currie, Janet, and Aaron Yelowitz. 2000. "Are Public Housing Projects Good for Kids?" *Journal of Public Economics* 75, no. 1: 99–124.

Ficke, Robert C., and Andrea Piesse. 2004. *Evaluation of the Family Self-Sufficiency Program: Retrospective Analysis, 1996–2000.* Research report prepared by WESTAT, in collaboration with Johnson, Bassin, and Shaw. U.S. Department of Housing and Urban Development, Office of Policy Development and Research.

Fischer, Will. 2000. "Labor Supply Effects of Federal Rental Subsidies." *Journal of Housing Economics* 9, no. 3: 150–74.

Gardenhire-Crooks, Alissa, with Susan Blank and James A. Riccio. 2004. *Implementing Financial Work Incentives in Public Housing: Lessons from the Jobs-Plus Demonstration.* New York: MDRC.

Goering, John. 2005. "Expanding Housing Choice and Integrating Neighborhoods: The MTO Experiment." In *The Geography of Opportunity: Race and Housing Choice in Metropolitan America,* edited by Xavier de Souza Briggs, pp. 127–49. Brookings.

Harkness, Joseph M., and Sandra J. Newman. 2006. "Recipients of Housing Assistance under Welfare Reform: Trends in Employment and Welfare Participation." *Housing Policy Debate* 17, no. 1: 81–108.

Jacob, Brian A., and Jens Ludwig. 2006. "The Effect of Means-Tested Housing Assistance on Labor Supply: New Evidence from a Housing Voucher Lottery." Paper prepared for Revisiting Rental Housing: A National Policy Summit. Harvard University, Joint Center for Housing Studies, November 14–15, 2006.

Kasinitz, Philip, and Jan Rosenberg. 1996. "Missing the Connection: Social Isolation and Employment on the Brooklyn Waterfront." *Social Problems* 43, no. 2: 180–96.

Kato, Linda Yuriko, and James Riccio, with Jennifer Dodge. 2001. *Building New Partnerships for Employment: Collaboration among Agencies and Public Housing Residents in the Jobs-Plus Demonstration.* New York: MDRC.

Kingsley, G. Thomas, and Peter Tatian. 1999. "Housing and Welfare Reform: Geography Matters." In *The Home Front,* edited by Sandra J. Newman, pp. 81–122. Washington: Urban Institute Press.

Lee, Wang, and others. 2003. *Impacts of Welfare Reform on Recipients of Housing Assistance: Evidence from Indiana and Delaware.* Bethesda, Md.: Abt Associates.

Lubell, Jeffrey M., Mark Shroder, and Barry Steffen. 2003. "Work Participation and Length of Stay in HUD-Assisted Housing." *Cityscape* 6, no. 2: 207–23.

Millennial Housing Commission. 2002. *Meeting Our Nation's Housing Challenges: A Report to Congress.* U.S. Government Printing Office.

Miller, Cynthia. 1998. *Explaining the Minnesota Family Investment Program's Impacts by Housing Status.* New York: MDRC.

Mills, Gregory, and others. 2006. *Effects of Housing Vouchers on Welfare Families.* Report prepared for the U.S. Department of Housing and Urban Development Office of Policy Development and Research.

Murray, Michael P. 1980. "A Reinterpretation of the Traditional Income-Leisure Model, with Application to In-Kind Subsidy Programs." *Journal of Public Economics* 14, no. 1: 69–81.

Newman, Sandra J. 1999. "From the Eye of the Housing Practitioner." In *The Home Front,* edited by Sandra J. Newman, pp. 221–35. Washington: Urban Institute Press.

———. 2005. "How Housing Matters: A Critical Summary of Research and Issues Still to Be Resolved." Johns Hopkins University, Institute for Policy Studies.

Newman, Sandra J., and Joseph M. Harkness. 2002. "The Long-Term Effects of Public Housing on Self-Sufficiency." *Journal of Policy Analysis and Management* 21, no. 1: 21–44.

Newman, Sandra J., and Ann B. Schnare. 1994. "Back to the Future: Housing Assistance Policy for the Next Century." Report prepared for the Center for Housing Policy, New Beginning Project. Washington: Center for Housing Policy.

———. 1997. " '. . . And a Suitable Living Environment': The Failure of Housing Programs to Deliver on Neighborhood Quality." *Housing Policy Debate* 8, no. 4: 703–41.

Olsen, Edgar O., and others. 2005. "The Effects of Different Types of Housing Assistance on Earnings and Employment." *Cityscape* 8, no. 2: 163–87.

Ong, Paul. 1998. "Subsidized Housing and Work among Welfare Recipients." *Housing Policy Debate* 9, no. 4: 775–94.

Painter, Gary. 2001. "Low-Income Housing Assistance: Its Impact on Labor Force and Housing Program Participation." *Journal of Housing Research* 12, no. 1: 1–26.

Patterson, Rhiannon, and others. 2004. *Evaluation of the Welfare to Work Voucher Program: Report to Congress.* U.S. Department of Housing and Urban Development, Office of Policy Development and Research.

Popkin, Susan J., and Elizabeth Cove. 2007. "Safety Is the Most Important Thing; How Hope VI Helped Families." Brief 2. Washington: Urban Institute, Metropolitan Housing and Communities Center (June 2007).

Public Housing Authorities Directors Association (PHADA). 2005. *Rent Reform: Fair and Simple Solutions.* Washington: Public Housing Authorities Directors Association.

Reingold, David A. 1997. "Does Inner City Public Housing Exacerbate the Employment Problems of Its Tenants?" *Journal of Urban Affairs* 19, no. 4: 469–86.

Reingold, David A., Gregg G. Van Ryzin, and Michelle Ronda. 2001. "Does Urban Public Housing Diminish the Social Capital and Labor Force Activity of Its Tenants?" *Journal of Policy Analysis and Management* 20, no. 3: 485–504.

Riccio, James, and Alan Orenstein. 2003. "Are Welfare Recipients in Public Housing Really Harder to Employ?" In *A Place to Live, A Means to Work: How Housing Assistance Can Strengthen Welfare Policy,* edited by Barbara Sard and Amy S. Bogdon, pp. 63–103. Washington: Fannie Mae Foundation.

Rohe, William M., and Rachel Garshick Kleit. 1997. "From Dependency to Self-Sufficiency: An Appraisal of the Gateway Transitional Families Program." *Housing Policy Debate* 8, no. 1: 75–108.

Sard, Barbara, and Amy S. Bogdon. 2003. "What Has Changed, What Have We Learned, and What Don't We Know?" In *A Place to Live, A Means to Work: How Housing Assistance Can Strengthen Welfare Policy,* edited by Barbara Sard and Amy S. Bogdon, pp. 3–19. Washington: Fannie Mae Foundation.

Sard, Barbara, and Margy Waller. 2002. "Housing Strategies to Strengthen Welfare Policies and Support Working Families." Research Brief. Brookings and Center on Budget and Policy Priorities.

Schone, Barbara S. 1992. "Do Means Tested Transfers Reduce Labor Supply?" *Economics Letters* 40, no. 3: 353–57.

———. 1994. "Estimating the Distribution of Taste Parameters of Households Facing Complex Budget Spaces: The Effects of In-Kind Transfers." Agency for Healthcare Research and Quality, Rockville, Md.

Shroder, Mark. 2000. "Social Experiments in Housing." *Cityscape* 5, no. 1: 237–59.

———. 2002. "Does Housing Assistance Perversely Affect Self-Sufficiency? A Review Essay." *Journal of Housing Economics* 11, no. 4: 381–417.

Smith, Robin, and Jennifer E. H. Johnson. 2001. *Welfare to Work Housing Voucher Program: Early Implementation Assessment, Final Report.* Washington: Urban Institute Press.

Solomon, Rod. 2006. Testimony before the House Committee on Government Reform, Subcommittee on Federalism and the Census (February 15).

Stoloff, Jennifer A. 2001. "Public Housing and Paid Work: Help or Hindrance?" Ph.D. dissertation, University of North Carolina, Chapel Hill.

Susin, Scott. 2005. "Longitudinal Outcomes of Subsidized Housing Recipients in Matched Survey and Administrative Data." *Cityscape* 8, no. 2: 189–218.

Turner, Margery Austin, and Lynette A. Rawlings. 2005. *Overcoming Concentrated Poverty and Isolation: Lessons from Three HUD Demonstration Initiatives.* Washington: Urban Institute Press.

U.S. Department of Housing and Urban Development (HUD). 2005. *Sixth Annual Report to Congress on Public Housing and Rental Assistance Programs: Demographics, Economic Viability, and Tenant Income and Rents.*

———. 2006. *Programs of HUD.*

U.S. House of Representatives. 2005. *State and Local Housing Flexibility Act of 2005.* HR 1999. 109 Cong. 1 sess.

———. 2006. *Section 8 Voucher Reform Act of 2006.* HR 5443. 109 Cong. 2 sess.

U.S. Senate. 2005. *State and Local Housing Flexibility Act of 2005.* S 771. 109 Cong. 1 sess.

Verma, Nandita, and James Riccio. 2003. *Housing Assistance and the Effects of Welfare Reform: Evidence from Connecticut and Minnesota.* U.S. Department of Housing and Urban Development, Office of Policy Development and Research.

7

From Hurdles to Bridges: Local Land-Use Regulations and the Pursuit of Affordable Rental Housing

ROLF PENDALL

Since the 1970s, affordable housing has shifted from a federal to a shared local, state, and federal issue. As coastal areas have experienced mounting affordability problems, their state and local governments have done much more than other states to promote and even require housing affordability. Three of these states—California, Massachusetts, and Florida—account for the vast majority of local affordable housing programs. Despite mounting interest over the past ten to fifteen years in local programs that encourage or even require construction of affordable housing, however, we still know little about the impacts of these programs on rental housing.

This chapter examines local housing policy in three cities: Pleasanton, California (in the San Francisco metropolitan area); Newton, Massachusetts (just outside Boston); and Coral Gables, Florida (adjacent to Miami). All these cities are affluent, job-rich suburbs where housing policy is either well rooted or newly emerging.

Local Governments and Affordable Rental Housing

Local governments influence housing tenure and housing affordability with regulations and expenditures. Many recent studies of affordable housing at the local level focus on inclusionary zoning—that is, city ordinances requiring that a certain portion of new construction be set aside for low-income households.[1] It is probably no accident that these programs have emerged in the states and regions with the most serious housing affordability problems and where local governments have been enthusiastic and empowered to adopt restrictive land-use regulations. But local governments also spend money on housing, both passed from federal and state governments and also generated internally, sometimes directed into local housing trust funds.[2] Land-use regulations affect tenure and affordability—often reducing the quantity and increasing the cost of rental housing; local governments use regulations and funding to make housing—especially rental housing—more affordable.

Exclusion as the Expected Norm

Local land-use regulations can make housing more costly by both restricting supply and increasing demand for housing.[3] Most studies of land-use regulations and housing affordability have asked whether and how land-use regulations raise the price of a single-family house. These studies suggest that regulations that raise single-family house prices will also raise rents because of connections between rental and ownership markets. Some regulations, however, can cause shifts between housing types by raising land prices and thereby encouraging higher density. A functioning urban growth boundary, for example, raises land prices, even absent changes in the demand for housing, and therefore creates pressure for higher-density housing types.[4] Multifamily housing tends to be rented, and renters operate in housing markets that are often only loosely coupled with owner-occupied housing markets.

Other studies provide more direct evidence about connections between local land-use regulations and rent. In a cross-sectional study of 1990 rents and housing prices in sixty large cities, Stephen Malpezzi finds higher rents in cities with strict state-level regulation but not in those with strict local regulation.[5] In earlier work, based on data from a 1994 survey of 1,160 jurisdictions in the twenty-five largest metropolitan areas, I find that very low density (or "exclusionary") zoning decreased housing supply in the 1990s, especially the supply of multifamily housing. In jurisdictions with limited housing supply, rental housing was, in turn, more expensive. Other growth-managing regulations had no such consistent effects on the local housing stock or prices.[6]

---

1. Brown (2001); Calavita, Grimes, and Mallach (1997); Calavita (1998).
2. Brooks (2002).
3. Nelson and others (2004).
4. Some urban growth boundaries are so loose that they do not work; see Pendall, Martin, and Fulton (2002). In some regions with functioning growth boundaries, lot sizes have declined, moderating price inflation in the house-plus-lot package, but an urban growth boundary that works necessarily imposes higher costs per square foot of land-plus-house.
5. Malpezzi (1996).
6. Pendall (2000a).

Local land-use regulations are also critically important in the location of households subsidized with federal and state funds. Local governments have long had the authority to approve or disapprove sites for subsidized housing, both in the era of public housing construction and in the present. And families with housing choice vouchers cannot live in areas without rental housing and are unlikely to choose jurisdictions whose policies have raised rents above fair market rents.[7]

Many observers contend that exclusion is not a coincidence but rather the consequence of deliberate and concerted actions by affluent suburban residents to control access to their communities. By doing so, these "home voters"[8] reduce congestion of their public services, thereby forestalling the need to raise taxes. They also encourage exclusionary zoning as a means of protecting their property values. To the extent that local communities are small, they will tend to be more internally homogeneous, attracting residents who want a particular mix of taxes and public services and who want to pay a certain amount for those services. Home voters are hypothesized to vote in local elections primarily to protect the status quo of property values, taxes, and services; metropolitan areas and states composed largely of small local governments dominated by home voters are, therefore, more likely to witness extensive exclusionary zoning at the municipal scale.[9]

Indeed, my colleagues Robert Puentes and Jonathan Martin and I have found that exclusionary zoning does dominate the landscape in the Midwest and the Northeast, where metropolitan areas are divided into a large number of small suburbs. Exclusionary local governments, by this definition, have low ceilings on permitted residential development and often proscribe development of apartments anywhere within their boundaries. In metropolitan Boston, for example, 70 percent of jurisdictions have zoning ordinances that limit development in residential zones to less than eight units an acre; about 55 percent would bar the development of a hypothetical apartment complex with eight units an acre, even by special permit. Exclusionary mechanisms are much less common at the jurisdictional scale in the South and the West, where metropolitan areas tend to have larger numbers of middle-sized cities and suburbanization happens under the governance of extensive and often populous counties rather than townships.[10] Despite expectations that suburban governments will cater to their home voters and do all they can to exclude low-income residents for class-based, consumption-based, or race-based reasons, however, suburban governments all over the United States are beginning to adopt programs and take action to grow a more diverse housing stock.

7. Pendall (2000b).
8. Fischel (2001).
9. Fischel (2001); Downs (1973); Danielson (1976); Tiebout (1956).
10. Pendall, Puentes, and Martin (2006).

Regulatory Affordable Housing Programs

Two local regulatory programs—inclusionary zoning and linkage fee programs—make demands on developers and, predictably, produce impressive results with respect to housing production. Inclusionary zoning (IZ) programs mandate the incorporation of affordable housing in otherwise market-rate housing developments. Some IZ programs allow developers to pay fees in lieu of providing housing; and some automatically provide a density bonus to compensate for the affordable housing mandate. Douglas Porter estimates that IZ and density bonuses have produced at most 90,000 housing units nationwide, most of these in states that require or encourage IZ programs.[11] This estimate seems low, however; in a 2003 survey, more than 100 California local governments reported having IZ beyond the requirements of redevelopment or coastal-zone law; in just a third of these jurisdictions, local programs had produced more than 34,000 units by 2003.[12]

Some of the earliest IZ policies were adopted around metropolitan Washington, D.C., in Montgomery County, Maryland, and Fairfax County, Virginia, but Fairfax County's mandatory policy was overturned by the Virginia state legislature. Other early adopters tend to be large cities like San Francisco and Boston. Linkage fees are charges on developers of nonresidential space to fund affordable local housing subsidy programs. The two best-known linkage fee programs are those in Boston and San Francisco; Boston's program generated $45 million from 1986 to 2000, helping fund nearly 5,000 housing units, and San Francisco's generated about $38 million between its adoption in 1981 and 2000.[13]

More politically palatable in most jurisdictions are incentive programs that encourage but do not mandate affordable housing production or contributions, usually by deregulating housing construction. The best-known of these is the density bonus, which offers density incentives without affordable housing mandates. But a host of other strategies has also been documented.[14] Probably the best-known of these are fast-track permitting, which places affordable housing development at the front of the development queue and expedites approvals, and waivers for development impact and permit processing fees.

Local Spending on Affordable Rental Housing

In addition to regulatory and deregulatory strategies for housing affordability, local governments spend money to subsidize the production, retention, and

---

11. Porter (2004).

12. California Coalition for Rural Housing and Non-Profit Housing Association of Northern California, "Inclusionary Housing in California: 30 Years of Innovation" (2003) (www.nonprofithousing. org/knowledgebank/publications/Inclusionary_Housing_CA_30years.pdf).

13. Boston Redevelopment Agency, "Survey of Linkage Programs in Other U.S. Cities with Comparisons to Boston" (May 2000) (www.ci.boston.ma.us/bra/PDF/ResearchPublications//pdr_534.pdf).

14. A large compendium of strategies is reported on the U.S. Department of Housing and Urban Development Regulatory Barriers Clearinghouse website (www.huduser.org/rbc/).

rehabilitation of affordable housing. Most of this money comes from federal and state governments. Two federal block grant programs—Community Development Block Grants and the HOME Investment Partnerships—pass money directly to local governments large enough to attain entitlement status. Some cities generate substantial funding from their own sources to expand their affordable housing programs, often directing these funds into dedicated local housing trust funds alongside funds from in-lieu fees and federal or state sources.[15]

Based on a 1994 survey with responses from 408 cities with at least 25,000 residents, Victoria Basolo has found mean local own-source expenditures on housing of about $2.5 million in fiscal year 1994–95, but the median and mode were both zero; a few cities, notably New York, drove up the mean. The mean expenditure of federal funds was $2.9 million, but the median was $333,000.[16] Large cities, those receiving substantial federal housing funds, and those with high median housing values were more likely to spend any of their own funds on housing; entitlement status, however, reduced own-source spending, suggesting that smaller cities substitute federal for local dollars on affordable housing. The number of local governments in the metropolitan area made local expenditures there less likely. The magnitude of local housing expenditures among cities that spent any funds responded to different forces, however. State mandates for housing planning and local fund set-asides tend to prompt higher local spending levels; smaller cities and those with higher rates of homeownership spend less of their own money on housing.[17]

New York City is the outstanding national example of local funding for subsidized housing, having spent more than $5 billion from 1985 to 1995.[18] From 1987 to 2002, New York City contributed capital to more than 33,000 new housing units, nearly 50,000 rehabilitated vacant units, and more than 120,000 rehabilitated occupied units, entirely rebuilding some neighborhoods that a generation earlier had been written off as doomed.[19]

How States Shape Local Affordable Housing Programs

Local governments do not adopt regulatory and deregulatory strategies or spend money to promote housing affordability in response only, or even mainly, to local constituencies; indeed, they are often forced or induced by their state governments to take on affordable housing programs. Although most states take a laissez-faire attitude toward local affordable housing programs and spending, a handful have intervened more forcefully to promote either or both density and affordability.

15. See Brooks (2002, p. 30) on housing trust funds.
16. Basolo (1999, p. 671).
17. Basolo (1999, p. 679.
18. Schwartz (1999, p. 840).
19. Schwartz (2005, pp. 198–99).

Table 7-1. *Summary of Local Housing Regulatory and Deregulatory Measures*

Measure	Description	Prohibits	Enables	Encourages or requires
Inclusionary zoning	Housing builders required to provide affordable housing or in-lieu fees	Oregon, Virginia	Louisiana (recent)	In specified municipalities: New Jersey, southern New England, Illinois; in redevelopment areas: California
Density incentive	Incentive encourages affordable housing construction or fee generation	Unknown	Most	California
Linkage fee	Commercial and industrial developers pay fees into a housing fund	Unknown	California, New Jersey, Florida, Massachusetts	None
Fee waiver	Affordable housing exempt from some local impact or application fees	Unclear for development impact fees	Most, for planning application fees	Unknown
Fast-track permitting	Affordable housing developments advanced in queue	Unknown	Unknown	Unknown

Some states, however, have foreclosed options for their local governments to adopt aggressive housing programs. Table 7-1 summarizes the main local tools and describes how states shape local governments' adoption of them; table 7-2 summarizes key state policy interventions in California, Florida, and Massachusetts.

About twenty-five states require their local governments to adopt comprehensive plans, which universally include land-use elements (or chapters) and almost universally include housing elements. In about a dozen of these states, local plans must meet state growth management requirements. But only five states—California, Florida, New Jersey, Oregon, and Washington—have aggressively required local governments to plan for affordable housing, through three

Table 7-2. *Main State Influences on Local Housing Programs, California, Florida, and Massachusetts*

Action	Impact	California	Florida	Massachusetts
Mandatory comprehensive plan with housing element	Increases attention to long-term need; builds constituencies; integrates land and housing planning	Yes	Yes, with review of entire plan	Cape Cod only
State review of local housing elements	Increases quality of local housing elements	Strong	Weak	None
Other planning	Special areas and circumstances encourage or require planning for housing	Redevelopment areas	Unknown	Chapter 40R areas may immunize against hostile 40B projects
Fair-share requirement	Requires localities to accommodate affordable housing	All local governments must respond to prospective regional housing needs in their housing elements	No provision	10 percent threshold to eliminate threat of hostile 40B projects
Builder's remedy	Court or administrative override of local actions or policies that constrain affordable housing development	In statute, but not used actively	None	Hostile 40B projects: builders can challenge local denials in state housing appeals board
Prodensity provision	Encourages or requires designation of sites at densities that support affordable types of rental housing	Implemented through state housing element review	In some areas (for example, South Florida)	None
Funding mandate	Requires localities to spend money on affordable housing	Mandate for jurisdictions with redevelopment areas (20 percent of Tax Increment Financing funds set aside)	No mandate; encouragement of local funding through state housing trust fund	None

main mechanisms: site adequacy requirements, sometimes coupled with fair-share provisions; density mandates; and requirements for housing subsidy programs.

Fair-share housing requirements, in place in New Jersey and California, allocate regional housing demand forecasts to local jurisdictions and require them to prepare to accommodate that housing. Local governments do so by adopting housing elements that identify sites where affordable housing is feasible; state agencies review local housing elements and judge whether they comply with state statute. New Jersey's fair-share allocations pertain only to housing for those earning less than 80 percent of the area median income, whereas California's pertain to both market-rate and low-income housing.[20]

California, Oregon, and Washington work most seriously to promote higher housing density, providing an impetus for the production of multifamily (and consequently rental) housing. Oregon, best known for its urban growth boundary requirement, also requires all its cities to adopt plans that meet the state's housing goal (Goal 10 of the 1973 Oregon Growth Management Act). Jurisdictions around Portland also must abide by the Metropolitan Housing Rule, which requires planning for high-density housing.[21] In some California metropolitan areas, the state's housing element law translates into density guidance from the Department of Housing and Community Development. Washington's Growth Management Act requires local governments to designate land in their comprehensive plans and zoning maps for multifamily and high-density single-family housing, based on local growth projections.[22]

States that require housing elements also typically require that local governments enact programs to foster affordable housing production. State review of local programs, however, varies widely across the nation and even within states.

Several states require or strongly encourage their local governments to enact inclusionary zoning or density bonuses. The strongest mandates are probably those in California, where redevelopment agencies are required to incorporate low- and moderate-income housing in new developments within project areas.[23] This requirement adds up to substantial production of affordable housing; in fiscal year 2004–05, for example, agencies reported having assisted in creating about 7,800 inclusionary units.[24] State reports suggest that all these inclusionary units

---

20. Meck, Retzlaff, and Schwab (2003).

21. *Oregon Administrative Rules,* chap. 660, div. 7, Metropolitan Housing, 2007 (arcweb.sos. state.or.us/rules/OARS_600/OAR_660/660_007.html).

22. Growth Management Act, chaps. RCW 36.70A and RCW 36.70B (1990).

23. California Community Redevelopment Law, *California Health and Safety Code,* sec. 33334.2, 2007 (www.leginfo.ca.gov/cgi-bin/waisgate?WAISdocID=91309129998+0+0+0&WAISaction= retrieve).

24. California Department of Housing and Community Development, Division of Housing Policy Development, *California Redevelopment Agency Housing Activities during Fiscal Year 2004–2005* (June 2006) (www.hcd.ca.gov/hpd/rda/04-05/rdasum04-05.pdf), pp. 12–13.

receive subsidy from the low- and moderate-income housing funds that agencies must set aside from tax-increment revenues. In addition, the California Coastal Act requires inclusionary units in new housing in the coastal zone.[25]

Another state intervention, the builder's remedy, is a key source of pressure for affordable housing in New Jersey, Massachusetts, Connecticut, and Rhode Island. In all four states, the state government establishes thresholds or benchmarks for affordable housing in all municipalities; when local governments have not surpassed that threshold, builders can challenge them for obstructing approval of projects that include affordable housing. In New Jersey, local governments can immunize themselves against such challenges by enacting a state-certified housing element; usually, certified elements incorporate inclusionary zoning with density bonuses. In the three southern New England states, municipalities face builder's-remedy challenges until at least 10 percent of their housing is subsidized. In the past five years, however, these provisions have been modified in Massachusetts and Rhode Island to encourage the integration of land-use planning and housing planning, thereby erecting hurdles to some builder's-remedy challenges. In August 2003, Illinois adopted a threshold-based statute that integrated both housing planning and IZ as mechanisms enabling local governments to protect themselves from builder challenges.[26]

Mandatory density bonuses have applied in California since at least the mid-1980s. Until 2004, developers could apply for a density bonus of 25 percent in exchange for a 10 to 20 percent affordability commitment; based on perceptions of the inadequacy of those incentives, the state legislature has sweetened the maximum bonus to 35 percent and requires additional concessions, in exchange for providing as few as 5 percent affordable housing units.[27]

A final area of state intervention into local land-use regulation grabs fewer headlines because, rather than a statutory provision, it comes from case law: limitations on local exclusionary zoning practices. Pennsylvania is probably the best-known example of this tendency; builders have historically won challenges against municipal zoning ordinances that exclude apartments.[28] (Recently, however, Pennsylvania's legislature relaxed its statutes to encourage cooperative planning among municipalities.)[29] In such states, the baseline practice of suburban zoning is not as aggressively antidensity as in southern New England and New Jersey, and as a consequence "anti-snob zoning" ordinances are not as obviously necessary a

25. California State Legislature, California Coastal Act, Public Resources Code, sec. 30000–12 (1976) (www.leginfo.ca.gov/cgi-bin/displaycode?section=prc&group=29001-30000&file=30000 30012), chap. 7, art. 1.

26. Meck (2003). For an early appraisal of the act in the Chicago area, see Hoch (2005).

27. Kautz (2006).

28. See, for example, *Surrick* v. *Zoning Hearing Board of Upper Providence Township*, 476 Pa. 182, 382 A.2d 105 (1977).

29. See Denworth (2002).

counterweight to exclusionary practices. One might expect a higher bar for exclusionary zoning in states with strong "Dillon's rule" traditions—that is, where courts proscribe local actions that are not expressly permitted by state law—and those with strong private property rights ideologies.[30] In others, where home-rule authority is strong and courts traditionally weigh community desires against those of landowners, exclusionary zoning can often continue to hold sway. The highest court in New York, for example, issued a decision in 1975 that appeared at first to limit exclusionary zoning, but the impact since then has been limited.[31]

California appears to be unique in the nation in requiring local expenditures for affordable housing. Specifically, when a local government captures rising property taxes in a designated redevelopment area, the redevelopment agency must set aside 20 percent of the increment to fund low- and moderate-income housing.[32] After the state legislature enacted this provision, many local governments set aside but then declined to spend the funds. A subsequent amendment to the legislation required them to spend the set-aside or redirect it to other agencies. In fiscal year 2004–05, $1.24 billion was generated by redevelopment agencies statewide, and $963 million was spent.[33]

States also shape enactment of local programs by prohibiting some of them, either by statute or through case law. At the top of the prohibited list is inclusionary zoning. In more than half the states, local government programs and activities must be authorized explicitly in statute. The extent of such authorization for local IZ and linkage fee programs is unclear and beyond the scope of this chapter but is likely to be modest, considering the politics of most of these states and the strength of the "growth machine" there. Oregon's state legislature banned inclusionary zoning in 1999.[34]

Typically, policies that promote affordable housing are the consequence of significant actions in state legislatures and courts by advocates of affordable housing, civil rights, and market-rate housing, sometimes working in coalitions to overcome resistance by municipalities and their lobbyists in the state capitals. In all cases, it appears that acquiescence, if not support, from market-rate home builders is a prerequisite for passage of state-level initiatives to promote affordable housing actions by local governments. In California, for example, the state's general plan

30. See Richardson, Gough and Puentes (2003) for more about Dillon's Rule.

31. *Berenson* v. *Town of New Castle* (341 N.E.2d 236 (N.Y. 1975); Span (2001).

32. California Community Redevelopment Law, *California Health and Safety Code*, sec. 33334.2 (1981) (www.leginfo.ca.gov/cgi-bin/waisgate?WAISdocID=91309129998+0+0+0&WAISaction= retrieve).

33. California Department of Housing and Community Development, Division of Housing Policy Development, *California Redevelopment Agency Housing Activities during Fiscal Year 2004–2005* (June 2006) (www.hcd.ca.gov/hpd/rda/04-05/rdasum04-05.pdf), pp. 1–2.

34. Oregon State Legislature, "Local Ordinances or Approval Conditions May Not Effectively Establish Housing Sale Price or Designate Class of Purchasers; Exception," H.B. 2658 (1999), sec. 197.309.

housing element law was strengthened in the early 1980s as a consequence of a coalition between advocates of affordable housing, both rural and urban, and the California Building Industry Association. Market-rate builders also were key players in the evolution of New Jersey's fair-share system, since they responded so hungrily to the incentives set out by the state supreme court in the *Mount Laurel II* ruling.[35] Florida's Sadowski Act, too, requires painstaking coalition building among an even broader group of interests that includes environmentalists (represented by 1,000 Friends of Florida), antipoverty and affordable housing advocates, and the Florida Home Builders Association. Oregon, too, provides examples of homebuilders' power; their support helped clinch two referendums on the state's growth management program in the late 1970s and early 1980s, but their opposition to inclusionary zoning led the state legislature to enact a preemptive statute in the late 1990s.[36]

Whereas home builders have played a powerful role in key moments by pressing for legislation to force local action on affordable housing, local governments—which ultimately must implement the policies—have tended to gain back ground over time. Nowhere is this clearer than in New Jersey, where legislators adopted the Fair Housing Act in 1985 to encourage less aggressive responses to regional housing needs than those set forth by the *Mount Laurel II* court. Since then, housing markets in New Jersey have shifted in ways that reduce the attractiveness of the attached single-family housing types commonly built to satisfy fair-share requirements, undercutting builder interest. Meanwhile, the state supreme court has become more respectful of local initiatives and restrictions, and the state has vigorously pursued growth management and open-space preservation to reduce development in suburban and exurban areas.

California's courts have tended to favor local governments in battles over their fair-share responsibility and treated the Department of Housing and Community Development's reviews of housing elements as merely advisory and not dispositive. The anti-snob zoning laws in both Massachusetts and Rhode Island came under severe attack in the late 1990s when market-rate developers began to use the appeals process to build projects with only a small share of affordable units. In both cases, the result appears to be the evolution of approaches that resemble New Jersey's Fair Housing Act, reducing the threat of builders'-remedy lawsuits in jurisdictions that plan for affordable housing. It remains to be seen whether this trend will so reduce the attractiveness of the states' housing policies that market-rate builders lose interest; if that were to occur, the long-term sustainability of any prohousing policy structure would be in question.

---

35. *South Burlington County N.A.A.C.P.* v. *Township of Mount Laurel,* 92 N.J. 158 (1983) (*Mount Laurel II*).

36. Knaap (1987); Multnomah County (2000, p. 5–3).

Unanswered Questions

Since the 1970s, local and state action on affordable housing in the United States has become more sophisticated. In perhaps a half dozen states with serious problems of housing affordability and (to a lesser extent) racial residential segregation, local housing programs have emerged that fuse land-use-based approaches with funding, sometimes even generated locally. Until this writing, though, there has not been an exhaustive national database allowing reporting on an inventory of local affordable housing programs, and so we do not really know the magnitude of these programs or the extent to which they are spreading.

It should come as little surprise, therefore, that there is little direct information on their impact on affordable rental housing. The most recent evaluation of IZ in California, for example, does not clearly specify the extent of rental versus ownership housing production.[37] Similarly, linkage fee programs have begun to mature—especially in San Francisco and Boston—but we do not know whether these programs aim to promote rental housing in particular.

Another gap in the current research is knowledge about how local housing programs fit together. Most studies have been conducted with reference to a specific housing approach, especially IZ. Although useful, these studies can miss the value of interlocking systems of programs in producing homes for those who are hard to house. High-quality tax credit projects for extremely low-income single mothers with teenaged kids need much more than IZ; they also need contributions from community development block grants, fee waivers, fast-track permitting, density bonuses, local redevelopment funding, available infrastructure, and collaboration among planners who regulate development, nonprofits that build the housing, and local housing planners who help negotiate the process.

Beyond the gaps in our knowledge of how local housing programs fit together, we also lack knowledge about how local housing programs fit into local development, redevelopment, and preservation strategies. Since housing is the single biggest user of urban and suburban land, much more needs to be known about the land-use context of local housing plans, policies, and programs. If mandatory programs like IZ and linkage fees add a layer of regulation in already complex and discouraging development environments, they are likely to further discourage development rather than produce much new affordable housing.[38] If local governments adopt housing programs within the framework of land-use policies that

---

37. California Coalition for Rural Housing and Non-Profit Housing Association of Northern California, "Inclusionary Housing in California: 30 Years of Innovation" (2003) (www.nonprofit housing.org/knowledgebank/publications/Inclusionary_Housing_CA_30years.pdf).

38. Powell and Stringham (2004); Victoria Basolo and Nico Calavita, "Policy Claims with Weak Evidence: A Critique of the Reason Foundation Study on Inclusionary Housing Policy in the San Francisco Bay Area" (2004) (www.nonprofithousing.org/actioncenter/campaigns/download/IH_ countering_critics.pdf).

encourage housing production more generally, on the other hand, mandatory programs can make a big contribution.

Research Questions and Methods

The remainder of this chapter is dedicated to filling some of these gaps by addressing two main research issues. First, what is the extent of adoption of local housing programs in the fifty largest U.S. metropolitan areas? How many local governments have programs? Which programs are most popular? And what is the geographic variation in program adoption? I answer these questions by referring to a 2003 mail survey of local governments in the fifty largest metropolitan areas in the United States. The survey was mailed to planners or elected officials in all jurisdictions with at least 10,000 residents and a sample of smaller jurisdictions in seventeen metropolitan areas in which large jurisdictions accounted for a small share of the metropolitan population or land area.[39]

Second, what are the histories and impacts of local housing programs in affluent, built-out suburban job centers? How have local politics and state law interacted to foster the emergence of these programs? What is the relationship between housing programs and land-use regulation more broadly? These cities make interesting studies because they are the sites of significant goal conflicts. They have substantial resources—staff capacity and tax base, in particular—and thus are able, if they choose, to develop sophisticated responses to development pressure and housing affordability problems. In some states, cities face increasing pressure from external forces (for example, state law and developers) to accommodate more affordable housing because the people who work there cannot afford to live there. Internally, however, their "home voter" residents often resist all forms of housing development, including both high-density housing and affordable rental housing. Increased density, in particular, can generate conflict not only because of concerns about anticipated impacts on property values but also because of impacts on traffic and community identity.

I answer this second question with case-study profiles of Newton, Pleasanton, and Coral Gables. I chose these cities because of their locations in metropolitan areas with substantial housing affordability problems but with different general approaches to land-use and development regulation. They are among the more affluent middle-sized cities in their regions (with populations ranging from 42,000 to 85,000), and each has at least 45,000 jobs, with many—and sometimes most—of their low-wage workers commuting in from lower-income cities. Newton and Pleasanton have long-standing affordable housing programs, while Coral Gables is currently considering an affordable housing program.

---

39. Survey questions are reproduced in the appendix and can also can be found at (www.brookings.edu/metro/pubs/20060810_Survey.pdf). For more details on the survey, see Pendall, Puentes, and Martin (2006).

Affordable Housing, Regulation, and Funding on the National Level

In 2003 an estimated 17 percent of jurisdictions in the fifty largest U.S. metropolitan areas had an incentive-based affordable housing program of some kind (see table 7-3); 10 percent of the total had only one incentive, 3 percent two incentives, and 1 percent had three or more incentives.[40] The jurisdictions with incentives are larger than those without; they account for 52 percent of the population and 27 percent of the land area in the United States.

Incentive programs are, however, largely confined to a few states. California, New Jersey, and Massachusetts account for an estimated 606 (56 percent) of the 1,089 jurisdictions offering any kind of regulatory incentive for affordable housing, even though they together account for only 19 percent of all jurisdictions.[41] These three states also lead in the share of all jurisdictions with incentive programs. Nearly nine out of ten California jurisdictions are estimated to have an incentive program, the next closest state being Massachusetts, weighing in with 46 percent of jurisdictions offering an incentive of some kind, and New Jersey and Connecticut following, in the mid-30 percent range.

An estimated 10 percent of jurisdictions offer a density bonus for affordable housing, making this the single most important regulatory program for affordable housing. The impact of density bonuses, however, far outstrips its incidence at the jurisdictional scale, since they are available in jurisdictions accounting for 35 percent of the population in these fifty metropolitan areas and 21 percent of the land area. Thanks to state mandates, California is the density bonus leader, with an estimated 81 percent of jurisdictions using them.[42] Between a quarter and a third of jurisdictions offer density bonuses in Massachusetts, Connecticut, Washington, and Delaware.

Only about 5 percent of the jurisdictions in the fifty biggest metropolitan areas are estimated to have mandatory inclusionary zoning; these jurisdictions include 14 percent of the metropolitan population and 5 percent of the land area. California again leads adoption of IZ, with more than 35 percent of jurisdictions (124) estimated to use IZ. Jurisdictions with IZ are mainly bigger cities, with 45 percent of the metropolitan population in the "big four" consolidated metropolitan statistical areas (Los Angeles, San Francisco, San Diego, and Sacramento) and only 10 percent of the land area. In San Francisco and Sacramento, more than half the jurisdictions had IZ in 2003, a much higher proportion than in San Diego (40 percent) or Los Angeles (22 percent).

40. Estimates of program incidence by metro areas within states are available at (www.brookings.edu/metro/pubs/20060810_50metros.htm).
41. For more data on the survey and its response rates, please refer to Pendall, Puentes, and Martin (2006).
42. California law requires local density bonuses; survey responses to this question must therefore be treated with caution.

Table 7-3. Incidence of Regulatory and Deregulatory Housing Programs, by Census Division, 2003[a]
Percent, except as indicated

		West		Midwest		South			Northeast	
Item	Total	Pacific	Mountain	West North Central	East North Central	West South Central	East South Central	South Atlantic	Mid-Atlantic	New England
Total (N)										
Jurisdictions	6,584	525	170	311	1,771	829	160	700	1,700	418
Population	161.5	33.8	8.7	3.6	26.0	18.3	3.5	29.0	29.6	8.9
Square miles	300.0	64.8	64.1	6.4	36.0	40.9	8.5	46.3	23.7	9.2
Density bonus										
Jurisdictions	9.7	60.1	6.1	6.9	1.1	0.5	3.4	11.0	4.4	26.0
Population	35.4	77.9	33.1	21.8	3.4	15.5	47.0	30.2	34.0	33.5
Square miles	20.7	47.4	13.4	5.4	2.1	2.2	18.7	30.6	10.2	26.9
Inclusionary zoning										
Jurisdictions	5.2	24.5	3.2	0.5	0.3	0.0	0.9	1.2	9.0	9.8
Population	13.9	38.3	10.8	0.7	0.6	0.0	25.0	8.7	10.2	21.8
Square miles	4.6	8.7	0.5	0.3	0.1	0.0	7.2	7.1	12.3	10.6
In-lieu fee										
Jurisdictions	4.2	17.5	3.2	0.4	0.2	0.0	0.0	2.5	7.3	7.6
Population	10.3	23.5	9.8	1.0	1.8	0.0	0.0	15.0	7.1	9.5
Square miles	4.2	7.5	0.4	0.3	0.3	0.0	0.0	8.5	12.2	6.9
Fast-tracking										
Jurisdictions	3.3	13.6	4.8	0.0	1.2	3.1	0.0	4.8	2.5	4.1
Population	11.8	25.5	29.6	0.0	0.5	5.5	0.0	17.1	4.5	4.8
Square miles	9.9	30.8	2.7	0.0	0.2	1.3	0.0	13.1	4.1	3.9

(continued)

Table 7-3. Incidence of Regulatory and Deregulatory Housing Programs, by Census Division, 2003[a] (continued)
Percent, except as indicated

		West		Midwest		South			Northeast	
Item	Total	Pacific	Mountain	West North Central	East North Central	West South Central	East South Central	South Atlantic	Mid-Atlantic	New England
Linkage fee										
Jurisdictions	1.6	4.8	0.6	0.0	0.3	0.4	3.9	1.4	2.7	2.3
Population	7.0	15.2	6.4	0.0	2.1	5.5	0.9	7.1	3.6	10.3
Square miles	2.4	6.3	0.2	0.0	0.4	0.9	0.2	2.2	5.0	2.1
Fee waiver										
Jurisdictions	4.0	18.7	5.7	4.4	1.2	1.6	4.7	6.1	1.9	5.3
Population	14.6	20.8	24.5	14.0	2.1	26.0	2.7	22.0	5.1	6.2
Square miles	7.7	13.0	2.5	3.1	0.7	4.2	7.5	18.9	3.9	5.2
Other incentive										
Jurisdictions	3.7	9.6	2.2	8.6	3.1	3.1	0.0	2.2	2.3	6.4
Population	11.4	25.0	4.5	6.3	1.5	14.8	0.0	16.1	4.0	3.5
Square miles	5.4	8.4	0.3	10.6	1.1	2.6	0.0	15.2	3.7	6.0
Any incentive										
Jurisdictions	16.5	67.1	14.6	11.4	5.7	5.4	9.7	16.0	14.6	36.9
Population	52.3	87.2	46.3	32.2	25.5	35.5	54.6	51.0	52.6	47.8
Square miles	26.8	52.5	16.3	8.0	7.1	7.5	26.1	40.6	22.8	37.5

One incentive										
Jurisdictions	9.8	35.5	5.7	6.4	2.6	3.6	6.3	9.9	9.2	27.5
Population	22.5	32.3	12.3	21.1	3.0	13.3	23.0	20.9	37.5	27.6
Square miles	11.5	14.5	13.6	5.1	2.3	2.2	11.7	16.8	13.0	27.7
Two incentives										
Jurisdictions	2.9	19.2	2.5	0.5	0.2	0.0	0.9	3.6	2.1	5.1
Population	13.1	37.7	19.4	0.7	1.7	0.0	25.0	12.5	4.3	5.0
Square miles	8.7	25.9	1.1	0.3	0.2	0.0	7.2	13.8	4.6	5.5
Three incentives										
Jurisdictions	1.0	6.7	0.6	0.0	0.0	0.1	0.0	0.4	1.1	1.5
Population	3.9	6.5	1.1	0.0	0.0	4.4	0.0	5.7	1.7	10.9
Square miles	1.5	3.3	0.0	0.0	0.0	0.7	0.0	2.9	2.1	1.6
Four or more incentives										
Jurisdictions	0.3	2.3	0.6	0.0	0.0	0.0	0.0	0.0	0.5	0.0
Population	1.9	7.4	6.4	0.0	0.0	0.0	0.0	0.0	0.2	0.0
Square miles	1.0	4.3	0.2	0.0	0.0	0.0	0.0	0.0	0.8	0.0

Source: Estimates of regulation compiled by author based on survey (January 2003) by Rolf Pendall and Jonathan Martin. For more details, see Pendall, Martin, and Puentes (2006). Population and land area estimates from Census Bureau (2000a, SF1).
a. Population is given in millions, square miles in thousands.

In New Jersey, about a quarter of 143 jurisdictions have IZ; these jurisdictions account for 27 percent of the population and 36 percent of the land area. These statistics show the impact of the *Mount Laurel* rulings, which essentially mandated IZ in "developing" suburban townships that had not yet accommodated much affordable housing. The surprise in New Jersey, however, is that only an estimated 11 percent of its jurisdictions offer density bonuses. In Maryland, well known for IZ because of Montgomery County's pioneering program, only an estimated four jurisdictions (18 percent of those for which estimates were made), with about a quarter of the state's metropolitan population and land area, now have IZ. The Massachusetts part of metropolitan Boston also had a fairly high incidence of IZ, with 14 percent of jurisdictions containing 35 percent of the metro area's population. In twenty-one of the thirty-seven states in which local governments were surveyed for this research, none of the respondents had IZ; most of these states were in the South and Midwest, but they also include Pennsylvania, Arizona, Oregon, and the District of Columbia.

How do jurisdictions with IZ differ from those without it? Considering that state policies tend to target different kinds of jurisdictions for policy interventions, it is appropriate to consider this question separately within the three states where the largest number of jurisdictions that responded to the survey have IZ: California, Massachusetts, and New Jersey. In California, 71 of 172 cities responding had IZ in 2003; 17 of the 97 respondents from Massachusetts and 30 of 101 New Jersey municipalities reported that they had IZ. Table 7-4 reveals few common factors across the three states that distinguish jurisdictions with and without IZ; in all three states, median contract rent is higher in jurisdictions with IZ. On a more limited level, the data suggest that jurisdictions with IZ have higher shares of white non-Hispanic (California, New Jersey) and Asian (Massachusetts, New Jersey) residents and lower shares of Hispanic residents (California, New Jersey). New Jersey jurisdictions with IZ also have significantly lower shares of African American residents than those without IZ. Localities with IZ also have higher incomes and newer housing stock in California and New Jersey and higher shares of housing in single-family detached stock and owner-occupied tenure in New Jersey. Massachusetts departs somewhat from these patterns, with lower shares of housing in single-family detached housing and higher shares of renters and with slightly older housing stock (the average median year of construction is 1955 for jurisdictions with IZ and 1960 for those without, $p = 0.116$).

The 2003 survey also asked whether local governments accepted in-lieu fees. An estimated 275 jurisdictions did so, 4 percent of the total, with 10 percent of the population and 4 percent of the land area. The geographic incidence of in-lieu fee programs parallels that of IZ and density bonus, with California (26 percent), New Jersey (22 percent), and Massachusetts (14 percent) at or near the top of the list. Within California, the San Francisco Bay Area again tops the list of jurisdictions with in-lieu provisions, 49 in all (43 percent of jurisdictions, 47 percent of

Table 7-4. *Average Characteristics of Jurisdictions with and without Inclusionary Zoning, California, Massachusetts, and New Jersey*[a]
Units as indicated

	California			Massachusetts			New Jersey		
Item	Inclusionary zoning	*No inclusionary zoning*	*Sig.*	Inclusionary zoning	*No inclusionary zoning*	*Sig.*	Inclusionary zoning	*No inclusionary zoning*	*Sig.*
In population (2000)	10.91	10.78	0.369	10.63	9.71	0.000	10.12	9.61	0.040
Percent white	61.1	49.2	0.001	86.1	91.1	0.149	81.6	73.6	0.035
Percent African American	3.6	4.9	0.156	3.3	1.4	0.206	5.1	10.7	0.021
Percent Asian	12.0	13.2	0.518	5.3	2.4	0.036	7.7	4.0	0.026
Percent Hispanic	19.6	29.2	0.003	3.4	3.3	0.953	4.3	9.9	0.001
Percent housing vacancy	4.1	4.5	0.533	3.5	4.0	0.638	4.0	9.3	0.004
Percent owner occupied	62.6	61.5	0.623	65.6	74.7	0.038	80.2	69.5	0.001
Median household income ($)	65,887	57,504	0.023	61,057	67,320	0.316	73,358	60,961	0.009
Percent single-family detached houses	57.0	60.3	0.174	54.4	67.9	0.023	71.0	61.7	0.026
Percent houses built in 1990s	15.6	11.9	0.072	9.7	11.7	0.306	15.0	9.7	0.012
Median year structure built	1972	1968	0.013	1955	1960	0.116	1969	1960	0.001
Median contract rent ($)	948	823	0.004	770	654	0.011	800	730	0.076
Median housing value ($)	363,742	287,570	0.012	260,741	236,595	0.441	214,897	192,324	0.267
Ratio of local income to metro income	1.20	1.16	0.462	1.17	1.29	0.316	1.46	1.22	0.005
Ratio of local rent to metro rent	1.20	1.15	0.306	1.23	1.04	0.011	1.23	1.15	0.118
Ratio of local value to metro value	1.29	1.22	0.527	1.37	1.25	0.441	1.16	1.10	0.561
Ratio of local value to metro income	6.54	5.73	0.134	4.98	4.52	0.441	4.27	3.85	0.286
Jurisdictions (*n*)	71	101	...	17	80	...	30	71	...

Source: Data from Census Bureau (2000a, SF3); author's survey.
a. Boldface type indicates a significant (sig.) difference at $p < 0.05$.

the population); in no other metro area in the United States did more than a third of jurisdictions take in-lieu fees. Virginia (16 percent) and Colorado (five jurisdictions estimated, 19 percent of the total) also appear to make extensive use of in-lieu fees for affordable housing.

Affordable housing linkage fees on commercial development, closely related to in-lieu fees and IZ, are again limited mainly to California, New Jersey, and Massachusetts. Linkage fees have spread beyond the big cities where they first garnered national attention; an estimated twenty-five California jurisdictions (7.5 percent of the total, with 18 percent of the metropolitan population) and forty-six New Jersey cities and townships (8.2 percent, with 14 percent of the population) have linkage fees. Ten Massachusetts cities and towns (4 percent, 19 percent of the population) had linkage fees in 2003. Florida and Kentucky were the only other states in which more than five jurisdictions were estimated to have linkage fees in 2003.

The final two incentives the survey asked about were fast-track processing (3.3 percent of jurisdictions nationally) and fee waivers (4.0 percent of jurisdictions). California again led states in the incidence of fast-tracking, but in this case the San Francisco Bay Area lagged the other metropolitan areas, with just 15 percent of jurisdictions offering a faster process for affordable projects; jurisdictions in Sacramento (30 percent) and San Diego (28 percent) evidently place a higher priority on "customer service" for affordable housing, with Los Angeles (20 percent) falling between San Francisco and the smaller metros. High-growth metropolitan areas where affordable housing incentives are otherwise uncommon also use fast-tracking more often than the national average. These include Phoenix, Las Vegas, Miami, Denver, Tampa, San Antonio, and Raleigh. Many of these are also among the metro areas leading the nation in offering fee waivers for affordable housing: Sacramento, San Francisco, Phoenix, Denver, San Diego, Orlando, Miami, and Raleigh.

Local Land-Use and Housing Policy in Built-Out Affluent Suburban Job Centers

The interplay between zoning, other growth regulations, local affordable housing programs, and the production and affordability of rental housing takes a distinctive shape in affluent suburban job centers. The coevolution of regulation, housing prices, and housing policies has had particular impacts in the three wealthy but built-up (and putatively built-out, according to their zoning and planning policies) suburbs that are the subject of the earlier case studies: Pleasanton, Coral Gables, and Newton.

These three cities are among the more affluent middle-sized suburbs in their regions, and each has a substantial number of jobs. In fact, they differ more in their population size than in their employment bases: in 2000 Newton had 83,829 residents, Pleasanton had 63,654, and Coral Gables 42,249, whereas the number

Table 7-5. *Population and Housing Statistics, Coral Gables, Newton, and Pleasanton, 2000*

Units as indicated

Item	Coral Gables	Newton	Pleasanton
Population	42,249	83,829	63,654
Household income (1999)[a]			
Median ($)	66,839	86,052	90,859
Metropolitan median ($)	38,632	52,306	62,024
Ratio of city median to metro median	1.73	1.65	1.46
Percent over $150,000	22.2	24.7	20.9
Housing units			
Total	17,796	32,112	23,987
Occupied (*n*)	16,734	31,201	23,317
Rented (*n*)	5,669	9,498	6,210
Percent rented	33.9	30.4	26.6
Single-family (detached or attached) (*n*)	11,098	19,392	18,347
Percent single-family	62.5	60.4	78.0
Multifamily, 2–4 units (*n*)	1,356	7,918	1,139
Percent multifamily, 2–4 units	7.6	24.7	4.8
Multifamily, 5 or more units (*n*)	5,316	4,793	4,045
Percent multifamily, 5 or more units	29.9	14.9	17.2
Built since 1990 (*n*)	1,469	1,127	6,072
Percent built since 1990	8.3	3.5	25.3
Median housing costs ($)			
Gross rent	754	1,083	1,219
Housing value	336,800	438,400	435,300
Monthly owner costs (with mortgage)	2,309	2,259	2,186
Jobs (2000) (*n*)[b]	49,215	45,775	55,140
Square miles (*n*)	12.4	18.1	21.7
Population per square mile (*n*)	3,407	4,631	2,933
Jobs per square mile (*n*)[b]	3,969	2,529	2,541

Source: Data from Census Bureau (2000a, SF3), extracted by the author; Census Bureau (2000b).

a. Boston metropolitan area median income (for Newton) is based on the Boston NECMA by 1993 OMB definitions; Miami and San Francisco metro areas (for Coral Gables and Pleasanton, respectively) are CMSA level.

b. Jobs are primary jobs and do not include second jobs.

of jobs ranged from 45,775 (Newton) to 55,140 (Pleasanton) (table 7-5). The 1999 median income of Coral Gables of $66,839 lagged that in both Newton ($86,052) and Pleasanton ($90,859), but it exceeded the Miami consolidated metropolitan statistical area median income by 75 percent, while Newton and Pleasanton had median incomes of 66 and 46 percent higher, respectively, than their metropolitan areas' medians. In all three cities, between 20 and 25 percent of households earned more than $150,000 in 1999. All three cities have populations that are more than 80 percent white (including Hispanic whites), and none is more than 4 percent black (table 7-6). In 2000, 47 percent of Coral Gables residents were Latino, and nearly one-fifth of the city's residents were born in Cuba; Pleasanton's population was 8.1 percent Hispanic (a much lower share than the 20 percent metropolitan level), and Newton's was 2.5 percent Hispanic.

Consistent with their relatively high incomes, the three cities have housing that is dominated by expensive owner-occupied single-family dwellings. Home ownership rates in 2000 ranged from 66 percent in Coral Gables to 73 percent in Pleasanton (table 7-5). Housing values in the three cities are very high, with median self-reported values in 2000 of roughly $337,000, $438,000, and $435,000 in Coral Gables, Newton, and Pleasanton, respectively; all three cities had median monthly costs for owners with mortgages of between $2,100 and $2,400. Gross rent in the three cities was $754, $1,083, and $1,219, respectively, well above the metropolitan area medians. Pleasanton has the largest share of single-family detached and attached housing (78 percent), the shares in both Coral Gables and Newton being about 60 percent. Newton stands out for its large share (about a quarter) of dwellings in two- to four-unit buildings, and Coral Gables for its number of large multifamily units (30 percent of the total, compared with about 15–17 percent in the other two cities).

Jobs in all three cities in 2000 paid lower wages than city residents earned. About half the jobs in Coral Gables paid wages less than $30,000 in 1999, but only 38 percent of Coral Gables residents earned wages that low (table 7-7). The corollary figures for Newton and Pleasanton were 44 and 37 percent of jobs, respectively, and 33 and 27 percent of resident workers. At the highest wage levels, that relationship was reversed, with between 27 and 32 percent of resident workers earning more than $75,000 a year but between 13 and 20 percent of local jobs paying that amount. The variation between local wages and local housing costs means that in all three cities, substantial numbers of low-wage workers commute in from elsewhere; in both Newton and Coral Gables, the largest source of low-wage workers (those with household incomes below $35,000) was their respective neighboring central city (Boston and Miami).[43]

In other respects, the cities differ from one another fairly substantially. Newton is an older city, having grown up around a series of about a dozen villages as a streetcar suburb in the late 1800s and early 1900s; as of 2000, only 3.5 percent of its housing stock had been built in the 1990s. Coral Gables is a postwar suburb, but it is the product of a 1920s master plan by Florida real estate magnate George Merrick, with strong design controls and a close association with tenets of the New Urbanism. About 8 percent of its 2000 housing stock was built in the

---

43. Data on California were not available.

Table 7-6. *Population by Race and Ethnicity, Coral Gables, Newton, and Pleasanton and Their Metro Areas, 2000*
Units as indicated

Item	City total			Percentage of city total			Percentage of metropolitan area total		
	Coral Gables	Newton	Pleasanton	Coral Gables	Newton	Pleasanton	Miami	Boston	San Francisco
Total	42,202	83,829	63,569	100.0	100.0	100.0	100.0	100.0	100.0
Not Hispanic or Latino	22,579	81,706	58,405	53.5	97.5	91.9	59.7	94.0	80.3
White alone	20,176	72,546	48,010	47.8	86.5	75.5	36.3	82.9	50.4
Black or African American alone	1,388	1,488	696	3.3	1.8	1.1	19.2	4.6	7.0
American Indian and Alaska Native alone	41	96	166	0.1	0.1	0.3	0.1	0.2	0.4
Asian alone	633	6,316	7,339	1.5	7.5	11.5	1.7	3.9	18.3
Native Hawaiian and Other Pacific Islander alone	0	0	53	0.0	0.0	0.1	0.0	0.0	0.5
Some other race alone	49	188	150	0.1	0.2	0.2	0.3	0.7	0.3
Two or more races	292	1,072	1,991	0.7	1.3	3.1	2.0	1.8	3.6
Hispanic or Latino	19,623	2,123	5,164	46.5	2.5	8.1	40.3	6.0	19.7
White alone	18,593	1,418	2,950	44.1	1.7	4.6	33.8	2.5	8.1
Black or African American alone	143	76	40	0.3	0.1	0.1	0.9	0.3	0.2
American Indian and Alaska Native alone	17	7	59	0.0	0.0	0.1	0.1	0.0	0.3
Asian alone	0	7	53	0.0	0.0	0.1	0.0	0.0	0.2
Native Hawaiian and Other Pacific Islander alone	0	0	0	0.0	0.0	0.0	0.0	0.0	0.0
Some other race alone	572	503	1,380	1.4	0.6	2.2	3.6	2.6	9.2
Two or more races	298	112	682	0.7	0.1	1.1	1.9	0.5	1.7

Source: Data extracted by the author from Census Bureau (2000a, SF3).

Table 7-7. *Jobs and Employed Residents, Coral Gables, Newton, and Pleasanton, 2000, by 1999 Wages*[a]
Units as indicated

	City total (N)			Percentage of city total		
Item	Coral Gables	Newton	Pleasanton	Coral Gables	Newton	Pleasanton
Jobs						
Total	49,215	45,775	55,140			
With earnings ($)	47,490	44,710	53,879	100.0	100.0	100.0
<10,000	7,360	6,855	5,770	15.5	15.3	10.7
10,000–20,000	8,965	5,925	6,570	18.9	13.3	12.2
20,000–30,000	8,110	7,025	7,394	17.1	15.7	13.7
30,000–50,000	10,910	11,715	13,905	23.0	26.2	25.8
50,000–75,000	5,595	7,320	9,770	11.8	16.4	18.1
75,000+	6,550	5,870	10,470	13.8	13.1	19.4
No 1999 earnings	1,730	1,069	1,285			
Employed residents						
Total	28,860	44,215	34,480			
With earnings (dollars)	28,218	43,290	33,855	100.0	100.0	100.0
<10,000	4,200	5,325	3,280	14.9	12.3	9.7
10,000–20,000	3,349	4,215	3,055	11.9	9.7	9.0
20,000–30,000	3,189	4,540	2,860	11.3	10.5	8.4
30,000–50,000	5,400	9,545	7,035	19.1	22.0	20.8
50,000–75,000	4,135	7,900	6,925	14.7	18.2	20.5
75,000+	7,945	11,765	10,700	28.2	27.2	31.6
No 1999 earnings	650	935	630			
Jobs per employed resident						
Total	1.71	1.04	1.60	. . .	. . .	. . .
With earnings	1.68	1.03	1.59	. . .	. . .	. . .
<10,000	1.75	1.29	1.76	. . .	. . .	. . .
10,000–20,000	2.68	1.41	2.15	. . .	. . .	. . .
20,000–30,000	2.54	1.55	2.59	. . .	. . .	. . .
30,000–50,000	2.02	1.23	1.98	. . .	. . .	. . .
50,000–75,000	1.35	0.93	1.41	. . .	. . .	. . .
75,000+	0.82	0.50	0.98	. . .	. . .	. . .
No 1999 earnings	2.66	1.14	2.04	. . .	. . .	. . .

Source: Data from Census Bureau (2000b).

a. Job count is of the number of people working in the city. Employed residents count is the number of workers living in the city.

1990s. Pleasanton combines aspects of an "edge city" at the crossroads of two outer-ring interstate highways (580 and 680) with a historic (late-1800s) downtown and its associated neighborhoods. As of 2000 about a quarter of its housing stock had been built in the 1990s. Despite these distinct growth histories, however, all three of the cities have policies that will hinder future housing growth; their residents and decisionmakers now consider the city mostly or entirely built-out.

A final difference is political. Party registration in Newton is heavily Democratic (47 percent in 2004, and only 10 percent Republican). Pleasanton and Coral Gables, by contrast, have heavier Republican registrations, at 39 percent and 44 percent, respectively, compared with Democratic registrations of 37 percent and 33 percent. All three are in predominantly Democratic counties (39 percent to 12 percent in Middlesex County, 55 percent to 18 percent in Alameda County, and 42 percent to 34 percent in Miami-Dade).[44]

Newton, Massachusetts

Newton's land-use pattern is typical of much of the Boston metropolitan area, with historic centers of settlement (villages) surrounded by lower-density residential neighborhoods. Interstates 90 (the Massachusetts Turnpike) and 95 (state Route 128) both traverse the city, with one interchange each, as does heavily traveled state Route 9. Newton is well served by the Massachusetts Bay Transit Authority, with three commuter rail stations, seven light rail (Green Line) stations, and ten bus routes.

Newton's draft comprehensive plan predicts that its population and housing stock will continue growing, although slowly. The plan positions Newton to return, in some ways, to its history as a streetcar suburb, protecting its single-family neighborhoods from change but encouraging intensification in mixed-use centers. Corresponding with this land-use shift is the city's hope for at least four new rail stations (two commuter stations, two Green Line) around which new mixed-use development centers (transit-oriented developments) would emerge. The land-use and transportation elements of the draft comprehensive plan have mutually supportive policies that support higher density, mixed-use development around transit, shared and centralized parking, and gradual replacement of single-story with multistory buildings in commercial areas and along commercial strips. In all, according to the comprehensive plan, the city can accommodate another 2,400 dwelling units under the current zoning, even assuming significant use of

44. Pleasanton data: Alameda County Registrar of Voters, "Report of Registration as of September 8, 2006" (www.acgov.org/rov/reg_statistics.htm); Newton data: Commonwealth of Massachusetts, "Enrollment Breakdown as of August 30, 2006" (www.sec.state.ma.us/ele/elepdf/stparty06.pdf); Coral Gables data: Miami-Dade County, "Elections Report: Registration Statistics" (2006) (elections.metro-dade.com/currstat.html).

discretionary special permits, which are required for all residential structures with three or more units.[45]

Under current zoning, residential density would increase mainly, if not entirely, under the business and mixed-use designations. Four of the five business districts allow dwelling units above the first floor. The tallest buildings allowed by the zoning ordinance occur in the Business 4 district, where a special permit could allow a structure of up to eight stories (ninety-six feet) with a floor area ratio of 3.0. The city has two mixed-use districts where housing is allowed either as of right or by special permit; the as-of-right height limits are two and three stories, respectively, but special permits allow a maximum of four stories in these districts. None of the exclusively residential zones allows such high densities or tall buildings.

Under what conditions would special permits be expected to be granted that would significantly increase the city's rental housing stock? The special-permit process—which is the trigger for the city's IZ policy—requires a two-thirds vote of the city's twenty-four aldermen, who may approve special permit only if they find that the site is appropriate, the use will not adversely affect the neighborhood, there will be no nuisance or serious hazard to vehicles or pedestrians, and access to the site over streets is appropriate for the types and numbers of vehicles involved.[46] Newton's comprehensive plan notes that auto registration in the city grew by 14 percent in the 1990s and total trip ends by 7 percent,[47] despite practically no growth in housing and jobs.[48] On the other hand, the plan also notes a decline in Newton's auto-based commuting in the 1990s (from 81 percent to 75 percent of workers), with a corresponding increase in walking to work and working at home, suggesting that traffic growth may decelerate soon.[49]

Newton has an active affordable housing program. It is the lead city in a HOME consortium; it also receives community development block grant funds as an entitlement city. It has its own housing authority, which owns 481 housing units and administers 442 Section 8 vouchers.[50] Even so, Newton has not met the threshold of 10 percent subsidized units that would protect it from challenges

45. City of Newton, Draft Comprehensive Plan, Housing Element (April 13, 2006) (www.ci.newton.ma.us/Planning/CPAC/com%20plan%202005/10102006update/5%20Housing.pdf), p. 3.

46. City of Newton, *City Ordinances,* chap. 30, art. 4, Zoning Administration, sec. 30-24 (2001) (www.ci.newton.ma.us/Legal/Ordinance/chapter_30_article_4.htm).

47. A trip end is either the starting or the ending point of a trip.

48. City of Newton, Draft Comprehensive Plan, Transportation and Mobility Element (April 13, 2006) (www.ci.newton.ma.us/Planning/CPAC/com%20plan%202005/10102006update/4%20Transport.pdf), pp. 2, 4.

49. City of Newton, Draft Comprehensive Plan, Transportation and Mobility Element (April 13, 2006) (www.ci.newton.ma.us/Planning/CPAC/com%20plan%202005/10102006update/4%20Transport.pdf), p. 3.

50. City of Newton, Draft Comprehensive Plan, Housing Element (April 13, 2006) (www.ci.newton.ma.us/Planning/CPAC/com%20plan%202005/10102006update/5%20Housing.pdf), p. 8.

under Chapter 40B.[51] Its affluence and location make it a potential target for hostile 40B challenges from private sector developers who hope to build a mainly market-rate development; indeed, twelve Chapter 40B projects with around five hundred affordable housing units were approved between 1977 and 2001.[52] Newton's large size, affluence, and liberal population also support a competent city planning staff and citizen boards of all kinds. Furthermore, the city has a small but successful nonprofit builder, CAN-DO, with a record of working for more than a decade within the city's rules.

In 1977 Newton became the first city in the Commonwealth to adopt an inclusionary zoning program, but it had an "informal" inclusionary policy even in the 1960s.[53]

> The original 1977 ordinance required all developments seeking a special permit to provide 10 percent of the units as affordable. The primary means of accomplishing this objective was to lease these units to the Newton Housing Authority (NHA) . . . as low-income rental units, but there also were other options available to a developer such as providing units off-site or making a cash payment in lieu of any units. In 1987, the Board of Aldermen wanted to provide more consistency in how this ordinance was applied and, perhaps, increase the amount of units being provided. The board modified the ordinance to require developers to set aside 25 percent of the bonus units allowed under a special permit as compared to the number of units allowed by right. . . . Additional language expanded the period of affordability, provided tighter regulations in lieu of fees and widened the applicability of the ordinance to other developments.[54]

All the units created under the 1987 version of the ordinance were rental units owned by the original developer and leased through the Newton Housing Authority to households earning less than 50 percent of area median income.[55] Residential builders did not like this arrangement: "The developer is . . . responsible for heating these large units and paying the condominium dues—which may or may not be covered by the lease payments. This makes the economics of the inclusionary ordinance a long, unnecessary burden on the developer."[56]

51. General Laws of Massachusetts, chap. 40B, Regional Planning, sec. 20-23, "Low and Moderate Income Housing."

52. Engler (2002, p. 18).

53. Horsley Witten Group, "Inclusionary Zoning Urban Case Study," report prepared for the Massachusetts Office of Environmental Affairs as part of the Smart Growth Toolkit (www.mass.gov/envir/smart_growth_toolkit/pages/CS-iz-newton.html); Engler (2002).

54. Engler (2002, pp. 18–19).

55. City of Newton, City Ordinances, chap. 30, art. 4, Zoning Administration, sec. 30-24(f) (2001) (www.ci.newton.ma.us/Legal/Ordinance/chapter_30_article_4.htm).

56. Engler (2002, pp. 18–19).

In 2003 the city amended the IZ ordinance for the first time since 1987, broadening the scope but making the affordability levels shallower.[57] Rather than requiring that 25 percent of the bonus density accommodated by a special permit be affordable, the new ordinance simply requires that 15 percent of all housing built under a special permit (that is, most of the city's new housing) be affordable. Additionally, at least 10 percent of the total habitable space in the development must be affordable, meaning the affordable units could be smaller than average. For the first time, however, the ordinance would yield both for-sale and rental units; in 2004 the aldermen clarified the 2003 amendments to ensure that the mix of inclusionary for-sale and rental units was the same as in the market-rate units. Two-thirds of the for-sale units would be affordable at 80 percent of area median income, with the remainder at 120 percent of area median income; the rental units would be affordable to a variety of households as long as the mean income of all assisted households did not exceed 65 percent of area median income. The developer must still own rental units for the forty-year affordability term and lease them to the Newton Housing Authority.[58]

Builders can also apply to build inclusionary units off-site (in partnership with a nonprofit), rehabilitate existing units, or pay an in-lieu fee. Developers of up to six market-rate units are required to make a "cash payment of three percent of the sales price for for-sale housing, or three percent of the assessed value of each unit for rental housing."[59] Proceeds of the funds are divided equally between the Newton Housing Authority and the City of Newton's planning and development department.

As of 2001, Newton's IZ policy and ordinance had provided about 225 units of affordable housing, about half the production of Chapter 40B units.[60] This low production partly resulted from the modest inclusionary requirement between 1987 and 2003:

> The city's zoning code allows multifamily development in relatively few areas of the city and at densities which are not conducive to producing much affordability. Because the density increases allowed by special permit are not significantly higher than those densities allowed by right, the formula tied to 25 percent of the increase simply does not create very many units. In

57. The text of the IZ ordinance includes both the 2003 amendment (X-48) (www.ci.newton.ma.us/Aldermen/ORD%20REVISIONS/x-48.htm) and the clean-up amendments from 2004 (X-125) (www.ci.newton.ma.us/Legal/Amendments/2004-2005_amendments/X-125.pdf).

58. Horsley Witten Group, "Inclusionary Zoning Urban Case Study," report prepared for the Massachusetts Office of Environmental Affairs as part of the Smart Growth Toolkit (www.mass.gov/envir/smart_growth_toolkit/pages/CS-iz-newton.html).

59. Horsley Witten Group, "Inclusionary Zoning Urban Case Study," report prepared for the Massachusetts Office of Environmental Affairs as part of the Smart Growth Toolkit (www.mass.gov/envir/smart_growth_toolkit/pages/CS-iz-newton.html).

60. Engler (2002, p. 18).

order to make it a more effective tool, zoning densities have to be increased under the special permit and the ordinance has to be made more inclusive, more flexible, with higher affordability requirements and with more administrative control in relation to city housing policy.[61]

It appears that the modification of Newton's IZ ordinance in 2003 made a trade-off. A larger amount of affordable housing would be required, and it would be required as a condition of approval for all development, but the affordability level is shallower. Since the inclusionary units are leased through the Newton Housing Authority, however, there is a chance that at least the shallowly subsidized rentals will be leased to families with vouchers.

The most recent addition to Newton's affordable housing tool kit is a local ordinance adopted in 2000, shortly after the legislature approved the Commonwealth's Community Preservation Act. Under the state act's terms, local governments are permitted to raise their own taxes to provide funding for open space, historic preservation, and affordable housing; at least 10 percent of the funds must be devoted to each of the three uses. Newton has far exceeded that mandate for affordable housing; as of fiscal year 2004–05, the city had spent $5.69 million for housing, $2.42 million for open space, $1.76 million for historic preservation, and $1.64 million for recreation.[62] The Community Preservation Act funds have assisted in the creation of eighty-one affordable units (all of which depend on multiple subsidy sources).

Pleasanton, California

More than many slogans, Pleasanton's—"City of Planned Progress"—describes the city well. Development in this eastern Bay Area city has been more closely planned and monitored than would be imaginable in many other states, driven by both elected officials and citizens at the ballot box. The city council adopted a building permit cap in 1978 to tie development more closely to infrastructure capacity, updating it periodically and closely tracking the progress of residential development.[63] A general plan policy restricts annual building permit issuance to a maximum of 750 units, but the implementing ordinance sets the cap at 350 units a year. City residents have also used their initiative and referendum powers aggressively to control the pace, location, quality, and ultimate amount of residential development in the city. In 1996 voters approved an ultimate cap of 29,000 housing units in the city.[64] Pleasanton also has a voter-approved greenbelt, limiting the

61. Engler (2002, p. 21).

62. City of Newton Community Preservation Committee, "Annual Report 2005" (www.ci.newton.ma.us/Planning/CPAC/FY05%20CPC%20Annual%20Report.pdf).

63. City of Pleasanton, *Pleasanton City Code,* "Growth Management Program," sec. 17.36.010 (2006) (66.113.195.234/CA/Pleasanton/index.htm).

64. Jason B. Johnson and Bernadette Tansey, "Voters Take Long Look at Sprawl," *San Francisco Chronicle,* November 4, 1999, final edition, p. A1.

outward extent of development. At this writing, Pleasanton is in the midst of a general plan update, but it is not considering an increase in its build-out.

Pleasanton's slow-growth attitudes have been nowhere more evident than in the city's plans for a flat, vacant, 508-acre parcel long owned by the City of San Francisco's water department just a few blocks from its historic downtown and bordering Interstate 680. A commission of Pleasanton citizens recommended in March 1993 the development of 3,000 housing units and 750,000 square feet of commercial space for the site, but successively hostile city councils pared back the housing to 581 dwellings and increased employment and public open space to 192 and 320 acres, respectively.[65]

Pleasanton's zoning ordinance allows multifamily housing in four zones, the densest of which allows one dwelling for each 1,500 square feet of lot area (twenty-nine units an acre) with a forty-foot height limit. Multifamily housing is also allowed under a Planned Unit Development (PUD) designation, where density varies according to negotiations between the city and builders. The general plan, by contrast, does not place an upper limit on density; its high-density category allows eight or more units an acre. No land is currently vacant and zoned for high-density development.

Pleasanton has at least a twenty-five-year history of planning for affordable housing. It has a housing specialist within its planning department; it also has a public housing authority with one fifty-unit senior project. The Department of Housing and Urban Development's 1998 "Picture of Subsidized Households" lists about forty vouchers in the city, most of them administered by the Alameda County Housing Authority.[66] The city's 2003 affordable housing inventory included 449 family units and 396 senior units, including the Pleasanton Housing Authority's project.[67] By June 2006, however, income restrictions had expired for 149 family units produced in response to growth management exemptions in the 1990s.[68] The remaining assisted family rentals produced under the exemption incentive have rents only $50–75 below market rates, because their rents were tar-

65. Bonita Brewer, "Bernal Property Options Explored," *Contra Costa Times* (Walnut Creek, Calif.), May 18, 2006, p. F4; Matt Carter, "Council to Weigh Future of Bernal Site," *Tri-Valley Herald* (Pleasanton, Calif.), June 30, 2003, More Local News section; Jason B. Johnson, "S.F., Pleasanton OK Plan for 1,900 New Homes," *San Francisco Chronicle,* March 6, 1998, p. A17; John King, "Field of Battle: Pleasanton's Slow-Growth Council Stymies S.F.'s Plan to Build Nearby," *San Francisco Chronicle,* June 16, 1997, p. A1; Michael Pena, "Final Hearings to Begin on Pleasanton Project," *San Francisco Chronicle,* August 2, 2000, Contra Costa edition, p. A17.

66. HUD (2004).

67. City of Pleasanton, *Pleasanton City Code,* sec. 17.36, Growth Management Program (66.113.195.234/CA/Pleasanton/index.htm), p. 33.

68. City of Pleasanton, *Pleasanton City Code,* sec. 17.36, Growth Management Program (66.113.195.234/CA/Pleasanton/index.htm), p. 52; City of Pleasanton, "Below-Market Rental Housing Opportunities" (n.d.) (www.ci.pleasanton.ca.us/community/housing/below-market-rental.html).

geted at 80 percent of area median income,[69] but those produced with the city's IZ program (adopted in 2000) have deeper affordability. A January 2000 rent survey showed two-bedroom rents in the most recent ninety-nine below-market-rate units as low as $845, compared with more than $1,500 for market rents.[70]

As an entitlement city, Pleasanton had access to community development block grant funds of about $300,000 in fiscal year 2005–06.[71] Since Pleasanton's voters have rejected proposals to form a redevelopment agency, no low-income housing funds are generated from tax increment districts. The city has been an active partner in at least a half-dozen affordable projects produced with for-profit and nonprofit builders, using a combination of bond finance, fee waivers, land donations, and leases.[72]

The most active affordable housing programs now are inclusionary zoning projects, dating from 2000, and the housing fund, which applies to most nonresidential development and was adopted in the 1990s.[73] The ordinance requires a set-aside of 15 percent of multifamily dwellings as affordable to low-income and very low-income residents, and 20 percent of single-family dwellings must be affordable to very low-income, low-income, and moderate-income households. *Affordable* is defined as having housing costs less than 35 percent of household income; the income ceilings are 50 percent, 80 percent, and 120 percent of the county's median incomes for those three categories of households, respectively, as established by the Department of Housing and Urban Development. Inclusionary units must be dispersed and identical to other units in their exteriors, but they may be smaller and have fewer amenities than market-rate units.[74] They must remain affordable in perpetuity.

The city has established incentives to encourage builders to build the housing instead of opting out with in-lieu fees; since adoption of inclusionary zoning in 2000, no residential builders have paid fees in lieu of building housing.[75] Builders may also propose alternatives to either incorporating units or paying fees, including building inclusionary units off-site, dedicating land, or transferring IZ units to other builders. Revisions to the condominium conversion ordinance currently under consideration would apply a 25 percent inclusionary requirement to condominium conversions;[76] the largest apartment project in the city, a 520-unit

69. Steve Bocian, Pleasanton assistant city manager, personal communication, July 19, 2006.

70. City of Pleasanton, "Average Vacancy Rates and Rents in Major Apartment Complexes" (January 2006) (www.ci.pleasanton.ca.us/pdf/housing-rents-0601.pdf).

71. City of Pleasanton, "Comprehensive Annual Financial Report for the Year Ended June 30, 2005" (2005) (www.ci.pleasanton.ca.us/pdf/cafr-2005.pdf).

72. Steve Bocian, Pleasanton assistant city manager, personal communication, July 19, 2006.

73. City of Pleasanton, *Pleasanton City Code*, Inclusionary Zoning, sec. 17.44, 2006 (66.113. 195.234/CA/Pleasanton/index.htm).

74. City of Pleasanton, *Pleasanton City Code*, Inclusionary Zoning, sec. 17.44.050, 2006 (66.113. 195.234/CA/Pleasanton/index.htm).

75. Steve Bocian, Pleasanton assistant city manager, personal communication, July 19, 2006.

76. City of Pleasanton, *Pleasanton City Code*, Inclusionary Zoning, proposed amendment, sec. 17.44 (June 7, 2006) (www.ci.pleasanton.ca.us/pdf/draft-res-condo-text.pdf).

development, obtained approval in summer 2006 for condominium conversion, but an affordable housing agreement was included as a condition of approval.[77]

The city's housing fee applies to commercial, office, and industrial development and to residential projects. Nonresidential developments currently pay $2.44 a square foot. Every single-family house of 1,500 square feet or more carries a charge of $9,166; smaller residences, including multifamily units, pay $2,272 a unit.[78] Residential projects are entirely exempt if they provide their mandatory inclusionary units as lower-income housing;[79] moderate-income units in single-family projects are exempt, but market-rate units in those developments are subject to the fee. Second units, one-for-one residential reconstruction, and churches are also exempt.[80] At the end of the 2004 fiscal year, the lower-income housing fund had a balance of $15.7 million.[81] The city's total affordable housing inventory in 2006 stood at 845 units, most of these for seniors.[82]

In the past, Pleasanton's affordable housing programs and policies have balanced affordable home ownership with rental housing, but in the last year or so the city council has recognized that home ownership is too costly to subsidize in such a high-cost market. Consequently, it decided to shift its emphasis; it adopted a policy that at least two-thirds of the housing fund should be spent on very low and low-income rental housing. With its flexible IZ ordinance, Pleasanton can also work with single-family housing builders to secure participation in the development of new rental housing to fulfill the inclusionary requirement. Additionally, the city council has added conditions of approval to recent rental projects that require the owners to accommodate users of housing choice vouchers, and the city is considering setting aside a portion of the housing fund as an annuity to capitalize a local housing voucher program.[83]

Pleasanton's annual growth cap and restrictions on density did not stop it from exceeding the overall housing supply allocation from the Association of Bay Area Governments' 1988–95 regional housing needs determination (or fair-share allocation). Like most Bay Area cities, however, Pleasanton far exceeded its

77. Steve Bocian, Pleasanton assistant city manager, personal communication, July 19, 2006.

78. City of Pleasanton, "Affordable Housing" (2006) (www.ci.pleasanton.ca.us/community/housing/); figures current as of 2006.

79. That is, affordable at 80 percent of area median income.

80. City of Pleasanton, *Pleasanton City Code,* Lower Income Housing Fees, sec. 17.40.040 (2006) (66.113.195.234/CA/Pleasanton/index.htm).

81. City of Pleasanton, "Comprehensive Annual Financial Report for the Year Ended June 30, 2005" (2005) (www.ci.pleasanton.ca.us/pdf/cafr-2005.pdf), p. 30.

82. Bay Area Economics, *Economic Development Strategic Plan Background Report,* report prepared for the City of Pleasanton (2006) (www.ci.pleasanton.ca.us/pdf/genplan-final-ed-background-060110.pdf).

83. Steve Bocian, Pleasanton assistant city manager, personal communication, July 19, 2006.

regional housing needs determination for moderate- and above-moderate income housing. By contrast, only 395 of the needed 497 low-income units and 83 of the 745 needed very low-income units were built. Availability of vacant and zoned sites also did not pose serious obstacles to rental housing construction; among the more significant events of the decade, in fact, was a successful appeal by the Hacienda Business Park developer Joe Callahan to convert some of the office park to multifamily housing in the early 1990s in the face of slack office demand.

Since 2000, however, growth restrictions in Pleasanton have begun to pinch more severely. The overall build-out limit of 29,000 units was enough, but only barely, to accommodate the city's fair share of the regional housing need for 1999–2006, assigned by the Association of Bay Area Governments at 5,059 units. The implementing ordinance for the building permit cap, however, sets a maximum of 350 units a year "until build-out."[84] This would keep the city from approving enough units to meet its fair-share assignment, but the city council has the option of overriding the ordinance as long as the city issues permits for fewer than 750 units (the ironclad cap provided by the general plan). The complex allocation rules in the ordinance sets aside 50 units a year for affordable housing projects in a fast-track process, but all other projects—even those incorporating inclusionary units—face the cap, which operates on a first-come, first-served basis and thus can exhaust all allocations partway through the year.[85]

When it reviewed Pleasanton's 2003 housing element, the state Department of Housing and Community Development initially ruled that the city could comply with state law provided that it rezoned sufficient sites to accommodate between 800 and 900 multifamily housing units by June 2004. The department specified that the city should carry out a program proposed in the housing element to rezone land for higher-density housing. The city now does not expect to carry out that program until at least 2007.[86] This led the Department of Housing and Community Development to decertify the housing element, making Pleasanton one of only six jurisdictions in the nine-county, 100-plus-jurisdiction Bay Area out of compliance with state law by the department's reckoning.[87] City staff assert

84. City of Pleasanton, *Pleasanton City Code,* Growth Management Program, sec. 17.36.060 (2006) (66.113.195.234/CA/Pleasanton/index.htm).

85. City of Pleasanton, *Pleasanton City Code,* "Growth Management Program," sec. 17.36.070 (2006) (66.113.195.234/CA/Pleasanton/index.htm).

86. Cathy Creswell, deputy director, California Department of Housing and Community Development, letter to Nelson Fialho, Pleasanton city manager, March 23, 2006.

87. California Department of Housing and Community Development, Division of Housing Policy Development, *California Redevelopment Agency Housing Activities during Fiscal Year 2004–2005* (June 2006) (www.hcd.ca.gov/hpd/rda/04-05/rdasum04-05.pdf).

that the rezoning will occur well before the next housing element is due in June 2009.[88]

Coral Gables, Florida

Coral Gables is almost completely developed; by 1995 only 20 acres of its 12.4 square miles were listed as vacant in its comprehensive plan. It has fairly intense residential development. Its zoning code restricts heights to three stories in most of the city but allows up to thirteen-story apartment buildings in certain areas with a maximum floor area ratio of 2.0 and density of sixty dwellings an acre.[89] The most intensive commercial development in the city would be in areas with a special mixed-use overlay, where the maximum floor area ratio is 3.5 and the maximum height is 100 feet; these mixed-use zones also allow residential development at up to 125 units an acre. One consequence of this intense development, combined with a road system sized for an earlier era, is that the service level on which most of its roadways operate has been graded as F.[90] To allow continued development, the city has received an exemption to the state's concurrency requirement for the Gables Redevelopment Infill District.[91] As elsewhere in southern Florida, Coral Gables has experienced substantial redevelopment pressure. One recent large project, for example, involves the demolition of an existing ten-story commercial building, a three-story commercial building, and several single-family homes to build ten- and sixteen-story mixed-use buildings and townhouses valued at $82 million.[92]

Unlike Massachusetts and California, both of which interject a regional component into local housing planning, Florida requires cities and counties to plan for the people who already, or are expected to, live there. State statutes (and a review by the Department of Community Affairs) require local governments to accommodate future growth and affordable housing needs based on projections that are in turn based on the municipality's recent past.

The history of housing policy in Coral Gables—in short, it has never had one until now—reflects these state-level rules. The city's 1995 housing element (certified by the state growth management agency along with the rest of the compre-

88. Steve Bocian, Pleasanton assistant city manager, personal communication, July 19, 2006. Although state law calls for a five-year housing element cycle, practically every round of housing elements has been delayed because of state budget cuts. Bay Area cities will next update their housing elements in 2009.

89. City of Coral Gables, *Zoning Code,* art. 3, sec. 3-11, Use District and Regulations: Special Uses (2004) (www.coralgables.com/CGWeb/documents/planning_docs/CGZC2004/06Art03Use DistRegs.pdf).

90. City of Coral Gables, "Comprehensive Land Use Plan Data Inventory and Analysis" (2006) (www.coralgables.com/CGWeb/documents/planning_docs/DIA.pdf), p. I-5.

91. City of Coral Gables, "Comprehensive Land Use Plan Data Inventory and Analysis" (2006) (www.coralgables.com/CGWeb/documents/planning_docs/DIA.pdf), p. I-5.

92. Deserae del Campo, "Commercial Development Booming in Coral Gables," *Miami Today,* September 22, 2005 (www.miamitodaynews.com/news/050922/story2.shtml).

hensive plan) concluded that it had a surplus of affordable housing because it had more low-income housing units than low-income households.[93] Coral Gables has accommodated little affordable housing in the past and has no federally subsidized housing.

By 2006, however, the city had to revise its comprehensive plan to account for the next ten years of growth. A new housing element was at the top of the list of needed revisions, partly because city planners understood that the Department of Community Affairs and the South Florida Regional Planning Council would not allow them again to ignore affordable housing needs.[94] To develop a new housing plan, Coral Gables hired Robert Burchell, a nationally recognized housing planner. A series of exemptions and conservative definitions of affordability led to a final estimate of 186 needed new affordable units and 2,111 existing burdened households.[95] The report suggests meeting all the need for new housing but only 106 units of the existing need in the next ten years.[96] Additionally, the report targets 145 units for rehabilitation or preservation in the next ten years.

In May 2006 city planners moved the report toward implementation by presenting the planning and zoning board with a new affordable housing ordinance containing inclusionary zoning and a nonresidential linkage fee. They gave the board two IZ options: apply a 10 percent mandate citywide for all single-family and multifamily development without any bonuses or apply IZ only in one mixed-use zoning district with a removal of density restrictions, increases in permitted heights, and substantial commercial-industrial density bonuses as incentives. Either option would allow developers to opt out with an in-lieu fee paid into a new affordable housing fund. The linkage fee program was presented in much less detail but provided only one affordable unit for every 15,000 square feet of nonresidential space.[97]

Several provisions of the proposed affordable housing ordinance might limit its effectiveness. First, the ordinance would apply to any household earning up to 120 percent of the city's median income, "as established by the U.S. Department of Housing and Urban Development."[98] Commentary by city staff on the

93. City of Coral Gables, "Comprehensive Land Use Plan Data Inventory and Analysis" (2006) (www.coralgables.com/CGWeb/documents/planning_docs/DIA.pdf), p. III-14.

94. Javier Betancourt, "Minutes of the Coral Gables Planning and Zoning Board (verbatim transcription)" (May 10, 2006) (www.citybeautiful.net/NR/rdonlyres/16505D86-0A99-4F19-94C8-F0D21AF8729F/489/051006PZBVerbatimMinutes.pdf), pp. 34–35.

95. Burchell, Dolphin, and Zhu (2006), pp. 36–37.

96. Burchell, Dolphin, and Zhu (2006), p. 48.

97. City of Coral Gables, "Planning Department Staff Report: Draft Affordable Housing Regulations" (May 10, 2006) (www.coralgables.com/NR/rdonlyres/69E1DDDC-E907-4E93-A419-3829E27E54A4/473/051006Affordablehousingregs.pdf), p. 2.

98. The draft ordinance does not clarify how the department makes determinations of a city's median income; see City of Coral Gables, Draft Ordinance as of May 10, 2006, Affordable Housing Programs (www.coralgables.com/NR/rdonlyres/F32ABFCA-9C47-4CF6-9820-FDBF79E2C463/475/051006ExistingCodeSection1113AffordableHousing.pdf), sec. 32-1.B.1.

ordinance, and in a planning and zoning board meeting on the programs in June 2006, stated that this would mean a maximum household income of $93,000. Second, for both the fee programs, the draft ordinance would allow Coral Gables to create partnerships with other jurisdictions and spend the funds not only within city limits but also within five miles of the city limits.[99] Third, the ordinance would give preference to senior citizens, residents, and workforce, in that order, with a requirement that a resident or worker demonstrate that he or she had lived or worked in the city for at least a year.[100]

Lessons from Affluent Suburbs

These three affluent, job-rich suburbs provide important lessons about the origins, impact, and trajectory of affordable housing programs and policies (summarized in table 7-8). In the end, these cities show the limitations of affordable housing policies in places that continue to consider themselves suburbs rather than central cities, even long after they have become job hubs in their own right. To have a serious impact on affordable rental housing, they will have to transcend their suburban roots and become new kinds of stars in their metropolitan constellations.

Impacts of Local Constituencies, State Law, and Professional Staff
on Local Housing Policy

How can the emergence of progressive local housing policies in these affluent suburban job centers be explained? In Newton, the answer seems obvious; it is a liberal city in a liberal region, 47 percent Democratic and 10 percent Republican as of 2004—only slightly less Democratic and more Republican than Boston (54 and 9 percent, respectively). Many of its residents are teachers and college professors who embrace an activist role for government in all respects. Core groups of affordable housing advocates and nonprofit housing developers have become key constituencies in the city, working to ensure that its housing element reflects their priorities. A series of mayors and city councils have carried forward the demands of these constituencies while bending where necessary to the will of local residents who prefer not to have affordable housing nearby. The city's special-permit process allows project-by-project review of almost all new development, slowing the approval process but still letting some development occur.

99. City of Coral Gables, Draft Ordinance as of May 10, 2006, Affordable Housing Programs (www.coralgables.com/NR/rdonlyres/F32ABFCA-9C47-4CF6-9820-FDBF79E2C463/475/051006 ExistingCodeSection1113AffordableHousing.pdf), sec. 32-1.E.4.
100. City of Coral Gables, Draft Ordinance as of May 10, 2006, Affordable Housing Programs (www.coralgables.com/NR/rdonlyres/F32ABFCA-9C47-4CF6-9820-FDBF79E2C463/475/051006 ExistingCodeSection1113AffordableHousing.pdf), sec. 32-1.B.

Table 7-8. *Main Lessons, Newton, Pleasanton, and Coral Gables*

Item	Newton	Pleasanton	Coral Gables
Impact on affordable housing			
	Long history of integrated programs yields around 1,000 subsidized units, mainly rental, by for- and non-profit developers; current shift toward balance of owner-occupied and rental housing	Integrated city plans, policies, programs yield around 1,000 units, mix of rental and ownership; early programs termed out, recent ones long-term; shifting from mixed own-rent to emphasis on rental	None yet; programs under discussion; no affordable housing in the city; likely emphasis is on owner-occupied housing for middle-income households
Factors underpinning and constraining success			
State law	Chapter 40B used to smooth approvals on "friendly" 40B projects; threat of "hostile" 40B projects maintains pressure to accommodate new affordable housing, devote CPA resources	State housing element law requires substantial action; viewed locally as toothless, but may be a tool to help local advocates keep housing on the agenda	State Growth Management Act is the principal motivation of adoption of new affordable housing policy
Local constituencies for housing	Citizen committees, locally based non-profit builder (CAN-DO), large body of selectmen usually includes some housing advocates	Citizen committee keeps housing on the agenda despite background conservatism; slow-growth movement gaining ground	None in evidence
Professional staff	City planning staff brokers IZ implementation; Housing Authority accepts and manages privately generated affordable units; dedicated staff for Commonwealth Preservation Act implementation	Assistant City Manager working on housing in the city since 1988; highly professionalized system for growth management, infrastructure; housing authority maintains senior complex	City used New Jersey consultant to develop housing action plan; little evidence of strong staff expertise on housing; no PHA
Development restrictions	Little developable land left; permitted density declining through time; high-density development allowed only under "special permit" system; future significant constraints to new development	City approaching ultimate housing limit of 29,000; annual 350-unit permit cap, with incentives for affordable housing; insufficient multifamily sites designated to accommodate "fair share"	Very high density permitted in some parts of city, but most of city is "built out" as the culmination of a cherished 1920s master plan

In Pleasanton, the answer is less obvious. Pleasanton has the highest Republican registration of any Alameda County city (at 39 percent) and the second-lowest Democratic registration (37 percent). Pleasanton's assistant city manager, however, notes that in the 1970s and early 1980s, a core group of longtime residents became concerned that their children could not afford to live nearby and that they themselves would find it difficult to remain in the city on fixed incomes in the future. Ever since, Pleasanton—like Newton—has had engaged citizens with concerns about affordability who have pressed for increasingly aggressive policies. But these citizens have not always won the battles; some of them strongly oppose the current housing build-out, and some tried to get the city to set aside land for affordable housing on the former San Francisco Water Department site but were defeated at the polls. Indeed, the citizen initiative has played a key role in setting land-use and housing policy throughout Pleasanton's recent history. Time and again, residents have gone to the ballot to reduce development capacity, protecting what they perceive as their quality of life by maintaining the density and landscape of suburbia. The city manager believes that Pleasanton's housing policies might not exist at all had the residents voted on all of them.

Coral Gables is even more Republican (42 percent) than Pleasanton. There is little evidence that an active citizenry has ever engaged the affordable housing issue there, and indeed, there are no affordable housing projects in the city.

There are also forces at work in all three cities, however, that both encourage the adoption of local housing programs and reinforce them once adopted. First, state housing policy sets the stage in all three cities. In Pleasanton and Coral Gables, state planning mandates provide a platform for active residents to come forward in support of affordable housing. These mandates also give convenient camouflage to elected officials and city staff who support affordable housing in spite of public sentiments against it. The same can be said for Chapter 40B in Newton; not just developers but also housing advocates and even city staff use it to counterbalance the exclusionary tendencies of home voters. It remains to be seen whether the nascent push for "workforce housing" by Florida's Department of Community Affairs and especially the South Florida Regional Planning Council will have such robust impacts in Coral Gables, especially in the absence of a strong citizen constituency for affordable housing.

Second, local affordable housing policies and programs have become professionalized in both Pleasanton and Newton. Pleasanton's assistant city manager has been working on affordable housing issues in the city since 1988; its previous planning director retired after a couple of decades' service to the city. Newton has city staff and an active local public housing authority, as well as locally based housing providers, with similar track records. The staff would prudently assert that they do not initiate policy, nor are they responsible for any aggressive programs, and that instead, they are responding to elected officials who in turn respond to their constituents; when these constituents want affordable housing programs, policies, and projects, however, the professional city staff are ready, willing, and able to make these ideas work effectively. Coral Gables, by contrast, lacks staff with a strong track record of efforts to make affordable housing work; in fact, the city contracted out its housing study to an out-of-town expert.

Tracking Impacts of Local Programs on Rental Housing

The three case-study cities show that it is difficult to link specific programs, such as IZ, to impacts on any particular component of the housing stock (rental, ownership, assisted living, and so on). One has to look more broadly at each city's land-use and housing policies and see how, together, they prepare the groundwork for affordable ownership and rental housing. In Pleasanton's case, inclusionary zoning is only one of a number of housing programs that get layered together, with efforts and funds commingled, to produce affordable housing. The city has been a partner in about a half-dozen low-income tax credit projects, providing fee waivers, housing fund contributions, land, staff time, and other contributions to hard and soft costs. In Newton, the story is similar and perhaps even more complex because the city and the housing authority both work—sometimes together, and sometimes separately—on housing.

Attributing specific results to programs is also complex because the programs evolve; in fact, the cases presented here suggest that adaptation and evolution are the rule and not the exception. Pleasanton had a weak, incentive-based IZ program from 1978 to 2000. In 2000 it enacted mandatory IZ with a substantial very low-income requirement and long (now perpetual) affordability terms. It has also shifted from a moderate preference for affordable home ownership toward a heavy recent preference for very low-income rental housing, mainly because city dollars can go further—especially when layered with other subsidy sources—in rental housing than in owner-occupied housing. Given the conservatism of the local electorate, these preferences could easily shift at any time, but state general plan housing element law might provide a counterweight to local politics. Newton also evolved from an informal IZ policy (in the late 1960s) to a formal ordinance in the late 1970s. In Newton, however, recent shifts have been toward shallower affordability for a larger number of units, and for the first time the IZ program will begin to produce affordable owner-occupied housing. Coral Gables, finally, has only an initial set of recommended programs, without any track record at all, but even these are undergoing modification during the process of adoption. They are almost certain to be massaged more in the future, and they may radically change if Florida's home builders win their legal assault on inclusionary zoning.

Influence of Underlying Land-Use Policies on Local Housing Programs

Both Pleasanton and Newton have housing policies that grew stricter while their land-use regulations tightened and vacant land was developed. If the suburban jurisdictions most likely to support intervention (absent a state mandate) are those with affluent residents and those with relatively high housing costs, and these tend to be precisely the jurisdictions that already have fairly restrictive land-use regulations (to protect and create amenities and infrastructure that such residents value), then there may be a built-in limit to the effectiveness of strong housing policy. In other words, it may be no accident that strong housing programs did not emerge in these affluent suburban jurisdictions while they could still have an appreciable impact on the supply of affordable housing.

Indeed, all three of these cities, but especially Pleasanton and Newton, are intensely difficult places in which to build new housing of any kind. Pleasanton has consistently delayed major developments, reduced permitted density on residential development plans after approving them, limited outward expansion, and reduced the number of building permits that can be issued each year and in total. With so many constraints on development and in such a strategic location, land costs in the city are astronomical; the market would most likely support mid- to high-rise residential development with a substantial affordable rental component. But city residents clearly reject the transformation of Pleasanton into a mixed-income jurisdiction, preferring instead to encourage the construction of large single-family houses selling for well over $1 million each.

Newton, like Pleasanton, still has land-use policies that reflect its self-image as a collection of villages connected by bucolic suburbia. A serious transformation of these villages to high-density, high-rise transit hubs may occur sometime in the future, but not until something occurs that shifts the city's politics in a fairly dramatic way. Even Coral Gables, which allows high densities and residential towers over 100 feet, is locked into a master plan developed in the 1920s for a different world; its citizens defend the image of the city handed down by that plan almost everywhere, leaving few sites on which redevelopment and densification can occur. Even there, high-rise and high density do not translate to low-cost rentals; owner-occupied condominiums and upscale apartments are the rule, and the city now must respond to needs for workforce housing.

Influence of State Policy on Local Action

These three cities sit in states with distinct approaches to local planning for land use and affordable housing. California requires a general plan and requires local governments to submit their housing elements for state review. It also has a strong tradition of home rule and citizen control over land use. Florida has a strong state growth management law and an affordable housing trust fund, but the trust fund is weakly linked to local planning, and the growth management law has not until recently been tightly linked to local programs for housing affordability. Massachusetts has historically had few mandates or controls on local planning for land use or housing, allowing local governments to experiment widely with their own programs but allowing builders to appeal local denials of affordable housing in jurisdictions with fewer than 10 percent subsidized units.

The housing programs in Pleasanton and Newton have much in common, despite their political differences and the differences in state governance of local housing and land-use policy. The main similarity between the approaches of California and Massachusetts is in the existence, at least in the background, of a threat that local governments could lose control over land development if they fail to accommodate affordable housing. Such a threat has not historically been prominent in Florida, where growth management has mainly served to ensure adequate infrastructure capacity and to protect the natural environment. Hence both Pleasanton and Newton might be expected to have more aggressive policies than Coral Gables. But now, largely because of pressure from the state Department of Community Affairs and the South Florida Regional Planning Council, Coral Gables is on the brink of adopting inclusionary zoning and linkage fees, which will constitute its first effort to bring affordable housing to the city.

Florida's laws, however, are too weak to resolve the limitations of policymaking for affordable housing in a context with a limited constituency and information base. As of this writing, Coral Gables planning commissioners believe they can meet the city's workforce housing needs by encouraging the development of housing for people earning more than $90,000 a year and that they can defensibly do even that much as far as five miles away from their city limits. Whether this will really pass muster with regional and state planners remains to be seen. Even assuming that state planning requirements really do give Coral Gables a mandate to create housing at all income levels within its own borders to satisfy demands for its future housing needs, that mandate will most likely be limited by at least two aspects of the state's planning laws. First, the laws do not—as California's do—allocate growth to jurisdictions according to a desirable land-use pattern at the regional level; instead, they require jurisdictions to meet population projections that are based on their own recent histories. Second, Florida's planning law projects the future need for affordable housing based on a jurisdiction's track record in accommodating low-income households in the past, again unlike California's process of determining regional housing needs, which is designed to assign more affordable housing units to jurisdictions that have not accommodated affordable housing in the past.

California's housing element law has problems of its own. It is weaker than the state's tradition of accommodating slow-growth sentiments at the ballot box and in city ordinances. After more than twenty years of growth restrictions, the planning and development process in Pleasanton has not been seriously affected by the housing element law, although compliance with the law does enter into the public debate. This is mainly because the bottom line for development has been set by voters at the ballot box, and no legal challenges have yet arisen that would rule such limits unlawful. Furthermore, housing element review is only one step in the process of affordable housing development. The Department of Housing and Community Development's reviews take in only the intended actions of local governments; implementation and long-term performance, however, usually occur out of view, if they occur at all. In Pleasanton, unusually, the department followed up to see whether a proposed program had in fact been adopted and only retroactively decertified the city's housing element. This decertification has brought threats of lawsuits but nothing concrete so far.

Conclusion

Cities, metropolitan areas, and states across the United States are currently in the midst of a revolution in affordable housing policy. Advocates for affordable housing convince more cities every day to adopt inclusionary zoning ordinances, and even when cities do not adopt IZ ordinances they extract affordability as a condition of approval for new development. At the same time, home builders are waging an equally or more ferocious campaign to discredit and defeat IZ in the courts and state legislatures. Once confined to California, New Jersey, and Maryland, by 2003 inclusionary zoning had become common in other states—especially Massachusetts. But already by 2006, new fronts had opened in the campaign over IZ, especially in Florida but also in Colorado.

Inclusionary zoning, while significant, constitutes only one part of the local housing agenda in the most active cities. Indeed, density bonuses are more common than IZ, though probably less effective; now, more cities are adopting linkage fees as well, and some are even putting their own money to work on affordable housing. The case studies presented here show some of the promise of aggressive IZ policies in fast-growth cities, but they also point up the limitations of IZ and the need to couple it and other affordable housing programs and policies with broader land-use policies. Pleasanton and Newton must be judged not only on the basis of what share of new development must be made affordable, nor even on the depth or length of the affordability terms in the new housing, but also on the gross production. The numbers from the local programs have been significant to date, but in neither city have local actions been enough to satisfy anything like the true housing need. In Coral Gables, of course, there is no track record because until now the city has had no programs.

State legislatures can and should take note of the impact of the differing housing policies of these three states. Much maligned though it is for being ineffective and costly, the California housing element requirement—and with it, the supply-oriented process of determining regional housing needs—has much to recommend it. Rather than simply encouraging local governments to adopt a "silver bullet" program like IZ, California's housing element mandate requires that local governments study their own housing needs, consider the needs of their regions, and adopt plans, programs, and policies to meet the needs. The housing element not only produces housing (especially shifting toward multifamily stock in jurisdictions with housing elements that comply with the law); it also creates constituencies for housing and professional local planning staff who can work to make housing happen. Massachusetts, by comparison, has a simple rule: if you have 10 percent affordable housing, you need not do anything else, and if you do not, you can either wait for a hostile project or try to collaborate for a friendly project. Thus far, Massachusetts policies have not been enough to push even an active city like Newton over the 10 percent threshold; Massachusetts lacks either an overall supply mandate or a planning requirement. Florida has a vaunted growth management program—a strong planning requirement—but it lacks a process that addresses supply or encourages a broad programmatic approach to affordable housing.

California's plan-heavy approach also is better suited than those of the other two states to addressing the crisis in rental housing. This is true, first and foremost, because most rental housing is still not built as affordable housing. Since California's housing policy begins with total supply and then breaks that supply into four income tiers, it nearly automatically points many local governments to high-density market-rate housing that has a high probability of being rented. These rentals might be opened for voucher users; local governments in California, and probably elsewhere, have the power to require managers to rent to housing choice voucher users as a condition of approval. A plan- and zoning-based approach, furthermore, establishes the necessary conditions for the development of projects with low-income housing tax credits, which most states (though not Massachusetts) will not award before local governments sign off on the proposed site.

The prospects for widespread adoption of California-style housing elements, however, appears to be remote; indeed, Illinois adopted the simple Massachusetts-style anti-snob zoning rule, not a planning mandate. In states without planning mandates, of course, legislatures cannot be expected to embrace housing plan mandates or regional housing needs determinations. In other states, planning more broadly remains under siege by property-rights advocates, and defenders of planning are understandably preoccupied with saving what they have. Even New Jersey appears to be shifting away from a planning approach toward a universal inclusionary requirement. These shifts promise to deliver more inclusionary zoning ordinances in the coming years, but the true impact of inclusionary zoning on affordability, and on affordable rental housing in particular, is likely to be disappointing in the absence of a broader local housing agenda.

References

Basolo, Victoria. 1999. "The Impacts of Intercity Competition and Intergovernmental Factors on Local Affordable Housing Expenditures." *Housing Policy Debate* 10, no. 3: 659–88.

Brooks, Mary. 2002. "Housing Trust Fund Progress Report 2002: Local Responses to America's Housing Needs." Center for Community Change, Washington (www.community change.org/shared/publications/downloads/HousingSurvey2002.pdf).

Brown, Karen Destorel. 2001. "Expanding Affordable Housing through Inclusionary Zoning: Lessons from the Washington Metropolitan Area." Brookings Center on Urban and Metropolitan Policy (www.brook.edu/es/urban/publications/inclusionary.pdf).

Burchell, Robert W., William R. Dolphin, and Chaolun Zhu. 2006. *Workforce/Affordable Housing: Study for the City of Coral Gables* (April) (www.coralgables.com/NR/rdonlyres/ F32ABFCA-9C47-4CF6-9820-FDBF79E2C463/445/PagesfromCoralGables11906 FINALv3part1.pdf).

Calavita, Nico. 1998. "Inclusionary Housing in California: The Experience of Two Decades." *Journal of the American Planning Association* 64, no. 2: 150–69.

Calavita, Nico, Kenneth Grimes, and Alan Mallach. 1997. "Inclusionary Housing in California and New Jersey: A Comparative Analysis." *Housing Policy Debate* 8, no. 1: 109–42.

Danielson, Michael N. 1976. *The Politics of Exclusion*. Columbia University Press.

Denworth, Joanne. 2002. "Planning *Beyond* Boundaries: A Multi-Municipal Planning and Implementation Manual for Pennsylvania Municipalities." Harrisburg: 10,000 Friends of Pennsylvania.

Downs, Anthony. 1973. *Opening Up the Suburbs: An Urban Strategy for America*. Yale University Press.

Engler, Robert. 2002. "An Inclusionary Housing Case Study: Newton, Massachusetts." *NHC Affordable Housing Policy Review* 2, no. 1: 18–22 (www.nhc.org/pdf/pub_ahp_01_02.pdf).

Fischel, William A. 2001. *The Homevoter Hypothesis: How Home Values Influence Local Government Taxation, School Finance, and Land-Use Policies*. Harvard University Press.

Hoch, Charles. 2005. "Suburban Response to the Illinois Affordable Housing and Planning Act." University of Illinois at Chicago (www.uic.edu/cuppa/upp/people/faculty/Hoch/ suburban_response_fulldoc.pdf).

Kautz, Barbara. 2006. "A Public Agency Guide to California Density Bonus Law, Adapted from Presentation for County Counsels' Association of California Land Use Fall 2005 Study Section Conference" (www.cacities.org/resource_files/24444.Analysis%20of%20Density%20 Bonus%20Law.pdf).

Knaap, Gerrit-Jan. 1987. "Self-Interest and Voter Support for Oregon Land-Use Controls." *Journal of the American Planning Association* 53, no. 1: 92–97.

Malpezzi, Stephen. 1996. "Housing Prices, Externalities, and Regulations in U.S. Metropolitan Areas." *Journal of Housing Research* 7, no. 2: 209–41.

Meck, Stuart. 2003. "Illinois Enacts Housing Appeals, Planning Statute." *Zoning News* 20, no. 6: 6 (www.planning.org/affordablereader/znzp/znoct03b.htm).

Meck, Stuart, Rebecca Retzlaff, and James Schwab. 2003. "Regional Approaches to Affordable Housing." In *American Planning Association Planning Advisory Service Report*, pp. 513–14. Chicago: American Planning Association.

Multnomah County. 2000. *Five-Year 2000–2005 Consolidated Plan*. Portland, Ore.: Bureau of Housing and Community Development.

Nelson, Arthur C., and others. 2004. "The Link between Growth Management and Housing Affordability: The Academic Evidence." In *Growth Management and Affordable Housing: Do They Conflict?* edited by Anthony Downs, pp. 117–58. Brookings.

Pendall, Rolf. 2000a. "Local Land-Use Regulation and the Chain of Exclusion." *Journal of the American Planning Association* 66, no. 2: 125–42.

———. 2000b. "Why Voucher and Certificate Users Live in Distressed Neighborhoods." *Housing Policy Debate* 11, no. 4: 881–910.

Pendall, Rolf, Jonathan Martin, and William Fulton. 2002. "Holding the Line: Urban Containment in the United States." Brookings Center on Urban and Metropolitan Policy (www.brookings.edu/metro/publications/pendallfultoncontainmentexsum.htm).

Pendall, Rolf, Robert Puentes, and Jonathan Martin. 2006. "From Traditional to Reformed: A Review of the Land Use Regulations in the Nation's 50 Largest Metropolitan Areas." Brookings Metropolitan Policy Program (www.brookings.edu/metro/pubs/20060810_landuse.htm).

Porter, Douglas R. 2004. "Promise and Practice of Inclusionary Zoning." In *Growth Management and Affordable Housing: Do They Conflict?* edited by Anthony Downs, pp. 212–48. Brookings.

Powell, Benjamin, and Edward Stringham. 2004. "Housing Supply and Affordability: Do Affordable Housing Mandates Work?" Policy Study 318. Reason Public Policy Institute (www.reason.org/ps318.pdf).

Richardson, Jesse J., Jr., Meghan Zimmerman Gough, and Robert Puentes. 2003. "Is Home Rule the Answer? Clarifying the Influence of Dillon's Rule on Growth Management." Brookings Center on Urban and Metropolitan Policy.

Schwartz, Alex. 1999. "New York City and Subsidized Housing: Impacts and Lessons of the City's $5 Billion Capital Budget Housing Plan." *Housing Policy Debate* 10, no. 4: 839–78.

———. 2005. *Housing Policy in the United States.* New York: Routledge.

Span, Henry A. 2001. "How the Courts Should Fight Exclusionary Zoning." *Seton Hall Law Review* 32: 1–107.

Tiebout, Charles M. 1956. "A Pure Theory of Local Expenditures." *Journal of Political Economy* 64, no. 5: 416–24.

U.S. Census Bureau. 2000a. Census of Population and Housing.

———. 2000b. Census Transportation Planning Package (CTPP2000).

U.S. Department of Housing and Urban Development (HUD). 2004. "A Picture of Subsidized Households" (www.huduser.org/datasets/assthsg/statedata98/allst.html).

Appendix: Survey Questions

Land-Use Policies and Housing:
A National Survey on Local Residential Development Regulation

This survey is part of a research project to identify local land-use and housing programs and policies in the 50 largest metropolitan areas in the United States. Please answer all the questions to the best of your ability. While accuracy is important to us, your time is also important, so please provide your best estimates for any information that is not readily available. If you wish to comment on any questions or qualify your answers, feel free to use the space in the margins; there is also space for comments on the back of the survey form. Your comments will be read and taken into account.

Thank you very much for your help.

Name of Respondent: _____
Title: _____
Name of Community: _____
City: _____ State: _____ Zip: _____
Telephone Number: ( ) ____-_____ Fax: ( ) ____-_____
E-mail: _____ Date of Response: _____

A. Planning and Zoning

The first two questions concern overall regulations, including comprehensive planning and zoning that are currently in force in your county.

1. Does your county have a comprehensive (master, general) plan?
   _____ No.   _____ Yes.
   If you answered "yes," what year was the Land Use element of the plan last updated?
   _____ (year)

2. Does your county have a zoning ordinance?
   _____ No.   _____ Yes.
   If you answered "yes," what year was the ordinance last updated? _____ (year)
   If you answered "no" to questions 1 and 2, please skip to Section C.

B. Zoning for Housing

Please answer questions 4–8 only for the areas to which the county zoning ordinance applies and not for townships or cities that have their own zoning ordinances.

3. What is the theoretical maximum number of dwelling units that may be constructed per net acre in areas to which your county zoning ordinance applies, in areas zoned in the highest residential density category?
   _____ Fewer than 4   _____ 4–7   _____ 8–15   _____ 16–30   _____ More than 30

4. How has the maximum permitted density changed since 1994?
   _____ Stayed approximately the same (within 10%).   _____ Reduced more than 10%.
   _____ Increased more than 10%.   _____ Don't know.

5. Does your county permit the placement of new mobile homes, either on a single lot or in a mobile home park?

_____ No.   _____ Yes; double-wide only.   _____ Yes; double- or single-wide.

6. Assume your county has a vacant 5-acre parcel. If a developer wanted to build 40 units of 2-story apartments and was flexible with planning, landscaping and building configuration, would there be an existing zoning category that would allow such development?

_____ No.   _____ Yes; by right.

_____ Yes; by special permit, PUD, or other special procedure.

7. Does your county require a popular vote of the county's residents as a precondition to rezoning?

_____ No.

_____ Yes, in open town meeting.

__ Applies to all rezonings __ Applies only to selected rezonings (describe below)

_____ Yes, ballot measure.

__ Applies to all rezonings __ Applies only to selected rezonings (describe below)

C. Jurisdiction Expansion Potential

These questions will help us understand whether development in your county can expand into unincorporated and undeveloped areas.

8. Is a popular vote required as a precondition to annexation in your county? (Please answer "no" if the only vote required is that of landowners or residents in the area to be annexed.)

_____ No.

_____ Yes, a binding referendum has been required since _____ (year).

_____ Yes, an advisory referendum has been required since _____ (year).

9. Does your county currently have any of the following? (Please check "yes" or "no")

_____No _____Yes   Urban service area/urban service boundary in place since _____ (year)

_____No _____Yes   Urban growth boundary in place since _____ (year)

_____No _____Yes   Greenbelt in place since _____ (year)

_____No _____Yes   Urban limit line in place since _____ (year)

_____No _____Yes   Other tool to control spread of development in place since _____ (year)

D. Other Regulations Pertaining to Housing

The next few questions concern other local regulations that your county uses for the management of residential growth, including growth (rate) controls, moratoria, and adequate public facilities ordinances.

10. Does your county currently have a measure that explicitly restricts the pace of residential growth?

_____ No.

_____ Yes; population growth limited to _____ percent per year; adopted _____ (year).

_____ Yes; residential building permit issuance limited to_____ (number) per year; adopted _____ (year).

11. Does your jurisdiction currently have a moratorium on issuance of new residential building permits or the processing of subdivision plats covering all or part of the county's unincorporated geographic area? (Please include moratoria imposed by either your county or another unit of government or utility district.)

    ____ No.

    ____ Yes; a jurisdiction-wide moratorium.

    ____ Yes; a moratorium covering part of the jurisdiction (specific zoning districts, geographic areas, environmental zones, etc.) that affects

        ____ Less than half of the jurisdiction's undeveloped land area.

        ____ More than half of the jurisdiction's undeveloped land area.

    Moratorium in force since _____ (year);

    ____ Moratorium will expire _____ (year).

    ____ Moratorium does not have a definite expiration date.

If you answered "no" to both question 10 and question 11, please skip the next question and go to question 13.

12. Does your current residential growth control or moratorium offer exemptions or incentives for affordable housing?

    ____ No.

    ____ Yes; projects that consist mostly (more than 50%) of affordable housing are exempt from the control.

    ____ Yes; the permit allocation system gives preference to affordable housing.

13. Apart from any residential-growth limiting measures currently in force, has your jurisdiction had growth-limiting measures that lasted more than a year since 1980?

    ____ No.

    ____ Don't know.

    ____ Yes; growth rate or building permit cap from _____(year) to_____(year).

    ____ Yes; permit or subdivision moratoria (including moratoria imposed by either your jurisdiction or another unit of government or utility district).

    ____ Yes; jurisdiction-wide moratorium from _____(year) to_____ (year).

    ____ Yes; moratorium on part of the jurisdiction from _____(year) to_____(year).

14. Does your jurisdiction charge impact fees?

    ____ No.

    ____ Yes; we impose fees based on a case by case review of project off-site impacts.

    ____ Yes; (we review projects) and fees are imposed at a flat rate of

    $_____ / square foot. $_____ / single-family unit. $_____ / multi-family unit.

    If so, fees apply to: (please check all that apply)

    ____ Schools   ____ Stormwater

    ____ Transportation facilities (roads, highways, transit)

    ____ Public safety facilities (police, fire stations)

    ____ Water supply and/or wastewater treatment, supply, delivery, and/or storage facilities

    ____ Parks, recreation and/or open space facilities

    ____ Water supply

    ____ Waste water treatment

    ____ Other: _____

15. Does your county have an adequate public facilities ordinance that makes development permission contingent on the levels of off-site public services?

_____ No.

_____ No, but we case review projects' off-site impacts on a case-by-case basis to estimate and mitigate impacts.

_____ Yes, an adequate public facilities ordinance was adopted in _____ (year) and applies to

_____ Schools   _____ Stormwater

_____ Transportation facilities (roads, highways, transit)

_____ Public safety facilities (police, fire stations)

_____ Water supply and/or wastewater treatment, supply, delivery, and/or storage facilities

_____ Parks, recreation and/or open space facilities

_____ Other:

_____.

If your county has an adequate public facilities ordinance, does it apply

___ in unincorporated areas only   ___ in both unincorporated and incorporated areas?

E. Affordable Housing

The final questions are on affordable housing in your county. (We define affordable housing as units guaranteed to remain affordable for at least five years to households earning less than 120 percent of area median income.)

16. Does your county use any incentives or requirements to encourage private-sector builders to develop affordable housing? (Please check all that apply.)

_____ No.

_____ Yes; residential density bonus (to developers of market-rate housing who agree to provide affordable housing units).

_____ Yes; inclusionary zoning (developers of market-rate housing are required to include affordable housing units in their developments); at least _____ percent of the units must be affordable.

_____ Yes; developers may satisfy this requirement by paying a fee instead of building housing on site.

_____ Yes, we provide "fast-tracking" (expedited permitting) for builders who agree to provide some affordable housing.

_____ Yes; we require linkage fees (monies collected to help support or develop affordable housing) from non-residential builders.

_____ Yes; other: _____.

17. What other programs does your county use to encourage affordable housing construction and substantial rehabilitation? (Please check all that apply.)

_____ We use public funds or provide staff to support local non-profits.

_____ We work with the local public housing authority to build new affordable housing and/or substantially rehabilitate existing uninhabitable units.

_____ We arrange for purchase of existing private-sector units for conversion to long-term affordability.

_____ We have adopted an ordinance providing for waivers of planning or development impact fees on affordable housing projects.

_____ Other programs in place (please list programs):

_____

18. Approximately how many affordable housing units (see definition above), assisted by either the public or private sector, are there in the unincorporated areas of the county? If you cannot answer this question, please indicate in the space provided below the name and telephone number of someone who can.

_____ There is no government-assisted affordable housing in the county's townships.

_____ # of units built or substantially rehabilitated by the public housing agency or a nonprofit with federal, state, or local subsidies (including existing private-sector units bought and made affordable).

_____ # of units built or substantially rehabilitated by private-sector developers as a result of a local government regulatory incentive or requirement (condition of approval).

_____ # of units built or substantially rehabilitated by private-sector developers with federal housing programs (e.g., LIHTC, HOPE VI, Section 235/236, etc.).

_____ # of units total.

_____ Number of these housing units built between 1990 and 2002 (inclusive).

_____ Please call _____ at (____)_____ to obtain this information.

19. Does your county have a local affordable housing funding mechanism (e.g., housing trust fund)?

_____ No.

_____ Yes; this fund is dedicated solely for affordable housing.

_____ Yes; this fund may also be used for projects other than affordable housing.

20. Compared to your jurisdiction's current level of regulation on land use and residential development, how would you describe your jurisdiction in: (please check)

	More regulated	About the same	Less regulated	No regulation
1970	___	___	___	___
1980	___	___	___	___
1990	___	___	___	___

PART **III**

Moving Forward: New Directions in Rental Housing Policy

8

Capital for Small Rental Properties: Preserving a Vital Housing Resource

WILLIAM C. APGAR AND SHEKAR NARASIMHAN

Nearly one-fifth of the rental housing stock in the United States is in smaller, multifamily apartment buildings with five to forty-nine units. Although relatively large shares of these units are occupied by lower-income families, the overwhelming majority is unsubsidized, and many are at risk of loss owing to disinvestment or conversion to higher-income occupancy. Unfortunately, little is known about the property ownership, management, and financial condition of this housing. What is known is that the scale and value of these properties makes it difficult for the current owners to achieve economies in property management and to absorb the high fixed cost of gaining access to debt or equity capital needed to operate, maintain, and preserve these units. Indeed, in a paper prepared for the Millennial Housing Commission, the Finance Task Force notes that financing for apartment buildings with five to forty-nine units "is one of the most significant gaps in the mortgage industry."[1]

Drawing on previous work by Shekar Narasimhan, this chapter explores the potential for developing innovative new housing and capital market strategies targeted to the small, unsubsidized multifamily rental stock.[2] We use the U.S. Census

---

1. Millennial Housing Commission, Finance Task Force, Policy Option Paper, "Small Multifamily Properties" (October 1, 2001) (govinfo.library.unt.edu/mhc/papers/smallmf.doc), p. 1.

2. Shekar Narasimhan, "Why Do Small Multifamily Properties Bedevil Us?" *Capital Xchange,* November 2001 (www.brookings.edu/printme.wbs?page=/es/urban/capitalxchange/article8.htm).

Bureau's Residential Finance Survey and other data to examine the ownership, management, and condition of the housing in five- to forty-nine-unit properties, both in general and in comparison with the same elements confronting owners of properties with fifty or more units. In many ways, the distinction between five- to forty-nine-unit properties and those with two to four units is an artificial one created by the secondary-market practice of combining single-family and two- to four-unit properties into a common category. Although they differ in terms of some aspects of financing, on the ground a four-unit and a five-unit property have much in common. Small multifamily rental properties, defined for this chapter as multifamily properties with less than fifty units, are important in meeting the housing needs of low-income households, and the owners of these properties face special problems.

What would it take to expand access to capital for this segment of the housing market? Currently, this market niche is filled by depository institutions at a relatively higher cost to the borrower. There is reason to believe, however, that investment and lending in the small-property market can be profitable. A number of creative lending institutions have engaged successfully with this sector, and the capital markets are now actively testing models.[3] Other new initiatives are under active consideration by industry leaders. These include expanding information sharing among lenders for benchmarking, improving mortgage insurance products, and creating a new rating system for small-property owners akin to the credit-scoring systems used to rate the likelihood that borrowers will repay home and consumer loans.[4]

Although most of the literature on small-property finance focuses on debt, this chapter explores the possible role that equity-side solutions could play. One solution proposed here is the creation of a federally sponsored small real estate investment trust (S-REIT) that would aggregate ownership of older, smaller multifamily properties with low or modest rents. Although this model has not been undertaken by the market, the concept makes economic sense. To test this proposition, we recommend piloting an S-REIT type aggregation strategy using an essential function bond approach, as the structural components are in place to begin executing this structure without regulatory changes.

An S-REIT structure would allow properties to be financed on a portfolio rather than a property-by-property basis and would bring economies of scale and professional management to what is generally a poorly managed segment of the housing market. This model also holds the potential to improve the efficiency of federal subsidy mechanisms, for example, by developing the potential for allocat-

---

3. Examples of these lending institutions include Shorebank (www.shorebankcorp.com) and the Community Preservation Corporation (www.communityp.com/).

4. Comments made at Improving Management and Capital of Mid-Sized Rental Property Owners and Developers, an off-the-record focus group discussion hosted by the Joint Center for Housing Studies, February 16, 2006.

ing low-income housing tax credits (LIHTCs) at the institutional level and thereby reducing the cost associated with allocating credits on a building-by-building basis.

The Continuing Importance of Small Multifamily Rental Housing

Whereas much of the housing preservation debate focuses on the subsidized inventory, the vast majority of low-income renters live in privately owned, unsubsidized single-family and small multifamily rental housing. With new production increasingly focused on the construction of either single-family homes or larger apartment buildings with fifty or more units, much of the vitally important small multifamily inventory is at risk of loss to disinvestment, demolition, and abandonment. Along with preservation of subsidized housing, preservation of unsubsidized but affordable rental housing must therefore be an important component of the nation's housing preservation agenda.

Overall, the privately owned, unsubsidized rental housing inventory is home to more than 80 percent (27.4 million) of all renters and nearly two-thirds (4.3 million) of the nation's lowest-income renters.[5] The vast majority of these unsubsidized rental units consist of single-family residences (including manufactured homes), two- to four-family units that filtered down to the rental market, and smaller apartment buildings of five to forty-nine units (figure 8-1).

Even allowing for the many large publicly assisted housing complexes, more than 39 percent of the assisted housing inventory is made up of single-family and two- to four-family homes, and 42 percent of subsidized units are in five- to forty-nine-unit apartment buildings. These include units rented by voucher holders as well as public housing and project-based developments located in smaller metropolitan and nonmetropolitan areas. Less than one-fifth of assisted rentals are in buildings with fifty or more units. These larger properties are typically older public housing and project-based development, as well as newly built low-income housing tax credit projects.

The dominance of small multifamily apartments persists despite the tendency of the building industry to focus on the construction of relatively high-quality units in larger apartment buildings. Over the ten-year period from 1994 through 2003, completions of multifamily rental units totaled 2.3 million. Of these, 1.1 million were in structures with twenty or more units, and another 1.1 million units were in apartment buildings with five to nineteen units (figure 8-2). Over the same period, completions of multifamily rentals in structures with two to four apartments—historically the mainstay of many urban rental markets—totaled less than 213,000.

5. Lowest-income renters have incomes that fall in the lowest quintile of the income distribution for renter households (Joint Center for Housing Studies 2006a, exhibit 26 and app. table A-6).

Figure 8-1. *Distribution of Renters in Subsidized and Unsubsidized Housing, 2003*[a]
Percent

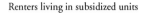

Renters living in subsidized units

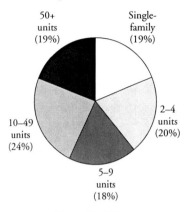

Total = 6.2 Million

Renters living in unsubsidized units

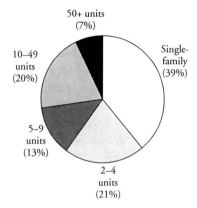

Total = 27.4 Million

Source: Joint Center for Housing Studies tabulations of the 2003 American Housing Survey.
a. Single-family units include manufactured housing.

Figure 8-2. *Distribution of New Multifamily Rental Properties,
by Number of Units, 1994–2003*

Thousands of units

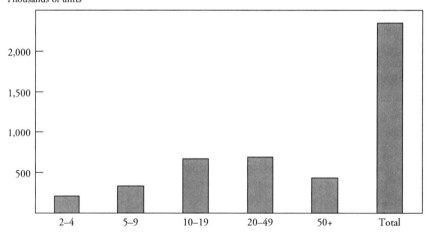

Source: Joint Center for Housing Studies (2006a, table A-7).

In part, these trends reflect advances in construction technology, the high fixed costs linked to land acquisition and permitting, and a growing acceptance of apartment living, but growth of the Low Income Housing Tax Credit program has also played a role. The U.S. Department of Housing and Urban Development reports that the average project size of tax credit developments has increased steadily since the program's inception and now stands at close to eighty units. With half of all tax credit units located in developments with fifty or more units, the large multifamily structures have become the fastest-growing segment of the rental housing inventory. Indeed, from 1999 through 2004 alone, the share of rental construction in apartments with fifty or more units grew from 13 to 24 percent.[6]

Even accounting for the presence of tax credit units, the asking rents for newly constructed rental apartments are far above what most renters can afford. Over the past ten years, the asking rent of new units moved up sharply to $974, more than 37 percent above the median for all units. At the standard of 30 percent of income, a household needs an income of $38,000 to afford a newly built apartment. As a result, the vast majority of newly constructed rental apartments are well out of reach for the 14 million renter households with incomes of less than $20,000.

With new construction focused on expanding the supply of more expensive apartments in large multifamily structures, the ongoing demolition and inventory losses of rental units in older small multifamily structures is rapidly depleting the available supply of affordable rental housing. Most of the privately owned small multifamily rental stock was built at least thirty years ago, when construction techniques and capital markets were less sophisticated and households were less affluent. Much of this inventory is now in need of substantial repair. According to the American Housing Survey, 3 million private market rental units have severe structural deficiencies and are at risk of loss (Joint Center for Housing Studies 2006a, p. 22).

Over the ten years beginning in 1994, an estimated 2.2 million rental units (6 percent) were demolished or otherwise permanently removed from the inventory (figure 8-3). More than half of these rentals were in older (built before 1960) one- to four-unit buildings located in the nation's most distressed neighborhoods. As might be expected, loss rates are higher for properties with such additional risk factors as low rent, long-term vacancies, and structural deficiencies. For older, smaller multifamily units, these added risk factors push the loss rate to 13 percent. Combining all the risk factors, including structural inadequacy, pushes the loss rate to more than 20 percent.

With new construction adding units mostly to the high end of the rent distribution and inventory losses draining units at the low end, it is little wonder that the inventory of affordable rental units is declining rapidly. For the ten-year period beginning in 1994, the number of units renting for $400 or less in inflation-

6. Joint Center for Housing Studies (2006b, p. 23, figure 31).

Figure 8-3. *Loss Rate of Smaller, Older Rental Properties, 1994–2003*[a]
Percent

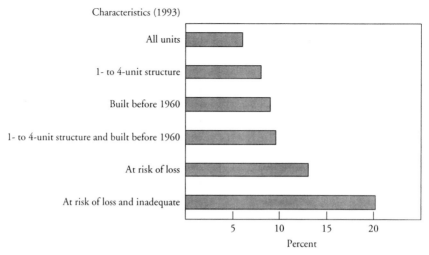

Source: Joint Center for Housing Studies (2006a, table A-10).
a. Loss rates defined as share of all units in 1993 that were reported as a Type C Non-Interview (permanent removal from stock) in 2003. At-risk units are those in 1-4 unit structures built before 1960, renting for under $300, and vacant for more than 6 months or reported as severely inadequate. Single family structures include manufactured housing.

adjusted terms fell by 13 percent—a loss of more than 1.2 million units. By comparison, the number of housing units renting for more than $800 a month increased by 1.7 million over the same ten-year period (Joint Center for Housing Studies 2006a, exhibit 19, p. 16).

The Changing Mortgage Environment

The changing structure of the banking industry has had a noticeable impact on the multifamily housing market. As in the single-family mortgage market, the past quarter century has seen dramatic shifts in the financing of multifamily apartments. Until the mid-1980s, local thrifts and savings banks were the largest providers. Following the industry shakeout from the savings and loan crisis of the 1980s, the historical role played by thrifts and savings banks in financing the acquisition and development of multifamily housing declined sharply, a trend that had particularly adverse consequences for the owners of smaller apartment buildings seeking financing. Indeed, by 2001, saving and loan banks provided just 17.2 percent of financing to properties with five to forty-nine units, compared with 36.9 percent in 1991.[7]

7. Census Bureau (1991, 2001).

Table 8-1. *Fixed-Rate Financing for Larger Multifamily Properties,*
by Size of Property, 1991 and 2001
Percent

	Property with mortgage		Mortgaged property with fixed-rate financing	
Number of units	1991	2001	1991	2001
5–9	65.8	57.7	57.6	58.6
10–19	74.6	60.3	61.6	60.2
20–49	81.4	75.4	56.6	67.3
50–99	87.2	84.7	63.1	72.1
100–199	88.6	87.7	66.4	79.7
200+	88.4	85.8	56.1	78.5
All	73.3	63.7	58.9	63.7

Source: Census Bureau (1991, 2001).

For the purposes of mortgage finance, the Federal Housing Administration and the government-sponsored enterprises (GSEs) define *multifamily* to include structures with five or more units, while the term *single-family* lumps single-family detached homes together with two-, three-, and four-unit buildings. Although government-backed mortgage insurance programs and secondary-market activities have greatly expanded access to capital for individual home buyers, they have done markedly less to expand access to capital for investors seeking to purchase, rehabilitate, or build two- to four-unit properties or smaller apartment buildings. In particular, following the collapse of large segments of the savings and loan industry in the 1980s and the rise of GSE financing in the 1990s, the mortgage market for multifamily apartment buildings has become bifurcated. As a result, by 2001 88.4 percent of large apartment properties (those with fifty or more units) had a mortgage, while a mere 57.7 percent of apartment buildings with five to nine units had one—well below the 65.8 percent figure recorded in 1991 (table 8-1).

Over the 1990s, the combination of the economic stress of the small-apartment sector of the housing market and the emergence of the GSEs as the primary source of apartment financing resulted in a dramatic decline in the number and share of smaller apartments with mortgages. According to the Residential Finance Survey, over the decade 1991 to 2001 the number of rental properties with five- to forty-nine units fell by 15 percent (from 557,000 to 473,000). The declining share of smaller multifamily properties with mortgages further added to the overall decrease in the size of the mortgage market for this segment, as the number of mortgaged apartment buildings with five to forty-nine units fell by more than 25 percent. Within the small multifamily segment, mortgage financing for five- to nine- and ten- to nineteen-unit properties experienced the sharpest decline. The number of mortgaged properties with five to nine units fell by 33 percent, while the number

Table 8-2. *Distribution of Mortgage Financing, by Lender Type and Size of Property, 1991 and 2001*

Percent

Lender type	Property with 5–49 units		Property with 50+ units	
	1991	2001	1991	2001
Commercial bank	23.0	23.6	17.3	17.9
Savings and loan, federal savings bank	36.9	17.2	20.9	11.0
Government-sponsored entity	5.5	27.1	13.8	38.6
Life insurance company	2.0	3.0	11.6	4.7
State and local housing finance agency	0.9	4.0	6.3	7.0
Individual	13.4	5.4	4.7	3.3
Other	18.3	19.8	25.4	17.6

Source: Census Bureau (1991, 2001).

of mortgaged properties with ten to nineteen units declined 27 percent (Census Bureau 1991, 2001).

During the 1990s, options for permanent financing of large properties expanded rapidly as secondary markets developed. Since that time, innovations in mortgage finance have helped to stimulate multifamily housing production. In particular, the share of multifamily mortgages (defined in the industry as loans on properties with five or more apartments) traded in the secondary market more than tripled, to more than 30 percent. However, growth was concentrated in mortgages for larger properties. The rising share of multifamily mortgage debt held in mortgage-backed securities, along with increased standardization of under-writing criteria and loan documentation, has created a larger, more stable, and less expensive supply of capital for developers and better diversification for investors. As a result, in 2001 funding by GSEs accounted for 39 percent of the mortgages made on all rental properties with fifty or more units, up sharply from the 1991 figure of less than 14 percent (table 8-2).

At the same time, the secondary market for construction and acquisition loans or financing of five- to forty-nine-unit buildings has been slower to develop, in large measure because these loans often lack standardized features important to the securitization process. By 2001, even after a decade of growth, the Residential Finance Survey recorded that GSEs served just 27.1 percent of all mortgages on properties with five to forty-nine units. Furthermore, loans for smaller investment properties tend to be more expensive and have less favorable terms than loans on larger properties. The higher costs of financing, along with the lack of project-based subsidies, prevent owners from either investing in capital improvements or selling their properties to more capable owners.

In evaluating the expansion of GSE activity in the small multifamily market, it is important to note that the 2001 data reflect the impact of special "bonus points" designed to spur GSE involvement in lending for such properties. In particular, from 2001 through 2003 GSE loans to owners of five- to forty-nine-unit properties serving lower-income renters received double credit in calculating GSE progress in meeting their federally mandated affordable housing goals. In a recent paper, William Manchester concludes that these bonus factors had the desired effect of expanding GSE activity in the small multifamily market. Manchester also notes that these gains were short-lived and the GSEs, particularly Freddie Mac, pulled back once the bonus factors expired in 2004.[8]

For owners of larger apartments, growing access to the secondary market provides significant advantages. Most securitized lending is at a fixed rate, with no right of recourse, and of intermediate to long term (ten to thirty years). For example, some 86 percent of all 200-unit apartment buildings have a mortgage, and some 79 percent of these mortgaged properties have longer-term fixed-rate financing. In contrast, only 58 percent of the five- to nine-unit apartments have a mortgage, and of these just 59 percent have longer-term fixed-rate financing. In absolute terms, over the 1991 to 2001 period, the number of five- to nine-unit apartments with longer-term fixed-rate financing fell by a third, to 88,000, while the number of apartment buildings of 200 or more units with longer-term fixed-rate financing nearly doubled, to more than 10,000.

Defining the Problem

Small properties pose significant challenges to a mortgage market that is increasingly driven by volume. In particular, a relatively large segment of the small-apartment inventory is owned by thousands of individuals, including many investors and owners who are reluctant to reduce their cash flow and assume the risk associated with debt financing. This fragmented ownership structure makes it difficult to achieve the scale economies that are associated with many elements of property management. Finally, many owners of small rental properties appear to be motivated by a complex set of social and emotional issues that may adversely affect their willingness to assume longer-term debt or to sell a property they lack the capacity to effectively operate.

Difficulties in Financing Small Multifamily Properties

There are many traditional lending reasons why accessing capital for financing small multifamily properties is legitimately more expensive. Many properties in this segment suffer from deferred maintenance that makes it difficult to charge rents sufficient to cover operating costs. Additionally, these older structures are typically energy inefficient and have faulty plumbing, resulting in excessive water use, while many provide limited cash flow. The Residential Finance Survey data

8. Manchester (2006. p. 11).

Figure 8-4. *Properties with Negative Net Operating Income, by Rent and Number of Units, 2001*

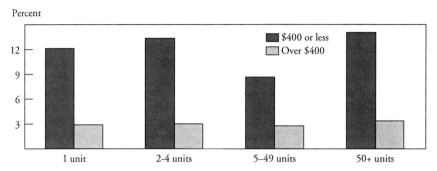

Source: Joint Center for Housing Studies (2006a, figure 33).

for 2001 indicate that fully 12 percent of all rental properties with average rents of $400 or less reported negative net operating income—an unsustainable condition that points to future accelerating losses of these low-cost units (figure 8-4).

Property owners with the ability to pay for debt service out of cash flow may be paying a premium for mortgage capital. Prospective investors or lenders often have difficulty establishing a property income valuation, assessing the property's physical condition, and ensuring that the property meets code requirements and regulations such as those governing lead paint. The general difficulties inherent in financing small, older properties that serve low-income markets are made greater by the fact that they are often located in deteriorating neighborhoods, making resale value difficult to judge. Compounding issues of overcrowding, code violations, tenant turnover, rent collection practices, lack of documentation, and problems associated with nonprofessional management make it difficult for prospective investors or lenders to assess the risk associated with the acquisition or finance of individual properties.

Finally, several factors limit the willingness of equity investors to participate in lending for small multifamily buildings and thereby impede the development of an active secondary market in mortgages for these properties. First, the size of these loans is an obstacle. Small multifamily loans lack the scale necessary to spread out the upfront costs of securitization across high-volume pools. Second, many owners of these properties do not keep detailed accounts of income and expenses that capital market investors require. Third, the secondary market imposes stricter underwriting standards and higher fees on a percentage basis for such properties, even on owners with well-documented income and expense histories to compensate for the costliness of doing full due diligence.[9]

9. Herbert (2001).

Figure 8-5. *Individual Ownership of Rental Housing, by Size of Property, 2001*[a]

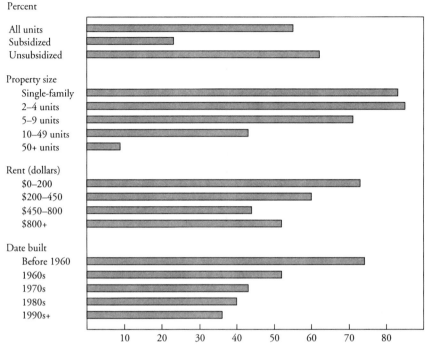

Source: Joint Center for Housing Studies tabulations of the 2001 Residential Finance Survey (Joint Center for Housing Studies 2006a, figure 28).

a. Single-family units include one-unit detached and attached structures and condominium units for rent. They do not include manufactured homes. "Individual" includes married couples.

Problems owing to Fragmented Ownership

Information on the characteristics of rental property owners is limited, but recently released data from the 2001 Residential Finance Survey suggest that many owners—and especially those with only a few units—are ill equipped to operate and maintain their properties profitably. Overall, the survey data indicate that close to two-thirds of the nation's nearly 26 million unsubsidized rental units are owned by individuals or couples (figure 8-5). The rest are owned by a variety of corporations and other entities, ranging from limited partnerships to churches and nonprofit organizations to real estate investment trusts.

For many of these individual owners, the rental business is a part-time activity that can provide supplemental income or housing for friends or relatives. The Joint Center for Housing Studies, citing tabulations of data from the 2003 Survey of Consumer Finance, notes that 4.3 million households reported receiving income from a rental property. Property revenue accounts for about 11 percent of household income for those less than sixty years of age and for as much as 25 percent of income for those in their seventies and older.

Most of these owners are not well diversified because they own too few properties to spread risks across market areas. Indeed, 3.4 million of the 4.3 million owners report having only one rental property.[10] These smaller owners seldom hire professional managers because to do so would require that they sacrifice some of their rental income. As a result, only one in five rental units owned by individuals and married couples are under professional management.

The fragmented ownership of relatively few properties also implies that the typical owner has limited capacity to realize the many economies of scale of management that are critical within the tight margins of tenant and property management. Indeed, owners of a limited number of units located in a handful of smaller properties are doubly disadvantaged in that they are unable to realize the scale economies that accrue to owners of larger buildings as they spread their attention over several buildings that may be geographically dispersed.

Although detailed data on operating costs of rental buildings of various sizes and characteristics are limited, the data that are available point to the existence of economies of scale in the operation of large apartment buildings. In a recent assessment, Jack Goodman observes that for properties with at least 200 units, average operating costs for each unit are from 4 to 8 percent lower than those recorded for smaller apartment buildings. Significant economies of scale are observed for most of the individual cost components, though controlling for other features that may influence per unit cost (such as property age or construction characteristics) makes this a challenging task. Even so, this analysis suggests that in areas such as property insurance, utilities, administration, and management, significant scale economies exist.[11]

Less is known about the economies associated with the ownership of a portfolio of smaller buildings. For buildings too small to support a resident manager, management is difficult, at best. Whatever the specifics of potential economies of scale, there is little doubt that most small-scale owners operate at the margin of profitability. The Property Owners and Management Survey conducted by the Department of Housing and Urban Development in 1995, though now a decade old, provides a comprehensive look at the economics of owning small rental properties. Overall, these data suggest that small properties are the least profitable, with average total costs slightly lower than total receipts.[12] Such budget stress adversely affects the maintenance and repair activities of absentee-owners

---

10. Joint Center for Housing Studies tabulations of data from 2003 Survey of Consumer Finance (www.census.gov/hhes/www/rfs/rfs.html).

11. Goodman (2004, p. 18).

12. Newman (2005, p. 22). See also Emrath (1997).

of one- to nine-family structures. Although their units are most likely among all property types to have structural deficiencies, 14 percent report spending nothing on maintenance, and 22 percent defer required major and minor repair.[13]

Risk Aversion among Owners

Small-scale owners are disadvantaged by definition: they are less well-capitalized and excluded from the economies of scale that are critical within the tight margins of tenant and property management. Competently managing rental housing requires expertise in many areas, and there is a history of lack of management capabilities in the low-rent inventory across the country.

Furthermore, many owners may be reluctant to assume debt, especially in situations in which the only debt available comes in the form of adjustable-rate, short-term loans. In his 1960s pathbreaking book *The Tenement Landlord,* George Sternlieb documents the operations of the owners of small apartment buildings in distressed neighborhoods. Although some financed their operations with debt, others avoided the risk associated with debt financing and instead operated their properties on a cash-and-carry basis. In this type of operation, steady cash flow is a key objective. With a lack of geographic diversification, many owners of just one or two small apartment buildings are reluctant to magnify this risk by leveraging their investment and exposing what may be razor-thin cash flows to the risks associated with short-term, adjustable-rate financing.[14]

The limited recent data on these topics paint a similar picture. In his study of owners of one- to four-family rental structures, Allan Mallach observes that many had once lived in their own properties, and many have family and friends that still do.[15] This social aspect of ownership may not only enhance their risk aversion when it comes to making decisions about how best to structure the financing on their apartment building, it may also influence their decision to sell. As a result, for at least a portion of the individuals who own rental properties, decisions concerning the operation, management, and potential sale of their investment property must be seen not only as economic decisions but as emotional decisions, as well.

Within the one- to four-family rental industry specifically, more than 40 percent of owners have no plans to sell their property in the next five years.[16] Another roughly 40 percent reported that they do not know their anticipated length of future ownership, and fewer than 16 percent planned on selling over the next five years. Like the owners of the overall single-family and small multifamily inven-

13. Joint Center for Housing Studies (2006b, exhibit 14 and app. table A-13).
14. Sternlieb (1966).
15. Mallach (2006).
16. Mallach (2006, p. 27) reports from the 1995 Property Owners and Managers Survey data that around 45 percent of owners anticipate owning for more than the next five years, and fewer than 40 percent do not know their anticipated length of future ownership.

tory, owners of one- to four-family units are mostly part-time owners and property managers with a high motivation for cash flow and with appreciation-related motivations such as retirement security and long-term capital gains.[17]

Given that approximately one-third of owners of these small rental properties acquired the units as their residence and became inadvertent landlords, many owners have an emotional attachment to the home, and any reluctance to sell may not be economically driven. Although many owners hold on to their real estate to either supplement their annual income or provide for future capital, the greatest number of these units are owner managed and often have substantial deferred maintenance issues.

Furthermore, owners may be influenced to hold on to their property to avoid paying taxes on the real gains of their property. This is a separate issue from that of the capital gains and exit tax related to subsidized housing, but there remains a perception that rental housing ownership is difficult to exit. The taxes owed at a profitable sale are not just on the gain but also on the depreciation claimed over the years. The most common methods to avoid paying capital gains are to move back into a unit for two of the five years before selling the property, so that it can be claimed as a primary residence, or to make a 1031 exchange for a like-kind property, rolling over the gain. As even the Dummies.com website states, the rules for properly executing a 1031 exchange are complex, and it is important to have an expert involved in these transactions, such as an attorney or tax adviser.[18] This complexity may deter potential sellers from marketing their properties.

However, these same owners might become motivated to sell if there were a way to replace the cash flow or have an immediate capital flow without the associated capital gains issues. Despite emotional ties, the difficulties associated with the management of rental property—the proliferation of regulations, difficulty in finding and holding reliable tenants who pay their rent on time, inability to provide cost-effective maintenance, or the aging of this housing stock—might encourage owners to sell in the near term if a suitable exit option existed.

The Small Real Estate Investment Trust

The host of issues threatening small multifamily properties scale up to create a greater capital problem that often keeps lower-cost financing at bay. Whether it is scale economies, uncertainty about management, unclear resale values, or deteriorating conditions, this capital problem is believed to be one of the principal causes of the loss of multifamily properties. Small multifamily housing is currently

17. Mallach (2006, p. 20).

18. From "Making and Managing Money," tab section entitled "Enjoying Rental-Property Tax Breaks" (www.dummies.com/WileyCDA/DummiesArticle/id-2418.html), which is adapted from *Investing for Dummies*, 4th ed., Hoboken, N.J.: Wiley (2005).

underserved by capital sources, and most of these properties that have financing typically have variable-rate, recourse, and shorter-term maturity (five years) on their debt.

To help overcome many of these barriers, Narasimhan first proposed in 2001 the concept of a small real estate investment trust as a new equity vehicle to help expand access to capital for small multifamily structures. The S-REIT structure would enable the owners to exchange (tax free) their small multifamily properties for S-REIT partnership units (figure 8-6). These units would, in turn, entitle the owner to a preferred cash flow and a share of potential appreciation rights and to the benefit of having the best local management, whether for-profit or nonprofit. In addition to being exempt from recording taxes and U.S. Securities and Exchange Commission and state registration costs, this S-REIT should have the ability to issue tax-exempt bonds and to obtain equity and debt financing at the corporate level so as to match assets and liabilities without the costs of single-asset financing. Ideally, this S-REIT would receive preference for other federal resources such as the LIHTC, funding from the Home Investment Partnerships program, and community development block grants and be able to negotiate for local government tax abatement support, so that cash-flow savings can be reinvested in the properties.[19]

The proposed structure solves many of the underlying problems that have hindered previous efforts to expand the availability of debt and equity capital for the preservation of small multifamily properties. These include using economies of scale to reduce operating expenses, avoiding the costs associated with single-asset financing, and encouraging owners to transfer properties. In his discussion of the S-REIT concept, Narasimhan underscores the importance of scaling up local, lean professional management services to address the real needs of the properties and the renters within these often urban locations. The aggregation of individual properties under a single management entity would provide scale economies that should substantially lower the operating costs. Examples of potential savings include bulk purchase of energy, other utilities, and building materials for maintenance and repairs. Better scheduling and other economies of scale could also reduce average personal and administrative costs for each unit; rather than requiring property insurance on a building-by-building basis, units in the pool could be covered by a less expensive bulk policy.

Although the exact savings from these economies will depend on a number of factors, Narasimhan presents a scenario for what he argues is a representative pool of twelve hundred units with an average monthly rent of $760, located in thirty buildings with five to forty-nine units each. Compared with the costs associated with individual ownership of these properties, Narasimhan estimates that under

19. Shekar Narasimhan, "Why Do Small Multifamily Properties Bedevil Us?" *Capital Xchange,* November 2001 (www.brookings.edu/printme.wbs?page=/es/urban/capitalxchange/article8.htm).

Figure 8-6. *The Small Multifamily REIT (S-REIT)*

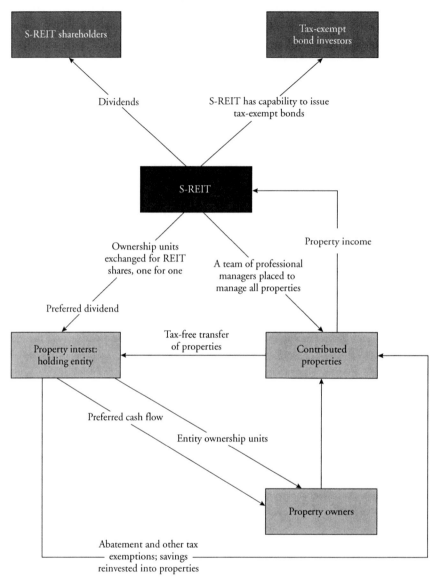

Source: Narasimhan (2001, p. 6, figure 3).

the S-REIT structure, monthly operating costs (not including local real estate taxes) could be cut 30 percent (or nearly $90) a month for each unit.[20] The potential to negotiate additional property tax abatement with local governments would only add to this potential cost savings.

Obtaining financing or securing subsidies for smaller multifamily properties is often difficult because the administrative complexity and costs may be as great for a ten-unit property as for one with a hundred units. Narasimhan gives three reasons that capital is currently expensive for these properties: the cost of due diligence, the perception of higher losses, and the unknown resale value of small multifamily buildings. By creating a portfolio of properties, the hope is that the scale will reduce due diligence costs and create a more stable structure to reduce losses.

As a result of the high fixed costs of single-asset financing, the market in small rental properties has yet to benefit from the expansion of financing options available through the burgeoning secondary market. Moreover, the high fixed costs also limit the ability of owners of smaller structures to use currently available supply-side housing assistance programs—including the Low Income Housing Tax Credit program. As is true with financing, the per unit costs associated with accessing equity investment through the LIHTC are prohibitively high, even though units in smaller multifamily housing account for the bulk of units at risk of loss from the affordable housing inventory.

Finally, Narasimhan's approach should help overcome what many view as the traditional reluctance of many small-property owners to sell. From the perspective of a broader national housing market, the current ownership structure is not efficient. Even as other sectors of the economy (for example, building-materials retailing) consolidated to generate economies of scale, the size distribution of ownership of the rental housing inventory has been slow to change. This may reflect the fact that while the current ownership pattern has obvious shortcomings, it still benefits many owners of small rental properties by providing a mechanism for wealth holding that has important social and economic benefits. Social benefits include the creation of a place to which the owner could return should the economic conditions change or a place to house needy families or friends. Although returns are modest, ownership of small multifamily units can also provide a small cash flow and potential appreciation gains.

By allowing owners to swap their units for a preferred premium and potential cash flow, the S-REIT enables owners to keep what they value in their current arrangements. Establishing a mechanism that would give owners the ability to trade their S-REIT shares for the right to move back into their building, or to provide some security of tenure for those family members and friends living in the

20. Shekar Narasimhan, "Why Do Small Multifamily Properties Bedevil Us?" *Capital Xchange*, November 2001 (www.brookings.edu/printme.wbs?page=/es/urban/capitalxchange/article8.htm), p. 7.

building, would most likely increase the willingness of some owners to convert to an S-REIT.

Prospects for Success of the Investment Trust Approach

The S-REIT creates an opportunity for securing the long-term affordability and improving the efficiency of the management structure of small rental properties by creating a structure wherein ownership transfers from individual to institutional hands. Through this pooling mechanism, small multifamily projects have access to affordable and flexible capital, professional management, and capital for minor rehabilitation while maintaining the present affordability. Available evidence suggests the presence of significant economies of scale in the operation of larger buildings, yet much less is known about the potential scale economies linked to the operation of a pool of smaller properties. That properties may be scattered over several locations adds further complexity to issues of coordinating and scheduling the labor and material used in building management and operations.

Recognizing the inherent difficulty of managing small multifamily properties, in the 1980s the Enterprise Foundation launched the City Homes Program, an effort to document the potential advantages of professional management in the operation of a portfolio of small rental properties.[21] Following a series of bulk purchases of Baltimore row houses, City Homes identified and documented cost-effective practices that could take advantage of the scale economies associated with the pooling of the management of small rental properties under a single entity. These ideas were catalogued in a widely distributed manual—*The Cost Cuts Manual*—that was used by for-profit and nonprofit entities seeking to enhance the quality and lower the costs of owning and operating rental housing targeted to lower-income occupants.[22]

Other efforts to manage portfolios of single-family and small multifamily properties continue today. For example, as part of an effort to deconcentrate assisted rental housing through construction of scattered-site units, many housing authorities and local community groups now have more than a decade of experience managing portfolios of small multifamily housing. Although scattered-site management is by no means easy, many of the best-managed entities provide examples of what is possible.[23] Adding to the mix of public and nonprofit agencies, various private sector firms are taking up the challenge of scattered-site management. For example, in 2004 Redbrick Partners launched a real estate investment trust designed to acquire, rehabilitate, and operate a pool of single-family rental housing. Through efforts to secure capital gains by turning around single-family

21. See Ellen (1991).
22. Santucci and others (1991).
23. For a summary of the issues, see Enterprise Foundation (1999).

properties, or by focusing on market areas with unrealized potential home-value appreciation, the Redbrick approach by design required that its partners effectively manage a pool of several thousand homes located in selected metropolitan areas.[24]

The same scale-economy issues also plague the resale of these properties, as there are fixed transactional costs whether the sale is four or forty units, such as appraisals, environmental reviews, and attorney opinions. These fixed costs, along with limited documentation and low fees related to the scale, are in part what limit the competition for financing, particularly in small, rural markets. Local depository institutions have overcome these barriers by using a more hybrid underwriting approach, relying in part on the creditworthiness of the borrower, and using a less costly evaluation process. Simplifying the appraisal and underwriting process has given depositories the greatest market share. Because of the lack of competition, these institutions can also charge higher fees and interest rates for these loans and constrain borrower choices regarding loan product.[25]

Often, however, programs remain hampered by size. The lauded LaSalle Bank program has a national multifamily Advantage Program that serves small-scale existing apartment properties with fixed terms up to fifty years, fully amortizing.[26] However, of the six projects they highlight on their website, the smallest multifamily project is thirty-three units, and the lowest size loan is $860,000; and most of the loans are adjustable-rate, interest-only, or short-term mortgages. Fannie Mae announced a plan to make available $25.6 billion for multifamily rental financing in 2005, of which $5.2 billion was targeted for small loans, up to $3 million in size, a number that is still quite large, given that many small multifamily properties sell for less than $100,000 for each unit. Absent implementation of a streamlined underwriting process, such small loans also carry with them high fixed costs.[27] Moreover, streamlining may remain a challenge, as principal-agent issues abound.[28]

Practical Alternatives for Showing Proof of Concept

Although the portfolio concept is compelling, the challenges of creating a congressionally chartered new equity vehicle are substantial. Alternatively, there already exist examples of market-driven efforts to use the real estate investment trust structure to aggregate single-family and small rental properties. Examples to date are profit driven and do not necessarily apply the concept in the most socially beneficial way. What is needed is a structure that combines public sector social responsibility with the best practices in capital market structuring.

24. James Hagerty, "Entrepreneur's Unusual Tactic: Buying Up Homes by Hundreds," *Wall Street Journal*, March 4, 2005, p. 21.

25. Herbert (2001).

26. LaSalle Bank (www.lasallerecm.com/l_multifamily.php).

27. See Fannie Mae's website (www.fanniemae.com/multifamily/index.jhtml?p=Multifamily).

28. See Herbert (2001, p. 21) for more discussion of overcoming these barriers, including bright-line tests, loss-sharing arrangements, and desire for repeat business.

One possibility is to build on the innovative practices of the nation's best local housing authorities (LHAs). Currently, many LHAs are in a period of reform and innovation as they reinvent themselves to be more entrepreneurial in serving their mission in an age of dwindling federal resources. Therefore an opportunity exists. Consider, for example, a property aggregation vehicle that uses the current capacity and financing authority available within the public housing authority structure: essential function bonds (EFBs). This bonding authority provides a steady stream of low-cost financing while using a "trusted partner" to reduce loan losses. Combined with the use of professional and lean management services that build on existing LHA experience of managing scattered-site housing, EFBs offer an opportunity to test-market many of the key principles embedded in the S-REIT approach.

Ongoing budget pressure has led many local housing authorities to rethink their strategy for how best to meet the housing needs of the very low-income people they serve. Unfortunately, some have been forced to retrench their activities, while others have found innovative ways to create new sources of capital to fund the development or preservation of affordable rental housing. Local housing agencies could use their capacity to issue essential function bonds to acquire and preserve a portfolio of currently unsubsidized small multifamily and single-family rental properties and in so doing provide a market test of the basic concepts of the S-REIT approach outlined in this chapter.

Although they are often examined only in terms of their involvement in the federally funded and regulated public housing and Section 8 programs, most LHAs, as state-chartered legal entities, have the authority to engage in a wide range of housing, community, and economic development activities, including financing and acquisition, along with the ownership and management of rental housing targeted to meet the housing needs of low- and moderate-income renters. Local housing authorities have long had the capacity to issue tax-exempt bonds, and over the past decade agencies across the nation have issued tax-exempt bonds for the purpose of financing housing owned by the agency and for other purposes linked to their "essential function." Under federal tax law, these essential function bonds are subject only to the same general restrictions as other government-purpose bonds and most significantly are not subject to federally imposed statewide bond caps.

In states that permit local housing agencies to issue bonds on their own behalf, the use of EFBs has soared over the past decade. Although not all states allow LHAs to issue bonds, a survey by the Joint Center for Housing Studies finds that as of July 2002, some sixty-four agencies in twenty-seven states had financed construction or acquisition of more than 40,000 units by issuing a total of $2.12 billion in EFBs—a substantial increase in total EFB activity over that recorded in a previous study done in 1995. Notably, six states (Washington, Illinois, Oregon, Maryland, Minnesota, and California) accounted for more than three-quarters of the EFB activity recorded in the 2002 survey. Although the precise definition of *essential function* varies from one state to the next, generally, state-enabling legislation authorizes LHAs to engage in a wide range of activities related to the construction, preservation, and ongoing ownership and management of housing affordable to low- and moderate-income households.[29]

The Quality Housing and Work Responsibility Act (QHWRA) of 1998 handed housing authorities a powerful new tool with which to address the modernization needs of conventional public housing. The 1998 legislation enabled local housing authorities to pledge future allocations from the public housing capital fund to secure private loan or bond financing. In a recent study funded by the Department of Housing and Urban Development, Harvard's Graduate School of Design documents several approaches to using the new financing tool (Harvard University Graduate School of Design 2003). In one model, EFBs are issued by a local housing authority, and the proceeds are used for capital fund–eligible activities. In combination with a growing investor belief that future capital fund appropriations are a reasonably secure source of funding, investment-grade bond ratings can substantially enhance the marketability of this new type of financial investment.

Whereas QHWRA expanded the ability of local housing authorities to issue EFBs to help finance public housing preservation efforts, the flexibility of the similar authority granted by states goes beyond simply revitalizing traditional public housing. For example, in 2000 the Housing Authority of the City of Santa Barbara used EFBs to purchase a sixty-unit senior development. Owing to its expiring affordability restrictions, the previous private owners had threatened to opt out and convert the property, a move that was avoided when the property was sold to the city's housing authority.

Because adding credit enhancement can increase the complexity and costs of bond issues, more than half of all EFBs covered by the Joint Center for Housing Studies survey reported having no credit enhancement in place, a tribute to the fact that many local housing authorities using the EFB tool are among some of the nation's best run. Indeed, the survey finds that it is not uncommon for EFBs without credit enhancement to secure investment-grade credit ratings.

Among those bonds with credit enhancement, local government guaranties can play a particularly important role. Close to 30 percent of all the bonds included in the survey were backed by local government, including through special tax pledges or other pledges that make repayment a general obligation of the city, county, or state government. By backing bonds with "full faith and credit," local housing authorities can substantially reduce borrowing costs in the tax-exempt bond market.

---

29. The general capacity to issue bonds is distinct from the more limited authority granted to states to issue special purpose bonds, such as tax-exempt multifamily revenue bonds that are subject to congressionally mandated bond caps; see Apgar and Whiting (2003) for more information about EFBs.

Finally, the flexibility of the essential function bond enables local housing authorities to finance a "pool" of properties with a single bond issue. As of 2002, for example, Dakota County Community Development Agency, in Minnesota, had constructed 711 units of senior housing using a single bond issue. Under the EFB bond structure in place, rental revenues from these projects are then pooled to pay for the expenses and debt service for all buildings, thereby reducing the risk to the lender.

Although the S-REIT concept has many good qualities, full implementation would require changes to existing federal tax and housing legislation—an unlikely near-term event, given the crowded federal legislative calendar and limited federal-level support for new housing initiatives of any type. Alternatively, it would be relatively simple for one or more local housing authorities—acting individually or in concert—to use their existing authority to issue essential function bonds and use the proceeds to acquire and preserve a portfolio of currently unsubsidized multi-family or single-family rental properties.

As noted earlier, many LHAs have experience with managing scattered-site units. Indeed, the application of best practices in portfolios of scattered-site properties acquired using the proceeds of essential function bonds could be superior, as they would not be subject to the same complex regulations that often hinder effective management of units operated under the Public Housing Scattered Site program. Alternatively, an LHA could partner with the growing number of private sector management entities with expertise in this area.

Although it would be helpful to layer this approach with rental subsidy, the reduced costs of tax-exempt bond finance combined with local property tax exemptions may well be sufficient to offer the units at modest rents. Even without subsidies, the approach would help stem the loss of many small multifamily properties. In so doing it would alleviate the ongoing pressure on market rents that undermines the well-being of the nation's lowest-income renters.

Conclusion

Although much of the national discussion of preservation of affordable housing focuses on the subsidized portion of the inventory, developing strategies to preserve the inventory of affordable but unsubsidized small multifamily properties is equally important. The potential for developing innovative new housing and capital market strategies targeted to the small, unsubsidized multifamily rental stock is clear. Although untested in their entirety, there is ample evidence that the most important elements of these new approaches are not only possible but ultimately desirable.

Unfortunately, lack of interest at the federal level may hinder full-scale implementation of these bold initiatives. By building on the best practices of local housing agencies and other local public and private entities, it is nevertheless possible to demonstrate the wisdom of these new approaches through a series of local demonstrations. The key challenge is to identify ways to bring the cost-reducing power of scale economies to the small multifamily housing sector that to date remains among one of the most fragmented segments of the overall housing market. Such efforts are not only key to creating a truly comprehensive national affordable housing preservation strategy but also hold the potential of unleashing a wave of innovative financing techniques similar to the wave of innovation that transformed single-family finance nearly two decades ago.

References

Apgar, William, and Emily J. Whiting. 2003. "Essential Function Bonds: An Emerging Tool for Affordable Housing Finance." Working Paper W03-2. Cambridge, Mass.: Harvard University, Joint Center for Housing Studies (February).

Ellen, Ingrid. 1991. "City Homes in Baltimore: Minimum Rehab to Combat Abandonment." Case Study 616-90-1010. Cambridge, Mass.: Harvard University, Kennedy School of Government (May).

Emrath, Paul. 1997. "Property Owners and Managers Survey." *Housing Economics* 45, no. 7: 6–9.

Enterprise Foundation. 1999. *Developing and Managing Scattered-Site Housing.* Columbia, Md.

Goodman, Jack. 2004. "Determinant of Operating Costs of Multifamily Rental Housing." Working Paper W04-7. Cambridge, Mass.: Harvard University, Joint Center for Housing Studies (July).

Harvard University Graduate School of Design. 2003. *Public Housing Operating Cost Study.* Research report prepared for the U.S. Department of Housing and Urban Development.

Herbert, Christopher. 2001. "An Assessment of the Availability and Cost of Financing for Small Multifamily Properties." U.S. Department of Housing and Urban Development.

Joint Center for Housing Studies. 2004. "Middle Market Rental: Hiding in Plain Sight." Cambridge, Mass.: Harvard University.

———. 2006a. "America's Rental Housing: Homes for a Diverse America." Cambridge, Mass.: Harvard University.

———. 2006b. "The State of the Nation's Housing." Cambridge, Mass.: Harvard University.

Mallach, Allan. 2006. "Landlords at the Margins: Exploring the Dynamics of the One to Four Unit Rental Housing Industry." Paper prepared for Revisiting Rental: A Symposium on the Importance of Rental Housing. Harvard University, Cambridge, Mass., November 14–15.

Manchester, Paul B. 2006. "Effectiveness of HUD's Housing Goal Incentives for Freddie Mac and Fannie Mae: Small Multifamily and Certain Single-Family Rental Properties." Paper prepared for the midyear American Real Estate and Urban Economics Association Conference, National Association of Home Builders. Washington, May 30.

Newman, Sandra. 2005. *Low-End Rental Housing: The Forgotten Story in Baltimore's Housing Boom.* Washington: Urban Institute.

Santucci, R. M., and others. 1991. *The Cost Cuts Manual: Nailing Down Savings for Least-Cost Housing.* Columbia, Md.: Enterprise Foundation.

Segal, William. 2003. "Segmentation in the Multifamily Mortgage: Evidence from the Residential Finance Survey." *Journal of Housing Research* 13, no. 2: 175–98.

Sternlieb, George. 1966. *The Tenement Landlord.* Rutgers State University Press.

U.S. Census Bureau. 1991. Residential Finance Survey (www.census.gov/hhes/www/rfs/rfs.html).

———. 2001. Residential Finance Survey (www.census.gov/hhes/www/rfs/rfs.html).

9

Just Suppose: Housing Subsidies for Low-Income Renters

JOHN M. QUIGLEY

I n most aspects of government policy, history matters. This is especially important in programs involving lumpy and costly investments with long, useful lives
and where political consensus is difficult to achieve. The importance of history—
or the path dependency of policy—is nowhere more apparent than in federal
housing policy. John Weicher observed in 1980 that housing programs "can only
be understood from a historical perspective" (Weicher 1980, p. 3). A quarter century later, having served in managerial and policy positions in three national
administrations, Weicher was even more convinced of the importance of historical accident in understanding current policies (Weicher 2006).

In this chapter, I deliberately ignore this path dependence. Instead, I ask, What
housing policies would we create if we were starting from scratch? I concentrate
on subsidies for rental housing. Rental housing represents a small fraction (about
a third) of federal government support for housing, and the configuration of
current policy is less dependent upon the political choices reflected in the original income tax statutes passed by Congress in 1913. Of course, even in rental
housing, one cannot completely ignore history in thinking about or advocating
good policy, so a brief history of federal subsidy policy toward rental housing is
in order.

Background

Programs

Direct federal expenditures on housing began with the Public Housing Act of 1937. The law, which was intended to "remedy the acute shortage" of decent housing through a federally financed construction program, sought the "elimination of substandard and other inadequate housing." Infrastructure investment in big cities was good fiscal policy in an economy with 17 percent of its workers unemployed, and the program provided shelter for some of those "temporarily" unemployed in the Great Depression. By some accounts, public housing was thought to be transitional housing, to be occupied by households for short periods of time until they could enter the economic mainstream.

For the next quarter century, low-rent public housing was the only federal program providing housing assistance for the poor. The dwellings built under the public housing program are financed by the federal government but are owned and managed by local housing authorities. The rental terms for public housing specified by the federal government (in return for financing) ensure occupancy by low-income households, currently at rents no greater than 30 percent of household incomes.

This program of government construction of dwellings reserved for occupancy by low- income households was supplemented by a variety of programs inviting the participation of limited-dividend and nonprofit corporations in the 1960s. These latter programs directly increased the supply of "affordable" housing but not the stock of government-owned housing. A series of programs offering loans at below-market interest rates to nonprofit and cooperative builders (in 1968), rent supplements on behalf of selected households (in 1969), and rental assistance (Section 236 of the National Housing Act of 1970) provided funds to developers to amortize investments in new housing while charging low-income tenants no more than a fifth or a quarter of their incomes in rent. These capital subsidy programs, designed for a low-interest-rate environment, proved unworkable as interest rates increased, and the programs were suspended in the early 1970s. But housing capital is long lived, and near the turn of this century the nation's housing stock still included more than half a million units subsidized by these programs (HUD 1998).

Section 8 of the Housing and Community Development Act of 1974 increased participation by private for-profit entities in the provision of housing for the poor. The law provides for federal funds for the "new construction or substantial rehabilitation" of dwellings for occupancy by low-income households. The federal government entered into long-term contracts with private housing developers, guaranteeing a stream of payments of fair market rents for the dwellings. Low-income households paid 25 (now 30) percent of their incomes on rent, and the difference between tenant payments and the contractual fair market rent was made up by direct federal payments to the owners of the properties.

Crucial modifications to housing assistance policy were introduced in the Section 8 housing program: the restriction that subsidies are paid only to owners of new or rehabilitated dwellings was weakened and ultimately removed, and payments were permitted to a landlord on behalf of a specific tenant (rather than by a long-term contract with the landlord). This tenant-based assistance program grew into the more flexible voucher program introduced in 1987. Households in possession of vouchers receive the difference between a locality's "fair market rent" and 30 percent of their incomes. Households in possession of a voucher may choose to pay more than the fair market rent (estimated regularly for each metropolitan area by the U.S. Department of Housing and Urban Development [HUD]) for any particular dwelling, up to 40 percent of their incomes, making up the difference themselves. They may also pocket the difference if they can rent a HUD-approved dwelling for less than the fair market rent.

In 1998 legislation made vouchers and certificates portable, thereby increasing household choice and facilitating movement across regions in response to employment opportunities. Local authorities were also permitted to vary their payment standards between 90 and 110 percent of fair market rent. The 1998 legislation renamed the Section 8 program the Housing Choice Voucher program.

In thinking about current housing policy choices, it is important to recognize that until thirty years ago, housing assistance to low-income renters was inextricably tied to investment in the construction of new dwellings. The voucher and certificate programs drastically reduced HUD's role in building housing for occupancy by low-income renters. It also reduced direct federal expenditures in building new dwellings for low-income households. But other forces increased the indirect subsidies provided to the construction of new housing to be occupied at low rents.

The Tax Reform Act of 1986 limited the power of state governments to issue tax-exempt debt to finance infrastructure investments for private purposes. Accordingly, state bonds issued for multifamily housing construction were limited in the legislation. However, the law also established the Low Income Housing Tax Credit (LIHTC) program to provide direct subsidies for the construction or acquisition of new or substantially rehabilitated rental housing for occupancy by lower-income households. The LIHTC program permits states to issue federal tax credits that can be used by property owners to offset taxes on other income or can be sold to outside investors to raise initial development funds for a project. To qualify, a specific proportion of a project's dwelling units must be set aside for lower-income households, and rents for these dwellings are limited to 30 percent of the tenant household's income. Qualifying owners may elect instead to set aside 20 percent of units for households with incomes below 50 percent of the median income in the local area, or they may set aside 40 percent of units for households with incomes below 60 percent of the area median. Qualification requires that these units be earmarked for occupancy by lower-income households for a period of thirty years.

The aggregate amount of tax credits authorized by the LIHTC program has been increased several times since its inception, to $1.75 a person in 2002, with automatic adjustments for inflation annually since 2003. With these adjustments, LIHTC credits increased to $1.95 per capita in 2006. Federal tax-credit authority is transmitted to each state, on a per capita basis, for subsequent distribution to developers of qualified projects.

The amount of tax credit that can be allocated to a specific project is a function of its (nonland) development costs, the proportion of units set aside for lower-income households, and its credit rate (4 percent for projects that are also financed by tax-exempt state bonds and 9 percent for other projects.) The credits are provided annually for ten years, so a dollar of tax-credit authority issued today has a present value of six to eight dollars.

The HOME Investment Partnerships program, authorized by the National Affordable Housing Act of 1990, provide some additional funds for supply-side rental programs. Funding through the HOME program comes as a formula block grant to local governments for the construction and renovation of rental housing and for tenant-based assistance (as well as the construction and renovation of owner-occupied housing and assistance to home buyers). The HOME block grant provides great flexibility to local governments in choice of programs, requiring a set-aside of funds for nonprofit community housing development organizations (see O'Regan and Quigley 2000).

Since funding began in 1992, jurisdictions participating in the HOME partnership have chosen to allocate about half of their grant proceeds to rental housing, but allocations to rental housing have been systematically reduced over time (to about 40 percent in 2002). Only 1 percent of grant proceeds are used for tenant-based rental assistance. Annual funding for the HOME program was $1.4 billion in 2004 (Turnham and others 2004).

Expenditures

Direct expenditures, tax expenditures, and guarantee costs are all public subsidies and thus liabilities of the federal treasury. However, only direct expenditures are observable in the annual budget adopted by the federal government. The budget reports government outlays (that is, actual expenditures) in any fiscal as well as budget authority (that is, the aggregate federal commitment of public funds available for expenditures in current and future years).

Table 9-1 reports the net budget authority and federal outlays for low-income rental assistance administered by HUD during the past three decades. As indicated in the table, federal expenditures on low-income rental housing (public housing, project-based assistance, and vouchers) since 1976 have more than quadrupled in constant dollars—from $7.9 billion to $31.5 billion. Despite this large increase in expenditures, net budget authority issued by Congress has declined substantially, by about 40 percent during the period, from $62.3 billion

Table 9-1. *Major HUD Programs for Low-Income Rental Assistance,*
Fiscal Years 1976–2007[a]
Millions of 2006 dollars

Fiscal year	Net budget authority	Federal outlays	Fiscal year	Net budget authority	Federal outlays
1976	62,330	7,902	1991	27,278	24,115
1977	85,096	8,664	1992	23,721	25,153
1978	89,988	10,084	1993	25,027	27,618
1979	63,384	10,974	1994	23,967	29,345
1980	64,789	12,877	1995	15,376	32,553
1981	56,411	16,045	1996	16,839	30,519
1982	28,455	16,891	1997	10,472	30,808
1983	19,480	18,527	1998	15,428	29,795
1984	23,363	19,867	1999	18,145	27,565
1985	45,652	43,269	2000	14,720	27,980
1986	19,545	20,746	2001	21,868	28,513
1987	16,181	20,761	2002	23,099	30,746
1988	15,369	22,053	2003	24,428	32,237
1989	14,203	22,568	2004	24,826	32,486
1990	15,873	23,607	2005	24,547	32,297
			2006	24,933	31,945
			2007	24,731	31,525

Source: U.S. Office of Management and Budget, Public Budget Database, *Budget of the United States Government, Fiscal Year 2007.*

a. Includes public housing, project-based assistance, and voucher programs.

in 1976 to $24.7 billion in 2007. This reflects the gradual shift in low-income housing assistance from project-oriented to tenant-oriented subsidies. New long-term commitments under production-oriented approaches were sharply curtailed in the early 1970s, but preexisting commitments under the public housing and Section 8 new-construction programs continue to provide shelter for a substantial number of low-income households.

Table 9-2 illustrates the evolution of new federal commitments for subsidized rental housing through the late 1990s using dwellings as the units of observation.[1] Two trends are apparent. First, the distribution of subsidy commitments between newly constructed and existing dwellings has changed markedly. In 1977 two-thirds of new funding commitments went to new construction. By 1997, almost

1. For some reason, data on subsidized units are no longer regularly published by the U.S. Department of Housing and Urban Development or by the U.S. House of Representatives Committee on Ways and Means.

Table 9-2. *New Commitments for Subsidized Rental Housing and Total Number of Rental Households Served, 1977–97*

Fiscal year	New commitments (number of units)		Households served (in thousands)	
	New construction	Existing housing	New construction	Existing housing
1977	247,667	127,581	1,825	268
1978	214,503	126,472	1,977	423
1979	231,156	102,669	2,052	602
1980	155,001	58,402	2,189	707
1981	94,914	83,520	2,379	820
1982	48,157	37,818	2,559	844
1983	23,861	54,071	2,702	955
1984	36,719	78,648	2,836	1,086
1985	42,667	85,741	2,931	1,180
1986	37,375	85,476	2,986	1,253
1987	37,247	72,788	3,047	1,366
1988	36,456	65,295	3,085	1,446
1989	30,049	68,858	3,117	1,534
1990	23,491	61,309	3,141	1,616
1991	28,478	55,900	3,180	1,678
1992	38,324	62,595	3,204	1,721
1993	34,065	50,593	3,196	1,900
1994	29,194	66,907	3,213	1,985
1995	19,440	25,822	3,242	2,081
1996	16,259	36,696	3,293	2,021
1997	14,027	36,134	3,305	2,051

Source: U.S. House of Representatives, Committee on Ways and Means, *Green Book, 1998*, tables 15-26, 15-25.

three-quarters of new federal commitments were made to preexisting units. Second, the net number of new federal commitments for housing has plummeted—by more than two-thirds from 1981 to 1997.

The legacy of previous program commitments, of course, means that the current mix of subsidized dwellings includes a larger fraction of dwellings newly constructed for occupancy by subsidized low-income households. Table 9-2 also reports these trends through the late 1990s. During the period covered, the number of subsidized renter households living in preexisting housing increased more than tenfold, to more than two million, but in 1997 more than 60 percent of subsidized renters lived in dwellings that had involved new construction at the time subsidized occupancy began.

For the more recent period, the available data reflect the growing importance of the voucher and certificate programs using the existing stock of housing.

Table 9-3. *Federal Outlays for HUD Supply- and Demand-Side Programs,*
Fiscal Years 2000–07[a]

Millions of 2006 dollars

Fiscal year	Supply side	Demand side	Fiscal year	Supply side	Demand side
2000	9,285	18,696	2004	8,625	23,860
2001	9,370	19,143	2005	8,259	24,037
2002	9,967	20,780	2006	7,908	24,037
2003	9,278	22,959	2007	7,428	24,097

Source: U.S. Office of Management and Budget, Public Budget Database, *Budget of the United States
Government, Fiscal Year 2007.*

a. Supply-side programs include public housing and project-based assistance; demand-side programs
include certificates and vouchers.

Table 9-3 reports trends since the turn of the century. During the past seven
years, reliance upon vouchers and certificates increased from two-thirds to three-
quarters of HUD outlays. In real terms, voucher outlays increased by almost
30 percent, while outlays for public housing and project-based assistance declined
by 20 percent. Table 9-3 also shows a marked decline in the growth of renter subsidies in the recent past. Since 2000, rental housing subsidies have increased by
about $3.5 billion in real terms, or about 1.7 percent a year.

Table 9-4 summarizes comparable information on federal government tax
expenditures for rental housing. Tax expenditures for low-income households
include tax credits distributed for the construction of low-income housing under
the LIHTC and the forgone revenue on tax-exempt multifamily housing bonds.
The LIHTC program has grown from $1.2 billion in 1991 to $4.1 billion in 2006
(in 2006 dollars). Multifamily housing bond programs adopted by the states are
smaller and declined from about a billion dollars to half that over the same period.
In part, this reflects cyclical declines in interest rates, which have reduced spreads,
making these bonds less attractive to investors.

For comparison, the table also presents the tax expenditures arising from the
special treatment of capital gains on owner-occupied housing. This tax expenditure (which reflects the fact that capital gains on owner-occupied housing are
accorded a special exclusion provision) is many times larger than the tax expenditures on rental housing reported in the table.[2] Tax expenditures associated with
capital gains for owner-occupied housing are estimated to be $39.8 billion in
2006, as compared with tax expenditures of $4.5 billion for rental housing. Tax

2. The table does not report the tax expenditures attributable to the exemption accorded to the
imputed rental income from owner-occupied housing (an additional $26.3 billion in 2004) or the
costs of federal guarantees arising from secondary market activities in support of owner-occupied
housing ($25.2 billion in 2004); see Jaffee and Quigley (2007).

Table 9-4. *Federal Tax Expenditures for Rental Housing, Fiscal Years 1987–2011*[a]
Millions of 2006 dollars

Fiscal year	Homeowner capital gains exclusion	Multifamily tax-exempt bonds	Low-income housing tax credit	Fiscal year	Homeowner capital gains exclusion	Multifamily tax-exempt bonds	Low-income housing tax credit
1987	7,765	2,271	49	2000	21,718	187	3,760
1988	10,570	1,966	255	2001	21,853	183	3,686
1989	23,371	1,873	437	2002	22,102	202	3,697
1990	23,578	1,575	171	2003	22,194	307	6,803
1991	22,592	1,460	1,153	2004	31,717	384	3,905
1992	24,136	1,487	1,542	2005	37,157	423	4,006
1993	24,019	1,343	2,074	2006 est.	39,750	430	4,060
1994	28,068	1,276	2,533	2007 est.	42,958	440	4,159
1995	24,841	1,188	2,903	2008 est.	47,449	489	4,364
1996	24,657	948	3,265	2009 est.	58,614	519	4,609
1997	30,474	998	2,834	2010 est.	77,167	528	4,844
1998	21,316	183	3,806	2011 est.	85,230	538	5,108
1999	21,630	186	3,389				

Source: Office of Management and Budget, *Budget of the United States Government,* fiscal years 1982 through 2007.
a. Figures for 2006–11 are estimates.

expenditures for capital gains on owner-occupied housing are currently about 25 percent larger than federal outlays on all HUD subsidy programs.

Why Subsidize Rental Housing?

Why should the federal government take an active role in devising policy for rental housing? As noted above, the initial rationale for the provision of public housing was the "acute shortage" of decent housing coupled with the "recurring unemployment" of the time. A combination of idle resources in the economy and a lack of effective demand arising from a calamitous recession launched a program of government-sponsored housing production.

With the postwar boom in the American economy, the comprehensive Housing Act of 1949 emphasized the goal of providing "a decent home and a suitable living environment" and "decent, safe and sanitary housing" for all Americans. Improved housing conditions formed the rationale for subsidy policies, and progress could be measured by noting the extent to which inadequate housing was eradicated. In 1975 about 2.8 million renter households lived in "severely inadequate housing," representing almost 11 percent of renter households. By 2001, the last year for which comparable data are available (see Quigley and Raphael 2004), the number of inadequately housed households by this standard had declined by 60 percent, and the fraction of renters living in severely inadequate housing was less than 3.5 percent of the population. Among dwellings affordable to the poorest households (those earning less than 30 percent of the local area median income), the fraction of severely inadequate housing was about 5.3 percent in 1999, according to the Millennial Housing Commission (2002, p. 93). Among dwellings affordable to low-income households (those earning 50–80 percent of local median income), the fraction classified as severely inadequate was 2.9 percent. Physically inadequate housing is certainly a concern for some households, especially the poorest renters. But among the very poorest households, only 5 percent of those who pay less than 30 percent of their incomes on rent live in severely inadequate conditions.

Until quite recently, it was widely presumed that the external effects of housing and bad neighborhoods were large and that neighborhoods with high poverty concentrations where housing was derelict were themselves a cause of social problems. Well-known studies, by John Kain (1968) and William Julius Wilson (1997) among many others, strongly suggest that unemployment, crime, and social disorder are causally related to bad neighborhoods and inadequate housing conditions.

However, this confident consensus has been disrupted by three developments. First, a series of careful studies of specific outcomes (for example, Mayer and Jencks 1990; Oreopoulis 2003) has failed to find strong and systematic empirical evidence of a causal nature. Although some detailed studies of public housing have documented statistical relationships between program participation and individual outcomes, they have not distinguished between effects of household income (arising because resources are transferred to the beneficiaries of housing programs) and the influence of housing or neighborhood conditions (see Newman and Harkness 2002 for a discussion). Second, methodological research by statisticians and econometricians suggests that a causal link would be quite hard to establish scientifically, if indeed it existed.[3] Third, extensive analysis of a real experiment in exposing households to better neighborhoods has failed to find much evidence of neighborhood effects.[4]

In any case, neither numbers nor quality provides a convincing rationale for public subsidies of rental housing in this century, and the results of the Moving to Opportunity experiments underscore the advantages of demand-side housing sub-

---

3. This has been termed the "reflection problem"; see Manski (1995); Durlauf (2002).

4. These Moving to Opportunity experiments, conducted in five cities from 1994 to 2002, are reviewed by John Goering and Judith Feins (2002). Jeffrey Kling, Jeffrey Liebman, and Lawrence Katz (2007) provide detailed evaluations: they review fifteen primary outcomes for adults and fifteen primary outcomes for youth and conclude that the experimental treatment had no effect upon the economic self-sufficiency of adults (in terms of earnings, welfare participation, and reliance on government assistance), little effect upon the physical health of adults, and quite mixed effects upon youth outcomes. In contrast, the effects upon the mental health of adults were consistently positive.

sidies, which facilitate dispersed residences. Indeed, this all seems well recognized now by politicians, scholars, advocates, and interest groups. For example, in its 2000 report to Congress, HUD emphasized high rent burdens as the source of "worst-case housing need" (HUD 2000). Since 2000, the Senate has directed HUD to compile and report the extent of worst-case housing needs annually. Because the extent of substandard housing is so small, these reports are essentially estimates of the fraction of households in various demographic groups paying in excess of half of their incomes on rent (see, for example, HUD 2005). "Worst-case housing need" has evolved into another way of describing poverty.

Affordability is clearly the most compelling rationale for polices subsidizing rental housing. The high cost of rental housing, relative to the ability of low-income households to pay for housing, means that these households have few resources left over for expenditures on other goods—food, clothing, medicine—that are also necessities. Because housing represents a large share of household expenditures in market-based economies—for the middle class as well as the poor—small changes in the rent burdens faced by households can have large effects on their levels of well-being. Improved outcomes in a variety of dimensions almost certainly arise if housing programs provide increased discretionary resources to recipients by reducing rent burdens. The affordability of housing is a legitimate rationale for housing subsidy policies. Indeed, as noted above, it seems to be the only surviving rationale for a large-scale subsidy program for rental housing in the United States. This suggests that rental housing programs for low-income households ought to be thought of as a part of the U.S. welfare system—in the same way that we think of income transfers, food stamps, and the earned income tax credit as components of that system.

This perspective highlights the egregious failure of the current system of historically evolving housing subsidy programs—the horizontal inequity accorded to similarly situated, otherwise identical, households. Under current programs, qualifying households obtain rental housing subsidies through some random process. Households apply for housing assistance through local housing authorities. Despite widespread presumptions to the contrary, virtually all local authorities have long waiting lists—eleven months, on average, in U.S. metropolitan areas (HUD 1999). Gary Painter (1997) reports that, for the largest public housing authorities, waiting times average almost three years. Indeed, in some housing authorities, waiting lists themselves are often closed. This means that qualifying households can wait years before obtaining rental assistance. Some may wait years before receiving permission to join the waiting list. Independent housing authorities have their own systems for ranking eligible households. Most authorities adopt some sensible procedure for granting priorities, but selection onto the waiting list and selection from the waiting list have many of the characteristics of winning the sweepstakes.

Compare this with the process of obtaining food stamps or medical assistance under Medicaid. Households are deemed eligible on the basis of income, house-

Table 9-5. *Rent Burdens and Subsidies for Low-Income Renters, 1978–2003*

Classification	Poor[a]						Very poor[b]	
	1978	1989	1995	1997	2001	2003	2001	2003
Renter households (*n*)	10,682	13,378	14,562	14,519	14,903	15,658	8,659	9,077
Renter households spending > 50% of income on rent (*n*)	3,226	5,056	5,927	6,395	6,022	6,105	4,838	4,945
Assisted households (n)								
Income below cutoff	2,094	3,933	3,772	4,077	4,234	4,256	2,942	2,986
Other	633	145	876	1,531	2,044	1,956	3,336	3,226
Assisted households (%)								
Actual	19.6	29.4	25.9	28.1	28.4	27.1	34.0	32.9
If targeted	25.5	30.5	31.9	38.6	42.1	39.7	72.5	68.4
Assisted households spending > 50% of income on rent (%)								
Actual	30.2	37.8	40.7	44.0	40.4	39.0	55.9	54.5
If targeted	24.3	36.7	34.7	33.5	18.0	26.5	17.3	18.9

Source: U.S. Department of Housing and Urban Development, Office of Policy Development and Research, *Rental Housing Assistance—The Worsening Crisis; A Report to Congress* (March 2001); *A Report on Worst Case Housing Needs in 1999* (January 2001); *Trends in Worst Case Needs for Housing, 1978–1999* (December 2003); *Affordable Housing Needs: A Report to Congress on the Significant Need for Housing* (2005).

a. Households with income below 50 percent of AMI.

b. Households with income below 30 percent of AMI.

hold size, and other demographics (such as disability), and all eligible households qualify for assistance. The only form of welfare assistance that is awarded under the sweepstakes model, rather than the entitlement model, is rental housing. Given that housing expenses represent a large fraction of the incomes of low-income households, the inequity is even more glaring. Some fraction of eligible households receives a large subsidy; a larger fraction receive nothing. The distribution is capricious. For example, under current rental subsidy policies, more than 70 percent of households below the poverty line are not served, and more than 40 percent of the households that are served are not in poverty (Currie 2006; Olson 2003). This is indefensible.

For 2003, it was reported that 32.8 percent of renters with reported earnings of less than 30 percent of local median income (roughly $18,500 for a family of four) received housing assistance, and 19.3 percent of renters earning 31–50 percent of local median income (up to about $32,000) received housing assistance (HUD 2005, pp. 50–55; also see table 9-5). Among the lowest-income households, that is, the 9.1 million renters with incomes below 30 percent of the local median, more than 6 million receive no housing assistance. Of those 6 million who are unserved, almost 5 million pay more than half of their incomes on rent.

Viewing rental housing subsidies as a part of the modern welfare system is very different from conceptualizing these subsidies as a part of an infrastructure investment program—the rationale for the program seventy years ago. Ensuring equal treatment of eligible households as part of a national welfare program is inconsistent with a policy of using rental subsidy funds to build innovatively designed new dwellings to be rented at below-market rents—at any conceivable budget. And the reason is obvious.

The cost of providing decent-quality housing through new construction is obviously much greater than the cost of providing it by using the existing depreciated stock of housing. This fact is well known to builders and developers, who almost never target new construction of rental units to the bottom half of the income distribution. (And this fact is also quite well known to slumlords, who offer small quantities of housing services to the poor, using the oldest and most obsolete portion of the housing stock.)

These cost differences in shelter provision for low-income households were thoroughly documented in conjunction with the Experimental Housing Allowance program a quarter century ago (see, for example, Mayo and others 1980). More recent analyses by the General Accounting Office (GAO 2001, 2002) suggest that the first-year costs of subsidizing rental households through new construction programs are from 49 to 65 percent more than the costs of subsidizing the same households using vouchers, and the present-value life-cycle costs are from 19 to 38 percent more than the costs of voucher programs for comparable housing.[5] No conceivable budget that sought to cover all renters below some low-income cutoff could make provisions for the expenditures required to provide newly constructed housing for assisted households.

A New Rental Housing Policy?

It is not clear that a rental housing subsidy program faithful to the analysis in the previous section could be implemented. In starting from scratch, there are many changes to existing programs to be considered.

First, eligibility rules for rental housing assistance would need to be tightened. Under current law, households with incomes below 80 percent of the area median income adjusted for household composition are eligible for rental housing subsidies. In 2006 this was an average cutoff income of $52,075 for a family of four. In contrast, current eligibility for food stamps for four-person households is confined to those with incomes less than half as large ($25,164). Eligibility for the earned income tax credit is limited to households (with one or more children)

5. Indeed, the recent analysis by Kling, Lieberman, and Katz of the Moving to Opportunity experiments concludes that these treatments pass the cost-benefit criterion because "the intervention[s] produced large mental health improvements and because other research suggests that it is cheaper to provide a unit of subsidized housing with vouchers than in a public housing project" (2007, p. 108).

earning a third less a year ($37,263). Eligibility for rental assistance would have to be tightened considerably to replace a national lottery program with an entitlement program for housing assistance for very low-income renters.

Second, passage of an entitlement program would require considerable support outside the policy community, and the continuity of the program would be problematic. One way to increase support, and to reduce administrative costs as well, would be to follow the politically successful program of subsidy for homeownership by using the Internal Revenue Service (IRS) to determine eligibility and to distribute the benefits.

Currently, the multibillion-dollar subsidies to homeownership in the United States are distributed largely by the IRS. Individual taxpayers need not report the dividend (that is, the imputed rent) on owner-occupied housing at all, and capital gains on sales are accorded special treatment in the computation of tax liability (on schedule D, by following the instructions on worksheet 2). The distribution of these large subsidies ($29.7 billion in 2006 from the imputed rent exclusion and $39.8 billion from the capital gains exclusion) is relatively painless. However, the subsidies provided under the tax laws for owner-occupants are not refundable to the taxpayer. Instead, the subsidy is paid implicitly as a credit against other tax liability.

In contrast, the earned income tax credit is fully refundable to the taxpayer. Eligibility for the credit can be established online.[6] Alternatively, the IRS will establish eligibility and will compute the credit due—and they will also send along a check—to any qualifying taxpayer. A refundable credit is not hard to administer.

In fact, there is already a housing program administered by the IRS that could be the template for this low-income housing subsidy program. The Mortgage Credit Certificate program authorized by the Deficit Reduction Act of 1984 entitles selected homeowners to claim a tax credit for some portion of the mortgage interest paid in any year, rather than the tax deduction afforded other homeowners.[7] A taxpayer in possession of a mortgage credit certificate issued by a unit of state or local government merely checks a box on his or her tax return (on line 54 of form 1040) and submits a brief form (form 8396, eleven lines long) to claim the nonrefundable credit.

To claim the low-income housing subsidy under the program proposed here, the taxpayer would need to submit a form issued by a local housing authority and check a box added to the current IRS form 1040. The form would simply certify that the household was renting a dwelling that met the minimum habitation standards imposed by the current voucher program. That form, together with the income reported by the household, the number of dependents in the household,

---

6. The form and worksheet can be found at (http://apps.irs.gov/app/eitc2006/showeligibility/tips.do).

7. See Greulich and Quigley (2003) for a detailed discussion.

and the postal address of the household, would be sufficient to compute the credit due any household. The computation could be made by any taxpayer (online) or by the IRS, as is the case with the earned income tax credit. Of course, the computations could also be made by any commercial tax preparer. The private sector would have an incentive to help in the administration of the program. The appropriate credit could be mailed in monthly installments to the low-income household or to its landlord (or to the local housing authority, for that matter).

Details

Of course, myriad details would need to be addressed before this sort of reform could be implemented. Households move during the year, and a changed postal code might entail a different fair market rent and area median income. Children are born; dependents are added. This means that settling up the monthly rent entitlement on an annual basis requires careful administration and attention to detail.

Then there is a question of costs. The precise costs to the Treasury depend upon two factors: the income cutoff for assistance and the payment standard employed. The income cutoff is conventionally represented as the ratio of household income to area median income (both adjusted for family size). The payment standard under the current voucher program is the HUD-computed fair market minus 30 percent of income.

Table 9-5 presents historical data from the worst-case housing needs reports for poor and very poor renter households. As the table indicates, from 1978 to 1989 there was an increase in the percentage of poor households (that is, those with incomes of less that half the local median) paying more than half of their incomes in rent, from 30 to 38 percent. The percentage of poor households spending more than half of their incomes on rent has remained roughly constant, averaging about 40 percent, since the late 1980s.[8] For 2001 and 2003, these worst-case reports also indicate that rent expenditures among very poor households (earning less than 30 percent of the area median) are about 55 percent of income.

The table also reports the fraction of these households assisted by low-income housing programs. This fraction increased from 1978 to 1989 and then remained roughly constant at 26–28 percent until 2003. The table also reports the fraction of these low-income households that could have been assisted if all rental housing assistance had been targeted to them. As the table indicates, targeting would have increased the population of assisted households, among those with less than half of local median income, by 6 percentage points in 1995 and by about 12 percentage points in 2003. Finally, the table reports the fraction of households in this category spending more than half their incomes on rent and the estimated fraction if hous-

---

8. These trends are confirmed using census data for renter households with incomes below the poverty line; see Quigley and Raphael (2004).

ing assistance had been targeted to the class. The portion of income spent on rent by these households would have been reduced by about 6 percent in 1995 and about 12 percent in 2003. If this targeting had been directed toward the very poorest of renters—those with incomes below 30 percent of area median—the fraction spending more than half of their incomes on rent could have been reduced from about 55 percent to less than 20 percent in both 2001 and 2003.

Greater precision in the targeting of subsidies would increase program costs for the same number of households served, since lower-income households receive more assistance. Without detailed information on the distribution of households by income across housing markets, it is not possible to estimate reliably the costs for any expansion of a more targeted program. However, some crude information is available from the 2000 census that may provide a rough estimate of costs. The census provides a national tabulation of household incomes and rents paid (HCT56, from the SF4 sample data). Household incomes of less than $20,000 were below 32 percent of the national median income (in 2000, for a family of four), and households in the lowest reported class, earning less than $10,000, had incomes below 16 percent of the median.

If a tax credit were introduced to subsidize households with annual incomes below $20,000 by paying them the difference between their reported rents and 30 percent of their incomes, and if this voucher payment were made by the IRS to all qualifying low-income households, the cost would be about $22 billion (in 2006 dollars) for the households that received subsidies. (Of course, this is an overestimate, since many households voluntarily pay more than 30 percent of their income on rent in order to receive more or better housing.) If housing prices increased by 10 percent as a consequence of the program, the cost would be about $26.2 billion in 2006.[9]

The rent subsidy program would provide assistance to about 8.0 million households with incomes below 32 percent of median household income, as against the assistance to 3.0 million households with incomes below 30 percent provided under the current programs (in 2003). The additional 5 million very poor households served would cost about $4,400 each. But savings could be achieved by withdrawing subsidies (slowly, to be sure) from the 3.2 million higher-income households currently subsidized by rental assistance programs and by redirecting costly rental construction programs (for example, the LIHTC, which costs $4.0 billion a year).

Of course, there is nothing sacred about a cutoff of 32 percent (or 30 or 16 percent) of median income. Nor is there any particular normative significance in the definition or computation of fair market rent.[10] The budget (any

---

9. If, instead, the credit were introduced for households with incomes below $10,000, it would cost $10.7 billion ($13.0 billion if rents increased by 10 percent).

10. Indeed, fair market rent was originally an estimate of monthly rent at the fortieth percentile of the rent distribution. It is now an estimate at the fiftieth percentile.

budget) can be accommodated—as an entitlement, beginning with the poorest households.

The introduction of the rental housing subsidy program outlined above would not be sufficient to replace all existing rental housing programs or the collateral functions of the U.S. Department of Housing and Urban Development. The vigorous enforcement of equal opportunity in housing, for example, is a precondition to the functioning of an expanded voucher system as an entitlement program for low-income renters. Low-income disabled households have special needs that could not be satisfied by participation in an expanded voucher program. Some fraction of the homeless is not only poor but disabled as well. These individuals require housing in a supportive environment that can best be provided collectively by government assistance. These considerations flow from recognizing that housing subsidies are better considered as a part of a welfare system, not an infrastructure investment program.

One aspect of current HUD activities would have to be increased substantially for this reform to be successful. Currently, HUD devotes some resources to the removal of regulatory barriers to the construction of new housing. Much of this activity consists of the identification of regulations and practices that increase housing costs, including zoning, building codes, and administrative processes. More federal resources would have to be devoted to removing local regulation that drives up the cost of new construction.[11]

Conclusion

Is this proposed reform a big change, or just a minor tweak, to existing rental subsidy policy? Under current law, local authorities are required to provide three-quarters of new rental subsidies to households earning less than 30 percent of local median income. This suggested reform would target a specific income cutoff and provide national entitlement to households of lower income. Under current policy, about three-quarters of HUD housing outlays are for demand-side subsidies, and the long-term trend has been to reduce systematically the importance of construction and supply-side subsidies. The proposed reform would accelerate this trend and would eliminate construction subsidies, but perhaps not tomorrow. Current policy uses local housing authorities as the rationing agents for housing subsidy, a legacy of the public housing initiative of seven decades ago. This reform would apply a national standard to determine eligibility and to award the subsidy. Local authorities would continue to inspect dwellings and certify compliance.

11. See Quigley (2007) for a discussion.

The device of achieving this through the IRS and a refundable tax credit is clearly a gimmick, employed, in part, to place the subsidy off-budget and to avoid the annual appropriations cycle. But the gimmick has proved to be successful and effective for other interest groups, even in the allocation of subsidies for housing. It has worked quite well for upper-income homeowners and for builders.[12] It is worth trying for the poor.[13]

The major barrier to this kind of reform would be the interests that could be offended by a simple and streamlined program providing vouchers as an entitlement. This is, of course, a major reason why history matters in the real world. Some builders might not immediately see such a program as really in their interest. Some local governments that currently use rental housing subsidy money to build ambitious urban monuments would object to such a program, and, of course, some government servants who would be made redundant might object to the program. All these interests are important players in the world of housing policy, and their potential objections are to be taken seriously.

However, the economic problem is that housing is unaffordable to low-income households, and they face extremely high rent burdens. We should transfer resources to those households so they can live in decent housing at expenditure levels they can afford.

References

Currie, Janet M. 2006. *The Invisible Safety Net.* Princeton University Press.

Durlauf, Steven N. 2002. "Neighborhood Effects." In *Cities and Geography,* vol. 4 of *Handbook of Regional and Urban Economics,* edited by J. V. Henderson and J. F. Thisse, pp. 2173–242. Amsterdam: Elsevier North Holland.

Fischer, Will. 2000. "Labor Supply Effects of Federal Rental Subsidies." *Journal of Housing Economics* 9, no. 2: 150–74.

Goering, John, and Judith D. Feins, eds. 2002. *Choosing a Better Life? Evaluating the Moving to Opportunity Social Experiment.* Washington: Urban Institute Press.

Greulich, Erica, and John M. Quigley. 2003. "Housing Subsidies and the Tax Code: The Case of Mortgage Credit Certificates." Working Paper W02-004. University of California–Berkeley, Program on Housing and Urban Policy (April).

12. Of the 46,335,237 individual tax returns filed in 2004, for example, 617,728 reported incomes in excess of $500,000. Of these, 421,141 reported home mortgage interest deductions totaling $11,245,360,000 (IRS 2006, table 2.1) At prevailing federal tax rates, the home mortgage interest deduction for the richest 1.3 percent of taxpayers yielded a revenue loss of $7.3 billion. This is between a quarter and a third of the total cost of the entitlement described above for all renter households with incomes below $20,000.

13. This device might also lead to a closer integration of housing subsidy policies and other parts of the welfare and income transfer system; see Fischer (2000).

Internal Revenue Service (IRS), U.S. Department of the Treasury. 2006. *Statistics of Income: Individual Income Tax Returns Complete Report 2004.* Publication 1304. Government Printing Office (September).

Jaffee, Dwight, and John M. Quigley. 2007. "Housing Subsidies and Homeowners: What Role for Government-Sponsored Enterprises?" *Brookings-Wharton Papers on Urban Affairs* 6, no. 1: 103–49.

Kain, John F. 1968. "Housing Segregation, Negro Employment, and Metropolitan Decentralization." *Quarterly Journal of Economics* 82, no. 2: 175–97.

Kling, Jeffrey, Jeffrey Liebman, and Lawrence Katz. 2007. "Experimental Analysis of Neighborhood Effects." *Econometrica* 75, no. 1: 83–120.

Manski, Charles. 1995. *Identification Problems in the Social Sciences.* Harvard University Press.

Mayer, Susan, and Christopher Jencks. 1990. "The Social Consequences of Growing up in a Poor Neighborhood." In *Inner-City Poverty in the United States,* edited by Laurence Lynn and Michael McGeary, pp. 111–86. Washington: National Academy Press.

Mayo, Stephen K., and others. 1980. *Costs and Efficiency.* Part 2 of *Housing Allowances and Other Rental Assistance Programs: A Comparison Based on the Housing Allowance Demand Experiment.* Cambridge, Mass.: Abt Associates.

Millennial Housing Commission. 2002. *Meeting Our Nation's Housing Challenges.* U.S. Government Printing Office.

Newman, Sandra J., and Joseph M. Harkness. 2002. "The Long-Term Effects of Public Housing on Self-Sufficiency." *Journal of Policy Analysis and Management* 2, no. 1: 21–44.

Olsen, Edgar O. 2003. "Housing Programs for Low-Income Households." In *Means-Tested Transfer Programs,* edited by Robert Moffitt, pp. 365–442. University of Chicago Press.

O'Regan, Katherine M., and John M. Quigley. 2000. "Federal Policy and the Rise of Nonprofit Housing Providers." *Journal of Housing Research* 11, no. 2: 297–318.

Oreopoulis, Philip. 2003. "The Long-Run Consequences of Growing Up in a Poor Neighborhood." *Quarterly Journal of Economics* 118, no. 4: 1533–75.

Painter, Gary. 1997. "Does Variation in Public Housing Waiting Lists Induce Intra-Urban Mobility?" *Journal of Housing Economics* 6, no. 3: 248–76.

Quigley, John M. 2007. "Regulation and Property Values: The High Cost of Monopoly." In *Land Policies and Their Outcomes,* edited by Gregory K. Ingram and Y. H. Hong, pp. 46–66. Cambridge, Mass.: Lincoln Institute of Land Policy.

Quigley, John M., and Steven Raphael. 2004. "Is Housing Unaffordable? Why Isn't It More Affordable?" *Journal of Economic Perspectives* 18, no. 1: 129–52.

Turnham, Jennifer, and others. 2004. *Study of Homebuyer Activity through the HOME Investment Partnership Program.* Cambridge, Mass.: Abt Associates.

U.S. Department of Housing and Urban Development (HUD). 1998. Office of Budget. *Annotated Tables for the 1998 Budget Process.* Government Printing Office.

———. 1999. *Waiting in Vain: An Update on America's Rental Housing Crisis.* Government Printing Office.

———. 2000. Office of Policy Development and Research. *Rental Housing Assistance: The Worsening Crisis.* Government Printing Office (March).

———. 2001. Office of Policy Development and Research. *A Report on Worst Case Housing Needs in 1999.* Government Printing Office (January).

———. 2003. Office of Policy Development and Research. *Trends in Worst Case Needs for Housing, 1978–1999.* Government Printing Office (December).

———. 2005. Office of Policy Development and Research. *Affordable Housing Needs: A Report to Congress on the Significant Need for Housing.* Government Printing Office.

U.S. General Accounting Office (GAO). 2001. *Costs and Characteristics of Federal Housing Assistance.* GAO-01-901R. Government Printing Office.

———. 2002. *Federal Housing Assistance: Comparing the Characteristics and Costs of Housing Programs.* GAO-02-76. Government Printing Office.

Weicher, John C. 1980. *Housing: Federal Policy and Programs.* Washington: American Enterprise Institute.

———. 2006. "Commentary on 'Federal Credit and Insurance Programs: Housing.' " *Federal Reserve Bank of St. Louis Review* 88, no. 4: 311–22.

Wilson, William Julius. 1997. *The Truly Disadvantaged: Crime and Family Disruption in U.S. Cities.* University of Chicago Press.

10

Rethinking U.S. Rental Housing Policy: A New Blueprint for Federal, State, and Local Action

BRUCE KATZ AND MARGERY AUSTIN TURNER

I n recent years, housing has all but disappeared from national-level debate except for occasional discussions of a possible housing "bubble" and the all-too-brief concern about emergency housing needs in the aftermath of Hurricane Katrina. Despite the lack of sustained attention, our country's housing challenges are changing in ways that not only affect an expanding segment of the population but also implicate other top domestic priorities. Some states and localities are starting to respond to these challenges in new and creative ways. But federal housing policy—particularly rental housing policy—is not getting the serious national attention it warrants.

One-third of all Americans rent the homes and apartments in which they live.[1] Some are renters by choice—because they are highly mobile or prefer not to assume the responsibilities of homeownership. But most who rent do so out of necessity—because they have limited savings or lack the income necessary to cover the costs of homeownership. And a growing share of renters cannot find homes or apartments that they can reasonably afford. As of 2005, more than 16 million households—up from about 13 million in 2000—spent more than 30 percent of their monthly income on housing, a cost burden defined as unaffordable by federal standards. Almost two-thirds of these cost-burdened renters had annual

---

1. According to the U.S. Census Bureau's American Communities Survey, 32.9 percent of all households—more than 36 million households—were renters in 2004 (Census Bureau 2005, table B11012, "Household Type, by Tenure").

incomes below $20,000. But the share of higher-income renters who are paying housing costs they can ill afford is also rising; from 2000 to 2005, the share of renters with incomes over $35,000 whose housing cost burdens were considered unaffordable climbed from 6.4 percent to 12.2 percent.[2]

Moreover, as metropolitan areas sprawl outward and jobs become increasingly dispersed, fewer low-wage renters can find housing near their work. While employment growth is fastest in the low-density counties on the fringes of America's metropolitan areas, affordable housing—and affordable rental housing, in particular—remains disproportionately located in inner-city and older suburban neighborhoods. In fact, in many metro areas, a substantial share of the affordable rental stock is concentrated in distressed, high-poverty neighborhoods.

Despite the magnitude and urgency of these problems, the current debate on federal housing policy amounts to little more than squabbling over crumbs. At present, federal policy seems defined almost exclusively by the fiscal imperative—that is, the pressure to reduce domestic discretionary spending—rather than by how best to address the nation's housing concerns. Moreover, today's congressional housing coalition is a mere shadow of its former self. Congressional response to the Millennial Housing Commission's report in 2002 paled in comparison with the reception given the National Housing ("Rouse-Maxwell") Task Force in the late 1980s. While that group's efforts resulted in the passage of the National Affordable Housing Act of 1990, the 2002 commission's findings have been all but ignored.

As long as the federal housing policy conversation remains limited to tinkering with existing programs, no real progress seems possible. But we are hopeful that federal housing policy can be reinvigorated. This optimism is founded in the efforts of many state and local governments to fill the void with imaginative solutions, thus acting as laboratories for innovative policies that might eventually succeed at the national level. Our optimism also stems from the vibrant state and local political coalitions that are successfully pushing through meaningful housing reforms and initiatives. Notably, these coalitions are using fresh language, deploying new arguments, and involving powerful partners from the business community in their push for change—a potential model for building broader support for a reinvigorated housing policy at the federal level, as well.

Inspired by this backdrop of state and local energy, we propose here a new blueprint for the nation's rental-housing policy. Our blueprint responds to the root causes of current challenges, respects the creativity and increasing capacity of state and local governments, and reconnects housing policy to the larger issues that Americans care about. This blueprint also aims to catalyze local markets—as fed-

2. Census Bureau (2000, table H73, "Housing Income by Gross Rent as a Percentage of Household Income"); Census Bureau (2005, table S2503, "Financial Characteristics").

eral homeownership policies historically have—rather than merely delivering a fixed volume of social housing.

Changing National Rental Challenges

The failures of today's rental housing market reflect a confluence of demographic, economic, and social forces that the current array of federal programs can no longer effectively address. Our country's greatest housing challenges occur at different levels: a nationwide housing affordability problem, insufficient housing supply in prosperous regions, a problem of housing location within metropolitan regions, and a neighborhood distress problem.

Nationwide Affordability

For a growing segment of the workforce, rents are rising faster than incomes. Gross rents (which include utility costs) have been growing faster than inflation, while the median renter's monthly income has declined 7.3 percent since 2000. As a result, average gross rents as a share of renter income have grown from 26.5 percent in 2000 to 30.3 percent today. In 2005, 45.7 percent of renter households were spending more than 30 percent of their income on housing costs (Census 2005). This trend is primarily the result of widening income inequality—with incomes rising much more slowly for low- and moderate-wage workers than for those in high-skill, high-wage jobs.

The fastest-growing segment of the U.S. economy today consists primarily of low-wage service jobs, and wages for these jobs are rising slowly. During the 1990s, wages at the very bottom of the distribution were stagnant, while those at the top rose rapidly. More recently, it appears that mid-level wages are also stagnating, while the top continues to gain (Autor, Katz, and Kearney 2006). In part, this is the result of economic restructuring: the decline in the traditionally high-paying U.S. manufacturing sector means that the economy has been shedding jobs that pay more than those that replace them. The median wages in industries that have added jobs since the 2001 recession are 21 percent lower than in industries that have shed jobs (Joint Center for Housing Studies 2004, p. 29).[3]

If all incomes were rising slowly, keeping pace with housing costs might be less of a problem, but incomes for highly skilled workers are in fact rising much more rapidly than others. In the Washington, D.C., metropolitan area, for example, average wage rates for high-level executive occupations were rising as much as three times faster during the early 2000s than wage rates for parking-lot attendants or food preparation workers (Turner and others 2004, p. 16). Rising incomes at

3. In addition, some economists argue that the immigration of unskilled workers into the United States—and the entry of Asian workforces into worldwide industrial markets—will continue to drag down wages at the bottom of the labor market over the long term; see Freeman (2005).

the top of the wage distribution put upward pressure on housing prices and rents, contributing to increases that outpace any wage gains achieved by workers further down the distribution. In tighter markets, housing costs are becoming increasingly unaffordable not just for the lowest-wage workers but for a broader swath of the workforce. The average rent for a two-bedroom apartment in the Washington metropolitan area is unaffordable for a family supported by a public school teacher, a firefighter, or a receptionist (Turner and others 2006).

Constrained Housing Supply

The problem of slow wage growth and widening income inequality is exacerbated in many housing markets by supply constraints on new housing units. Although the overall housing supply is still expanding, its growth is not keeping pace with population and household growth, so that the net stock of low- to moderate-cost rental units is steadily shrinking (Joint Center for Housing Studies 2006). Local zoning laws, land-use controls, and other regulatory barriers limit total housing production, raise the costs of new units, and often prevent the production of low-cost units. As population expands in a market with constrained supply, the increased competition for units causes prices to rise, even for households that do not typically rely on new construction for their housing. In effect, the traditional filtering process—by which older housing units become more affordable over time while the most affluent households trade up to new units—cannot function properly when supply is so constrained relative to growing demand (Glaeser and Gyourko 2002; Glaeser, Gyourko, and Saks 2005).

Because of these supply constraints, most of the unsubsidized rental housing being produced in the United States today consists of high-cost luxury rentals; for example, only 12 percent of units produced in 2004 had rents below $650 (Joint Center for Housing Studies 2006, p. 23). Some affordable rental housing is also being produced, subsidized primarily through the Low Income Housing Tax Credit (LIHTC) and HOME Investment Partnerships programs and targeted explicitly to low-income households. Although the LIHTC subsidizes the production of around ninety thousand units of affordable rental housing a year, this is not enough to offset losses. Two million low-cost units were demolished or withdrawn from the rental housing inventory between 1993 and 2003—an average of 200,000 losses a year (Joint Center for Housing Studies 2006, p. 24). Meanwhile, rental housing that is affordable to moderate- and middle-income households is simply not being produced.

The combination of rising income inequality and constrained housing supply is evident throughout the country but plays out differently in different metropolitan contexts. The problems outlined here are particularly intense in economically prosperous areas, where expanding employment opportunities attract in-migration and businesses pay top dollar for highly skilled workers. Weaker labor markets do not face the same growth pressures, so in some areas housing costs are not rising as fast. In these markets, however, unemployment is higher and wages are lower, making the housing affordability pinch just as severe for those with low-wage jobs. As a consequence, in markets across the country, growing shares of low- and moderate-income households have rent burdens that are considered unaffordable by federal standards. In fact, in 2005 more than half of all renter households with annual income below $35,000 were paying more than 30 percent of income toward housing costs in 118 of the nation's largest metropolitan areas.

Housing Location within Metropolitan Regions

While housing costs are rising more rapidly than incomes for many renter households, affordable rental housing is especially scarce in communities where job opportunities are most plentiful. Historically, both jobs and affordable rental housing were concentrated in central-city locations. But over the last few decades, employment growth has become increasingly dispersed, while exclusionary zoning laws have limited the development of rental housing in many suburban communities (Pendall, Puentes, and Martin 2006).

Population and employment have become increasingly decentralized over the past three decades. In 1970 half of all households in the nation's ninety-one largest metropolitan areas lived within 8.9 miles of the central business district. By 2000 that boundary had moved out to 12.2 miles (Joint Center for Housing Studies 2006). Today, employment growth is fastest in the low-density counties on the fringes of America's metro areas. And in many metros, entry-level and low-wage jobs are more widely dispersed than high-wage jobs. For example, the District of Columbia accounts for 34 percent of its region's high-wage jobs (paying over $75,000 annually) but only 20 percent of low-wage jobs (paying under $35,000 annually). In fact, in the Washington metro area as a whole, low-wage jobs are twice as dispersed spatially as are high-wage jobs (Turner and others 2004).

The suburban jurisdictions where job opportunities are most plentiful offer relatively little affordable rental housing. The same regulatory barriers that constrain housing supply overall also severely limit the production of modest, higher-density rental housing in these job-rich jurisdictions. Suburban land-use regulations can inhibit the production of affordable housing by imposing direct costs (such as administrative fees, impact fees, and environmental mitigation requirements) or by constraining the range of allowable development types (through large-lot zoning ordinances, inflexible building codes, density restrictions, and outright bans on multifamily housing).

Of course, many regulatory barriers reflect competing priorities about land use and development. Many local building code provisions are intended to ensure the safety and structural integrity of housing construction. Some development restrictions are designed to preserve wetlands or protect open spaces for everyone to enjoy. Many zoning provisions focus on subdivision design features such as sidewalks,

street width, and other neighborhood amenities that enhance neighborhood quality. All of these are legitimate policy objectives, even if they have the effect of limiting housing production and increasing housing costs.

However, some regulatory barriers are, in fact, intended to prevent low-cost
housing from being built in a local community, to exclude lower-income (and
minority) households, and to maintain high property values for current residents.
Unfortunately, local governments (which usually control land-use decisions) have
no incentive to face up to the trade-offs between housing affordability and other
legitimate objectives. In fact, political incentives encourage each individual jurisdiction to satisfy existing property owners by attracting jobs while at the same time
imposing controls on residential development in ways that enhance community
amenities, maximize property values, and exclude lower-cost housing options
(Nelson and others 2002; Downs 1994).

Central cities, then, remain the primary source of affordable rental housing
within most metropolitan regions. Nationally, 45 percent of all renters and two-
thirds of poor renters live in central-city jurisdictions (Joint Center for Housing
Studies 2006). In the early to middle twentieth century, the concentration of
affordable rentals in central cities—typically, in close proximity to manufacturing
centers—made sense. But in the aftermath of economic restructuring, most of
those jobs have long since dispersed, leaving the affordable rental stock behind. In
many metropolitan regions, rental housing can also be found in some segments
of the inner suburbs, typically in older jurisdictions, close to the central city, where
few jobs are available. Rents also remain relatively affordable on the urban fringe,
where jobs have not yet located and land is still cheap. Much of the rapid population growth since the 1990s is occurring in exurban places as moderate-income
families leapfrog over existing suburban communities to find more affordable
housing.

Neighborhood Distress

The clustering of affordable rental housing in central-city neighborhoods has
served to reinforce concentrations of poverty and exacerbate racial segregation.
Although most poor Americans live in nonpoor neighborhoods and the incidence
of concentrated poverty declined in the 1990s, 7.9 million poor people still lived
in "extreme poverty" census tracts in 2000 (Jargowsky 2003).[4] Neighborhoods of
concentrated poverty are disproportionately minority; more than half of all high-
poverty neighborhoods in 2000 were predominantly (more than 60 percent) black
or Hispanic (Pettit and Kingsley 2003). Nationwide, 19 percent of poor blacks
and 14 percent of poor Hispanics lived in high-poverty neighborhoods in 2000,
compared with only 6 percent of poor whites (Jargowsky 2003, p. 10). Within

---

4. This report defines "high-poverty neighborhoods" as those with poverty rates above 30 percent and "extreme-poverty neighborhoods" as those with poverty rates above 40 percent.

metropolitan areas, these disproportionately poor neighborhoods perform unfavorably across a sampling of social indicators. For example, 45 percent of adults in extreme-poverty tracts lack a high school diploma, compared with only 19 percent across the wider metropolitan area. The share of households with children that are headed by single females is 54 percent in extreme-poverty tracts but only 24 percent metrowide (Pettit and Kingsley 2003).

It is unsurprising, then, that residents of such neighborhoods often fall victim to a host of undesirable outcomes. As Paul Jargowsky has noted, "Concentrations of poor people lead to a concentration of the social ills that cause or are caused by poverty" (Jargowsky 2003, p. 2). These ills include higher rates of crime, teenage pregnancy, and educational failure; higher prices for basic consumer goods; reduced private sector activity; poor health outcomes; and higher fiscal burdens on local government.[5]

Lamentably, federal housing policy has actually fueled the problem of concentrated poverty—for example, through the siting of public housing and, more recently, LIHTC units within large developments in isolated, distressed neighborhoods (Schill and Wachter 1995; Freeman 2004). More than half of public housing residents still live in high-poverty neighborhoods, and only 7 percent live in low-poverty neighborhoods (where fewer than 10 percent of residents are poor) (Newman and Schnare 1997; Turner and Wilson 1998). Federal programs to assist low-income renters have also exacerbated residential racial segregation. In fact, public housing handbooks originally encouraged local authorities to assign households to projects based on their race and the racial composition of the surrounding neighborhoods (Massey and Denton 1993; Hirsch 1983). Once the public housing system became intensely segregated, it proved to be extremely difficult—both politically and practically—to desegregate it, and efforts to do so have had little impact (Popkin and others 2003). The clustering of subsidized housing into neighborhoods of concentrated minority poverty undermines the economic and social viability of these communities (Massey and Denton 1993; Wilson 1987).

Housing Matters

For the most part, the three broad challenges outlined above have been narrowly conceived of as housing issues to be discussed and debated by self-described housing advocates and practitioners. Increasingly, however, researchers, policymakers, and advocates outside traditional housing policy circles are recognizing that housing is critical to advancing other national issues and agendas. In general, the lack of affordable housing stands in the way of economic productivity and undermines the fundamental premise that full-time workers should be able to achieve a decent standard of living for themselves and their families. More specifically,

5. For a short survey of these social ills, see Berube and Katz (2005).

the concentration of affordable housing in distressed inner-city neighborhoods traps low-income children in places where public schools are failing and life chances are limited. The lack of affordable housing in the right places also contributes to environmentally and fiscally wasteful patterns of sprawl and decentralization.

Maintaining Economic Competitiveness

High housing costs, sprawling development patterns, and long commutes undermine the economic competitiveness of urban regions and reduce productivity for the nation as a whole. A shortage of affordable housing may inhibit the economic dynamism of a metropolitan region by reducing its capacity to accommodate new growth, either through the expansion of existing firms or by attracting new ones. More specifically, when reasonably priced housing is in short supply and households have to spend large shares of income for housing, a region becomes a less attractive place in which to live and invest. In addition, high housing costs create pressures on employers to increase wages as jobs go unfilled at lower wages and as current employees demand higher wages to accommodate their high costs of living. Commutes from home to work become longer as families locate farther from their jobs in order to obtain affordable housing, increasing congestion costs, reducing productivity, and possibly contributing to employee turnover. Ultimately, these trends may constrain or even destabilize a region's labor market, particularly for low- and moderate-wage labor as people quit their jobs, existing residents leave the region, and prospective residents choose not to move into the region (Glaeser, Gyourko, and Saks 2005). Some economists argue that the impacts of high housing costs on regional economies may even undermine overall national productivity.[6]

Making Work Pay

Affordable housing is essential to fulfilling the implicit promise of welfare reform: that Americans who work hard should be able to achieve a decent standard of living. Today's high housing costs create hardship and instability for families of low-wage workers who "play by the rules" but still do not earn enough to afford decent housing. This failure is particularly distressing because a growing body of evidence suggests that living in decent, affordable housing may provide a platform upon which low-income families can build their incomes and achieve financial security. Simply living in decent, affordable housing constitutes a critical support for work because families living in unaffordable housing are financially insecure, vulnera-

6. NY-NJ-CT Regional Plan Association, "Out of Balance: The Housing Crisis from a Regional Perspective" (April 2004) (www.rpa.org/pdf/outofbalance_paper.pdf); Pill (2000); Family Housing Fund, *Workforce Housing: The Key to Ongoing Regional Prosperity* (2001) (www.fhfund.org/_dnld/reports/Workforce%20Housing_Full%20Report.pdf); Feather O. Houstoun, "Integrating Affordable Housing with State Development Policy," National Governors' Association (2004) (www.knowledgeplex.org/showdoc.html?id=72004).

ble to unexpected increases in other costs, and more likely to move frequently (Mills and others 2006). This insecurity may make it more difficult for them to get and keep jobs, work extra hours, or advance to higher wages. In addition, the extra income freed up when housing is affordable may enable families to pay for reliable child care, transportation to a better job, additional training, or professional clothing—all investments that can enhance employment success. Several recent studies suggest that people who receive assistance to make their housing costs affordable are more likely to benefit from workforce or welfare-to-work programs than people without housing assistance. Thus affordable housing serves to buttress social programs that encourage work and self-sufficiency.[7]

Improving Access to Opportunity

The concentration of affordable rental housing in pockets of poverty isolates residents from social and economic opportunities. A growing body of social science research indicates that living in a distressed, high-poverty neighborhood undermines the long-term life chances of families and children.[8] In particular, children who grow up in distressed neighborhoods and attend high-poverty schools are less likely to perform at grade level, complete high school, or go on to college. Moreover, young people who are surrounded by drug dealing and crime are more likely to become caught up in dangerous or criminal activities. Concentrated poverty also exacerbates the housing-jobs imbalance through which residents of poor neighborhoods are isolated from opportunities for employment and advancement because of distance or poor access to transportation. This is particularly true for African Americans, whose housing options are most constrained by long-standing patterns of discrimination and segregation (Turner [forthcoming]; Raphael and Stoll 2002).

The damage caused by concentrated poverty creates ripple effects extending far beyond the distressed communities themselves. For example, high-poverty neighborhoods lead to increased demands on local government for public safety, child protection, and other social services. Cities often must raise taxes or divert resources from other priorities to fund these necessary spending increases, which in turn encourages the flight of middle- and higher-income taxpayers out of the city (Pack 1998). Less tangible but more important, the isolation of residents of high-poverty neighborhoods far from mainstream social and economic opportunities perpetuates inequality, reinforces racial separation, and fuels social polarization (Polikoff 2006). These effects all undermine social cohesion in a country that is fast becoming majority-minority and endanger our success as a diverse and open society.

7. Sard and Lubell (2000); Barbara Sard and John Springer, "Affordable Housing: One of the Keys to Self-Sufficiency," *Housing Facts and Findings* 4, no. 1 (2002) (www.fanniemaefoundation.org/programs/hff/v4i1-affordable.shtml); Sard and Waller (2002); Newman and Harkness (2006).

8. For a comprehensive review of the empirical literature on neighborhood effects, see Ellen and Turner (1997).

Fighting Sprawl and Promoting Environmental Sustainability

There is a strong connection between the concentration of affordable rental housing in central cities and the sprawling development patterns on the fringes of American metros. This connection is best understood by examining the locational decisions of moderate- and middle-income families. When deciding where to live, these households usually shun poorer areas within central cities based on perceptions (and often realities) of high crime, failing schools, heavy tax burdens, and reduced public amenities. Because such families usually cannot afford to live in high-priced areas, however, they are forced to move to the outer suburbs and beyond, thus fueling new residential development on the urban fringe. This game of leapfrog unfortunately characterizes most, if not all, American metropolitan areas.

These sprawling patterns of development yield a host of adverse environmental consequences. In many cases, the conversion of greenfield sites to urbanized land endangers fish and wildlife habitats, exacerbates erosion, and increases pollution from storm-water runoff, among other effects (Benfield and others 1999; EPA 2001). In addition, as traffic congestion increases, air quality worsens (Schrank and Lomax 2005). The vast quantities of fossil fuels that Americans consume just to drive from place to place are contributing to global warming and climate change through the emission of carbon dioxide and other greenhouse gases (Kahn 2001). Americans account for around one-quarter of worldwide greenhouse gas emissions, with the transportation sector representing the nation's single largest end-use source of carbon emissions.[9] Matthew Kahn (2006) has argued that sprawling, low-density development generates environmental costs on a global scale. When affordable housing is concentrated in distressed, high-poverty neighborhoods rather than neighborhoods of opportunity, the outcome is not only more decentralization and sprawl but increased environmental degradation, as well.

The Federal Response to the Affordable Housing Challenge

Over the past seven decades, the federal government has created a complex web of spending, tax, and regulatory programs for financing and subsidizing the production of affordable rental housing, providing rental assistance for tenants to use in the private market, and revitalizing distressed neighborhoods by demolishing public housing and constructing economically integrated housing in its place. These policies have a substantial record of achievement and accomplishment. Yet current and past programs also suffer from serious deficiencies of scale, design, and implementation that need to be remedied.

9. U.S. Energy Information Administration, "Emissions of Greenhouse Gases in the United States, 2004" (2005) (www.eia.doe.gov/).

What Federal Housing Policies Have Achieved

Federal housing policies have three central accomplishments. Since the 1930s, federal production programs have stimulated the construction of millions of affordable rental housing units and built networks of private and public practitioners, skilled in the financing and development of affordable housing. Since the 1970s, federal demand-side rental assistance has helped millions of renters afford privately owned housing, often in neighborhoods with quality schools, safe streets, and functioning local markets. And since the mid-1990s, the demolition of distressed public housing and its replacement with economically integrated rental housing is transforming the economic and physical landscape of some of the most distressed neighborhoods in the United States.

RENTAL PRODUCTION PROGRAMS. Federal rental production policy has gone through three distinct phases. During the first phase, dominant from the 1930s through the 1960s, the federal government financed the construction of more than a million units of public housing. The federal government contracted with local public housing agencies to produce and manage these units. In effect, these contracts required the agencies to maintain the affordability of public housing units in perpetuity.

During the second phase of rental production policy, dominant from the 1960s to the early 1980s, the federal government subsidized the construction of more than 1.3 million units of privately owned affordable housing through a combination of below-market financing, income tax preferences, and operating support. The focus on private sector delivery altered both the means of production and the management of the built product. Under these programs, the federal government executed contracts directly with for-profit and nonprofit developers of affordable housing, rather than with local public housing agencies. The terms of contracts generally limited the period during which affordability restrictions needed to be maintained.

The current phase of federal production policy, dominant since the mid-1980s, has delegated key decisions to state and local governments. These governments are vested with responsibility for allocating federal tax credits and block grant funding in accordance with federally mandated affordability plans. In general, these federal resources have been used to produce quality affordable housing in low-income neighborhoods of distress, often through community-based housing providers. The key subsidy programs of this period (which are still in use) are the LIHTC program, the Community Development Block Grant program, and the HOME Investment Partnerships program. These programs have been complemented by federal regulatory efforts under the Community Reinvestment Act and by government-sponsored enterprises to encourage the provision of private debt capital. In addition, the National Community Development Initiative, a joint effort involving large philanthropic foundations, major financial institutions, and the federal government, builds the capacity of community development corporations and the national housing intermediaries—the Local Initiatives Support Corporation and the Enterprise Foundation—that support them.

These federal programs and policies have been very successful at stimulating the production of affordable housing. The Low Income Housing Tax Credit program, for example, has created more than a million units of affordable rental housing since its inception. The HOME program, often used in conjunction with the LIHTC, committed close to $13 billion from 1992 to 2003 and supported more than 750,000 affordable units of housing. Significantly, state and local governments reserved 19 percent of their federal rental housing resources for nonprofit organizations during this period (HUD 2004). HOME grants and the low-income housing tax credits have also helped build and sustain a national network of community development corporations with increasing proficiency in the production, preservation, and management of affordable housing. According to a 1998 national census, some 3,600 community development corporations in the country had produced about 550,000 units of affordable housing (about one-fifth of which were located in rural communities) (Steinbach 1997).

DEMAND-SIDE RENTAL ASSISTANCE PROGRAMS. Beginning in the mid-1970s, rental housing vouchers emerged as the most substantial form of subsidized housing in the United States. They now serve some 2.1 million households. In general, housing vouchers pay the difference between 30 percent of a recipient's income and the rent of a qualifying, moderately priced house or apartment. Vouchers are the most direct way of meeting the principal housing challenge facing very low-income renters: affordability. Unlike production programs, vouchers can be delivered quickly to families who need assistance. They also enable their users to adjust rapidly to changes in local and metropolitan housing and job markets.

The Housing Choice Voucher program is unique among federal housing programs in that it allows the recipient rather than the developer to decide where the low-income household will live. Voucher recipients can even receive their assistance in one jurisdiction and take it to another as they search for housing that best fits their family needs. Not surprisingly, many voucher recipients exercise this choice, and they are dramatically less likely than public housing residents to settle in high-poverty neighborhoods. Only 14.8 percent of Section 8 voucher recipients live in high-poverty neighborhoods (neighborhoods that are more than 30 percent poor), compared with 53.6 percent of public housing residents (Newman and Schnare 1997).

By helping families relocate from high-poverty to low-poverty neighborhoods, the housing voucher program has the potential to lead to significant improvements in families' well-being and long-term life chances (Katz and Turner 2000). Findings from Chicago's Gautreaux initiative, a court-ordered program to help desegregate public housing, suggest that using housing vouchers to help families move away from a distressed, high-poverty neighborhood can provide a route to economic independence. Low-income families who used the Chicago vouchers to move to resource-rich white suburbs were less likely to receive welfare and more likely to have jobs than their counterparts who remained in low-income black neighborhoods. Children of families who relocated to the suburbs were less likely to drop out of school and more likely to enroll in college than their urban counterparts (Briggs and Turner 2006; Cove and others [forthcoming]). Emerging evidence from the recent Moving to Opportunity (MTO) demonstration is also encouraging.[10] Participants received vouchers that could be used only in low-poverty neighborhoods, and rigorous research finds evidence of dramatic gains in perceived safety and in mental and physical health. Although the evidence is mixed with respect to employment and earnings effects, some findings suggest that families who move out of central-city neighborhoods may also achieve significant wage gains (Briggs and Turner 2006).

PUBLIC HOUSING TRANSFORMATION. Over the past decade, the federal government has embarked on an ambitious effort to demolish the worst public housing projects in the country and replace them with housing that is economically mixed, better designed, less dense, and fundamentally integrated into the fabric of local neighborhoods and city economies. Called the Housing Opportunities for People Everywhere (HOPE VI) program, this transformation effort includes funding for supportive services to help former public housing residents make the transition to work. Congress also appropriated funds for a separate pool of housing vouchers to aid the relocation of residents who choose to move out of the neighborhood.

The new housing developments produced under HOPE VI differ dramatically from earlier generations of public housing. Not only are they generally well constructed, but the best among them have also successfully applied the latest thinking on housing and community design. These improvements include improving security through smarter building layouts (for example, private entrances that face the street); connecting new units to the neighborhood through sidewalks and street grids; and improving building exteriors by adding front porches and landscaping (Holin and others 2003).

Socioeconomic integration has become a central feature at many HOPE VI sites across the country. The expectation is that properties that have to attract and retain higher-income tenants will be better managed and maintained over time and that a mix of income levels creates a healthier social environment and brings better services—especially schools—to the surrounding neighborhood from both local government and the private retail sector. Some developments are even

10. Under MTO, residents of high-poverty public housing projects who volunteered to participate were divided into several groups: experimental households, who were given vouchers but were only allowed to move to neighborhoods of low poverty; households who received a standard voucher and could move to any apartment of their choice; and in-place households, who remained in public housing.

experimenting with mixed-tenure approaches, with a portion of the new housing reserved for homeowners rather than renters.

The new developments are leveraging substantial resources from the public, private, and philanthropic sectors—resources that were virtually absent (and, in some cases, prohibited) from former public housing developments. They are also experimenting with a range of management approaches: many have employed private sector property management firms on-site (and at risk) rather than relying on remote public agencies. Such firms are using basic management techniques—lease enforcement, enhanced screening procedures, improved amenities—to attract and retain a broad spectrum of residents (Popkin and others 2004).

The quality of many of the new HOPE VI developments is sparking significant improvements in the surrounding neighborhoods. Case studies almost uniformly show substantial declines in neighborhood crime and unemployment and substantial increases in income, property values, and market investment. In several high-profile developments, HOPE VI investments have been accompanied by significant improvements in the quality of the local schools and the educational performance of low-income children (Turbov and Piper 2004). With some of these findings, of course, cause-and-effect is not entirely clear. It is as yet hard to tell how much of the steep decline in crime, for example, derives primarily from the demolition of the dilapidated public housing projects rather than the construction of the new, economically integrated developments. Only the passage of time will enable these more nuanced questions to be fully answered.

Where Federal Housing Policies Fall Short

Despite this record of accomplishment, the current mix of federal housing policies is ill equipped to address today's affordable housing challenges. The failure of current housing policies is partly a result of the modest scale of the federal investment, which is simply insufficient to meet the scale of need. Yet the failure of current housing policies is also the result of flawed design and implementation.

PROBLEMS OF SCALE. The gap between federal housing resources and the needs of low- and moderate-income renters is steadily widening. As discussed earlier, an increasing share of low- and moderate-income renters face serious affordability challenges. Since federal housing assistance is not an entitlement, however, only about one-third of eligible households receives assistance.[11] In essence, low-income renters participate in a national "housing lottery" that has ceased to be fair or rational in its distribution.

However, even the current system seems laudable compared with what could emerge over the next decade. Unless current trends are reversed, we can expect the

---

11. This estimate is derived by dividing the total number of directly assisted rental units (4.9 million) by the total number of extremely low-income (below 30 percent of area median income) and very low-income (below 50 percent of area median income) households (13.7 million), given that most direct federal assistance programs target these income levels.

gap between resources and needs to widen even further, for several reasons. First, the inventory of federally subsidized affordable housing is shrinking, and the share of eligible households receiving assistance will necessarily decline because of these predictable losses.

Second, the federal housing budget is under enormous pressure. For the past several years, the U.S. Department of Housing and Urban Development (HUD) has been targeted for significant budget reductions. The present administration's fiscal year 2007 budget, for example, requests only $33.6 billion in discretionary budget authority for the department, compared with fiscal year 2006 appropriations of $34.3 billion. In a sharp departure from the past, significant reductions have been proposed even for the highly cost-effective voucher program.[12] In recent years, the budget for vouchers has grown only enough to renew existing, in-use vouchers (accounting for inflation) and to offer replacement vouchers to households that are deprived of other forms of federal housing assistance (for example, public housing demolished through HOPE VI).[13] Moreover, statutory changes have shifted vouchers from a unit-based program to a dollar-based program, compelling local housing agencies to choose between renewing all vouchers at reduced subsidy levels or renewing a smaller number of vouchers at full subsidy.

The absence of incremental vouchers means that, in the end, most remaining federal housing dollars will be used to build new housing for the working poor rather than to accommodate households with extremely low incomes. The LIHTC and HOME programs, for example, target their housing to families at 60 percent of area median income, compared with vouchers, which largely serve poorer families, with incomes at 30 percent of area median income or below.

Finally, in contrast to the federal government's ten-year plan to end chronic homelessness, there is simply no long-term plan to address the widening gap between resources and needs for low-income renters. This is partly because both political parties in Congress have focused disproportionately on expanding the ranks of homeowners and partly because the cost of closing the renter affordability gap is perceived as exceedingly high given current fiscal realities.[14]

IMPENDING LOSS OF AFFORDABLE RENTAL UNITS. The growing gap between housing needs and federal resources is exacerbated by the state of the inventory of federally subsidized affordable housing, much of which is at risk of loss, either

---

12. Over a thirty-year period, tax credit and production programs cost roughly 110–140 percent of the cost of vouchers on a per unit basis (GAO 2002, p. 52, table 5).

13. Cushing N. Dolbeare, Irene Basloe Saraf, and Sheila Crowley, "Changing Priorities: The Federal Budget and Housing Assistance, 1976–2005," National Low Income Housing Coalition (www.nlihc.org/pubs/cp04/ChangingPriorities.pdf); Crowley (2004); Will Fischer and Barbara Sard, "HUD Data Show Housing Voucher Costs Leveled Off Starting in 2003 as Rental Market Cooled" (2005) (www.cbpp.org/3-16-05hous.pdf).

14. Systematic research has made a compelling case that investment in stable housing for the homeless actually saves public resources over the long term (Culhane, Metraux, and Hadley 2002). The same case has not yet been made for affordable rental housing.

through deterioration or gentrification. The public housing inventory currently has a backlog of unmet capital modernization needs of $18 billion to $20 billion, and new capital needs are accruing at $2 billion to $3 billion a year (McCarty and others 2006). The president's fiscal year 2007 budget request provides only $2.1 billion for the public housing capital fund, an 11 percent reduction from the previous year and the third straight annual decrease.[15] These capital needs are essentially the legacies of bad policy and implementation—poor-quality construction, the concentration of public housing in distressed inner-city neighborhoods, and insufficient funding for operating and modernization costs (Millennial Housing Commission 2002).

The story of potential deterioration and obsolescence in public housing is mirrored in a portion of the federally assisted inventory. According to the Millennial Housing Commission (2002, p. 14), "Hundreds of thousands of federally subsidized apartments are in very poor physical condition, starved of cash flow to meet backlogged repairs so that they are at a risk of loss." In 1995 nearly one-quarter of private federally assisted units were "distressed" because they were underbudgeted for operations, maintenance, and renovations. Owners of such properties have limited incentives to maintain properties in good condition, given the limitation on profits built into the program design.

In contrast, another substantial portion of the federally assisted, privately owned stock is threatened with loss through gentrification. Subsidy contracts for 196,000 of these units are due to expire over the next ten years, after which owners will be allowed to "opt out" and convert their properties to market rate.[16] About two hundred thousand units with project-based assistance have already been lost to opt-out since the mid-1990s (National Low Income Housing Coalition 2006). For owners who want to renew their federal subsidy contracts, Congress currently provides for one- to twenty-year renewals at market rate. However, current federal policy related to affordable housing preservation suffers from a number of weaknesses. First, all funding for housing subsidy contracts must be reallocated from discretionary funds each year and is subject to the availability of sufficient appropriation, thus creating a risk that Congress might fail to distribute necessary funds.[17] This "appropriations risk" prevents owners from obtaining advantageous multiyear financing from lenders and provides a serious disincentive for owners to renew their contracts or improve their properties (National Low Income Housing Coalition 2006; Millennial Housing Commission 2002).

15. National Low Income Housing Coalition, "Overview of the President's FY07 Request for the Department of Housing and Urban Development" (2006) (www.nlihc.org/news/020906.html).

16. Another 200,000 units financed by forty-year Section 236 mortgages are at risk of loss over the next ten years (Joint Center for Housing Studies 2006).

17. U.S. Department of Housing and Urban Development, "Project-Based Assistance: Housing Assistance Payment Contract" (2006) (www.hud.gov/offices/hsg/omhar/readingrm/section8/attach18.PDF).

Second, Congress has defunded many federal programs for preservation of affordable housing that once existed. Since 2002, the federal government no longer provides direct grants or loans for the rehabilitation of the existing affordable housing stock (although many states and localities use low-income housing tax credits or block grants for this purpose) (National Housing Trust 2006). Additionally, the federal capital gains "exit tax" currently penalizes property owners who choose to sell their properties, even if they sell to a nonprofit preservation entity that could guarantee long-term affordability. In weak real estate markets, this tax makes it more economical for owners to disinvest in their properties rather than sell them, leading to eventual deterioration and abandonment (Millennial Housing Commission 2002).

The preservation of federally subsidized rental housing looms as a major policy challenge in coming years, given the structural changes in housing markets throughout the country and the simple fact that it is significantly less expensive to preserve an existing unit of affordable housing than to create a new one. Although the federal housing tax credit program currently adds around ninety thousand units a year to the affordable housing stock, this amount is more than offset by the loss of units owing to opt-out or deterioration and removal. All told, an estimated 2 million low-cost units were demolished or withdrawn from the rental housing stock between 1993 and 2003, resulting in a net loss of more than a million affordable rentals (Joint Center for Housing Studies 2006). Smaller, older, and privately owned properties are at greatest risk of removal.

GEOGRAPHIC CONCENTRATION OF AFFORDABLE RENTALS. Federal rental production programs have a long history of concentrating assisted units in inner-city neighborhoods—contributing to the concentration of poverty rather than enhancing access to opportunity. As discussed earlier, the location of conventional public housing contributed substantially to the rise of high-poverty neighborhoods. We now know that concentrating large numbers of poor families in a few square blocks undermines almost every other program designed to help them—making it harder to find jobs and placing extraordinary burdens on the schools and teachers that serve poor children (Ellen and Turner 1997; Jargowsky 2003).

Troubling signs suggest that the newer forms of affordable rental housing production are still reinforcing concentrated poverty in inner-city neighborhoods, though at lower levels than in prior public housing and assisted-housing programs. A recent analysis of the performance of the tax credit program in the 1990s reveals that central cities (where, again, poverty rates are much higher than the national or suburban average) received a disproportionate share of the units. Central cities contained 58 percent of all metropolitan tax credit units built during the 1990s despite the fact that they housed only 38 percent of metropolitan residents. At the neighborhood level, the spatial distribution of tax credit housing presents a mixed picture. As of 2000, the average LIHTC unit was located in a census tract with a poverty rate of 19 percent. Among central-city units, the average tract poverty rate was higher (24 percent)—but not as high as the tracts where other types of federally subsidized rental units are located (average poverty rate of 28.9 percent). In addition, one out of every seven tax credit projects sited in a central city is in a neighborhood of extreme poverty (Freeman 2004).

Comparable detail on the spatial distribution of HOME units is not available, but the patterns appear to be similar. As of the late 1990s, the average tract poverty rate for HOME-funded rental projects in cities and urban counties was 26.6 percent, and the average within central cities was even higher—31.2 percent (Walker and others 1998). Moreover, more recent data indicate that about two-thirds of the HOME units developed in metropolitan areas are located in central-city jurisdictions (Herbert and others 2001). These figures should not be surprising. Community development corporations build affordable rental housing in the neighborhoods they serve because that is what the federal government pays for and because they believe that housing production stimulates neighborhood revitalization. They rarely question the legitimacy of consigning low-income families to neighborhoods that do not offer what most middle-class families seek in their housing: good schools, proximity to quality jobs, and quality services.

NO INCENTIVES FOR LOCAL REGULATORY REFORM. As discussed earlier, a panoply of state and local regulations and administrative practices substantially increases the cost of producing rental housing and limits where affordable units can be developed. For the most part, federal rental production programs have ignored this reality, providing few incentives to states and localities to remove regulatory and administrative barriers and reduce the costs of production. In the end, scarce federal production resources do not go as far as they could, with per unit costs of production increased by adherence to burdensome local regulations and administrative procedures. Moreover, exclusionary practices have contributed to patterns of racial and ethnic segregation, since minority households have lower incomes than whites, on average, and are more likely to be renters.

The current state of federal oversight is fairly limited. The federal government requires local and state governments that receive federal block grant funding to conduct a process to identify and ameliorate local regulatory barriers and impediments to fair housing as part of the comprehensive housing affordability strategy within their consolidated plans (Turner and others 2002). However, current regulations do not impose any consequences if a local government fails to remove the barriers it has identified or if it fails to identify any barriers in the first place.[18] The weakness of existing federal oversight reflects a widely held view that affluent suburban jurisdictions would balk at receiving federal housing funds if compelled to overhaul regulatory and other practices that constrain the development of afford-

18. Stowell and Shelburne (2004).

able housing. To a large extent, therefore, the federal government looks the other way when local jurisdictions act in an exclusionary manner. In most metropolitan areas, the absence of any regional mechanism to ensure a fairer and more equitable distribution of affordable housing resources is also a factor.

In recent years, the federal government has stepped up its efforts to collect and disseminate information about promising practices in regulatory reform. In 2005 HUD awarded the first annual Robert Woodson Awards, given to state and local governments that exemplify the best efforts in regulatory reform. While these initiatives are helpful, they appear to be primarily geared to removing regulatory barriers to the production of single-family homes rather than rental housing. In addition, they provide few incentives (besides public accolades) for states or local jurisdictions to address the regulatory barriers that constrain rental housing supply.

THE LIMITED SUCCESS OF RENTAL VOUCHERS. Despite strong evidence of success, the performance of the federal voucher program has been undermined by the exclusionary nature of rental housing markets, fragmented delivery systems, and the lack of supportive services like counseling. First, not all voucher recipients are successful in finding a house or apartment that qualifies under the program. The latest available evidence indicates that in large metropolitan areas, only about two-thirds (69 percent) of voucher recipients are successful in finding qualifying units, down from the 81 percent success rate of the late 1980s. As one would expect, success rates vary across metropolitan areas and are influenced by a wide range of factors, including the general tightening of housing markets across the country, exclusionary zoning practices in suburban communities, and the competence and capacity of local housing authorities (Kennedy and Finkel 1994).

Second, housing vouchers do not provide equal access to low-poverty and low-minority neighborhoods for all poor households. They produce better locational outcomes for suburban recipients than for central-city residents, for white recipients than for African Americans and Hispanics, and for the elderly than for nonelderly families and disabled people. Voucher holders appear to be significantly underrepresented in low-poverty neighborhoods relative to the availability of potentially affordable rental housing. Vouchers still consistently outperform public housing, even in central cities, even among African Americans and Hispanics, and even among families and disabled recipients. But they clearly have the potential to offer better locational outcomes for these groups (Turner and Wilson 1998; Turner and Williams 1998; Newman and Schnare 1997).

The stock of rental housing for which vouchers can potentially be used is widely dispersed. Within the fifty largest metro areas, virtually all census tracts contain at least some units of below-fair-market-rate rental housing, and more than eight of every ten tracts are home to at least some voucher recipients (Devine and others 2003, p. 11). Overall, vouchers are generally not clustered geographically: in two-thirds of all tracts with voucher recipients, the program accounts for less than 2 percent of all households (Devine and others 2003, p. 64). However, where vouchers are clustered, the clustering is in high-poverty, mostly minority, central-city neighborhoods. Specifically, in tracts where voucher recipients account for more than 25 percent of households, the poverty rate averages 40.4 percent, compared with 19.5 percent where they account for less than 5 percent of households (Devine and others 2003, p. 66). Most of the voucher recipients who live in these tracts (83 percent) are minorities (Devine and others 2003, p. 68).

Part of the explanation for the voucher program's inconsistent performance is that its administration is highly fragmented and insular. Since the inception of the program, local public housing authorities have enjoyed a near monopoly over voucher administration. Rarely does the administrative geography of the housing authorities match the metropolitan geography of rental markets. In the Detroit metropolitan area, for example, thirty-one separate authorities administer public housing; in Philadelphia, nineteen do; and in Chicago, fifteen. In these and other metropolitan markets, "too much" devolution has made it difficult for low-income families to know about suburban housing vacancies and exercise choice in a metropolitan housing market (Hughes 1997).

The absence of competition for voucher administration has also, arguably, stifled innovation and accountability. Public housing agencies essentially operate this program in a closed system, where high performance is rarely rewarded and bad performance is rarely punished. Voucher administration has, therefore, failed to realize the benefits of competition that have influenced other areas of domestic policy—such as education or welfare—where administrative responsibilities have been opened up to a wide array of public, nonprofit, and for-profit entities (Katz and Turner 2000).

CHALLENGES FOR THE ORIGINAL RESIDENTS OF HOPE VI DEVELOP-MENTS. Although HOPE VI has had a demonstrably positive effect on the economic vitality and social diversity of distressed inner-city neighborhoods, questions have been raised about the effect of this effort and similar mixed-income housing initiatives on the original low-income residents of troubled housing projects. From the beginning of the HOPE VI program, it was assumed that many residents would not return to the revitalized sites because fewer public housing units would be available there, because some families would choose to receive vouchers and move out of the neighborhood, and because some would not be capable of meeting the tightened screening procedures in the new developments.

The evidence on tenant return—a currently contentious issue—is mixed. The most comprehensive tracking report on tenant outcomes from eight early HOPE VI sites has found that 19 percent of the households surveyed were living in a revitalized development, 29 percent were living in other public housing properties, 33 percent were renting units using housing vouchers, and 18 percent had left assisted housing altogether (Buron and others 2002). A recent U.S. General Accounting Office study, using data from the 165 project applications, reported a wide variance of expectations regarding the return of existing residents, with applicants expecting, on average, 46 percent of residents to return (GAO 2003).

The evidence on residents who decided, for whatever reason, not to return to revitalized sites is also mixed. In general, residents who received vouchers were able to move to neighborhoods of much lower poverty. On average, the census-tract poverty rate for voucher recipients dropped from 67 percent to 27 percent. Yet many housing authorities failed to plan adequately for relocation or provide sufficient support to residents (with vouchers and without vouchers) during the process. Particular concern surrounds the treatment of "hard to house" families, many of whom cannot meet the screening criteria in the new developments and frequently end up in distressed public housing or outside the system entirely. These families include custodial grandparents, large families, and "multiproblem" households—those with members who have mental and physical illnesses, substance abuse problems, or criminal records (Popkin and others 2004).

BALKANIZATION OF ADMINISTRATION WITHIN CITIES. The administration of federal housing assistance is compartmentalized and inefficient, with various funding streams flowing independently of one another to state housing finance agencies (tax credits and bonds), local public housing authorities (vouchers and public housing), private owners (project-based subsidies and mortgages), and state and local departments of housing and community development (community development and HOME block grants). However, the balkanization of administration can be even worse at the municipal level. Cities often have distinct agencies for the separate but overlapping tasks of housing finance, housing production, housing preservation, housing regulation, public housing administration, community development, neighborhood redevelopment, planning and zoning, and other special initiatives.[19] Federal programs exacerbate this problem rather than creating mechanisms and incentives for local agencies to coordinate essential housing investments and regulations.

State and Local Policy Innovation

In recent years, owing to the absence of federal leadership on rental housing policy, many local and state governments have stepped into the void, mostly where hot market conditions have made housing an issue of widespread concern. Significantly, state and local leaders increasingly recognize the connection between the availability of affordable housing and future economic vitality. In California,

19. Within Washington, D.C., alone, for example, seven separate organizations are all significantly involved in housing production and development: the Department of Housing and Community Development, the Housing Finance Agency, the District of Columbia Housing Authority, the National Capital Revitalization Corporation, the Anacostia Waterfront Corporation, the Housing Production Trust Fund, and the Office of the Deputy Mayor for Planning and Economic Development—yet there is no single "housing czar" to coordinate or hold accountable the activities of these related agencies.

for example, a convening of civic leaders has declared that housing affordability is a "key component of the state's economic engine." High housing costs, they argue, prevent the state "from being competitive in attracting and retaining skilled workers."[20] The latest generation of state and local policies focuses primarily on three interconnected objectives: boosting incomes (so that more working families can afford the cost of housing), expanding the supply of moderately priced housing, and reorienting the regulatory environment.

On the income side, a growing number of states—currently eighteen plus the District of Columbia, constituting 46 percent of the U.S. population—are enacting minimum wages higher than the federal standard, some of them significantly so.[21] Twenty-one states plus the District of Columbia now have their own earned income tax credit (EITC) programs, which—like the federal program—supplement the incomes of workers who earn up to double the rate of poverty with a refundable year-end tax credit (Nagle and Johnson 2006). Although local governments generally have less capacity to act on this issue than states, advocates in many communities have campaigned for living wages for public employees, and some jurisdictions have even moved toward enacting local EITCs.[22]

States and localities have also taken major steps to expand the supply of affordable housing. Most prominently, thirty-seven states and more than 350 counties and cities have used dedicated sources of public revenue like taxes and fees to create housing trust funds that collectively spend nearly $1 billion annually on the production and preservation of affordable housing. Over the past five years, housing trust funds have grown radically in both size and number. In late 2002, for example, California voters approved a $2.1 billion bond measure to endow a new state trust fund. In Los Angeles—where the homeownership rate is 40 percent and only 12 percent of households can afford to buy a median-priced home—the city's housing trust fund will soon have $100 million in annual dedicated revenues, enabling it to fund 4,000 to 5,000 units of affordable housing annually, making it the largest local trust fund in the country.[23]

In New Jersey, Governor John Corzine has increased funding for the State Rental Assistance program to provide an additional 1,500 vouchers and adopted

20. California Center for Regional Leadership, "Report on the San Francisco Bay Area Regional Economic Vitality Conversation" (June 2004) (www.calregions.org/pdf/SFEVCReport.pdf).

21. The U.S. Department of Labor maintains a current list of minimum wage laws in each state (www.dol.gov/esa/minwage/america.htm). It is likely that the federal government will increase the national minimum wage in 2007. At the time of this writing, both the House of Representatives and the Senate have passed legislation increasing the minimum wage to $7.25 an hour. The Senate bill, however, would make changes to tax and immigration laws that are not addressed in the House bill and includes an $8.3 billion package of small-business tax cuts.

22. Tim Flacke and Tiana Wertheim, "Delivering a Local EITC: Lessons from the San Francisco Working Families Credit" (2006) (www.brookings.edu/metro/pubs/20060516_SFWorks.htm).

23. Randall C. Archibold, "Problem of Homelessness in Los Angeles and Its Environs Draws Renewed Calls for Attention," *New York Times,* January 16, 2006; Jessica Garrison, "Villaraigosa Announces Plan for Affordable Housing," *Los Angeles Times,* January 21, 2005; Goodno (2002).

an aggressive plan to produce and preserve 100,000 units of affordable housing over ten years. He has directed the New Jersey Department of Community Affairs and the New Jersey Housing and Mortgage Finance Authority to develop a comprehensive state housing plan to expand the state's supply of affordable housing by fostering mixed-income housing development in close proximity to jobs and existing infrastructure, coordinating housing development with public transportation systems to minimize traffic congestion, energy consumption, and carbon emissions, and encouraging walkable mixed-use communities.[24]

Moreover, many states are seeking ways to expand the use of tax credits in the production of affordable housing, building off their responsibility for administration of the federal LIHTC program. Several have shown interest in launching tax vehicles that promote employer-assisted housing. In Illinois, for example, a "donation tax credit" provides donors (both corporations and individuals) with a fifty-cent tax credit for every dollar donated to an eligible housing project, including employer-assisted housing and homeownership counseling as well as traditional programs to develop affordable rental and owner-occupied housing.[25]

Finally, on the regulatory side, more than 130 localities nationwide have taken affirmative steps to mandate the production of affordable housing through inclusionary zoning ordinances. The first such ordinance was passed in Montgomery County, Maryland, in the mid-1970s. Today, around 5 percent of the U.S. population lives in a community that requires affordable housing to be built in any new development.[26] In 2004 Madison, Wisconsin, became the second city in the Midwest to adopt inclusionary zoning. Its ordinance—aimed in part at making it possible for public servants to live closer to work—requires all new developments including ten or more contiguous units, whether rental or owner occupied, to set aside at least 15 percent of units in the development for affordable housing. Households earning below 60 percent of area median income qualify for the set-aside rental units, and those earning below 80 percent of area median income for the owner-occupied units.[27]

New York City has pulled all these pieces together: a higher minimum wage, expanded affordable supply, and reduced regulation.[28] Mayor Michael Bloomberg's ten-year housing plan—the largest municipal housing plan in the country's history—represents a $7.6 billion commitment to build and preserve 165,000

24. It should be noted that in January 2007, a state appeals court invalidated the state's plan for providing affordable housing under the *Mount Laurel* decisions. The court gave the state six months to develop new rules that would ensure that towns meet their obligations to provide an adequate supply of affordable housing.

25. For more information, see the Illinois Housing Development Authority website (www.ihda.org).

26. More than 100 of these localities are in California, with most of the others clustered around Boston and Washington, D.C.

27. For more information, see the discussion of inclusionary zoning on the City of Madison's website (www.cityofmadison.com/cdbg/iz/).

28. The minimum wage—$7.15 as of January 1, 2007—is set by the state of New York.

units of affordable housing. According to the mayor, "Affordable housing is fundamental to [the city's] long-term economic prosperity."[29] Among other steps, the ten-year plan establishes a New York City Housing Trust Fund to subsidize low-income housing development; creates a New York City Land Acquisition Fund to prepare new development sites and finance other predevelopment costs; reforms the city's historic Section 421-a tax exemption; incorporates the principles of inclusionary zoning and density bonuses; and streamlines other regulatory barriers. In addition, the city's Housing Development Corporation—an entity independent of the city's budget—has now become the nation's largest issuer of bonds to finance lower-cost housing, with $4.8 billion in bonds outstanding at the end of 2005.

Innovations in regulatory reform have also occurred at the state level, where both California and Illinois have compelled suburbs and other localities to open up to affordable housing. In California, for example, every city and county must develop a "housing element" that identifies sites appropriate for new affordable housing. Anti-NIMBY ("not in my back yard") laws prohibit local governments from withholding approval for new low-income housing developments unless certain narrowly drawn conditions exist. The state also has a density-bonus law requiring local governments to grant up to a 35 percent increase in allowed density if a prescribed minimum percentage of affordable units in each development is attained. In Illinois, the 2003 Affordable Housing Planning and Appeal Act requires most communities to develop affordable housing plans and provides an affordable housing appeals process, which enables developers whose low-income projects are denied by local authorities to appeal the decision to a state-level board. Illinois is the fourth state in the country—and the first outside New England—to create such an appeals system.

A New Rental Housing Policy Blueprint

The burst of state and local energy around housing bodes well for federal policy. Most significant, state and local efforts illustrate the potential of affordable housing to garner the support of a diverse set of influential constituencies. The political coalitions that have pushed housing innovations across the country draw from interests far beyond the narrow confines of traditional housing advocates: business leaders who see the connection between the costs of housing and employers' abilities to attract and retain skilled workers; advocates for working families who fear that high housing burdens will hinder efforts to grow a strong and resilient middle class; and environmental advocates concerned with the impact of sprawling development patterns on air and water quality and climate change. To a large extent, the success of these broad-based coalitions harkens back to earlier periods

---

29. "Housing Plan for New York City's 21st Century Neighborhoods," remarks presented to the New York Housing Conference–National Housing Conference Twenty-Ninth Annual Luncheon, Sheraton New York Hotel, December 10, 2002.

when national housing policy innovation was intimately connected to other clear national priorities, such as economic competitiveness, support of returning veterans, and alleviation of racial injustice.

On a substantive level, state and local efforts provide the core elements of a policy framework that can be replicated at the national level: boosting income to ensure that a broader portion of the American workforce can afford housing; growing and maintaining the supply of affordable housing to meet the increasing demand of the American workforce; and shaping housing markets to ensure that new affordable housing is located close to employment and educational opportunities.

Yet state and local efforts, for all their political potency and policy innovation, will never be sufficient to address the breadth and depth of today's affordable housing challenge. The nature, scope, and complexity of the challenge require a federal response that recognizes both the achievements and the drawbacks of past and current interventions. Instead of quibbling over funding levels for today's programs, we need a new approach that learns from the experience of the past century, builds on state and local policy innovations and political ingenuity, and tackles today's challenges more effectively. Federal rental policies should work to catalyze local markets to produce more housing, at lower costs, and in the right locations.

The Big Picture

No single level of government can or should tackle today's rental housing challenges on its own. Federal, state, and local governments all have essential roles to play. We propose a new division of responsibility—and accountability—between the federal government and states and localities.

Only the federal government has the fiscal capacity to address the consequences of stagnant wage growth and income inequality nationwide. As long as incomes for a substantial segment of the population fall short of what it takes to cover the costs of adequate housing, state and local governments simply cannot afford to close the affordability gap for enough households. Therefore, federal policies should target the demand side of the housing affordability equation, ensuring that all households have sufficient income (or a housing voucher) to make minimally adequate housing affordable.

If the federal government addresses the demand side of today's housing affordability crisis, state and local jurisdictions can and should assume lead responsibility for the remaining, supply-side challenges. Using both regulatory policies and supply-side subsidies, states and localities should create incentives that induce private market actors (both for-profit and nonprofit) to produce and maintain rental housing that is affordable at moderate-income levels. In principle, the federal government should not have to address these supply-side challenges once it has tackled the demand side of the problem.

However, under this basic framework, the federal government would still have a strong interest in the effectiveness of state and local supply-side policies, because federal policies to boost incomes will ultimately be ineffective if the supply of housing in some markets is still artificially constrained, pushing up rents and distancing affordable housing from work opportunities. Therefore, the federal role with respect to supply-side policy must create strong incentives for states and local jurisdictions to reduce regulatory barriers that unnecessarily constrain market supply and inflate costs; produce affordable rental housing where it is most needed; and ensure that families are not excluded from opportunity-rich communities based on their race or ethnicity.

The new policy framework outlined here effectively addresses today's housing market challenges, substantially expanding opportunities for low-income households to obtain decent and affordable shelter in safe and healthy neighborhoods. But our proposed strategy goes beyond narrow housing goals to advance a broader set of national priorities that are currently being undermined by the failures of federal housing policy. By expanding the availability of affordable housing in regions where jobs are plentiful and population is expanding, this strategy enhances the economic productivity and competitiveness of the nation as a whole. By raising after-tax wages to a level sufficient to cover the cost of decent housing, it lives up to the fundamental premise that people who work full-time should be able to provide their families with a decent standard of living. By tackling the regulatory barriers that have concentrated affordable rental housing in distressed central-city neighborhoods, it expands opportunities for low-income families to raise their children in safe and healthy communities with high-performing public schools.

The Demand-Side Strategy

Ensuring that people who work full-time earn enough to make decent housing affordable is the critical first step in a twenty-first-century housing policy. The federal minimum wage standard and the earned income tax credit both represent powerful tools for accomplishing this goal. Currently, a full-time worker would need to earn close to $16 an hour (more than three times the current federal minimum wage) in order to make the average rent for a modest, two-bedroom house or apartment affordable at 30 percent of gross income (National Low Income Housing Coalition 2005). Clearly, a substantial increase in the federal minimum wage is required as part of a strategy for ensuring that full-time workers can afford minimally adequate housing.[30]

---

30. The current federal affordability standard, which considers housing costs "unaffordable" if they exceed 30 percent of household income, may warrant reconsideration. One alternative is to focus on whether a household's income net of housing costs is sufficient to cover basic necessities. This standard yields a smaller total number of households currently paying unaffordable housing costs (Kutty 2005). In addition, some households pay unaffordable housing costs for only a year or two, while others are more permanently cost burdened. Focusing on eliminating permanent housing affordability problems may represent a more realistic policy goal.

However, the minimum wage alone cannot fill the entire gap. Currently, the federal earned income tax credit provides a substantial supplement to wages for many working families. In fact, estimates indicate that the EITC already reduces the number of households with severe housing cost burdens by 18 percent (Stegman, Davis, and Quercia 2003). Increasing the tax credit, extending its coverage to include childless workers, and expanding participation would substantially reduce the number of working families paying unaffordable housing costs, even at the current minimum wage. Combining a modest increase in the federal minimum wage with a substantial expansion of the EITC offers an administratively efficient strategy for boosting the after-tax incomes of working households and thereby making housing more affordable for many.

One of the limitations of a national, income-based strategy is that it fails to reflect variations across markets in the cost of decent housing. In other words, the combination of a higher minimum wage and an expanded earned income tax credit could effectively address housing affordability problems in some low-cost markets, while still leaving working families in high-cost markets with unaffordable rent burdens. One option would be to adjust EITC payments to reflect variations in local housing costs, in effect making the credit more generous in high-cost market areas than in low-cost areas. However, the federal government's primary responsibility should be to bring working people's incomes up to a single, national standard while creating incentives for state and local governments to reduce the costs of housing locally and to expand the availability of units that are affordable at this income level.

What about households headed by elderly or disabled people—who cannot work—and families with children where adults are not working (or are not working full-time)? For these households, we recommend targeted pools of housing vouchers, linked to appropriate incentives and services. One pool might be designed to provide a dignified safety net for households who cannot work and who lack the resources to obtain decent housing. Elderly and disabled households could use these vouchers to live in conventional rental housing or to move into supportive housing facilities that provide health-related services and assistance in conjunction with decent housing. Another pool of vouchers might be targeted to families leaving welfare, with a rent formula that encourages work and a requirement that families enter into a self-sufficiency contract in order to make the best possible use of housing assistance. A third pool of vouchers might be targeted to families with young children living in severely distressed neighborhoods, providing support and help to relocate in communities where their children will be able to attend good schools.

A potential strategy for encouraging states and localities to expand production of rental housing and reduce market rent levels would be to set a single national payment standard for these new vouchers in conjunction with a supplemental fund that local authorities would be required to use to "top up" vouchers to a level sufficient to cover the costs of adequate housing in the local market area. As other state and local policies brought local housing costs down and expanded the stock of moderately priced units, money from this fund that was not needed to supplement federal voucher payments could be redirected to other, locally determined housing purposes.

These federally funded vouchers should all be administered at a regional scale, not by individual, local jurisdictions (as the current Housing Choice Voucher program is). The current system of administration by local public housing agencies fragments the metropolitan rental market, making it difficult for low-income families, particularly minority families living in central cities, to know about and act on the full range of housing options that a voucher makes affordable. Moreover, by automatically assigning responsibility to local public housing agencies, the current system prevents other capable public and private sector entities from administering the program, stifling the innovation that competition can bring. Therefore, we recommend that vouchers be administered regionally rather than locally in urban areas, and by a state-level entity for nonmetropolitan areas (Katz and Turner 2000).

Experience confirms that metropolitan-wide administration of federal housing vouchers is feasible and that it has the potential to address many of the pitfalls created by the current system of localized administration. However, there is no single right answer to the question of what type of organization is best qualified to administer housing vouchers for any given metropolitan region. Under these circumstances, one strategy for accomplishing a shift in governance would be to conduct a competitive process that is open to a wide array of public and private entities, with either the federal or state government selecting one well-qualified organization to administer the program for each metropolitan region. This would shift the governance of the housing voucher program from the parochial to metropolitan level and open up the administration of vouchers to a wider variety of public, for profit, and nonprofit entities.

The Supply-Side Strategy

Under this new demand-oriented approach, federal supply-side interventions would become more deliberate and focused. It is inconceivable that the federal government can subsidize the production of a sufficient volume of affordable housing to meet demand. Simply put, the federal government cannot build its way out of the nation's affordability problem. The role of federal production programs must, therefore, be more targeted, namely, to leverage the full panoply of state and local powers and activities.

State and local governments wield enormous influence over the quantity, location, and quality of affordable housing production because of their role in regulating the real estate market, administering federal tax and spending programs and, increasingly, designing and implementing their own production efforts. Federal production resources should be designed to encourage state and local governments to be "affordable housing–friendly" in the design and application of their regulatory regimes. In this way, federal programs will catalyze the production of substantially more affordable housing than is possible given current or even substantially higher funding levels. Federal production resources should also be allocated so as to ensure that affordable housing is built in the right places—in communities of choice and opportunity that can boast of good schools and quality jobs.

What combination of carrots and sticks could the federal government deploy to effectively guide state and local action? We propose to start by providing metropolitan planning organizations (MPOs) with federal funding (and technical assistance) to prepare regional housing strategies that complement the regional transportation plans already mandated by federal law. These housing strategies would be designed to ensure that all communities in a metropolitan area, including those that are economically prosperous, participate in the production of housing that is affordable to families with a broad range of incomes. Metropolitan planning organizations are a logical choice for the development of regional housing strategies given that they are generally governed by elected representatives of city and county governments, have been responsible for metropolitan transportation decisionmaking since the early 1990s, and are increasingly staffed with professionals with planning expertise.

To complement the metropolitan focus of the MPOs, new federal resources would also be made available to support and nurture the creation of nonprofit regional housing corporations. These corporations would have the principal task of developing and preserving affordable rental housing in growing suburban areas. Some of these regional housing corporations would, by necessity, be new nonprofit entities; others would most likely evolve from existing community development corporations.

Within this new regional planning framework, cities and urban counties would continue to receive HOME and community development block grants but would be required to implement housing programs in ways that further and are consistent with regional housing strategies. Metropolitan planning organizations would have the authority to certify compliance, and cities and counties that were found in noncompliance with these metropolitan strategies would be given a designated period of time to correct the identified deficiencies. Failing that, the jurisdictions would no longer be eligible to receive either federal housing production funds or federal transportation resources.

In order to induce more affordable rental production in suburban communities— many of which do not currently qualify for funding from either HOME or community development block grants—we propose a new federal incentive fund. Jurisdictions would be eligible to receive awards from this fund if they reduced regulatory barriers and expanded the supply of moderately priced rental housing within their borders.

States would continue to administer the LIHTC, but the formula for allocating credits would be recalibrated to increase the availability of credits where new rental production is demonstrably needed. And LIHTC income limits and targeting incentives should be adjusted so as to discourage the concentration of more affordable housing in distressed neighborhoods and support both developments serving a broad range of incomes within revitalizing communities and developments that expand the availability of rental housing for low- and moderate-income households in opportunity-rich communities.[31]

Getting There from Here

The policy framework proposed here represents a fairly radical shift from the array of federal programs that exist today. Even if the basic thrust of our proposal gained wide acceptance, it would take time to transform federal programs and incentives and to build local, state, and regional capacity to perform more effectively. Moreover, the transition to a new system of federal responsibilities would have to include a responsible strategy for dealing with the existing stock of federally subsidized housing units, including both public housing and the privately owned stock of housing that receives federal project-based rent subsidies. In the short term, therefore, we recommend four priority next steps that could begin the process of transitioning to a more rational and effective system of federal rental housing policies.

First, we recommend that the federal government require existing metropolitan planning organizations to produce regional housing plans in conjunction with their already-mandated transportation plans. This requirement would begin the process of linking regional housing and transportation plans and could encourage some metropolitan regions to begin addressing regulatory barriers and other rental housing supply constraints. To support MPOs in this expanded mandate, the federal government should provide funding (to hire qualified housing staff) as well as technical assistance.

Second, we recommend the creation of new pools of federal housing vouchers, to be awarded competitively to local and regional entities that can demonstrate their capacity to implement innovative programs linking vouchers with effective support services. Three decades of experience with the federal housing voucher program have shown that providing rental assistance directly to tenants is an effective and efficient mechanism for addressing the basic housing needs of low-income families. Most households that are given a voucher are successful in finding a house or apartment for which they can use the voucher (Kennedy and Finkel 1994). Vouchers enable recipients to live in better-quality housing, with more affordable rent burdens, than otherwise similar but unassisted households (Schussheim 1998).

---

31. For an excellent review of the strengths and weaknesses of the LIHTC program and recommendations for reforms, see chapter 5 in this volume.

Moreover, vouchers provide a potentially powerful tool for addressing the failures of past housing policies. Effectively implemented, they can promote mobility and location choice, helping to deconcentrate poverty and enabling poor households to find affordable housing in safe neighborhoods with effective public schools and better access to areas of job growth.

The new voucher pools would be explicitly targeted to promote two goals: encouraging and supporting work among people leaving welfare and enabling low-income families with children to relocate from distressed communities to communities with high-performing public schools. Given limited resources, it makes sense to shift from the current lottery system for allocating vouchers to a system that prioritizes recipients who are prepared to make the best possible use of housing assistance. Research suggests that when families receive housing assistance in conjunction with case management many are able to improve their education or skills and enter the labor market, and some are able to increase their earnings and assets.[32]

There is a strong case to be made for limiting the use of federal housing vouchers to neighborhoods served by good public schools. Many of the central-city neighborhoods in which affordable rental housing is currently concentrated are served by failing schools, which leave children unprepared for success in today's labor markets. While efforts to improve the performance of these schools deserve support, federal housing assistance resources should not be subsidizing families with children to live in neighborhoods with failing schools. Research evidence suggests that when families use vouchers to move to communities with effective public schools, their children benefit. But vouchers alone do not necessarily result in families' moving to neighborhoods served by quality schools or enrolling their children in those schools (Briggs and Turner 2006; Briggs, Ferryman, and Popkin 2007).

Our third priority recommendation is to expand and retarget the Low Income Housing Tax Credit program. The nationwide pool of LIHTC resources should be retargeted to provide more credits to states in which rental housing is in short supply and fewer credits to states with sufficient (or excess) supply. In addition, we recommend adjustments to LIHTC income limits so that credits can be effectively used to produce both mixed-income housing in distressed communities (where the broadest possible mix of incomes is needed) and affordable housing in opportunity-rich communities (where more of the LIHTC units should be targeted to low- and moderate-income levels, within the context of mixed-income neighborhoods).

In conjunction with these LIHTC reforms, the nonprofit housing delivery system should also be expanded beyond the current network of community development corporations. Production and other funds should be invested in

32. Blomquist, Ellen, and Bell (1994); Jeffrey Lubell and Reid Cramer, "Shoring Up HUD's Family Self-Sufficiency Program: Recommendations for Congressional Action" (2005) (www. newamerica.net/Download_Docs/pdfs/Doc_File_2627_1.pdf).

creating a network of regional housing corporations to develop and preserve affordable rental housing in suburban areas. A national network of regional housing corporations can build on the achievements of community development corporations, many of which can naturally graduate to operate at the metropolitan level. A recent study of a national network of large-scale housing nonprofits finds that these organizations are substantial producers of affordable rental housing and have the capacity to operate effectively in their metropolitan regions, developing and managing units in suburban as well as central city communities (Mayer and Temkin 2006).

Finally, we recommend that the federal government implement new initiatives to preserve and transform the current inventory of public and federally assisted housing. With regard to public housing, the successful HOPE VI program should be renewed for another decade of investment. As with the current program, heavy emphasis should be placed on quality design, integrated approaches, and public-private partnerships. Special preference should be given to proposals that use housing redevelopment efforts to leverage school reform. In addition, broader public housing reforms are needed to accelerate the shift to project-based management that has the power and tools necessary to maintain affordable housing for the long haul. On the financing side, the notion of converting operating and capital funding to long-term project-based rental assistance should be explored. Such conversion would enable public housing agencies to secure private financing for rehabilitation purposes.

With regard to the federally assisted inventory, ambitious efforts should be made to preserve currently affordable units. As the Millennial Housing Commission has argued, "U.S. housing policy must recognize that preservation is cheaper than new construction, that the rehabilitation and preservation of units returns the units to lower-income use faster than new construction can provide such units, and that maintaining and renovating existing units combats blight and contributes to healthy communities" (Millennial Housing Commission 2002, p. 33). An effective federal preservation policy would include three essential elements. First, the federal government needs to appropriate funding for the renewal of Section 8 contracts in a timely and predictable manner. Given the vagaries of the appropriations process, it would obviously be best to eliminate appropriations risk and shift the renewal of project-based contracts to the mandatory side of the budget. Absent that, the federal government, perhaps in concert with state or local governments, could offer some form of guarantee to minimize risk and encourage for-profit owners to renew their contracts for as long as practicable.

Second, the federal government should enact a separate block grant for the preservation of federally assisted housing. Such resources, matched with state and local investments, could be used to provide low- or no-interest loans to finance the acquisition and recapitalization of affordable housing by qualified preservation entities. Such preservation entities would be required to maintain the affordability restrictions

Table 10-1. *Estimated Cost of "Next Step" Recommendations*
U.S. dollars

Policy	Year 1	Year 5	Five-year total
Incremental vouchers	766,400,000	4,229,810,997	12,284,243,897
LIHTC	850,000,000	1,044,000,000	4,718,000,000
HOPE VI	500,000,000	500,000,000	2,500,000,000
Preservation grants	500,000,000	500,000,000	2,500,000,000
Exit-tax relief	28,400,000	28,400,000	142,000,000
	2,644,800,000	6,302,210,997	22,144,243,897

of the transferred housing for a prolonged period, say fifty years.[33] Finally, the federal government could eradicate or significantly reduce the tax liabilities that owners of federally assisted housing face upon sale or transfer of their properties. The provision of exit-tax relief could be triggered by the sale or transfer of a property to a nonprofit preservation entity that commits to guarantee long-term affordability.

These steps, all of which could be implemented immediately and at varying scales, offer the potential to begin moving federal rental housing policy in a new direction—toward a framework that addresses the fundamental market challenges facing the country today. How much would these initiatives cost the federal government? Although the scale of each of our proposals is flexible, we recommend a package that would include 1 million new incremental vouchers (phased in over ten years), a 20 percent expansion in the LIHTC, restoration of the HOPE VI program to its original scale of $500 million a year, a comparable annual investment in preservation matching grants, and exit-tax relief for the owners of older subsidized properties. The estimated cost of this package totals about $2.6 billion in the first year, rising to $6.3 billion in year 5 (see table 10-1).

One potential source of funding for an increase at this scale could come from a modest adjustment to the homeowner capital gains tax exclusion (not the deductibility of mortgage interest or property taxes). This exclusion was expanded in the mid-1990s in part to assist older owners of large, high-valued homes who wanted to downsize to smaller, lower-valued homes. The cost of the capital gains exclusion is estimated to climb from $35 billion in 2006 to $47 billion by 2012.

Political Feasibility of the Plan

Our recommendations draw from a rich and growing store of housing literature and practice. Given the diversity of experience and perspective, we have no doubt that advocates, practitioners, and policymakers will debate both our choices and priorities. Yet in the current environment, the most serious question facing any pro-

33. In the 109th Congress, legislation was introduced in the House and Senate to create such a block grant program.

posal for federal housing policy reform is whether it is politically feasible. Can rec-ommendations that call for significant new federal investments in housing (even when potentially offset by reforms to housing tax expenditures) be taken seriously in an era of federal deficits, ideological polarization, and partisan gridlock?

We fully understand the impediments to change. It has been almost a decade since Congress engaged in a serious discussion on housing policy, and the politi-cal and fiscal environment has worsened considerably since then. Yet we firmly believe there are signs of hope and that many of the transition recommendations we have made can be enacted in the aftermath of the 2008 presidential election.

First, the burgeoning of state and local innovation and investment offers lessons on issue framing, issue labeling, and political coalition building that provide a road map for federal action. As indicated by myriad state and local examples, housing advances are being made under the broad rubric of enhanc-ing economic competitiveness and rewarding work rather than the traditional frame of enhancing social equity. In fact, political, business, and even advocacy leaders are increasingly using terminology like "workforce housing" to emphasize this shift in focus and positioning. The result, not surprisingly, is that strong, pow-erful coalitions are being forged across disparate constituencies that reach far beyond traditional affordable housing advocates or even real estate interests.

The heavy involvement of business leaders and major employers in these new coalitions alters the political calculus in important ways. Most important, busi-ness engagement signals to elected officials that supporting housing is good poli-tics as well as good policy. It also enables elected officials in an increasing number of metropolitan markets to position affordable housing as an issue of job growth, job retention, and economic competitiveness.

As with other domestic issues, state and local innovations and coalitions are likely to bubble up to the national level, particularly as state and local leaders find that their interventions require federal engagement to be fully successful. The issue, therefore, is not whether state and local housing efforts will influence fed-eral engagement but when and to what extent.

Second, the political geography of housing is shifting across and within met-ropolitan areas in some salutary ways. In the 1980s a few major metropolitan areas like New York, San Francisco, and Boston drove national housing policy, because the lack of affordable housing had reached crisis proportions there. The number of metropolitan areas facing a crisis in housing affordability has grown dramati-cally in the past five years, from only two metropolitan areas in 2000 to sixteen today. When rent burden is analyzed as a percentage of income, the weight on low- and moderate-income renters is clear: in sixty-two metropolitan regions, more than half of renter households with incomes below $75,000 a year were pay-ing more than 30 percent of their income in housing costs in 2004.[34] The new

---

34. Census Bureau (2004, table B25074).

political geography of the housing affordability crisis stretches from Cleveland and Akron, Ohio, to Tucson, Arizona; Lancaster, Pennsylvania, to Jacksonville, Florida. The geographic—and political—diversity of these metros has significantly expanded the potential coalitions in both the House and the Senate.

Similarly, past housing coalitions tended to be led out of the central cities, where the bulk of housing needs were traditionally felt. Today, the reality of high housing costs and the mismatch between the location of moderately priced rental housing and the location of jobs is being experienced in both cities and suburban areas, thereby expanding the legislative coalition for a new federal engagement.

Third, the housing needs of immigrants increasingly alter the political calculus of housing. In a growing number of states and metropolitan areas, both political parties are competing intensely for the votes of these new citizens and have been compelled to dedicate greater attention to basic issues like access to health services, education, and child care for this population. Housing should be no different: because many immigrants have lower incomes and fewer assets, this population lives in rental housing in higher numbers than the general population. Fully 45 percent of the foreign-born population lived in rental units in 2004. In addition, immigration has played a significant role in buoying the total number of renters nationwide over the past decade. New immigrants prevented a decline in the number of renters nationwide. Rather than the projected loss of 2 million renters, over the past decade we saw a slight increase in the number of renters nationwide. Immigrants filled the gap created by growth in homeownership and then some (Joint Center for Housing Studies 2006). Reducing the rent burden for these households is necessary to help new citizens build assets and become homeowners.

Fourth, a decade of public housing demolition has begun to remove from national consciousness the very projects that shaped the negative image of affordable housing for the past generation. These projects, when they stood, were stark reminders of the mistakes of past housing policies and fueled community opposition to new affordable housing across the nation. With their demise—and the emergence of replacement housing that is well designed, livable, and economically integrated—housing advocates have the potential to take the offensive and cite the positive, value-enhancing, market-shaping effect of new affordable housing.

Fifth, the 2008 presidential election promises to inspire intense competition for ideas at the federal level—since this is the first time since 1952 that neither ticket will have an incumbent running. This has already set off a scramble for ideas as individual "unannounced" candidates struggle to distinguish themselves from the pack. In June 2006, for example, former senator John Edwards gave a major policy address at the National Press Club calling for a radical overhaul of HUD by placing work at the center of our national housing policy.[35] His plan would create

35. John Edwards, National Press Club Policy Address, June 22, 2006 (johnedwards.com/news/speeches/20060622/).

1 million new housing vouchers for working families over the next five years by cutting back HUD's role in managing public housing, slashing the number of HUD-retained contractors, and reducing the size of the agency by at least 1,500 employees. On the Republican side, former Massachusetts governor Mitt Romney has been recognized for his Office for Commonwealth Development, a state agency promoting smart growth through the integration of housing, transportation, energy and environmental policies, programs, and investments.

Finally, we believe that our proposed reformulation of federal housing policy has the potential to appeal to a robust coalition that crosses partisan and ideological lines. Our program blends ideas espoused by liberals, centrists, and conservatives: increased investments in programs that work, carrots and sticks for regulatory streamlining, a shared responsibility for housing among different levels of government, and an emphasis on individual responsibility and self-sufficiency. Housing has a long history of bipartisan support at the federal level, and it is possible to imagine a fresh start for housing in the aftermath of the 2008 presidential election.

Conclusion

Since the 1930s, federal rental housing policy has been constantly evolving, responding to new market trends, changed political circumstances, and the shifting philosophies of the day. We argue that the pressing housing challenges facing the nation at the start of the twenty-first century require federal rental housing policy to renew itself once again and become relevant to the realities of a dynamic period in American life.

A new federal, state, and local housing partnership will demand, first and foremost, a full understanding of the nature and scope of the rental housing challenge, including the state and local restrictions that hinder production and the federal housing policies that often limit individual choice and family success. It will necessitate a repositioning of the housing issue as one that, left unchecked, undermines other national economic, social, welfare, educational, and environmental priorities. And it will compel a fundamental reimagining of the federal role in housing as one principally of supporting and supplementing the incomes of low-wage workers rather than subsidizing the production of rental housing in which these workers can live.

Our recommendations build on the energy and innovation that is emerging from state and local leaders across the country. In that spirit, they are meant to be federalist rather than federal and fully acknowledge the preeminent role of state and local governments in setting the rules of housing production in this country. The recommendations focus primarily on closing the growing gap between wages and rental prices in the country and, as such, must be seen as one of a series of responses to globalization and our changing economic landscape. They also require that the federal role in producing affordable housing must be clear and structured to catalyze markets, stimulate the overhaul of regulatory restrictions, promote mixed-income housing, decommission federal enclaves of poverty, support city and suburban collaboration, and diminish the ill effects of balkanized, duplicative, and fiscally wasteful administration.

There are no doubt risks to pursuing this strategy, and many constituencies will find greater comfort in protecting their piece of a shrinking pie than in striking out for new, uncharted territory. Yet political risk and political leadership are essential if the current stalemate over housing policy is to be broken. We call for a new national compact on housing and hope that this proposal and others can help unleash a period of meaningful policy debate, reform, and action.

References

Autor, David H., Lawrence F. Katz, and Melissa S. Kearney. 2006. "The Polarization of the U.S. Labor Market." Working Paper 11986. Cambridge, Mass.: National Bureau of Economic Research.

Benfield, F. Kaid, and others. 1999. *Once There Were Greenfields: How Urban Sprawl Is Undermining America's Environment, Economy, and Social Fabric.* New York: National Resources Defense Council.

Berube, Alan, and Bruce Katz. 2005. *Katrina's Window: Confronting Concentrated Poverty across America.* Brookings.

Blomquist, John D., Ingrid Gould Ellen, and Stephen H. Bell. 1994. *Program Impacts.* Vol. 2 of *Operation Bootstrap.* U.S. Department of Housing and Urban Development, Office of Policy Development and Research.

Buron, Larry, and others. 2002. *The HOPE VI Resident Tracking Study.* Washington: Urban Institute.

Cove, Elizabeth, and others. Forthcoming. "Moving on Over, Moving on Up? Employment Outcomes for MTO Relocatees." Washington: Urban Institute.

Culhane, Dennis P., Stephen Metraux, and Trevor Hadley. 2002. "Public Service Reductions Associated with Placement of Homeless Persons with Severe Mental Illness in Supportive Housing." *Housing Policy Debate* 13, no. 1: 107–63.

de Souza Briggs, Xavier, and Margery Austin Turner. 2006. "Assisted Housing Mobility and the Success of Low-Income Minority Families: Lessons for Policy, Practice, and Future Research." *Northwestern University Journal of Law and Social Policy* 1, no. 1: 25–61 (www.law.northwestern.edu/journals/njlsp/v1/n1/index.html).

de Souza Briggs, Xavier, Kadija Ferryman, and Susan J. Popkin. 2007. "Can Better Housing Choice Improve School Outcomes for Low-Income Children? New Evidence from the Moving to Opportunity Experiment." Washington: Urban Institute.

Devine, Deborah J., and others. 2003. *Housing Choice Voucher Location Patterns: Implications for Participant and Neighborhood Welfare.* U.S. Department of Housing and Urban Development.

Downs, Anthony. 1994. *New Visions for Metropolitan America.* Brookings.

Ellen, Ingrid Gould, and Margery Austin Turner. 1997. "Does Neighborhood Matter? Assessing Recent Evidence." *Housing Policy Debate* 8, no. 4: 833–66.

Freeman, Lance. 2004. "Siting Affordable Housing: Location and Neighborhood Trends of Low-Income Housing Tax Credit Developments in the 1990s." Brookings.

Freeman, Richard. 2005. "What Really Ails Europe (and America): The Doubling of the Global Workforce." *Globalist* (June 3).

Glaeser, Edward L., and Joseph Gyourko. 2002. "The Impact of Zoning on Housing Affordability." Discussion Paper 1948. Cambridge, Mass.: Harvard Institute of Economic Research.

Glaeser, Edward L., Joseph Gyourko, and Raven E. Saks. 2005. "Why Have Housing Prices Gone Up?" Discussion Paper 2061. Cambridge, Mass.: Harvard Institute of Economic Research.

Goodno, James B. 2002. "Affordable Housing: Who Pays Now?" *Planning* 68, no. 11: 4–9.

Herbert, Christopher E., and others. 2001. *Study of the Ongoing Affordability of HOME Program Rents.* Cambridge, Mass.: Abt Associates.

Hirsch, Arnold. 1983. *Making the Second Ghetto: Race and Housing in Chicago.* Cambridge University Press.

Holin, Mary Joel, and others. 2003. "Interim Assessment of the HOPE VI Program Cross-Site Report." Report prepared for the U.S. Department of Housing and Urban Development. Cambridge, Mass.: Abt Associates.

Hughes, Mark Alan. 1997. "The Administrative Geography of Devolving Social Welfare Programs." Brookings.

Jargowsky, Paul. 2003. "Stunning Progress, Hidden Problems: The Dramatic Decline of Concentrated Poverty in the 1990s." Brookings.

Joint Center for Housing Studies. 2004. *The State of the Nation's Housing 2004.* Cambridge: Harvard University (www.jchs.harvard.edu/publications/markets/son2004.pdf).

———. 2006. *America's Rental Housing: Homes for a Diverse Nation.* Cambridge, Mass.: Harvard University.

Kahn, Matthew. 2001. "The Environmental Impact of Suburbanization." *Journal of Policy Analysis and Management* 19, no. 4: 569–86.

———. 2006. *Green Cities: Urban Growth and the Environment.* Brookings.

Katz, Bruce, and Margery Austin Turner. 2000. "Who Should Run the Voucher Program? A Reform Proposal." *Housing Policy Debate* 12, no. 2: 239–62.

Kennedy, Stephen D., and Meryl Finkel. 1994. *Section 8 Rental Voucher and Rental Certificate Utilization Study: Final Report.* U.S. Department of Housing and Urban Development, Office of Policy Development and Research.

Kutty, Nandinee K. 2005. "A New Measure of Housing Affordability: Estimates and Analytical Results." *Housing Policy Debate* 15, no. 1: 113–42.

Massey, D. S., and N. A. Denton. 1993. *American Apartheid: Segregation and the Making of the Underclass.* Harvard University Press.

Mayer, Neil, and Kenneth Temkin. 2006. *Housing Partnerships: The Work of Large-Scale Regional Non-Profits in Affordable Housing.* Washington: Urban Institute.

McCarty, Maggie, and others. 2006. "Housing Issues in the 109th Congress." Report RL32899. Congressional Research Service.

Millennial Housing Commission. 2002. "Meeting Our Nation's Housing Challenges: Report of the Bipartisan Millennial Housing Commission Appointed by the Congress of the United States." Government Printing Office (govinfo.library.unt.edu/mhc/MHCReport.pdf).

Mills, Gregory, and others. 2006. *Effects of Housing Vouchers on Welfare Families.* U.S. Department of Housing and Urban Development.

Nagle, Ami, and Nicholas Johnson. 2006. "A Hand Up: How State Earned Income Tax Credits Help Working Families Escape Poverty in 2006." Washington: Center for Budget and Policy Priorities (www.cbpp.org/3-8-06sfp.htm).

National Housing Trust. 2006. "State and Local Housing Preservation Initiatives." Washington (www.nhtinc.org/documents/Pres_Scan_March2006_Final.pdf).

National Low Income Housing Coalition. 2005. *Out of Reach 2005.* Washington (www.nlihc.org/oor2005/introduction.pdf).

————. 2006. "2006 Advocates' Guide: Project-Based Rental Assistance." Washington (www.nlihc.org/advocates/projectbased.htm).

Nelson, Arthur C., and others. 2002. "The Link between Growth Management and Housing Affordability: The Academic Evidence." Brookings (www.brookings.edu/es/urban/publications/growthmanagexsum.htm).

Newman, Sandra, and Joseph Harkness. 2006. "Rental Housing Affordability and Children's Outcomes." Paper prepared for Revisiting Rental Housing: A National Policy Summit. Harvard University, November 14–15.

Newman, Sandra J., and Ann B. Schnare. 1997. " '. . . And a Suitable Living Environment': The Failure of Housing Programs to Deliver on Neighborhood Quality." *Housing Policy Debate* 8, no. 4: 703–42.

Pack, Janet Rothenberg. 1998. "Poverty and Urban Public Expenditures." *Urban Studies* 35, no. 11: 1995–2019.

Pendall, Rolf, Robert Puentes, and Jonathan Martin. 2006. *From Traditional to Reformed: A Review of the Land Use Regulations in the Nation's 50 Largest Metropolitan Areas.* Brookings.

Pettit, Kathryn L. S., and G. Thomas Kingsley. 2003. "Concentrated Poverty: A Change in Course." Washington: Urban Institute.

Pill, Madeleine. 2000. "Employer-Assisted Housing: Competitiveness through Partnership." Working Paper W00-8. Cambridge, Mass.: Harvard Joint Center for Housing Studies (www.jchs.harvard.edu/publications/mpill_W00-8.pdf).

Polikoff, Alexander. 2006. *Waiting for Gautreaux: A Story of Segregation, Housing, and the Black Ghetto.* Northwestern University Press.

Popkin, Susan J., and others. 2003. "Obstacles to Desegregating Public Housing: Lessons Learned from Implementing Eight Consent Decrees." *Journal of Policy Analysis and Management* 22, no. 2: 179–99.

Popkin, Susan J., and others. 2004. *A Decade of HOPE VI.* Washington: Urban Institute.

Raphael, Steven, and Michael A. Stoll. 2002. *Modest Progress: The Narrowing Spatial Mismatch between Blacks and Jobs in the 1990s.* Living Cities Census Series. Brookings.

Sard, Barbara, and Jeff Lubell. 2000. "The Value of Housing Subsidies to Welfare Reform Efforts." In *The Increasing Use of TANF and State Matching Funds to Provide Housing Assistance to Families Moving from Welfare to Work,* pp. 3–14. Washington: Center on Budget and Policy Priorities (February).

Sard, Barbara, and Margy Waller. 2002. "Housing Strategies to Strengthen Welfare Policy and Support Working Families." Brookings Institution and Center on Budget and Policy Priorities (April) (www.brookings.edu/es/urban/publications/sardwallerhousingwelfare.pdf).

Schill, Michael H., and Susan M. Wachter. 1995. "The Spatial Bias of Federal Housing Law and Policy: Concentrated Poverty in Urban America." *University of Pennsylvania Law Review* 143: 1285–342.

Schrank, David, and Tim Lomax. 2005. "2005 Urban Mobility Study." Texas Transportation Institute, College Station.

Schussheim, Morton J. 1998. "Housing the Poor: Federal Housing Assistance for Low-Income Families." CRS Report 98-860E. Congressional Research Service.

Stegman, Michael, Walter Davis, and Roberto Quercia. 2003. "Tax Policy as Housing Policy: The EITC's Potential to Make Housing More Affordable for Working Families." Brookings (www.brookings.edu/metro/publications/200310_stegman.htm).

Steinbach, Carol. 1997. *Coming of Age: Trends and Achievements of Community-Based Development Organizations.* Washington: National Congress of Community Economic Development.

Stowell, Candace, and Mark Shelburne. 2004. "Responding to HUD's Affordable Communities Initiative: Will It Make a Difference?" *Practicing Planner* 2, no. 4 (www.planning.org/affordablereader/pracplanner/hudvol2no4.htm).

Turbov, Mindy, and Valerie Piper. 2004. *Hope VI as a Catalyst for Neighborhood Change.* Brookings.

Turner, Margery. Forthcoming. "Residential Segregation and Employment Inequality." In *Segregation: The Rising Costs for America,* edited by James H. Carr, Nandinee K. Kutty, and Shanna L. Smith. New York: Routledge.

Turner, Margery Austin, and Kale Williams. 1998. *Housing Mobility: Realizing the Promise.* Washington: Urban Institute Press.

Turner, Margery Austin, and Charlene Wilson. 1998. *Affirmatively Furthering Fair Housing: Neighborhood Outcomes for Tenant-Based Assistance in Six Metropolitan Areas.* Washington: Urban Institute Press.

Turner, Margery, and others. 2002. *Planning to Meet Local Housing Needs: The Role of HUD'S Consolidated Planning Requirements in the 1990s.* Washington: Urban Institute (www.huduser. org/Publications/pdf/local_housing_needs.pdf.).

———. 2004. *Housing in the Nation's Capital 2004.* Washington: Fannie Mae Foundation.

———. 2006. *Housing in the Nation's Capital 2006.* Washington: Fannie Mae Foundation.

U.S. Census Bureau. 2000. *Census 2000.*

———. 2004. *Census 2004.*

———. 2005. *American Communities Survey.*

U.S. Department of Housing and Urban Development (HUD). 2004. "Congressional Justifications for 2005 Estimates" (www.hud.gov/about/budget/fy05/main_toc.cfm).

U.S. Environmental Protection Agency (EPA). 2001. "Our Built and Natural Environments: A Technical Review of the Interactions between Land Use, Transportation, and Environmental Quality" (January) (www.epa.gov/dced/pdf/built.pdf).

U.S. General Accounting Office (GAO). 2002. "Federal Housing Assistance: Characteristics and Costs of Federal Housing Programs." Report GAO-02-76 (www.gao.gov/new.items/d0276.pdf).

———. 2003. "HOPE VI Resident Issues and Changes in Neighborhoods Surrounding Grant Sites." Report GAO-04-109 (www.gao.gov/new.items/d04109.pdf).

Walker, Christopher, and others. 1998. *Expanding the Nation's Supply of Affordable Housing: An Evaluation of the Home Investment Partnerships Program.* U.S. Department of Housing and Urban Development.

Wilson, William Julius. 1987. *The Truly Disadvantaged: The Inner City, the Underclass, and Public Policy.* University of Chicago Press.

Contributors

William C. Apgar
Harvard University

Eric S. Belsky
Harvard University

Jackie M. Cutsinger
Wayne State University

Anthony Downs
Brookings Institution

Rachel Bogardus Drew
Harvard University

Ingrid Gould Ellen
New York University

George C. Galster
Wayne State University

Bruce Katz
Brookings Institution

Jill Khadduri
Abt Associates

Ron Malega
University of Georgia

Shekar Narasimhan
Beekman Advisors

Rolf Pendall
Cornell University

John M. Quigley
University of California–Berkeley

James A. Riccio
MDRC

Stuart S. Rosenthal
Syracuse University

Margery Austin Turner
Urban Institute

Charles Wilkins
Compass Group

Index

CPSIA information can be obtained at www.ICGtesting.com
Printed in the USA
270130BV00004B/1/P